CAROLINE MOOREHEAD

Human Cargo

A Journey Among Refugees

With a new introduction by the author

VINTAGE

10

Vintage
20 Vauxhall Bridge Road,
London SW1V 2SA

Vintage is part of the Penguin Random House group of companies
whose addresses can be found at global.penguinrandomhouse.com.

Penguin
Random House
UK

This edition reissued in Vintage in 2016
First published in Vintage in 2006
First published in hardback by Chatto & Windus in 2005

www.vintage-books.co.uk

A CIP catalogue record for this book
is available from the British Library

ISBN 9781784703615

Printed and bound by Clays Ltd, St Ives PLC

MIX
Paper from
responsible sources
FSC® C018179

Penguin Random House is committed to a sustainable future
for our business, our readers and our planet. This book is
made from Forest Stewardship Council® certified paper

Contents

To Lyndall

Permissions

I would like to thank Eva Hoffman, for permission to quote from *The New Nomads*; Mandla Langa, for permission to quote from *The Naked Song*; Random House, for permission to quote from Giuseppe Lampedusa's *The Leopard*. Parts of then prologue are based on an article that appeared in the *New York Review of Books* in 2001. Every effort has been made to trace the holders of copyright material and any omission or error will be put right in future editions.

Definitions

Asylum-seeker: a person who is in the process of applying for asylum.

Refugee: the 1951 United Nations Convention Relating to Refugees defines a refugee as a person who, 'owing to a well-founded fear of being persecuted for reasons of race, religion, nationality, membership of a particular social group, or political opinion, is outside the country of his nationality, and is unable to or, owing to such fear, is unwilling to avail himself of the protection of that country . . .'

Migrant: a person who leaves his or her country of origin voluntarily, in search of work, to join family, to study.

Illegal immigrant: a person residing in a foreign country without permission.

A Refugee Story

One day a man in a country in Africa was arrested and accused of belonging to an illegal opposition group. He was sent to prison and tortured. In his cell was a very small window. By standing up very straight in the far corner of the room, he could just see a field outside. From time to time, cows came to graze in it. As the weeks passed, he grew to recognise their shapes and colours. One in particular pleased him, and he gave her a name. From that day on, whenever she passed his window, he talked to her. He told her about his wife and children ·who had disappeared, about his house and his parents, and the village where he grew up.

The day came when he was freed. He left his African country and went into exile, taking his cow with him. In his new country, he was offered an appointment with a doctor to talk through his experiences. On the first day, he arrived in good time, leading his cow behind him. When the receptionist ushered him into the consulting room, he made sure the cow had plenty of room to follow him. Week after week, the man and his cow attended sessions together.

Several months went by. One day, the doctor suggested that the moment had come for the man to bid farewell to his cow. He replied that it was too soon. Several more months passed. Then the morning came when the man accepted that he could keep his cow with him no longer. That day, he was extremely sad. He brought the cow with him as usual, and then, crying, told her that the time had come for her to go home. Saying goodbye to his cow made him weep more than he had wept for many years.

Introduction

In 2005, when *Human Cargo* was first published, 20,000 refugees were crossing the Mediterranean every year from North Africa, for the most part landing on the shores of Sicily and Italy's southernmost islands. In 2015, a decade later, this figure has grown over ten-fold, to 239,000, in the first seven months of the year alone. Now they land as often in Greece, where during the summer months they have arrived on the islands of Kos, Samos, Megisti, Agathonisi, Leros and Farmakonisi up to the rate of 2,000 people a day. Europe is living through a refugee crisis the like of which it has not seen since the end of the Second World War, with implications for regional stability and humanitarian action that have no end in sight. As Angela Merkel declared in August, it is neither the ailing Greek economy, nor the ongoing financial fluctuations, but the migration issue that will define this decade.

While the causes of displacement have not changed greatly – conflict, persecution, racism, poverty, natural disasters – the numbers of those fleeing their homes reflect the world's current state of chronic instability. When I started work on *Human Cargo*, there were an estimated 17 million refugees, displaced people and asylum-seekers in the world; today there are 59.5 million, the highest figure on record and over 8 million up on last year alone. Some 42,500 people leave their homes every day to seek protection, either within their own borders or in other countries. If they were a nation, the population of displaced and dispossessed people would be the 24th-largest country in the world. And it would be a young nation, for over half of all refugees today are under the age of eighteen.

From danger at home to danger at every stage of the road to freedom: the journeys that may carry people to safety are themselves desperately unsafe, whether across countries at war or in boats so leaky that at least 3,000 people are known to have drowned in the straits between North Africa and the island of Lampedusa last year, up from 700 in 2013 – but since no one knows how many boats cross and who is on them, the figures are certainly higher. Fighting in Syria and Iraq and the rise of Isis saw 15 million people driven from their homes – 3.9 million of them are now refugees in 107 countries; and as the fighting intensifies, so these numbers will rise. Isis, the latest and most successful incarnation of the Jihadist movement that has been building up for several decades, already controls, with a degree of organisation and efficiency, an area roughly the size of Britain.

New conflicts in the Central African Republic, South Sudan, Ukraine, Libya, Yemen and Burundi have pushed many millions more to seek safety elsewhere. The fact that Libya is now beyond government control, that hundreds of different groups are struggling for territory and influence, that its borders are porous, and its long and lawless coastline lies a few hundred kilometres from the southern shores of Italy, have made it the easiest way to reach Europe from Africa.

In the refugee world, the vocabulary is all about growth: more child refugees, more asylum applications, more migrants in detention, more refugees in more long-term camps; over 4 million today and increasing all the time. Nor is it just the scale of the problem, but the speed at which it is growing.

What do not grow, of course, are the funds with which to look after them, or the spirit of generosity and responsibility with which many of the rich, developed, conflict-free countries approach the crisis. Not long ago, because of a drop in donations, the World Food Programme announced a severe cut in food supplies. UNHCR, just about struggling to keep pace with its commitments in 2005, now no longer has the resources or the capacity to respond even at a minimum level to the calls for protection and assistance from these displaced populations. As of the summer of 2015, it was £2 billion short of what it needed to keep camps functioning in Lebanon, Iraq, Egypt, Jordan and Turkey.

Faced by hungry and desperate people trying to force their way into Europe, governments have responded by putting up fences and walls, increasing border police, tightening up asylum procedures and visa applications, and investing in the capacity of neighbouring countries to detect, detain and deter migrants. Between 2010 and 2011, Australia increased its detention centres for asylum-seekers and migrants from ten to twenty-one. When, in August 2015, people arriving in Greece tried to cross into Macedonia, the army closed the border and police fired tear gas and stun grenades, then spread razor wire over the rail tracks. Slovakia has announced that it will consider only Christian refugees. Spain has built border fences around its North African territories of Ceuta and Melilla against refugees arriving from the south. Hungary has put up a fence along its 175-kilometre border with Serbia, its southern neighbour. Meanwhile the Gulf states decline to take all but a handful of refugees.

Throughout Europe, as right-wing parties make gains in elections, governments respond with varying degrees of panic. Scenes of frenzy, rioting and anger at borders, in train stations and sea ports lead to more barbed wire and security cameras, more squabbling among member states, more fodder for populist politicians, more attacks on refugees – by August Germany alone had registered 336 assaults on shelters in the first seven months of the year, 100 times more than in the whole of 2014. But desperate people find other crossings, and fences and walls are no more than symbols, illusions for domestic audiences promoting the fallacy that what is happening is a temporary phenomenon, easily checked by such short-term measures.

And as yet more bedraggled and dehydrated Africans are rescued from sinking boats in the Mediterranean, so they are further demonised in the popular mind by being greeted by officials in full protective clothing. It is as if they were contaminated aliens, come to spread disease.

By the summer of 2015, Syria had displaced Afghanistan as the world's top 'source' country, a position the latter had held for thirty years. As a result, Turkey displaced Pakistan as the top host country, followed by Lebanon, Iran and Jordan. What has not changed in the last decade is the most overlooked of facts: that over 85 per cent of the world's refugees remain in their own regions. Europe's burden is minimal. The United Kingdom is home to less than 1 per cent of the world's forcibly displaced people (and is the only European country to practise the indefinite detention of migrants). It is the global south, not the north, which bears the brunt of the problem. 4 million displaced Syrians are already living in UN refugee camps in Lebanon and Syria.

People on the move in this decade have few rights and little protection. Under the UN 1951 Convention and its 1967 Protocol, states recognise and are obliged to offer asylum to people judged to have a 'well-founded fear of persecution' if they return to their own countries. The Convention has been signed and ratified by 142 of the world's 195 nations, but almost every one of them, one way or another, violates its terms. In any case, it does not recognise conflict and violence as a valid reason for granting asylum, though it is accepted under the African and Latin American charters. More so than ten years ago, the very terms 'refugee', 'migrant' and 'asylum-seeker' have become inextricably entwined, used interchangeably to prove every turn and twist in the argument. Far more than was the case ten years ago, the words themselves have become loaded. Who, in a world riven by religious and territorial conflict, is a refugee? What makes him deserving of acceptance? The fact that he belongs to the wrong political party, the wrong sect? That his village was washed away in a hurricane and his children have nothing to eat? That his country is in a state of permanent civil war? The clarity that seemed to exist when the Convention was framed has long since disappeared in a fog of conflicting claims.

Germany is expected to receive 800,000 asylum-seekers in 2015 – about four times the number it took in 2014 and more than all the other European states combined. Only Sweden comes anywhere near the same level relative to population size. The UK's commitment is the second lowest among EU members after Hungary, which has refused to take any.

Were I starting *Human Cargo* today, it would not have been possible to leave out the climate-change refugees, the people made homeless by increased droughts, desertification, the rise in sea levels and the disruption of seasonal weather patterns. The term 'environmental refugee' was first coined in 1976, but it was not until the mid-1990s that environmentalists began warning that more people might soon be displaced on account of natural disasters than because of conflict and persecution. Half the population of Bangladesh lives less than 5 metres above sea level. The US state of Louisiana loses 65 square kilometres to the sea every year.

And as the numbers keep rising, so do the profits of the people who prey on them. Organised criminal networks mastermind many of the sea crossings in the Mediterranean, with revenues said to exceed those of some of the drug cartels. The smuggling and trafficking of people have become big business, and those who run the gangs are seldom caught. Syndicates have taken to online advertising to attract would-be migrants, including information on which countries have the best welfare and education provisions. On Facebook it is possible to learn how to obtain a false passport. In a world in which a passage can cost anywhere from a few hundred to a few thousand dollars, sea crossings have become more expensive since the better-off Syrian families came looking for escape routes. African refugees have little hope of securing a place on the more seaworthy boats.

Solutions to this crisis are not simple, but some can be identified. While development aid could be used to keep people in their own countries, it cannot be delivered to countries in the throes of conflict. But it could be used strategically elsewhere. Recent rescue programmes put in place by the European Union are reducing the number of deaths at sea, but fewer people would need to take to leaky boats if legal routes were opened whereby asylum-seekers could apply for protection without having to embark on perilous journeys.

A common strategy on refugees and migration, with a system of mandatory quotas across the twenty-seven EU states, is being urged by Angela Merkel, despite the proposal being rejected in a series of acrimonious debates by EU leaders at a world summit in June 2015. But there have now been moves from the UK and France to increase the numbers they take. This would protect fringe countries – notably Italy and Greece – from bearing most of the costs of receiving those who cross the Mediterranean, and is made more urgent by the fact that some 1.5 million people asked for asylum in 2014 – the highest figure ever recorded and one which will rise sharply in 2015. It would also prove that Europe could live up to the humanitarian values that underpinned its creation.

Nor is managed migration without self-interest. Europe's populations are aging rapidly; they need the skills and labour of young migrants to boost their own economies. As recent surveys have shown, refugees and migrants, far from imposing costs on hard-pressed public and welfare budgets, contribute more in taxes and social contributions than they receive in benefits. The 'human rights-based, coherent and comprehensive migration policy' being called for by the UN, with mobility its central concept, is the one way that the EU can reclaim its borders, combat smuggling, and give migrants a voice.

As António Guterres, the UN High Commissioner for Refugees, told a meeting held at the Ditchley Foundation in July 2015, the world is now facing 'the most serious refugee crisis for twenty years'. Unless it is addressed, it can only get worse. The moment may have come to stop spending fortunes on preventing people from arriving, be they migrants or refugees, and to start putting in place safe and fair solutions. After a boat capsized off Lampedusa, leaving many people drowned, the new Pope Francis made the island his first pastoral visit in July 2013. There he inveighed against 'the globalisation of indifference'. Speaking of the fragile, leaky boats as vessels that had once been 'vehicles of hope' and had become 'vehicles of death', he warned that when humanity loses its bearings, these tragedies result. In April 2015, he told the crowd in St Peter's Square: '[The migrants] are men and women like us, our brothers seeking a better life, starving, persecuted, wounded, exploited, victims of war.' It is a question not simply of the moral obligation to save people in need, but a collective realisation that the world has entered a new era, and it is in its own interest to face up to it.

Though the countries from which people flee today have often become more violent, and the journeys they are forced to make more frightening, the experiences themselves – of loss, fear, poverty, humiliation – have not in essence changed. What has changed is the way refugees and migrants are perceived: as an invading force, which justifies states in taking whatever measures they choose to 'protect' their borders. The outpouring of collective indignation and generosity after the death of a small boy in the waters off Bodrum in Turkey caused a sudden change of popular mood, in a way that the horrifying statistics and numbers had failed to. But it is one that can change quickly again, as more and more people keep coming. Action for refugees means not simply welcome when they arrive, but an international solution to the conflicts and persecution that made them refugees in the first place. It is a truism never sufficiently repeated that no one wants to be a refugee, that all dream of going home, and that what they need until that moment is to be safe. Survival, not greed, lies behind flight. The task now is to manage, humanely and practically, a crisis of unprecedented dimensions, one that cannot be wished away or wait until treaties and summits.

When I wrote *Human Cargo* in 2005, I wanted to try to turn refugees and asylum-seekers from statistics and faceless numbers into real people, with their own lives and families and pasts. The stories in this book are being lived and repeated, every day, in most parts of the world.

Caroline Moorehead, August 2015

Prologue: The Lost Boys of Cairo

Refugees live in a divided world, between countries in which
they cannot live, and countries which they may not enter.
Elie Wiesel

When Musa Sherif arrived at the house of his friend, a tailor from Sierra
Leone, early in February 2000, he found no one there. He was surprised
because his friend was nearly always at home, waiting for him with his
supper, but he reasoned that the tailor might have had to make a long
journey to the other side of Cairo for a fitting with a client. The room
looked unusually neat and empty, but his place was laid, and there was
dinner in a pot on the stove. On the table sat a brown paper parcel, tied
with string. Musa sat and waited. When some time had passed, he began
to grow anxious. He needed to eat and leave so that he could find
somewhere to sleep that night; as a Liberian asylum-seeker in Egypt he
had no money for a place of his own. And, this being his only meal of the
day, he was hungry. Finally, he ate, sitting uneasily at a corner of the table.
Then he waited some more.

It was now that he suddenly noticed that the brown packet had his
name on it. He opened it. Inside were a newly made pair of trousers, a shirt
and a tie, folded neatly, with a letter on top. 'Dear Musa,' it said, 'here is
a present for you. Forgive me. I have wanted to tell you every day for many
weeks now, but I have been too cowardly. I was chosen for resettlement
in Canada. Today I am leaving.' Musa took the clothes his friend had
made for him, put them on, threw away the frayed and filthy ones that he
had been wearing for many months, and went back to the streets. Unlike
his friend, he had not yet even been recognised as a refugee.

Musa is one of the 'lost boys' of Africa. Though the phrase has come to
be used specifically for the young Sudanese separated from their families
during their flight from the civil war of the 1990s, who grouped together
and eventually made their way to the United States, Cairo is full of lost
boys, though most are no longer boys now, but young men, from Sierra
Leone and Liberia, Ethiopia and Eritrea, Sudan, Guinea, the Ivory Coast,

Rwanda and Burundi. Over the last ten years they have come to Cairo by a hundred different paths, on foot, by ferry, in aeroplanes, on trucks and trains, by camel and horseback, believing that, for all its horror, life was still worth living, that Egypt would be the gateway to a future, and that their past, as victims of the savagery of civil war and modern conflict, was somehow their passport to that future. If the lost boys have something in common, beyond a look of stunned and mistrustful defeat, it is that they have all witnessed acts of unconscionable cruelty, which they alone, out of their large families, have inexplicably survived. Fate – luck – has a particular meaning for them.

I met Musa Sherif for the first time in the late afternoon of 5 February 2000, shortly after his friend's departure for Canada. It was my first day in Cairo. I wouldn't have noticed him – for he was one of fifty-six young Liberians gathered in the office of the African Studies Department of the American University in Cairo – had it not been for his pressed, almost starched new trousers. He was also the only young man in a tie. Later, I would see him in very clean denim dungarees, and in a baggy suit of trousers and bomber jacket, in a fashionable military colour, with striking emerald-green leather trainers: clothes, for Musa, as for many of the other young men, were a symbol of possibility, of belief that there was some order in a profoundly disordered world, and still some hope of being able to make an impression on it.

On this afternoon in early February, Musa had followed the other young men to a meeting called by Barbara Harrell-Bond who, as Emeritus Professor in Refugee Studies at the American University and long a defender and protector of refugees, had become a point of reference for asylum-seekers in Cairo. They were sitting on the floor, pressed closely one next to the other, for the office was too small for such gatherings, in a room of faded elegance, its ornate latticed doors and decorated tiles remnants of Cairo's earlier grandeur. Musa was one of the young men who spoke. His English was good and his voice clear and precise. With his shirt and tie and his overly big glasses with their round frames, he had the look of a bookish, eager accountant or librarian. What I didn't then know was that Musa had been a schoolteacher until the nightmare of his current life overtook him, and that, as the brightest and most promising in a large family of sons, he had been selected by his father as the one to study and make his way in a world beyond their farm and village. Nor did I know then that peculiar-looking little Abdullai, with his bright pink woman's quilted jacket and children's furry earmuffs, to which were attached wire antennae which quivered as he moved his head, was not yet fifteen and living in a derelict car abandoned beyond the airport, and that he was often hungry; or that Abdularam, sitting crosslegged in the front row and asking a stream of highly technical questions about the Refugee Convention, spoke such unfathomable English because he had no back teeth on either side from years of violence and neglect. Later, all these Liberians would become people familiar to me. I carried their stories around with me in my head, stories of murdered parents and burnt-out homes, of terror and flight. And I slowly pieced together – fragment by fragment, offered tentatively as bits in a vast, uncompleted jigsaw in meetings or calls late at night from public telephone boxes – the map of each one's particular odyssey. In the same way, Liberia itself would later become a real place for me, a country of rivers and mountains and towns, but also a place of war and violence, of military commanders, rebel checkpoints and random, hideous brutality. Unschooled, and for the most part on the run and lost for several years, these young men turned out to be keen historians of the civil wars that had destroyed their families and their childhoods.

That late afternoon in February, as the winter sun went down, as the light in the small cramped room faded, and the noises from the narrow street of car-repair shops outside began to grow faint, the Liberians talked on and on about themselves and their fears about what was happening to them. It marked a particular moment in the lives of these fifty-two young men and four girls. Until that afternoon, these young people had been drifting along the margins of Cairo's immense refugee population in search of help, teaming up sometimes, like Musa, with other asylum-seekers from other African countries, but for the most part totally alone. After this time, they would become a band, with the rivalries and animosities inevitable among people so anxious and so destitute, but a band nonetheless, looking after the interests of the others, so that when Abudu was the first to be accepted for resettlement in the United States, and Amr went to prison on obscure charges of spying for Israel, these events would be personal in the lives of each one of them.

It was on that late February afternoon in Cairo that I started to keep notes and that this book began. I wanted it to be about the refugees and asylum-seekers whose stories I had been hearing over twenty years of writing about human rights. It would be, I hoped, a record of what happens to people when their lives spiral out of control into horror and loss, of the lengths they will go to in order to survive, of the extraordinary resilience of ordinary men, women and children when having to accept the unacceptable, and also an account of how the modern world is dealing with exoduses that far exceed in complexity and distance anything the world has known before. I covered both those who travel to flee torture and persecution and those who move to escape poverty and failed lives. And as the months went by and I got to know the Liberians, and then travelled to other places in search of other refugees, the book grew to take in their journeys and their expectations, their former lives, their destinations, and the experiences of those working with them and struggling to formulate coherent policies for the future. I started with no preconceived ideas, beyond a recognition that among the asylum-seekers there are certainly people who have no history of persecution, and that not everything said to me would be true. Without attempting either to cover all parts of the world or all facets of the subject, I listened to their stories and followed wherever they led: the whole journey of exile, from flight to resettlement or return home. I described only what I saw and heard.

Among the young Liberians, Musa's story is remarkable only for the remorselessness of the horrors that overtook him. The brightest boy in a Mende family of four wives and a prosperous farmer in Grand Capemount County, he was sent away to Sierra Leone to train to become a teacher. He was studious and learnt good English and Arabic. When he was seventeen, he went home to teach in the local school and to prepare to succeed his father as village elder. In the photograph taken of him at the time, which he has carried with him all these years, he looks absurdly small and young: short, stocky, with a very round face and an almost jaunty manner. Musa was at home in the large family compound with his new, pregnant wife, sixteen-year-old Zainab, when in 1997 Charles Taylor's second wave of civil war brought marauding killers to Grand Capemount County. Taylor's soldiers wanted no elders and no educated Mendes in the new Liberia. The killing was slow and deliberate. First the women and the girls, after raping them; then the elders, using machetes to chop off arms and legs; then the young men, shot with Kalashnikovs. Musa, in a line with four of his brothers, was the last. By the time the soldiers reached him, an officer had arrived. The killing was stopped. His brothers were all dead, along with his mother, father and sisters. Musa was alive.

He fled. Three days later, at the border with Sierra Leone, he found his wife; she had been raped twice but had not been killed and had not lost the baby. They crossed the frontier and wandered in the bush, eating grass and roots, with his wife's mother and a little girl of five found abandoned along the way, whose parents had been murdered in front of her. One day rebels – bands of soldiers roamed both sides of the border – caught his mother-in-law as she was gathering berries; they raped and mutilated her, and, in great pain, she died. Then Musa was captured, slapped about and scarred with the blade of a bayonet. But Zainab hid in the bushes with the little girl, and their baby, a boy, which had been born under a tree shortly before and survived. Musa escaped and found them and they pressed on, hiding in the undergrowth, begging food from villagers. At last they reached a refugee camp, but they were turned away: it was full, and those who ran it by now feared that all young Liberian men might be killers with tribal scores to settle.

And so they wandered on, stopping from time to time to rest, until one day, on the outskirts of Liberia's capital, Monrovia, they met a friend of Musa's father, a Lebanese trader. Knowing that Musa could not survive for long in a country run by Charles Taylor's men, then hunting down all they suspected of being rebel fighters, he bought him a plane ticket and a visa for Egypt. Musa's wife, first child, adopted daughter and their new baby found refuge with an aunt. Musa was now twenty-two. In Egypt, he believed that he would find asylum; the United Nations High Commissioner for Refugees (UNHCR) would surely grant him refugee status and bring his wife and children to join him. He flew to Cairo, expectant, exhausted by months of fear and frantic with worry about his family.

That was in 1999. By the time I reached Cairo in 2000, Musa was still alone, stateless, without papers, work, a home or his family. UNHCR had neither interviewed him nor recognised his claim to be a refugee. He had lost touch with Zainab and his children; he believed they had fled over the border into Guinea, where the camps for those who escape Liberia's continuing carnage are renowned for rape and casual murder. The politics of the modern refugee world are not on Musa's side. He arrived in Egypt too late. By 1999, all Africa seemed to be on the move, running from the civil wars that are consuming the continent, and many other desperate people had been drawn north by Egypt's open-door policy, not knowing that the country has neither the means nor the intention of looking after those they so hospitably allow in, and that the rest of the world has few plans to give them refuge either.

Over the next three years, shocked by what he felt to be betrayal, Musa slowly shed his hopes one by one. He accepted that he had nowhere to sleep, but had to move from week to week to the floors of other refugees' rooms, always hiding, and knowing that if he was picked up by the police without papers he might be deported or imprisoned. He understood that he would have to wait, perhaps for years, for UNHCR to decide whether or not what he witnessed and endured amounted to the 'justified fear of persecution' that alone would grant him refugee status and the possibility of resettlement in the West. He accepted that he would find no work other than an occasional day as a labourer in the black economy, for as an asylum-seeker with no papers he could not officially work. He concentrated only on one thing: finding his wife and children and bringing them to live with him on the streets of Cairo.

Among the small community of Liberian lost boys, Musa was seen as a loner; he preferred to put his energy into his dreams, alongside which Cairo, with its overcrowding and its incessant noise, its poverty and racism, its bullying police and indifferent aid workers, was a passing nightmare. The boyhood image he had of himself as a teacher and future village elder remained as real to him as it had ever been; he could not and would not give it up, just as he would not learn Egyptian Arabic, for to do so meant that he had accepted that he would never leave. And so he preferred not to seek out the company of the other Liberians with similar pasts, young men like Abdula, who made jokes in an American accent learnt from the tourists who used to come to Egypt before the spectre of terrorism destroyed the holiday market, and who once saw rebel soldiers burn his father over an open fire before hacking him into little pieces, or Mohamed, a tall boy with a moon-like face and frightened eyes, who watched as his godmother's head was kicked about like a football, or Abu, the boy-soldier whose rite of passage included the slitting open of a pregnant woman's stomach. What these lost boys have seen and been forced to do is not something others care to hear about.

In autumn, the early mornings in Cairo are almost cool. The pollution, which normally hangs over the streets like a heavy yellow blanket, is light and at this hour the city is still and quiet. Long before it is properly day, the asylum-seekers gather at the gates of the offices of UNHCR. There are the Dinkas from Sudan with their very long legs, and the elegant, high-cheekboned Somalis; some of the Sierra Leoneans have no arms or hands, their rebels having decided that mutilating civilians is an effective way of terrorising those who might be tempted to support the government. Then there are the Ethiopians, whose ancient allegiance to Haile Selassie has branded them as traitors to the new regime, and men and women from Rwanda and Burundi, where massacres became a way of life, and other Sudanese, dissident survivors of torture in Khartoum's security headquarters. They come at dawn to wait, in the hope that their names may feature on the new lists of those called for interview, to hand in documents, or to jostle for a slip of paper with a date on which they can collect a form which will allow them to apply for an interview, many months, even years, into the future. Documents of any kind, even scraps of paper with a number on them, are infinitely precious: they suggest identity, a possible existence. Tattered high-school certificates, old driving licences, envelopes with addresses on them, preserved against all odds during flight, are guarded and produced with pride. At UNHCR's gates all fear that they may learn that their appeal has failed and their file is closed, so that the future contains only statelessness or deportation. 'CLOSED FILE', the terrible words that signify the end of this particular road, are written in large black capital letters.

Since the middle of the 1980s, Egypt has opted for the solution – adopted by forty-one countries – of having UNHCR interview its asylum-seekers in order to decide whether their fear of persecution is well-founded, with the result that the UN body, once revered for its mandate of protecting refugees, is, in Egypt, both prosecution and defence, an anomalous and uneasy position it occupies today with growing prickliness and paranoia. In 2000, 3,057 refugees left Cairo for new lives in the United States, Canada and Australia, the vast majority to the USA. But after 11 September 2001, President Bush declined to fix a quota for the year's intake, thereby closing the door not only to the refugees who hoped to win places, but also to all those who had already been accepted but had not yet left; they have now been told they need to be vetted again for possible terrorist links. No one really thinks that the United States will ever again be very welcoming to those persecuted in other lands.

Inside UNHCR's offices, where only those called for interview ever penetrate, there is an embattled air. It is not easy to be a gatekeeper to the future of so many desperate people; nor is it easy to keep in mind the intricacies of the civil wars and political repression across much of the African continent. Not all the young Egyptians employed to vet cases enjoy pronouncing on whether the violence suffered and remembered constitutes a degree of persecution extreme enough to make return too dangerous. In this daily listening for the nuances of deceit – the little lies that will mark a claim as false – something of UNHCR's noble mandate is being lost. But it is perhaps wrong to blame those who listen, for hour after hour, to these tales of bloodshed and torture. There are too many cases, too much suffering, too little time. What is happening in Cairo today is happening all over the world, and as the funds are cut, the number of asylum-seekers keeps on growing and the West becomes more fearful and more isolated, so those who man the gates in Cairo are under pressure to search ever more keenly for lies and inconsistencies. And so the refugees despair.

Fear, memory and expectations, endlessly deferred, rule in the quick-sands of Cairo's refugee world. Psychiatrists say that it is important for peace of mind to live in the present, to come to terms with daily existence, and neither brood about the past nor attach too much meaning to the future; but the refugees trapped in Cairo today, haunted by terrifying memories of loss and savagery, seduced by a longing for a world they perceive as stable and fulfilling, cannot accept the present. Cairo is a prison sentence, to be endured because there is no option. They simply wait. 'The problem for refugees here,' a young man told a church-worker not long ago, 'is that they have no real existence: they live in their head.' Like Musa, no African will consider learning more than the few words of Arabic they need to live: it is too potent a symbol of failure. The few lucky enough to have the desperately desired blue refugee card are not always the happiest. Gone are the terrors of sudden arrest, but resettlement is never automatic and it can take many years; the waiting becomes almost too painful as the image of the West becomes more glorious month by month. There have been suicides, people unable to wait any longer; they have no courage left, having used it up on their torturers and the long, frightening journeys to safety. When the refugees decide to die, some do so by jumping from the balconies of Cairo's tall buildings; a ten-year-old boy killed himself this way not long ago.

Cairo is not just one of the most polluted cities in the world; it is dirty, intensely overcrowded, broken down and full of rubble, with roads built up on legs above other roads in an attempt to dispel the traffic jams that paralyse the city for all of the day and most of the night. Occasionally, between the brick and the cement, you catch glimpses of filigreed minarets, delicately carved porticoes and arcades, stately facades and the traces of sumptuous courtyards, earlier Cairos of the Islamic master-craftsmen and Coptic merchants, when the city was a splendid place of pleasure gardens and cool palaces, civil servants in their red fezzes strolled along tree-lined avenues and visitors drank sherbet in famous tearooms. It is the utterly derelict nature of the city today that partly makes possible its absorption of so many refugees – 200,000? 500,000? No one can say for sure. Around the city's edges, entrepreneurs keep constructing identical breeze-block buildings in ever widening circles, leaving the top floor unfinished so that other floors can be added year by year. From the top of the buildings along the Nile, on the rare moments when the smog evaporates and the setting sun lights up the horizon, you can see the Pyramids at Giza, framed by the jagged edges of yet more unfinished blocks. Wherever the buildings are most derelict, the electricity supplies most sporadic, the water least reliable, there the refugees live.

Donzo is another young Liberian, an almost jaunty, good-looking Mandingo with deep regular gashes along both his cheeks. He was one of the first of the young men to bring me his testimony, so that I could turn it into a formal application for refugee status with UNHCR. When he was sixteen Donzo was caught by Charles Taylor's men. They didn't want him for a boy-soldier, but they wanted information about the Mandingos. He had none to give. Before letting him go, a soldier took out his knife and, getting his companions to hold the boy still, carved slits across both sides of his face. Six years later, having lost his grandparents, parents, seven brothers and sisters, several aunts and uncles, and many cousins, he fled to Cairo and went to live with eleven other young Africans on the seventh floor of what must once have been a fine apartment block. This was soon after the meeting in the offices of the African Studies Department at the American University in Cairo in February 2000, when the young Liberians took to living in groups and I started visiting them at home so that they could show me, with a mixture of pride and embarrassment, how they were coping with their lives.

In two high-ceilinged rooms with cornices and the remains of parquet floors, these eleven young men have two broken beds, two chairs, three blankets, a light bulb and a very old, erratic television set. The glass in the windows up the staircase has long since broken, leaving a few splintered edges. A lift, its mahogany doors wrenched off, dangles from one rusting pulley. Rubbish fills every corner and down the wide marble stairs, chipped and blackened by filth, trickles an open sewer. The banisters have gone. It is almost completely dark. Donzo and his companions live on $40 a month, the allowance received from UNHCR by the one Sierra Leonean recognised as an official refugee. At the beginning of the month when the money comes, Donzo tells me, they eat rice and some vegetables cooked in oil; by the end they are down to just bread. They seldom leave the building for fear of arrest, preferring to spend the months of waiting in the semi-dark, almost comatose with boredom and inertia. Izako, Donzo's friend and a former customs officer, had left a wife and two children in Monrovia after he had been tortured and raped by Charles Taylor's soldiers: he worries, during the long empty days, about whether they are still alive. If the figures of acceptance by UNHCR remain the same, I write in my notebook after this first visit to their rooms, seven of these eleven boys will never leave Cairo.

Asylum-seekers with families, like the thousands of Sudanese who have arrived since the war intensified in southern Sudan in the late 1990s, prefer to live in shanty towns on the outskirts, where widows share rooms without light or water. TB among these families is endemic; the children have open sores and scabies; they cough and scratch constantly. They do not go to school, for school is not available to asylum-seekers, and a whole generation is growing up illiterate. When the Sudanese women find work as maids, they lock their children for safety into the almost empty, dusty, box-like rooms, where they lie on blankets on the dirt floor. Apart from the shafts of light that filter through cracks in the door, it is dark; they stay there all day. At Arba Nos, where the desert begins, 300 Sudanese families live and wait. At least 200, I work out, will never get away.

Over the next three years, between the spring of 2000 and late 2003, I went back to Cairo four times with Lyndall Passerini, a writer friend. We returned to help set up a legal-advice centre for asylum-seekers to prepare their submissions and their testimonies for their interviews with UNHCR, and, with money from friends, to start a number of small educational projects among people for whom schooling is often the only symbol of a possible alternative future. We found the money to provide teachers for classes of young Somalis, held in the homes of those fortunate enough to have them, to fund a nursery school at Arba Nos for Sudanese children up to the age of four, giving them food and medical care and somewhere to spend the days so that their mothers did not have to leave them locked in dark and airless huts, and to support English classes for adult Sudanese who, hoping for eventual resettlement in Australia, Canada or the United States, knew that speaking English was a first step to getting there. But it was the Liberians who, day after day, brought us their stories and proved the most engaging and demanding students.

By the spring of 2001, exactly a year after my first visit to Cairo, a flat had been rented in one of Cairo's poorest and most distant suburbs, two classes formed with blackboards and plastic chairs, maps of Africa pinned to the walls, and books brought out from England. A teacher had been found, and Mohamed Bafalie, a tall, responsible young man who had been a teacher in Monrovia before having to flee, was appointed director of the school. Bafalie's wife, Khalidatou, who had followed him to Cairo after being persecuted by soldiers, was forced to leave their small son and daughter behind with her mother.

From the first day the young Liberians were absolutely clear about their school: they wanted to learn everything. Asked to make lists of what they wished to be taught, they wrote down: engineering, psychiatry, car maintenance, political science, economics, media studies, philosophy, law, history, medicine, creative writing. Most could read and write, but very few had completed more than a couple of years of elementary school. They accepted with good grace when offered English grammar, literature, a little modern history and politics. Given their fares by bus to this distant flat, they came assiduously, though their journeys, as the only black people in crowds of often hostile Cairenes, were frightening: Mohamed, the moon-faced boy, was attacked one day on a bus by a group of teenage boys, who beat him about the head with a stick with a nail in it. Early gatherings were polite, subdued; as the months passed, as they felt safer, the young men began to challenge and argue. They began to want things. They were always polite, but they were now also firm. In class, they asked questions, demanded tests; they wanted, always, more: more homework, more classes, more information. They wanted the internet and new computers, they wanted certificates, they wanted assurances that they would not be abandoned.

And, slowly, they advanced up the uncertain and interminable queue at UNHCR. By the time of my third visit, in the spring of 2002, all fifty-six had had their first interview, and five had been accepted for resettlement in the West. Their pleasure, their relief at such good fortune, spread through the group: it had happened to five, it could happen to them all. Though they were still living on the edge of destitution and subject to occasional casual racist attacks, the mood within the group began to change. It became lighter. They gave out a sense that the future had opened again. Now, emailing me when I was back in London, they tentatively asked for things, impossibly ambitious, often, but a sign that they imagined a life in which they might really become engineers and lawyers. Kabineh, a short, very young-looking boy, with cropped hair and a childish grin, wrote: 'I am sleeping from place to place with a lot of disturbance. 2 books I really wished you could send for me: (1) mass communication, (2) Business Management.' Bility, who always wore a brown woolly hat, whatever the heat, wondered whether he could have a shortwave radio to listen to the news from Liberia. All longed for computers.

Then, in the autumn of 2002, something happened that changed the Liberian story. One of the young men, Amr, was arrested. For a while, no one could discover why. It became known that he had been taken to the

Mogamma, the ministry of foreign affairs, a vast ugly building that faces Cairo's fine Museum of Antiquities in Tahir Square. There were rumours that he had been tortured. At a first court appearance, he had bruises on his face and neck, and he appeared confused and fragile. Then it transpired that the security police had spotted him outside the Israeli Embassy, decided that he had been spying for Israel, and further suspected that he was involved in a money-laundering operation. The charges were absurd; but in the volatile world in which Cairo's asylum-seekers exist, they were terrifying. If the Egyptian police could really imagine that a Muslim Liberian was helping the Israeli secret police, then which one of them might not be a target next?

Other arrests followed. One of the first was Kono, a short, thickset, phlegmatic boy of twenty, one of the group's only two Christians. He was solid, slow moving and very sad. I knew Kono from my first visit to Cairo, when he came to my flat one day and described his childhood: how he was the only son of parents who had both worked for Samuel Doe, President of Liberia until ousted by the rebels, and how, when the rebels closed in on the presidential palace, they arrested everyone they found with any connection to the dead president, and killed both his parents. Kono had then gone to live with a much-loved uncle and aunt, who brought him up as their son, until the day that his aunt went to the market and was captured by rebels and raped before being killed. His uncle survived for a while longer, but then he too was seized in one of the frequent outbreaks of violence that consumed Monrovia in the 1990s, and killed. Kono was then twelve.

In Cairo, awaiting news of his UNHCR interview, Kono had decided, for reasons he was never able to explain to anyone, to accept an offer made to young Muslims from Africa to study at Al Azhar, Cairo's Islamic university, and to take a place in the dormitory they provided for homeless students. He did not, of course, tell them that he was a Christian. However, someone told on him. He was immediately arrested by the university's guards and turned over to the police, who announced that he would be deported. Unusually, he was left in a corridor while arrangements were being made to take him to a prison; he escaped. As he told the story later, he made his way to the offices of UNHCR, where an outraged young Egyptian interviewer told him that she wanted nothing more to do with him, as he was clearly a liar, and as such ineligible for any kind of UNHCR assistance. Kono disappeared into hiding.

The next to go was a wiry, bookish boy called Mustafa Kromer. Mustafa had once explained to me that, as the youngest son of a man with many wives and many children, he had never been quite sure how many of the boys and girls who thronged the family compound in Liberia were his full brothers and sisters. His own mother died when he was seven, and he had been cared for by a grandmother. Mustafa was out fishing when the rebels came to Grand Capemount County in 1991. His grandmother, fearing the advance of the soldiers, took him to hide in the bush, but the life was very hard, she was elderly, and died soon after. Mustafa returned to his village and found his father, and with him and other children he moved from village to village across north-western Liberia in search of safety. He was eleven when he saw his first killing – a cousin beaten to death in front of him when he failed to answer questions from rebel soldiers. The rebels now advancing their way through Grand Capemount County towards Monrovia were led by a man called Alhaji G. V. Kromah. Anyone bearing the name Kromah or Kromer was suspect in the eyes of the government forces sent out to confront the rebels and, one by one, members of Mustafa's large family were captured and killed. Mustafa himself was picked up with two of his brothers and taken to an army camp, where he was beaten and questioned. Mustafa's testimony, told to me over several weeks, runs to many pages: it is a slow, sad story of flight, violence and the gradual destruction of a once happy and united family, as one by one adults and children disappeared, were killed or simply died from hunger and exhaustion. By September 1998 Mustafa was the only survivor. A family friend, finding him wandering on the streets of Monrovia, smuggled him to Cairo. He was seventeen.

Mustafa spent three weeks in an Egyptian cell behind a police station in the spring of 2002. He was given only water for the first five days and kept permanently blindfolded. He was not allowed to use the lavatory. He was also slapped and kicked, something he made little of, being accustomed to physical brutality. In Cairo, prisoners call the room set aside in prisons and police stations for questioning and physical brutality the 'freezer'. Mustafa was not subjected to the electric shocks given to many taken into detention, but when they took off his blindfold after five days they put him into a small cell and left him there. It was not empty; on the contrary, it held about fifty people. There was no room for the prisoners to do anything but stand. They took it in turns to sit down.

Mustafa was eventually released; he was not told why he had been arrested. By now, however, there was a rumour going round the Liberian community that they were being singled out for persecution by the Egyptian police because Charles Taylor, then President of Liberia, had publicly announced his support for the Israeli Prime Minister, Ariel

Sharon. It was now widely suspected that the Liberian boys were spies for Israel.

As more arrests took place, as more of the young men were taken in for questioning, slapped about, held overnight, threatened with deportation and indefinite detention in one of Egypt's infamous jails, in which prisoners remain for years without charge or trial, as Amr remained inside and was known to have been tortured again, as Kono disappeared altogether, so fear began to spread among the Liberians. The fact that Amr had been an accepted refugee, with his blue card from UNHCR and the possibility of resettlement before too long in the West, and yet was still not safe from police brutality, added to the tension. UNHCR, whose mandate of protection for refugees should in theory have saved Amr from torture and arbitrary detention, was able to do nothing. Edgy and fearful, the young Liberians began to fall out among themselves, accusing each other of absurd and random misdemeanours, watching over their shoulders for betrayal. A feeling of panic seized the group. Musa, the outsider, the young man who had held aloof from the classes and avoided all overtures of friendship, suddenly disappeared from Cairo. He was reported to have returned to Liberia to look for his wife and children, but a rumour started going round that he had become a spy for the Egyptian secret service in return for food and a place to sleep. He was said to have been sighted talking to a stranger near the Mogamma. His ticket to Monrovia was said to have cost $650, and the fact he could find such a sum was proof, said the others, of his guilt. I had last seen him walking along the towpath by the Nile in his emerald-green trainers, talking feverishly about his rejection by the group, like an animal expelled from a pack. He was defiant and agitated.

Towards the end of July 2002, a month when temperatures in Cairo rise to over 40°C and the normally frenetic city is stunned into inertia, six more Liberians lost their nerve. Approaching one of the foreign smugglers and traffickers who prey on refugees and asylum-seekers everywhere, they were directed to catch a bus to Nueba, one of Egypt's resorts on the Red Sea. The plan was for them to cross by night into Israel, something of an irony given the suspicions already existing. Before they were able to slip across, as they were leaving their hotel in the dark, the Egyptian security police arrived and arrested them. Two of the group were married, a young couple called Gedaweh and Mahmada. They had been forced to leave their two children behind in Liberia when fleeing in 1999. They were both recognised refugees, but had already waited for over three years for their promised resettlement in the West, from where they would be able to bring their children to join them. They were now afraid that if arrested they might never see their children again. Gedaweh, like Musa, was a teacher. He later told a friend what happened to them in Nueba. They were just leaving their rooms in the hotel when the security men arrived. Mahmada was pushed back into the room and on to the bed, with such force that she fell to the floor. The Liberians were then taken to the local police station, and next morning they were interrogated. 'They asked us,' Gedaweh told his friend, 'what we were doing in Nueba. We said that we were tourists. They insisted that we were spies for Israel. When we asked for some water to drink, because it was very hot and we were very thirsty, they gave us sea water. For three days, all we were given to drink was salt water.' Later, Gedaweh heard one of the policemen say to his superior officer: 'Captain, you're wasting your time with these people. If it was me, I would open fire on them, and that would be the end of it.' The six were freed.

By the time I returned to Cairo in November 2002, Gedaweh and his wife had gone. The trafficker had found a better route across the Sinai and they were in hiding in Tel Aviv, paying off the smuggler's fee in hard labour, laying a new water pipeline for the settlements. They were living, so word reached Cairo, in a disused hangar, under guard, and working twelve-hour days. They were said to be hungry. They had taken with them Fumbe, a footballer, who had cleaned our kitchen during our first visit to Cairo in 2000; and also a shy and gentle boy called Mamadu, with his rather small head and very cropped hair, who had been badly beaten up by the police on their first attempt at escape. Mamadu was one of the Liberians I knew best. He was one of the first who came to talk to me, and having come once, came back again and again, adding details to his original testimony that he had been at first too ashamed and too afraid to recall. Mamadu had been a boy-soldier. A small, myopic child, he had seen his parents and his three younger brothers and sisters dragged out of their house in Monrovia and killed in front of him, his mother and father shot, the children battered to death. At least, he said, he hadn't actually *seen* this happen, because the rebels had pulled him behind their Jeep; but he had heard it, the shots and the sounds of bodies being hit and the cries. He was then eleven. The rebels took him back with them to their camp to join the other children they intended to turn into soldiers. What happened to him next was something I only slowly pieced together as I got to know him and he began to trust me, and after I had finally understood how very short-sighted he was and taken him to an oculist who told me that he could barely see across a room.

For a while, the rebels left Mamadu with the girls they had captured on earlier raids. The children prepared food for the rebel leaders, fetched wood and washed clothes. But the day came when Mamadu was ordered to follow the soldiers on a raid, and a day soon after when he was given a Kalashnikov and told to shoot one of the captives, a terrified woman with a small child clinging to her. Mamadu refused. He was beaten, slapped, denied food. Later, he was again taken on a raid and given a gun. He was told that if he refused to shoot, he would be killed. The captives this time were all men. Mamadu shut his eyes and fired. He never asked if he had killed anyone; he didn't want to know. He suspects that he did. The raids went on. Mamadu spent his days planning his escape. At last the day came when he was trusted sufficiently to be sent to a nearby village in search of food. When he got there he found a woman in the market and begged for help. She took him in, hid him, and later helped him to make his way to Monrovia. Behind the fragility, the short-sighted stare, the gentle manners, lay an absolute will to survive. In Cairo, this became a desperate need to be educated, as if only an education could redeem the horror of the past. It was all he wanted to talk about when I saw him on my visits to the rented Liberian classrooms, where he was one of the most eager and dedicated students, attending every session, whatever it was about. Now, having heard that he had been taken by the smugglers to Tel Aviv, I tried to find him. I could only imagine how frightened he must have been, how very close to the edge of endurance, to have taken the decision to flee. His last email from Cairo had been sad, but then I had not known what he was planning. 'We do promise to never forget about you. Especially me, Mamadu. You know it's just such kind of cruel juke of nature to suddenly surprise us with such big and ugly separation.' In Israel, friends tried to trace him. He seemed to have disappeared.

In November 2002 I started to keep a proper diary. Eleven Liberians were by now in Israel, among them probably Donzo, the boy with the scars across his face. Two had left for resettlement in the States. Two had vanished, rumoured to have been deported back to Liberia. Musa was still missing. Abdula, the charming, jaunty boy, with his American accent and his spiky hair, who had watched his father burnt very slowly to death over an open fire, was in hospital, seriously ill with tuberculosis and pneumonia. 'The Liberians are frightened,' I wrote in my notebook. 'Amr is in prison, Kono in hiding, Mamadu has fled. No one feels safe.' The Liberian flat had been closed down after the security police called in the teachers for questioning. The classes had been transferred to a room in the American University, but only half the Liberians were now attending, and when they came they were anxious and distracted. The others were staying at home, not daring to be seen on the streets. At UNHCR, in the wake of Septembetr 11 2001, the refugees said that the emphasis during interviews was on lies, how best to catch out the asylum-seekers, find holes in their testimonies so that they could be turned down. I learnt that a new stamp had been devised – LOC, 'lack of credibility' – and that it was now stamped onto most of the files as a reason for rejection. 'But who is to say what is credible,' I wrote in my diary,

> when you have been shot at by rebels, when you have seen your mother raped and your brothers and sisters burnt to death in your house, when your father has disappeared and you are now alone in the world? When you are ashamed to describe to the young woman sitting across the desk from you with her tapping pencil and her inquisitive eyes what the soldiers did to you and how you are afraid that you may have Aids from being raped by the guards and how you ache for news of your family who you really know perfectly well that you will never see again? How do you explain that the journey from your village in Africa to Cairo took everything you had in terms of money, and more than money, courage, imagination and hope? That if the woman sitting at the desk turns you down, you have no idea what you will do next, and that your reserves of hope have gone? That though you look tidy, well turned out, this is because you have spent the money you borrowed on soap with which to wash yourself and your clothes for this interview, and that you are absolutely terrified that you may not be saying the right things?

I wanted to see Amr, still in a police lock-up on the edge of Cairo. There was talk that he would soon be released, after almost a year in prison, for lack of evidence. One morning, I had a call from Fofana, the most qualified of the young Liberians. He had gained a First in law, having completed his degree at Al Azhar after arriving in Cairo, and had recently been told that his resettlement application for the US had gone through. With his serious, even ponderous, manner, he had become something of a legal spokesman for the group. He would, he said, take me to the police lock-up, where we would at least be able to call to Amr through a fence.

Later, I wrote:

> Amr's name is called. I see his fingers first, clutching at the top

of a black painted iron gate covered with thick wire netting, where there is an 18-inch gap between the gate and the ceiling. After his fingers, the top of his head appears, and then his eyes, as he pulls himself up by his arms, helped by other prisoners below. We call out to each other. I have brought him a belt, to hold up his trousers, because his own has been taken away from him, and some food. It is passed from hand to hand, from guard to guard, and then given to Amr, whose arm can just squeeze through the gap. Since I can only see the top of his face, I cannot tell how he is.

Going back into Cairo by bus, we passed the City of the Dead, the great Cairo cemetery of houses and mausoleums and mosques, built for the bodies and spirits of the departed. Fofana told me that it now had six million people – a figure I find almost impossible to believe – living in it, people who can find no housing among the living.

Six months later, in the spring of 2003, I was back in Cairo. Amr had been released. A Spanish woman, Ana Liria-Franck, had been appointed to head UNHCR's Cairo office and with her had come more generous policies towards the asylum-seekers. Some groups were now being accepted de facto as refugees under the 1951 Convention, by virtue not of their individual fears of persecution, but because of where they had come from and the continuing turmoil inside their countries. First interviews had speeded up considerably, and by now all the Liberians were through the first stage, and some were on their way to resettlement in the West. Those destined for America were full of excited dreams, and had taken to carrying American comics and magazines around with them. For those who remained in Cairo, better things were promised. In UNHCR, Ana Liria-Franck and her colleagues were trying to make plans – 'durable solutions' in the language of the UN – for those whose cases were not strong enough to win them full status under the 1951 Convention but who nonetheless were unable to go home. Among the Liberians, now down to thirty-four – the other twenty-two scattered between Israel, the United States, Canada and a handful back in Liberia – the mood was buoyant. 'Group very depleted,' I wrote. 'Most of those who remain are excited, talkative. But some are still worried. Bility, in his brown woolly hat, says that he can't talk about English grammar any longer when he has nowhere proper to live and often nothing to eat.' Bility told me that he had been buying chicken carcasses from restaurants, on which the wings are usually left, and that he made soup from them.

Just the same, for the most part the young Liberians were reclaiming their lives, one by one. All, that is, except for those who had fled across the desert and into Israel and who now found themselves in a limbo. After many months, news had reached the group in Cairo that they had worked off their smugglers' fees and were now free. Accorded the lowest rung of recognition by the Israelis, they were safe to stay, but they still had no proper papers, no right to travel and their prospects for an education were very poor. Gedaweh and Mahmada, having now not seen their children for almost four years, had no possibility of having them join them. Like Fumbe, the young footballer, what they felt most bitterly was that, had they stayed in Cairo, they would by now have been on their way to the US, Australia or Canada, with Kono and Mohamed, to be resettled in new lives. But it was from Mamadu, the short-sighted boy-soldier from whom I had heard nothing in almost a year, that I had the saddest news.

Having reached Tel Aviv on his second attempt, Mamadu was still working off his smuggler's fee in a cement factory. His health was poor and made considerably worse by the dust, and he had lost many days of work through illness. He wheezed constantly and was sleeping on the floor of a disused warehouse; he seldom had enough to eat. 'I feel myself growing older and do not know anything,' he wrote. When I sent him money, partly for a doctor for a rash that had spread across his face, he wrote again, about 'repairing wounds from my face ... There is no way I can pay you back for everything that you've done for me, you are a special credited person from the deepest part of my heart and someday I believe you will be proud of me ... hopefully I will be fine as long as I know myself.' A few months later, he emailed me to say that he had found work washing up in a hotel. 'Am quite sure some day things are going to be much better with lots of fun and joye. A day that one does not have to always worry about how life is going to be tomorrow. Pretty soon that day will arrive.' This was soon after his twentieth birthday. He had been alone for nine years. His dream was to become a mathematician.

The refugees are not absolutely without help in Cairo. There is something in the utter desolation and loss of the refugee existence, the courage of the stories of endurance, that strikes a chord among those drawn to the world of human rights. Lawyers and doctors, teachers and a few social workers, both Egyptian and foreign, struggle to find answers to a situation that appears more intractable with every passing week. In shabby offices in various parts of the city I discovered people helping the asylum-seekers with their testimonies so that no opportunity would be lost when the date for an interview with UNHCR finally arrived; doctors who, in their spare time, treated those who had been most profoundly tortured and worried about increasing alcoholism among the men and how to alleviate the profound depression that afflicts so many refugees; priests who collected money and unwanted clothes to give to the most destitute; church-workers who ran small feeding programmes. Like charitable endeavour everywhere, it touched only the very edges of what was wrong. Lying at a crossroads for the flow of Africa's displaced people, Cairo is a staging post for refugees, a step on a journey that should, but seldom does, move from terror to safety. Neither the beginning nor the end of their odyssey, the city is where the policies and the resolutions succeed or fail, where all that is expected of UNHCR is most visibly exposed. In the great international debate about the future of asylum, the trading in quotas, the many arguments about mandate and responsibilities, the haggling over economic migrants, the seminars about 'irregular movers' and the internally displaced, Cairo provides one view of the collapse of this ideal.

Not long ago a Sudanese man, carrying a small girl in his arms, managed to get past the guards at UNHCR and into the office of a member of staff. The child was crying loudly. The man was also crying. Arriving before the interviewer's desk, he drew back the skirt of the girl's dress and pointed to her legs: they were covered in open, bleeding, infected sores. 'Help me,' he said to the woman. 'Help me to do something, help me to go to a doctor.' The woman, it seems, sat frozen, speechless. The man grew more agitated and insistent. Still, she did nothing. At last, despairing, beyond endurance, he pulled from his pocket the blue refugee card he had fought so long and so hard to obtain, and tore it in shreds. 'Now I am . . .' he cried out, trying to explain an act so symbolic and so momentous in words that could never be strong enough, '. . . I am ashamed to be a refugee.'

Part One

A View of History

Chapter One

The Homeless and the Rightless

Displacement is like death. One thinks
it happens only to other people.
Mourid Barghouti

When Henri Dunant arrived home from the battle of Solferino in June 1859, full of disgust and pity at the treatment of wounded soldiers, Geneva was a small, pious, scholarly city, where people lived modestly and regarded themselves as enlightened conservatives. In the narrow streets of the fine old town, up and down the Grand Rue where the rich, established families lived, they had long felt pride not only in the number and variety of their philanthropic endeavours, but also in the welcome they extended to the people they called 'aliens', the foreigners and political refugees such as Voltaire and Jean-Jacques Rousseau who had come to settle along the shores of their lake, and whom they regarded as assets, not liabilities.

For all their instinctive misgivings about Dunant's impetuousness and touches of vanity, the Genevois quickly perceived that there was much lustre to be gained for their city in his impassioned pleas for humane action in the conduct of war. Soon, committees were meeting to draft articles on the laws of war, on the care of wounded soldiers, and on injuries caused by particular kinds of weapons. They were not the first proposals dealing with the regulation of warfare, but they were more ambitious than most that had gone before, and the timing was right. By 1864, the Red Cross movement was born, and the first Geneva Convention had been drafted and presented for signature to the nations of the world. The Genevois took immense pleasure in their new initiative, though by now Dunant himself was an outcast, victim of a foolish financial speculation and consigned to obscurity until unexpectedly awarded the first Nobel Peace Prize as an old man over forty years later.

Geneva's credentials for the new humanitarian movement were excellent. Switzerland was a neutral country strategically placed at the heart of Europe, its absolute neutrality sanctioned by the Treaty of Westphalia in 1648 and again by the Treaty of Vienna in 1815, since when it had welcomed a steady flow of people at times of European unrest. It was prosperous and it was pacifist. Not surprising, then, that in 1920, when millions of people were made stateless by the dismantling of the Ottoman and Austro-Hungarian empires and the collapse of Tsarist Russia, it was to Geneva that the world looked for the creation of an organisation to care for those fleeing chaos, famine and persecution. By then the League of Nations had been set up in the Palais des Nations, not far from the lake. For the International Committee of the Red Cross, just up the road, deeply involved in refugee matters and enjoying considerable international prestige as a result of its work during World War I, it was an obvious step to put pressure on the new League to care for refugees.

In 1921, the League persuaded the Norwegian explorer Fridjof Nansen – he was sixty and would have preferred to pursue his scientific interests – to take the job of negotiating the repatriation of some 500,000 Russian prisoners of war; the following year, he was appointed first High Commissioner for Refugees. Nansen received little funding, but he possessed a great deal of passion and energy. He persuaded governments to recognise travel documents for stateless Russians – the Nansen passport – and then turned his attention to the problem of the hundreds of thousands of Bulgarians, Romanians, Magyars and Armenians, survivors of the Turkish massacres, now wandering Europe and constantly turned away at borders. 'Once they had left their homeland,' wrote Hannah Arendt in the 1950s, 'they remained homeless; once they had left their state, they became stateless; once they had been deprived of their rights, they became rightless, the scum of the earth.'

Nansen worked extremely hard all through the 1920s. By his death in 1930 he had almost single-handedly helped a large number of people and established a principle of moral responsibility for the displaced, but the organisation had as yet very little bite and could do little to help the Jews, who by the early 1930s were already looking for safety from Nazi rule and finding the doors of Western states closed against them. In 1933, the League of Nations set up a High Commissioner for Refugees from Germany, but so anxious was it not to offend the German government, still at this point a member of the League, that it agreed to regard the matter solely as an internal affair and to confine its attentions to emigration and travel documents, with no questions asked about the conditions and causes for flight. An outspoken early commissioner, James G. McDonald, resigned in despair in 1936. Two years later, the Germans left the League, but even so the Western governments remained reluctant to offend them. When it came to human lives, McDonald said bitterly but without effect, 'considerations of diplomatic correctness must yield to those of common humanity'.

The economic depression that spread across North America and Europe in the 1930s did much to set back the refugee cause. National interests, governments argued, would be best served by imposing tough limits on immigration. One by one, ever more restrictive laws, aimed at keeping out all but carefully selected groups, were passed. It was only after considerable pressure from Jewish associations that President Roosevelt agreed, in 1938, to call an international conference at Evian to discuss ways to resettle the Jews now trying to escape Austria and Germany. Evian is a shameful milestone in the history of refugee affairs. It was there that delegates from most of the major Western powers rose, one after the other, to talk about their own national levels of unemployment and to argue that the movement of so many Jewish refugees could only be 'disturbing to the general economy'. Evian offered no lifeline to the Jews of Europe. All it achieved was the creation of a feeble intergovernmental committee on refugees. It was unable either to persuade Germany to allow their Jewish citizens to emigrate with money or possessions, or to convince Great Britain not to curtail the immigration of Jews into Palestine. Germany, encouraged by the world's evident indifference to the suffering of the Jews as well as the other unwanted members of its population, stepped up its own punishments and restrictions. Nansen's dream, of a world that took responsibility for the fate of those who fell victim to human-rights abuses and were forced to flee their homes, lay in ruins.

By early 1945, there were over 40 million people drifting about Europe, stateless, displaced, lost. There were Germans trying to go home; there were survivors of the concentration camps; there were those whose countries and homes had been swallowed up, as borders had been redrawn and territory had changed hands. Many of these people, Russians and Czechs, Poles and Hungarians, Ukrainians and Romanians, gathered in Germany, a country in which almost everything – houses, roads, railway lines, water supplies, industry and agriculture – had collapsed.

The Western powers had been preparing for this moment. As early as November 1943, meetings had been held by the Allies to discuss what relief measures would be necessary when the Axis countries were at last defeated. Mindful of their lack of generosity in the pre-war years and appalled by the stories now emerging from the occupied countries of German atrocities, forty-four states agreed to donate large sums of money to assist and return home those who had been displaced by war. Between the autumn of 1943 and the summer of 1947, a UN Relief and Rehabilitation Administration, employing at its peak over 27,000 people, spent $3.6 billion, the bulk of it given by the United States. One of UNRRA's many tasks, debated at some length at both the Yalta and the Potsdam conferences, was how to repatriate as quickly and as efficiently as possible all those wanting to return home at the end of hostilities. Unlike its predecessors, UNRRA proved effective. In the first five months of peace, three-quarters of the displaced went home.

However, it soon became apparent that not everyone actually wanted to go home, particularly as news began reaching the West that Stalin was sending many of those who returned straight to the gulags. By 1946 repatriation had all but stopped, and a million people were still in Europe's refugee camps.

It was in New York and Washington, rather than in Geneva, that the next step in the refugee story took place. At the heart of the post-war sessions debating the new United Nations, and among those drafting the Universal Declaration of Human Rights, the talk was all about the rights of people, their right to flee from oppression, to express their own views, to practise their own faiths, and to choose for themselves where they wanted to live. Refugees, lacking protection, became people of international concern and protection. And it was no longer simply a matter of groups of people, fleeing and being assisted together, but of individuals with their own cases, their own choices and fears and anxieties. According to Article 14 of the Universal Declaration, every individual was to have the 'right to seek and to enjoy in other countries asylum from persecution'.

UNRRA had been established to deal with repatriations. As its chief funder, America now decided to wind up its activities. In the face of bitter opposition from the Eastern bloc, which continued to call on its former citizens to come home, the US voted to create a new body, the International Refugee Organisation. The IRO's mandate was subtly different: to 'resettle' people uprooted by war. The Soviets refused to join, accusing the West of turning the camps into centres of anti-communist propaganda and using them to recruit the forced labour they needed to rebuild their shattered countries. But an important step had been taken. Under IRO's mandate fell a vital new element, the protection not merely of groups but of individuals with valid objections to being repatriated. During the four and a half years of its existence, barely 50,000 people returned to their former homes in central or eastern Europe.

The question now was what to do with those who remained in the camps. The fit and healthy were soon recruited by the very labour schemes so condemned by the Russians. In return for volunteering to build roads, or to work in the mines, industry or agriculture in the West, refugees could apply for citizenship in the countries that offered them work. No one, however, wanted the sick or the elderly, and as the Cold War dragged on, so 400,000 cases lingered on in the camps. Before finally winding up its operations – which, at $428.5 million had proved expensive – IRO officials warned that what once had seemed a temporary phenomenon would in time turn out to be a very permanent one.

It was now 1950. The US, having spent many millions of dollars on refugees in Europe, decided that the problem was no longer theirs to deal with, particularly as they were now helping European countries directly through the Marshall Plan, which would in turn, they argued, benefit the refugees. What neither they nor it seems anyone else envisaged was a world in which refugees would keep on coming, as the IRO had warned. War, famine, violence and poverty would send people fleeing across borders, and as fighting broke out in Korea and the Palestinian territories and starvation spread across China, so it became plain that yet another measure would be needed to counter these new flows of displaced people. In the United Nations, talks began about the setting up of a new body, an Office of the UN High Commissioner for Refugees (UNHCR), and a new convention that would spell out their rights. Louis Henkin was a young lawyer at the State Department, interested in international law, when he was invited by his boss, Dean Rusk, to sit with the US team negotiating the 1951 convention. With him were delegates from twenty-six countries. Professor Henkin, a courteous, upright man now in his late eighties, is the only member of the committee still alive. What he remembers are the many hours devoted to the meaning of the word 'refugee', and a general, ill-defined feeling that the topic did not have great significance for the modern world. There was much talk about whether there should be a 'right' to asylum, or only the right to 'seek' it. The all-important Article 33, about *non-refoulement* – not sending refugees back to countries where they faced persecution – was only pushed through by the French, who reminded the others of the fate of the Jews trying to flee the Nazis during World War II. Eastern Europe declined to attend the sessions, saying that the refugees left in the camps in Europe were all traitors, and the US argued strongly that the new organisation's mandate should be one of protection only, without assistance or relief, and that its budget should be limited. The meetings, Professor Henkin recalls, which took place in Washington and on the shores of Lake Geneva, were on the whole good-tempered, but not without argument, for the British (who at the time had very few refugees) wanted host states to bear responsibility for the refugees on their territory, while the French (who had many refugees) wanted other countries to share the burden. Germany, Austria and Italy, all overwhelmed by the large numbers of refugees still living in camps, had no voice at the table.

The document that emerged in a surprisingly short space of time – little more than six weeks – was a simple reflection of the immediate post-war world. The terms it came up with remain in use to this day. The definition of a refugee, according to Article 1 of the Convention, revolved around the idea of persecution, 'a well-founded fear of persecution on account of race, religion, nationality, membership in a particular social group, or political opinion'. The words 'asylum-seeker' would apply to those seeking refugee status. The persecutors, it was tacitly agreed, were the totalitarian communist regimes, and the refugees were therefore, by definition, 'good'. 'Bad' refugees lay well into the future. In the 1950s, 'good' refugees were seen to be useful pawns in Cold War diplomacy. Migrants, it was spelled out, were people who could go home: refugees were those who could not. That there would soon be people fleeing in great number from poverty, generalised violence, or lives without bearable futures, was not foreseen. The 'durable solutions' to the lives of refugees, which UNHCR undertook to explore, included resettlement in another country, integration nearby, or repatriation – but only if the refugee so wished it. In 2004, the Refugee Convention, together with its 1967 Protocol which extended its scope beyond Europe to take in the rest of the world, remains the most important international document on refugee protection. It is, for example, the foundation of EU policy towards refugees, and ratification is a condition of European Union membership.

In 1951, however, it reflected the concerns of the day. The decision was taken not to include the 458,000 exiled Palestinians who, for political reasons, were to be assisted by the United Nations Works and Rehabilitation Administration, with the result that there would be no international organisation to protect them. And there was much discussion about whether UNHCR should concern itself with anyone but European refugees. Those 'internally displaced' people – later called IDPs – who had not crossed an international border in their flight were eventually excluded. Sovereignty was not challenged. While the new agency could assist or at least protect refugees once they had fled over a border, it was not invited to concern itself with the reasons they had left home in the first place. UNHCR, opening its doors for business in Geneva, not far from the Palais des Nations and in the company of a growing number of agencies and international organisations now clustering together in Switzerland, was given a very small budget, an emergency fund to be used only in dire necessity, a few rooms and a handful of staff.

In 2001, UNHCR celebrated its fiftieth birthday. No international organisation, argues Gil Loescher, author of a comprehensive and authoritative evaluation of its achievements, has ever had such an inauspicious beginning, nor been born of such inherent paradoxes. Apolitical, it acts as chief advocate for the refugee cause. Forbidden to challenge governments over their internal affairs, it has a mandate to protect those that governments persecute. The world it looked out on in 1951 was divided, deeply respectful of the sovereign right of states, and little interested either in refugees or in their futures. The United States, from the beginning, was so suspicious of entrusting responsibility to a United Nations body that it immediately set up an International Office for Migration to ensure that its influence remained strong in the world of displacement and the movement of people. What UNHCR had not been given was power; the question was: how far could it get with persuasion?

The first High Commissioner for Refugees was Gerrit Jan van Heuven Goodhart, a shrewd, modest and eloquent man who had spent the war in the Dutch resistance and who liked to remind people that he had been a refugee himself. The US, who had wanted an American commissioner, showed their irritation by marginalising the agency while he remained in office. The original International Refugee Organisation were also annoyed by having their position usurped. Goodhart further alienated some of the donors by his determination to include relief in his mandate, and he had considerable trouble raising the necessary funds until bailed out by the Ford Foundation. Goodhart died suddenly in 1956 of a heart attack, but even his critics reluctantly admitted that he had managed to make much of the Western world aware that they owed a measure of responsibility to refugees.

The next few years were crucial. The second High Commissioner, Auguste Lindt, was a Swiss diplomat, popular with the Americans and a personal friend of Dag Hammarskjold, the second Secretary General of the UN who was killed in a plane crash while seeking peace in the Congo. Lindt and his successor, another Swiss diplomat called Felix Schnyder, negotiating their way delicately through the minefields of the Hungarian revolution and the Algerian war of independence, cleverly turned UNHCR into the genuine focal point of the refugee world, while shifting its concerns away from Europe and towards Africa, where one country after another was battling with the turmoils of ex-colonial rule. It was not quite enough for the nascent African states, however, who complained that UNHCR's tight definition of a refugee failed to reflect the conditions on their continent. In 1964, the Organisation of African Unity appointed a commission which in time drew up its own refugee convention with a more generous interpretation of the word 'refugee', to take in not only those fearful of individual persecution, but all who were driven to flee their homes because of war and civil conflict. Wars, violence and ethnic fighting would all now enter the refugee debate, to be reaffirmed – though not by Western nations – when in 1984 ten Central American states signed the Cartegena Declaration on Refugees.

The fourth High Commissioner of UNHCR was a man with excellent contacts in the developing world. Suave and gregarious, Prince Sadruddin Aga Khan had once shared a room with Edward Kennedy at Harvard, where he attended lectures by Henry Kissinger. He spoke perfect French and English. He had not long stepped down, after ten generally well-regarded years, yielding his place to the former Danish Prime Minister Paul Hartling, a clergyman with progressive views, when the flight of people from Vietnam, Laos and Cambodia, which had begun in 1975, intensified sharply. Under Hartling, who ruled more democratically than the somewhat cliquish Aga Khan, more than two million refugees, the boat people of Indo-China, were resettled in the West. It was under Hartling too that there was a global surge in refugee numbers. Vast camps were set up in Africa and Asia, later to prove hard to dismantle. 'Refugee warriors', operating from camps across borders, became players in regional struggles for power. During the 1980s, refugee numbers rose from 10 to 17 million; contributions from reluctant donors failed to keep up with the needs of those who fled.

But something else was also happening. As more and more refugees, driven by violence and human-rights violations, left their homes in the developing world, so they began to travel further afield, arriving in ever greater numbers in European countries to claim asylum. Until now, requests for asylum had been few and confined to dissident scientists and ballet dancers whose defections from the Eastern Bloc made headlines in national newspapers. With political upheavals across Africa, Asia and the Middle East came a surge of arrivals, by plane, lorry and boat, people who bypassed normal channels, often with the help of newcomers on the refugee scene, the traffickers and smugglers of illegal travellers. They came from Ethiopia, and what was then Rhodesia, from Sri Lanka, Iran, Iraq and then Somalia. In 1976, 20,000 people asked for asylum in Western

Europe; by 1981 the figure had reached 158,500. By now, UNHCR was having to struggle to keep its position as main arbiter over asylum policy.

Right through the 1970s and early 1980s, European bureaucracy had coped well with immigration. Faced by this sudden surge of unexpected arrivals, however, the system crumbled. Waiting times for decisions became longer, and appeals banked up. There were growing doubts about the nature of the asylum claims, and questions about the extent to which the newcomers were valid refugees under the 1951 Convention. The idea of the 'bad' refugee took shape, that of a person not so much in flight from persecution as actively in search of work and a better life, using the asylum route as his way into Europe. The words 'economic migrant' entered the jargon of refugee affairs. While UNHCR in Geneva kept urging European governments to be generous, arguing that even if some of the claimants were not strictly speaking Convention refugees there was still too much danger at home for them to risk returning, states responded by drafting ever tighter restrictions. By the mid-1980s, most European countries, agreeing that the best way to stem the flow was to prevent people arriving in the first place, were drawing up measures to deter them. Soon, with the advent of the European Union, an outer European perimeter was defined, a larger fortress barricaded against newcomers. Financial support was withdrawn from asylum-seekers who were deemed not to meet the criteria; detentions and deportations began. When UNHCR complained, Western governments paid no attention and concentrated on their own refugee policies. No one listened when Hartling pleaded that those who sought asylum should be seen as victims, not abusers.

By the late 1980s, UNHCR had reached a low point, excluded from many of the worldwide refugee debates. In any case, faced by the political upheavals and natural disasters of the day, the donors wanted relief operations, and they were prepared to pay for them, particularly when the relief kept vast numbers of refugees from arriving at their doors. Under the next High Commissioner, Jean-Pierre Hocké, they went some way to get them. Hocké had been head of operations for the International Committee of the Red Cross in 1967 at the time of Biafra and knew all about the logistics of relief. He was decisive, even authoritarian, and he wanted to see an end to the long-term camps that had by now become such a permanent aspect of the refugee world. These camps, said Hocké, with considerable reason but ahead of his time, crushed 'human dignity' and reduced the 'human capacity for hope and regeneration'; what the West should be doing was not keeping them afloat, but attacking the root causes of the exoduses. Hocké also longed to revise the 1951 Convention, to bring its definition of a refugee into line with that of the Organisation for African Unity, in order to take in all those affected by the wars and civil conflicts now endemic in much of the world. But Hocké was too dictatorial, and his style of leadership offended many. In any case, Cold War politics continued to dominate the regional conflicts of Africa and Asia. Shortly into his second term, in 1989, he resigned after a bruising scandal over his expenses. Few were sad to see him go.

And as it happened, Hocké's departure coincided with another event that transformed the refugee world. With the collapse of the Berlin wall, the very nature of the refugee question altered again. Gone were all the old Cold War certainties about the 'good' refugees fleeing communism. In their place came a decade of unprecedented violence, ethnic conflict, ecological disaster and spreading poverty. The 1990s saw war in Iraq and Chechnya, ethnic cleansing in the Balkans, genocide in Rwanda, the collapse of Sierra Leone and Liberia, the disintegration of Somalia, the transformation of the Great Lakes of Africa into an area of barbarity and anarchy, and the targeting of civilians, and later aid workers. In Rwanda, almost all girls past puberty were raped – and many were then murdered. Of twenty-seven major conflicts in 1992, only two were actually between states. By now, around 90 per cent of the casualties of war were civilians.

Hocké's successor, Thorvald Stoltenberg, a Norwegian former minister of defence, stayed in office just a year. He was replaced by a small, determined, elderly Japanese professor of international relations called Sadako Ogata, the first woman and the first Asian to hold the post. Japan was recognised as an important funder and Ogata's American education and academic background were seen as useful. She was also hard-working, politically astute and keen to avoid confrontations, arguing that over such prickly matters as asylum policy it was better to be tactful than morally superior. 'The real problem,' she announced, 'is saving lives. We can't protect dead people.'

Faced with the killings in Rwanda, Somalia and the Balkans, watching refugees flowing in rivers across borders or trapped in desolate areas of no man's land, hungry, desperate and confused, Ogata turned to relief operations. Relief, she announced, was protection. Bosnia in 1992 transformed UNHCR into the world's largest emergency relief agency, at its peak delivering food, tents and medicines to over a million and a half 'war-affected' people – almost the entire population, along with returnees, the internally displaced and refugees. Repatriation, long considered a sensitive subject, became another of Ogata's goals. During her time in office tens of thousands of people went home to Ethiopia, Eritrea, Angola, Cambodia, Mozambique and Namibia.

Building on Hocké's logistical skills, Ogata changed the agency into a more broadly based humanitarian organisation, helping not only the traditional Convention refugees, who had been able to cross borders, but the internally displaced, who had remained within their own countries. Donors liked Ogata. They preferred to give money to relief, rather than being forced to address the root causes of the emergencies that drove people into becoming refugees, or to consider too closely the ethics of their increasingly restrictive asylum policies. The media liked her too. They welcomed her open manner and her obvious desire to attract their attention. Within the UN, UNHCR became the most admired of all the agencies, and, at the height of the Yugoslav refugee crisis, the one with the biggest budget.

And Ogata's interests, as it happened, matched the mood of the times. In 1992, the Secretary General of the UN, Boutros Boutros-Ghali, announced that the 'time of absolute and exclusive sovereignty' was over, and that intervention against repressive regimes was a necessary component of international politics. For the first time, collective interventionist policies were seen to be legitimate to prevent refugee flows. For Ogata, intervention, which she welcomed, would take the form of preventative diplomacy and human-rights concerns, all designed to make it easier for the victims of war not to have to flee their homes. But it was not always easy. Faced with the moral choice of whether – in effect – to collaborate in ethnic cleansing by helping people to leave their own countries, or to abandon the defenceless to die, Ogata acted decisively. She would help people survive, whatever the implications. She would even work with the military if she had to, especially after aid workers began themselves to be targeted. As she had said, she could do nothing for the dead. But nor could she always do much for the living. Rwanda proved a bitter failure for many UN agencies, UNHCR among them. Neither were the *genocidaires* halted as they killed, nor were the camps housing survivors later prevented from being militarised. The question faced by Ogata and her colleagues was painful: to what extent does relief make things worse by prolonging conflict?

Not everyone was sad to see Ogata leave. People had liked her personally and found her style of leadership friendly. But she had stayed a little long. By the end of the 1990s the mood was again changing. Protection for refugees was felt to have suffered during her tenure, when so much emphasis had gone on relief. In Kosovo, which saw the largest mass refugee movement in Europe since World War II, UNHCR was accused of having been poorly prepared and acting too slowly. For its part, the organisation felt itself to have been sidelined by states and forced to stand by while basic standards were violated and competing parties followed their own agendas. Donors moved away, preferring to invest funds in bilateral agreements or non-governmental organisations. UNHCR was not the only agency to suffer, but between 1992 and 1997 its budget dropped by 21 per cent. The principal loser, as ever, was Africa, where by 1999 UNHCR was spending just one-tenth of what it spent in the Balkans. And by now Africa, with 12 per cent of the world's population, had nearly half of its displaced people.

In January 2001, Ruud Lubbers, a former Dutch Prime Minister, became the ninth High Commissioner for Refugees. As a man with the political stature and confidence to meet world leaders on equal terms, Lubbers was perceived as someone able to confront Western governments over their ungenerous asylum policies and their reluctance to honour their refugee commitments, and at the same time as decisive and clear-headed enough to reform a large and unwieldy office that had grown unaccountable during the years of major relief operations. It was hoped that he would persuade more countries to provide UNHCR's funds, 94 per cent of which still came from the US, Japan and the European Union, and which had fallen from $1.25 billion in 1996 to $911.6 million in 1999. Possibly even more important than all these things, Lubbers was determined to restore to UNHCR its primary function as a protector of refugees, rather than see it eroded further in all-consuming relief operations. Hocké's reign, say the experts, was flawed by his manner and his mistakes; but he had been right in his insistence on protection. Mrs Ogata, though admired for the tenacity with which she kept the agency at the very frontline of the humanitarian world, had made a fundamental mistake in letting the commitment to protection slip, so that success came to be measured only in terms of how much relief could be delivered how quickly. To fill the vacuum, non-governmental organisations working with refugees, of whom there were now a very great number, had themselves begun to move into protection.

The new millennium, as faced by Lubbers, contains huge challenges. Though refugee numbers are actually down, from a peak in the early-1990s of 19 million to around 12 million today, and though the number of asylum claims in Europe has dropped to the lowest in four years,* global attitudes towards refugees have degenerated into chaos and panic. Governments, having allowed asylum-seekers to become scapegoats, have effectively marginalised them and made it harder for them to integrate. Though refugee protection, drawing on many different strands of international law, is now embedded in human-rights and humanitarian treaties and agreements, restriction, not generosity, has become the order of the day. The talk is all of 'humanitarian pragmatism'. Refugees, accused of using scarce resources at times of high unemployment, have been exploited by xenophobic politicians. International humanitarian action to prevent mass exoduses has never seemed so severely limited by lack of political will or money.

About half of the world's refugees today are under the age of eighteen, and almost 5 per cent of these are unaccompanied minors, travelling the world on their own. Like adults, they are obliged to prove that they meet the definition of a refugee under the 1951 Convention, whose adult-centred approach fails to take into account the fact that some abuses of our times are aimed specifically at children. Child-soldiers have no special claims. Child refugees are to be found in prisons and detention centres in many parts of the world, including Australia and the United States.

As Jeff Crisp, an Englishman who for a while ran UNHCR's evaluation and policy unit, sees it, refugee matters have reached a 'profoundly dysfunctional' state, failing to provide protection to those most in need of it, and condoning discriminatory practices that ensure that only people with access to considerable amounts of money can hope to escape from unstable countries by paying smugglers. Large sums are spent on keeping small numbers of refugees out, and small sums on protecting large numbers of refugees in distant camps. Never, he believes, has there been so much hypocrisy. Countries happy to profess their support for the 1951 Convention at meetings, hurry home to do all they can to obstruct the arrival of the asylum-seekers whose rights they have just upheld. UNHCR, once regarded as a teacher and keeper of refugee standards, has lost much of its former credibility. There has been some talk about the need for UNHCR to be more accountable, and much debate across the aid world generally about how to incorporate the protection of human rights into the wide sweep of humanitarian work. The Refugee Convention is in the odd position of being the only major human-rights treaty that is not

---

* In 2002, there were 587,400 applications for asylum to 37 countries, down 5.4 per cent on 2001; the decline was highest in Australia (−50 per cent), followed by the US (−11 per cent).

externally supervised – all other key UN human-rights accords have some
mechanism to ensure that states are held accountable for what they have
signed up to.

Not the least of Lubbers' challenges is what to do about all those who
have fled their homes but not crossed international borders, either
because they have not been able to or because they do not want to. There
have always been people displaced within their own countries by war,
disaster and poverty, but they came late to international attention, and it
was not until 1992 that the UN General Secretary appointed a former
Sudanese diplomat, Francis Deng, as his representative on IDPs
(Internally Displaced People). In 1998, Deng presented the UN with a
definition – someone 'forced to flee on account of armed conflict,
violence, violation of human rights, or natural or man-made disasters', but
who has not crossed a recognised state border – and a set of guiding
principles. But there is still no treaty on IDPs, and though UNHCR is not
mandated to take responsibility for them, no other agency has been willing
to step forward, and in practice it frequently falls to UNHCR to fill the
gap. Although in January 2000 the then Ambassador to the UN, Richard
Holbrooke, declared that to use initials to talk about any one group of
people was unhealthy, and urged the world to stop distinguishing between
victims in such an arbitrary way, and in 2001 the UN set up a special unit
to better coordinate assistance, the 'displaced' remain the poor relations of
the refugee world. According to the Global IDP Database run by the
Norwegian Refugee Council in Geneva, there are 25 million IDPs in the
world today, scattered across fifty countries. Over half of them – some 13
million people – are to be found in Africa, in camps, on the edge of cities,
in shanty towns and condemned buildings, where they have become
indistinguishable from the urban poor, victims of violence and civil
conflict, of floods and tropical storms, droughts, famines and deforestation,
epidemics of measles and cholera and Aids.

Though funds have not actually grown under Lubbers, they have at
least stabilised. He has proved good at attracting new sources: in 2003
Russia gave $1 million for the first time and Kuwait $2 million. However,
refugee crises today attract a huge, uncoordinated mixture of multilateral,
national and non-governmental initiatives and organisations, each of them
raising money separately from donors, and large sums of money are spent
every year both on special units to satisfy lobby groups – women, children
or the environment – and on the organisation itself. Refugee emergencies
and long-term camps continue to eat most available money, making it hard
for the High Commissioner to expand the more abstract idea of protection

he has consistently championed since his arrival. Few people inside UNHCR today question the need for more staff, better training in protection matters and human-rights education, or for the kind of programmes that will reduce the need for people to flee. But UNHCR is under constant pressure from governments, from its executive committee, EXCOM, and from the UN itself, and its position is being seriously weakened by the increasing perception of refugees as a threatening and destabilising force. The whole notion of security, once seen as being about keeping refugees safe – during flight, in camps, waiting for the outcome of their asylum applications – has shifted. Now it is the refugees themselves who are seen to pose the danger, particularly in the wake of September 11 2001. Since the attack on the Twin Towers, human smuggling routes are increasingly referred to as 'routes for international terrorists'.

Nowhere, however, is the challenge to UNHCR's authority more visible than over current asylum policy. Asylum has always posed difficulties – of definition, of determination, of outcome – but while numbers were small and posed little threat, and the asylum-seekers were the 'good' refugees fleeing communism, the issue assumed little importance. But as requests for asylum in Europe, North America, Australia and Japan rose through the 1980s – to reach around 700,000 in the European Union in 1992, the year that UNHCR also recorded a peak of 19 million refugees throughout the world – so Western states intensified their efforts to stop the refugees arriving, investing millions in complicated entry rules which in turn led to backlogs. And, as it became harder to send people home, so pressure grew to make asylum unattractive, and to prevent people from arriving. Barriers erected to keep out those in search of work – the so-called 'economic migrants' – became barriers to those fleeing persecution. As states fought to appear in control of their borders, visa requirements were introduced, then made stricter. Airlines transporting illegal immigrants became liable for fines. The industrialised world, country by country, closed its doors to asylum-seekers, leaving no legal way for them to enter.

Today there is no alternative for asylum-seekers but to enter the European Union illegally, a fact that has played into the hands of smugglers, whose business is flourishing as never before, with strong links to the criminal underworld of drug smuggling and the trafficking of women and children for prostitution. Eight hundred thousand people are estimated to be transported each year across international borders, at a turnover of some $10 billion. In 2000, two UN protocols to the Convention on Transnational Crime were drafted, declaring that those 'trafficked' for clearly sexual purposes were to be considered victims and entitled to assistance, while those who paid to be 'smuggled' were deemed only to require 'humane treatment'. To this day there is virtually nothing to protect asylum-seekers who use smugglers, though in practice they are often drawn into a web of exploitative relationships in order to pay off their debts.

Not surprising, then, that untruths surround refugees. As hostility towards those who arrive without documents has grown, so anti-immigration campaigners have manipulated statistics to paint a picture of the West under siege from an invasion of greedy migrants, and so the asylum-seekers themselves have resorted to embellishing their pasts, the better to merit acceptance. It is not easy for people who have fled violence or persecution, or even just poverty, to handle truth. A story is often told about the boat people arriving in their thousands in Hong Kong and Bangkok in the late 1980s. UNHCR staff were sent out to interview them in order to decide whether or not their fear of persecution at home was such that they were entitled to refugee status and resettlement in the West. The screening of the boat people became the largest and the most expensive of UNHCR's operations at the time. Among them were many unaccompanied children, some as young as six or seven. UNHCR staff quickly realised that the story these children told was always the same: their parents were dead. Word, it seemed, had reached Vietnam that orphans would be quickly resettled, and that they would then be an anchor for their siblings and eventually their parents, who would later turn out not to be dead at all, and who would then rejoin them in the West. In practice, only a quarter of these children were accepted; the rest were sent home. UNHCR staff working in the camps at the time remember how hard they tried to get close to the children, to explain to them that their parents had sent them off on the boats not because they did not love them, but because they were to be their passports for a future.

And it was not just the children. Women of a certain age arrived in the company of small children claiming to be their grandmothers. They had been told, it seemed, that their chances of resettlement were far better if they had infants in their care. When it became clear that it made no difference to their chances, they reappeared at the registration offices to say that the children were not theirs after all, and that they would prefer not to be burdened by having to look after them.

In Geneva, London and Washington, in circles where refugee policy is made and discussed, the mood is one of despondency and confusion, fed by the anti-immigration lobby which in turn feeds growing xenophobia.

The gap between reality and Western rhetoric has never been wider; the need for coherent and harmonised global asylum policies – for burden sharing, for generous yet realistic measures – has never been greater. Fewer than half the people applying for asylum get it, leading governments to conclude that the process is being abused by economic migrants not in need of protection. No European country has proved able to establish fair, fast and efficient systems to determine refugee status, and their inability to return failed asylum-seekers has undermined their credibility. Deportation is expensive and almost impossible to enforce, particularly now that decisions can take several years to reach, by which time the asylum-seeker has laid down roots. Over-stayers, those who fail to leave when their visas or papers run out, are simply tolerated, making it possible for the public to argue that governments are incompetent. The situation also encourages asylum-seekers to regard their journeys as worthwhile, given that deportation may never happen. In any case, airlines are reluctant to accept deportees, who may refuse to board unless handcuffed, while fellow travellers object strongly to becoming witnesses to forcible deportations.

Some $10 billion is being spent annually by governments on dealing with what is a relatively small number of asylum-seekers,* while humanitarian organisations find it impossible to raise a fraction of that money for the considerably larger number who remain in camps in the developing world. This $10 billion is about 12 times what UNHCR receives to look after over 17 million refugees, displaced people and others 'of concern' to them around the world. Whether in Europe or North America, large sums go each year to patrolling borders: Canada takes in 13,000 refugees each year, but spends $300 million controlling its borders – ten times what it contributes to UNHCR. Today it is the world's poorest countries, in Asia, Africa and the Middle East, who bear the burden of the displaced: 90 per cent of refugees in fact stay in their own regions. In 2000, when the countries of Western Europe were complaining most loudly about the sacrifices they were making and the money they were spending on asylum-seekers, the top receiving countries for refugees were in fact Iran, Pakistan and Tanzania. In 2003, the Ivory Coast, Guinea, Liberia, Tanzania, Yemen, Burundi and Sierra Leone all reported the arrival of substantial numbers of refugees.

*In 2003–4, the cost of handling asylum-seekers in the UK was estimated to be £835m – the equivalent of £34 for every household in the country. In the same year, the UK contributed 5 per cent of UNHCR's budget. In 2003, 807,000 people applied for asylum in 141 countries.

Confronted by the global spirit of intolerance and unease, mindful of the ways in which Western states have taken to manipulating the definition of a refugee to suit themselves, Lubbers has launched a series of new initiatives – global consultations, a 'Convention Plus', bilateral agreements, joint papers with the International Office for Migration – intended to make governments reaffirm their commitment to UNHCR's original mandate and to pay for a fairer share of the world's refugees. In the wake of criticisms about UNHCR's failure to analyse and reflect on its own performance, its embroilment in scandals involving the sexual exploitation of people in camps and its apparent reluctance to contemplate institutional change, there has been much talk about improving and strengthening the implementation of the Convention through monitoring bodies or special rapporteurs. These initiatives are said to have left many of the staff exhausted and confused. When, on 12 December 2001, ministers from eighty-five countries gathered in Geneva to renew their pledges to refugees, President Vaira Vilke-Freibergen of Latvia described her own childhood as a refugee, and declared that the existence of so many refugees in the modern world was proof 'that something is very wrong somewhere on the international scene'.

In 2004, the fact remains that only about 145 countries of the world's 190 have signed the 1951 Convention, and even those that have violate its articles every day.

Part Two

Leaving

Chapter Two

The Extracomunitari: *Sicily's Boat People*

We are old, Chevalley, very old. For over twenty-five centuries we've
been bearing the weight of superb and heterogenous civilisations, all from
outside, none made by ourselves, none that we could call our own.
Giuseppe di Lampedusa, *The Leopard*

Nene and Vera Sciortino were watching television when the storm broke.
It started abruptly, a sudden downpour of torrential rain, and by midnight
a great gale had got up and hail began to fall, solid balls the size of potatoes
as Nene would later tell visitors when he showed them the holes in the
table on his terrace. The noise these hailstones made on the plastic terrace
roof was so loud that the Sciortinos were obliged to increase the sound on
their television, and it was some time before they heard the cries coming
from the beach. At first, Nene thought these shouts were all part of the
programme, a gameshow that he and Vera usually watched on a Saturday
night. Nene is an actor, a singer of Sicilian folk songs, a ruddy-faced
friendly man in his mid-thirties, and, when he is not travelling around
Sicily talking at conferences and seminars about the need to preserve the
Sicilian language and popular culture, he and Vera put on theatrical
sketches for school children in the Greek temples at Agrigento and
Selinunte.

As the cries and shouts continued, Nene got up and went to the window
that looks out of their sitting room directly onto the long sandy beach at
Realmonte, not far from Agrigento, on Sicily's southern coast. Peering into
the utter darkness, he could make out only the white crests of the waves
breaking over the sand. But then he saw some people running along the
water's edge. How absurd, he said to Vera, to go swimming on a night like
this. The hail was still crashing down, and there was also lightning and
thunder. But then more people came running, and it was now that Nene
saw that they were gathering in a circle, just in front of La Playa, a new bar
that jutted out onto Capo Rossello, where on summer evenings foreign
tourists come to dance to a small band. Being a Saturday in the middle of
September the dancefloor was crowded, and when he and Vera put on

their rubber boots, found an umbrella and trudged through the wet sand, they discovered the dancers standing at the water's edge in the pouring rain, pulling from the sea a number of gasping, sodden, half-naked young Africans, their clothes hanging in rags about them, their teeth chattering from the cold. As it happened, one of the members of the band spoke some English, and when the strangers had stopped panting and shaking and were able to speak, they explained that they were asylum-seekers and that their boat had struck the rock that juts out above the reef just offshore, not a hundred metres from La Playa. There were, said the young Africans, gesticulating frantically towards the sea, still many others on board, and the boat was sinking. They had reached the shore because they were swimmers. They didn't think anyone else on board could swim. Some said they had sisters and brothers on the boat; one said that his wife was there.

The onlookers, peering into the darkness, could see nothing, though by now the hailstones were no longer crashing down. The night's weather was catastrophic, as Nene explains when he talks about the long night of the *naufragio*, the shipwreck, as the people of Realmonte describe the night of Saturday 14 September 2002, when a boat carrying 150 Liberian asylum-seekers, *extracomunitari*, went down off their popular beach. It was a freak storm, the like of which he had not experienced in all his twelve years in his beach house, and the unfortunate Liberians were *disgraziati*, uniquely unlucky, to have tried to come ashore that very night.

When the dancers had at last understood what had happened, when the terrified Liberians had told them, again and again, the story of what had befallen them and it had been translated into Italian, the police were called, and soon the beach was covered in police cars and *carabinieri* and marines from the Guardia Costiera stationed not far away at Porto Empedocle. The fishing boats pulled up on Realmonte's beach were too small to make any headway against the surf still breaking on the beach, and when a lot of calls had been made over the walkie-talkies and the *telefonini*, as the Italians call their mobile phones, it was found that there wasn't a working rubber dinghy with a big enough outboard along the whole of the coastline. By now, it was nearly three o'clock in the morning. A powerful searchlight was at last produced by the police, and when its beam was cast towards the rock, not only could the boat itself be seen, tipped far over on its side and half underneath the water, but, to the horror of the onlookers, people could be spotted clinging to the rock. As Nene watched, first one and then another slipped beneath the waves. It made him think of ants, running around in fear. The thunder had stopped, and in the lulls between the crashing waves he could hear cries coming from the reef. It was now that the *Vice Questore* from Agrigento appeared, took off his clothes and swam out in his vest and pants to the wreck. When he returned to shore he was able to tell the crowd that help was needed for at least a hundred people. Boats from the various naval services stationed at Porto Empedocle at last came in sight, and it was not long before other sodden, bedraggled, gasping Liberians were being helped into La Playa and given hot coffee and blankets, though not one of them would take off their trainers, even though they were full of water, because it was there that they kept their money, saved up with such painful slowness for this one, illegal, dangerous journey to the shores of Europe. Their eyes, Nene remembers, were very red, bloodshot, almost like fire.

The only person who would remove his shoes was a portly, fair-skinned man with a large inflatable lifejacket, whose pockets rather than shoes were found to be bulging with dollar bills. He was assumed to be the *scafisto*, the trafficker, and the police led him to one side, where he sat in silence, refusing to answer any questions. Eventually taken to prison and repeatedly questioned, he began to talk, but then abruptly fell silent again and has remained silent ever since, because, say the police, he was in some way got at by the mafia, who are known to run the network of *scafisti* along the shores of Tunisia. Some say he was Egyptian, others Libyan. Early on, he told a policeman that he was Palestinian, from Gaza, but when they questioned him about Gaza he was vague.

As for the *extracomunitari*, they were only too happy to talk, but only about the horrors of the shipwreck, the hours of pitching at sea, the fear, the lack of water and food, the nightmare moment when the boat hit the rock and began to sink, for on the question of where they came from and who owned the boat and where they were going, they would say nothing at all. By six o'clock on Sunday morning, there was very little left for anyone to see. The boat had by now partly sunk to the bottom of the shallow beach. Realmonte returned to the closing days of its long, hot summer. For a few weeks, fragments of clothes were washed up at the water's edge and even part of a torn lifejacket, but the people who collect Realmonte's rubbish eventually took them away when it was felt that they looked bad for the tourists. Though no one was ever able to say precisely how many people had been wedged onto the Liberians' boat – what the Italians call a *carretta di mare*, a sea chariot, some ten to twelve metres long and open but for a very small cabin – ninety-five had been saved, and at least thirty-five were known to have drowned. One of the bodies was that of a girl the police doctor thought was no older than fifteen. Most of the dead had no names, the survivors being unable or unwilling to say who they were. One or two, taken to identify the bodies, hesitated; then said nothing. Francesco di Salvo was on duty with the ambulance that night, and saw the bodies lacerated by the sharp rocks. As he sees it, they must have been truly desperate to risk so much. He is haunted by the memory of a very young girl brought to shore already dead, clinging so tightly to her sole possession, a small handbag, that her fingers could not be prised loose from its handle.

When early on the Monday the partly submerged boat was pulled to shore, another body was found on board. The police banged on Nene's door and asked whether he had any plastic bags to cover it with. Vera was disgusted. She gave them a sheet, and the Sciortinos were upset to find that the police planned to leave the body there all day, lying in the sand just in front of the terrace, until the proper authorities could be persuaded to come to collect it later in the afternoon.

But it was still not quite all over for Nene and Vera. Four days later, at ten o'clock on the Wednesday morning, a fine calm day when the tourists were all back on the beach, Vera saw a body floating in the water about twenty yards from the shore in front of the house. She called Nene, and together they stood at the water's edge. A second body bobbed to the surface, not far from the first, and then a third. Over the next two hours, as they stood watching with horrified fascination, nine other bodies, bloated and purple, the skin flailed away by the sharp volcanic rock, shot like corks to the surface of the flat sea. From a distance the Sciortinos thought they looked rather like the tourists peacefully floating in the warm, still water. By then, the shore was once again crowded with onlookers, and the police sent frogmen to bring in the bodies and look for others. This was the worst moment of the whole *naufragio*, and for several days neither one of them could sleep for the horror of what they had seen, though it helped when Don Giuseppe, Realmonte's parish priest, held a mass on the beach exactly a month after the shipwreck, and the villagers threw flowers into the water where the boat had gone down. And it helped, too, that journalists and tourists curious about the *naufragio* came by and banged on Nene's door and he was able to tell them what had happened, although he was very angry when a cartoon appeared in the scurrilous local *La Sicilia* showing a peddleboat with two tourists, corpses floating by their side, under the words '*turismo macabro*'.

By Christmas, Nene had been able to put it all behind him, but Vera had decided that she could no longer eat fish, not knowing what flesh they might have fed on, and when Nene goes out fishing in the small, red-bottomed wooden boat he keeps pulled up outside their house, Vera will cook the catch he brings back, but she will not put it in her mouth. She says that she will never eat fish again.

For the young Liberians whose savings had gone into this journey to a new life, whose families had sold their houses and lands and animals to pay smugglers to take them to a continent where they would not be persecuted and where they would be safe and prosperous, this last lap, on a boat carrying ten times the number of people it was built to carry, had been a time of terror.

For Mercy, Happy and Roland, a brother and two sisters from a town called Maryland, not far from Liberia's capital, Monrovia, the journey had started many weeks before, on a lorry that carried them to the coast, then on a ship which paused after five days, they do not know where, to transfer them to a second boat, which itself paused, some four days later far out at sea, to transfer them to yet another boat, this time the small, open wooden boat on which they had been standing and crouching for almost five days, thirsty and very hungry, when the storm got up. Clinging to the boat's wooden rim, too closely packed and too frightened to move, as the storm gathered strength and the hailstones began to pound on to their heads and shoulders, they could see the lights from La Playa and, between the gusts of wind and the thunder, could just hear snatches of music from the dancefloor. Mercy, clinging to her sister, remembers the moment of impact with the rock, when the small boat, with a sudden shuddering lurch, crashed against something hard, and those on board were flung violently to one side. She saw some of her companions lose their hold and slip over the side into the darkness. Almost at once, she lost sight of Happy, and in the jostling, crying, flailing crowd, found herself pushed to the very edge of the boat and, as it began to tilt and sink, start to slip over the side herself.

Mercy cannot swim. When I went to find her, she was still living in Realmonte, some 300 yards from the beach of Capo Rossello. She told me that she could remember the water seeming to draw her down, and then feeling a sharp edge of rock just under the surface. She reached out and grasped it with all her strength, as those around her slipped past and disappeared. She is short and slight and does not look very strong, but because she was young, just twenty, and because she simply could not bear for all the months of skimping and saving and planning and indecision and longing to be thrown away so casually on a single moment of disaster, she went on clinging to her small piece of rock, and she was still there, four hours later, when the rescue boats from Porto Empedocle arrived and sailors pulled her on board and took her to land, where ambulances were waiting with blankets and hot, sweet coffee. What she did not know then was that she was two months pregnant. The father of her baby was a boy from Maryland whom she had planned to marry, but who had not got together enough money for the journey by the time that she and Happy and Roland set out to make their new lives in Europe.

For her sister Happy, the *naufragio* was the end of that dream. Mercy never saw her again after that moment when, clinging to each other, the two sisters felt the terrible crash against the rock. Roland saw her once more, when he was taken to a mortuary in Porto Empedocle and asked to look at the dead Liberian refugees lying side by side in their torn clothes. Happy was the first body he saw. She was twenty-two.

After my visit to Mercy and Roland, I drove back along the *superstrada* towards Agrigento, a city built, as Plato noted, as if its people would never die, while they ate as if they had not an hour to live. I was directed to the wrecker's yard where, as the Italians put it, a 'cemetery' has been created for the boats which carry the *extracomunitari* to their shores. There, in between the smashed Fiats and BMWs, lay the Liberians' boat, tilted over to one side, wedged between two other similar, wrecked boats, scraps of netting still hanging from their sides, what remained of their decks littered with empty plastic water bottles, a couple of torn jackets, a dirty blanket. Happy's boat looked absurdly small to have carried so many people, and almost festive, with its bold stripes of blue, yellow and red paint, and its name, a flourish of Arabic lettering along one side; it was not easy to imagine it at sea, tossed around in the dark and the hail with 150 terrified people clutching the sides and each other. Salvaged by the coastal police when the summer resumed its fine days, and taken to the wrecker's yard to await any subsequent enquiry into the shipwreck, the boat sits with some dozen others, a few smaller, one or two larger, wrecks of boats condemned as unseaworthy long before their final journeys, gaudy yet infinitely sad. Beyond the yard lies a meadow which in spring is bright with yellow daisies and the deep red of the wild clover that covers this part of southern Sicily, while above rises the rocky escarpment that leads, not half a kilometre away, to the ridge on which stands the Doric Temple of Concord, which held out against the Carthaginians for eight months, perfect against the clear sky.

Even Don Giuseppe, the priest of Realmonte, feels that there was something demonic in the fury of the storm that hit his parish on the night of the *naufragio*. He has lived in and around Agrigento for many years, but he has known no weather as terrible or as ferocious as on that night. Don Giuseppe is proud of the way that his parishioners behaved at the time, the way they hastened to the shore when they heard about the shipwreck, carrying with them blankets and coats, and he admires the insistence with which they pressed him to find a house not only for Roland and Mercy, but for Daniel and Adrean, the only married couple among the survivors, who were expecting a baby. In Sicily, he says, 'we are used to strangers. We've had Arabs, we've had the Spanish, we've had the Greeks, we've even had the Americans. And now we have Liberians.' Realmonte is very poor, and though the people do not go hungry, unemployment is as high here as in all parts of Sicily, and there is very little luxury to be had. As it happens, Realmonte has within its *comune* a salt mine, and a second, smaller mine of malachite, which could give work to a number of the villagers; but some years ago a dispute broke out between an industrialist from the north who wanted to buy them, and the Italian authorities, who refused to let him begin mining until favourable terms were worked out for profit-sharing. The mines have stayed closed ever since.

On the night of the storm, the single young men were sent off to a hostel in nearby Racalmuto. The Misericordia, Italy's voluntary ambulance service, decided to give the two couples the use of a flat off Realmonte's main square. By the time Mercy realised that she was pregnant, not long after the shipwreck, Adrean was about to give birth. When her little girl was born prematurely in January 2003 and had to stay in the hospital for several weeks, Realmonte's women took it in turns to visit her and help her plan the baby's return to the village. Mercy's baby, Angela, arrived in April, after a Caesarean birth, and when Mercy brought her home the women again visited to show the young mother how to care for her child, though they worried that she seemed curiously uninterested in feeding the baby, and not as attached to her as they expected her to be. As Mercy and Roland are Christians, Angela was baptised by Father Giuseppe in Realmonte's church. All through the autumn and winter neighbours dropped by with vegetables from their plots of land outside the village, with baby clothes and toys and even a pram.

Roland is as reluctant as all the survivors to go into the details of his escape, but he is eager to talk about the conditions that drove him and his two sisters to flee: the marauding bands of rebels who descended on Maryland, his fears of being forcibly recruited as a soldier, the collapse of his business selling building materials. He does not speak about the terror and cold of the long journey at sea with too little food and water and no knowledge of where the boat was heading. Like many of the young

Liberians in Cairo, Roland and his sister are Mandingo, among the most persecuted of the ethnic groups. Since his rescue, though not yet officially recognised as a refugee and so not in theory permitted to work, Roland has been able to do casual work in Realmonte's supermarket, the villagers feeling only too conscious of his need for money, being so constantly in need of it themselves. However, he still cannot bring himself to write to tell his widowed mother, who stayed behind in Maryland with a cousin while her three children set out for their new life one hot August morning, of Happy's death. He thinks she would prefer not to know.

It is quite possible that Happy and Mercy's boat was not heading for Sicily's southern shore at all. Roland told me that the first he knew that his destination was not Africa was when, swimming to shore after the shipwreck, he saw that the people on the beach were white. There is a joke, repeated with pleasure by Sicilians: Not long ago, a young Senegalese man was brought by a smuggler to within a hundred yards of shore, pushed overboard and told to swim. He climbed out of the water on the beach and approached a fisherman working nearby. '*Wo ist der Bahnhof?*' he asked, having been assured by the trafficker that he was being landed in Germany. The same joke is told, with equal pleasure, by the inhabitants of Capri, off the coast of Naples.

It is more likely, as Dr Moscat of Agrigento's police prefecture explains, that Roland and Mercy's boat was destined for Lampedusa, the island that lies 180 kilometres still further south, and it was here that I went next, looking for other refugees from Africa's civil wars. Though none of the Liberians in Cairo had travelled this particular route, some had made long sea journeys, terrifying and bewildering experiences that were somehow rites of passage to their new lives, the journey itself becoming a kind of passport which, unlike those they shed along the shore and in the sea, confers dignity and promise. Very few of the refugees coming from landlocked Africa have ever seen the sea and few can swim, making the prospect of crossing these great expanses of often rough water truly terrifying.

In 2002, 8,000 *extracomunitari* arrived on Lampedusa from Turkey, Malta and the ports and beaches of North Africa, where they had collected and waited until enough were assembled to make up a boat. Sfax, a known gathering point for the Tunisian smugglers, lies barely 110 kilometres from Lampedusa, and it is here that the would-be asylum-seekers learn how much their journey will cost them and what their destination might be. It is the traffickers, said to operate in mafia-like associations, who tell the asylum-seekers to give away as little as possible when they land, to get rid of all their documents so that they can lie about where they have come from and so cannot then be sent home or the traffickers themselves traced. In the symbiotic process which seems to govern southern Italy's response to the asylum-seekers and migrants who flock to their shores – in which coast guards, *carabinieri*, harbour police, immigration authorities and the *scafisti* themselves all play their interlocking parts – Lampedusa has taken on a vital role.

Lampedusa is Europe's southernmost tip, the first toehold towards northern Europe. A spit of barren, flat, rocky land, the island looks on a map like the skull of a primitive, long-jawed creature, its nose tapering to a thin wedge. The property of the feudal princes who had founded Palma in the early seventeenth century, the island is bare, baked hard and dry for many months of the year into a uniform stony whiteness. Lampedusa is neither pretty nor, with its jagged, limestone cliffs, hospitable. The author of *The Leopard*, last in the line of Lampedusas, never even visited it, though the family retained a rampant *gattopardo*, more properly translated as ocelot, on their coat of arms. According to legend, the founder of the Lampedusas was Tommaso, 'the leopard', commander of the Imperial Guard of the sixth-century Byzantine Emperor Tiberius, whose daughter Irene he married, and the island had been a gift in recognition of services rendered.

Lampedusa was once thickly wooded. Today, the dozen or so stunted pines that are its only trees lie almost parallel to the ground, bowed by the winds that blow from the west. Although in the autumn hunters come from Sicily and the mainland to slaughter the protected hoopoes and golden orioles as they fly south in flocks to winter in Africa, leaving their spent cartridges scattered between the rocks and wild herbs on the low hills, Lampedusa is popular mainly with scuba-divers, fishermen and tourists in search of sun, heat, and the deep, unpolluted waters that surround it. Once a NATO base, it was discovered by Italians overnight in the summer of 1986, after Colonel Qaddafi fired two missiles towards Italy which landed twenty kilometres off the coast of the island, bringing journalists and in their wake several thousand tourists, who slept on mattresses on the ground until enough rooms and hotels could be built to absorb them. Drystone walls, demarcating plots of land long since abandoned to stones and wild flowers, stretch away from the single small town, where the uncontrolled building of summer shacks has given the island the look of much of the rest of Italy's ruined coastline.

Lampedusa is where Italy ends and where Africa begins. Spring and

summer, on the long calm days, it is where the refugees arrive almost daily
in their battered and crumbling boats, frightened, unsure, expectant.
Experts in asylum matters who study the flows of refugees and their
journeys to the north, call it the blue route after the waters of the
Mediterranean, and it has become a lucrative source of the estimated $5 to
$7 billion revenue from the world's traffic in smuggled people. Gangs,
often reported to belong to the same mafia as those that traffic in drugs,
run complex shipping networks that involve large boats carrying 600 or
more *clandestini* for the first part of long journeys, transferring them to
small, ancient and no longer seaworthy crafts for the final stretch to shore.
Since arrivals seem to mesh neatly with available space in Lampedusa's
single reception centre, it is said that there is a *basista*, a spy or a look-out,
for Tunisia's mafia on the island who phones to say when Lampedusa is
ready to absorb more newcomers.

On Lampedusa, I looked for people to tell me about their boat journeys
from Africa, and found Alex. A twenty-three-year-old Liberian who lost
most of his family in the civil war, he spent eleven years with his sisters as
a refugee in Ivory Coast, before deciding to escape the constant fear that
he would be picked up by rebels and forced to become a soldier. He
described a journey that began in Monrovia with twenty others, hidden on
a large ship and not being told its destination by their trafficker, to whom
they had each paid $200. For four days, while it was still tied up in port,
the young men hid in different corners of the boat without food or water.
After it set sail, they were gathered together, then transferred, far out at
sea, to a smaller boat. This took them to Turkey, where three of them
were dropped off on a remote beach. They made their way to the nearest
town, where they found some 'black brothers' who put them in touch with
a new set of smugglers. They paid over $1,000 each, then went into hiding.
A few nights later, they were led back to the coast, put onto a small boat
and taken out to a larger one. On board were eighty-five other
extracomunitari, all Africans, from Nigeria, Ghana, Sudan, and Tunisia; all
but four were men, reflecting the fact that the asylum-seekers who make
these hazardous journeys tend to be young men in their twenties and
thirties, while the refugee camps across Asia and Africa are full of women
and children for whom the journeys are too difficult.

The asylum-seekers had been told to bring food and water for eight
days. The weather was very bad, the sea rough, and the boat developed
engine trouble. It floated without power for two days, sprang a leak and
began to sink. A fishing boat appeared, came alongside and was able to
take eleven people off – Alex among them – before the boat went under,

drowning all the rest, including the four women. Alex, who could not swim, broke his hand when being pulled on board; his two friends were drowned. The fishing boat was extremely crowded, but it took them into Lampedusa, and Alex was taken to hospital and his hand treated. He still had $800, the rest of his life's savings, hidden in his shoes. 'They asked me a lot of questions,' he says, 'but I didn't really have much to tell them. I had planned for my life to be secure, and I wanted a place with peace of mind.' The Italians have given Alex a humanitarian permit to remain, a halfway measure that ensures him protection for a year and permission to work, and is renewable. But he has changed his mind about escape and has not found the life of an exile what he imagined it would be. 'I want to go home to my sisters and my farm,' he says. 'I don't want to be alone.'

Rarely, in fact, do those arriving at Lampedusa make it to shore under their own steam. More often their boats are spotted by the helicopters which patrol these coasts, or are picked up on the radar screens of the coastguards, who go out to meet them as they near the land. They do so both in the hope of netting a *scafisto* bringing his cargo in to land, or of helping a sinking craft by taking its passengers on board and taking them into a secluded corner of Lampedusa's large natural port, far from the eyes of tourists who might be offended by the spectacle of such bedraggled and confused new visitors.

Comandante Rino Gagliano is the captain of one of the Italian coast-guards' middle-sized motor-launches that do their share of patrols on Lampedusa, though the more exciting tours of duty are those conducted further north, along the Albanian coast, where traffickers have taken to putting four powerful engines onto their fast rubber dinghies, with which they can more easily outmanoeuvre the slower police launches. Never-theless, Italy and Albania's bilateral agreement to try to stem the flow of migrant workers has succeeded in diminishing the numbers who manage to get out. But the comandante is not really after excitement. His wife taught history at Lampedusa's one secondary school until her early death not long ago, and he has a particular fondness for the island's low white houses and its stark shoreline. He talks with sympathy about the desperate people he regularly fishes from the water, and the cups of good Italian coffee he takes pleasure in giving them, for, like all Sicilians, he is baffled by the idea of countries where coffee is not a staple of life. He says that rescuing boats about to sink takes priority – as it does under all the laws that have governed seafaring for many generations – over arresting *scafisti* as they hasten back towards international waters. Like all the sailors and coastguards who work these parts, he tells stories of asylum-seekers flung into the sea at gunpoint so that the trafficker can get away faster, of boats so old and ailing and crowded with people that even small waves can sink them, of headless bodies found floating at sea. What haunts him is those he never learns about: the refugees who are known to have drowned in these stretches of water, whose names are never recorded and whose bodies are never found. The *canale di Sicilia*, he says, has become a cemetery. Of the 3,000 known deaths recorded by human-rights groups of people trying to enter Europe in the last ten years, many have drowned in the waters that separate Italy and Spain from North Africa.

The comandante, like most of the islanders, feels mostly sympathy for those so desperate that they will risk their lives in this way. To suffer so much is to merit recognition, assistance: the more the suffering, the swifter and greater should be the recompense. The tales of these travellers have come to fascinate the local people, for whom shipwrecks and endurance are all part of the fabric of their history, reflecting the strength and vigour of their island, both in its robustness in withstanding cycles of invaders and newcomers and in providing pioneers for new worlds elsewhere. The fact that the *extracomunitari* arrive with nothing, sometimes virtually naked having shed or lost their clothes in rough seas – shorn, as it were, of their pasts – makes them appealing. There is pride in being the first to show off Europe, to vaunt all that it has to offer, as if to reassure the survivors of such terrors and hardships that the journeys have been worth it. The past is truly another country, and their hosts intend to make it so.

In Italy, a country renowned, with exasperation and affection, for the confusion and corruption of its bureaucracy, the operation to corral and process asylum-seekers appears almost streamlined. On Lampedusa, the *extracomunitari* are marched off to a Centro di Permanenza Temporanea, a 'permanent temporary centre', the absurdity of its name belying the claim that the system is both humane and practical; since 2002 it has been cracking under the strain of growing numbers. Here, in a former military barracks, new arrivals are briefly interviewed, provided with clothes and a few necessities, and given cigarettes and permission to use a telephone. There is a sense of pride among the island's residents that they have responded so calmly and generously to their unexpected visitors. Father Francesco, Lampedusa's young and eager second priest, who for three months in 2002 became acting director for the island's CPT, speaks of a larder always kept full in anticipation of new refugees, of doctors on duty to care for those who have been at sea for many weeks, of having to fend off journalists after a sudden influx of boats. Though few of the asylum-seekers describe their reception so glowingly, Father Francesco talks about his permanent temporary visitors indulgently and says that they are given forks but no knives, and the services of the local barber but no razors, though there have been no attempted suicides on the island. Macaroni with meat sauce, he volunteers, is their preferred dish. Some arrive with scabies, others with malaria and heart disease, and many of the women are pregnant, but all are treated kindly, and those few who have died while he has been on Lampedusa have been given a corner of the town's cemetery, where they lie together under plain wooden crosses in a plot covered with geraniums and wild flowers.

Because of its geographic position and its long coastline – over 7,000 kilometres – Italy has now become the first country of arrival for more asylum-seekers than any other of its European Union partners. A few go overland from the former Yugoslavia, but most arrive by sea, making the boat people of Italy – 18,000 arrived in 2002 on the coasts of Sicily alone and 20,000 in 2003 – the seafaring refugees of our times. Europe's earliest migrants came by sea to Sicily, perhaps as early as 20,000 BC, and later by sea and land came Greeks, Carthaginians, Phoenicians, Romans, Saracens, Normans, Hohenstaufens, Angevins, Aragonese, Castilians, Austrians, Piedmontese and the Neapolitan Bourbons. Over the centuries, Sicily was conquered, abandoned, colonised and recolonised by tyrants, kings, mercenaries, dukes, plenipotentiaries and emperors. There is probably less Italian blood, so Sicilians say, in their veins than there is Greek, Arab, Norman or Spanish. Positioned on the east–west and north–south routes of the Mediterranean, the island is fertile, with excellent natural harbours, although Goethe, on his travels at the end of the eighteenth century, described it as a morose place, even before Palermo's vast palazzi had crumbled, the fortunes of their families eaten up through feuds and generations of squabbling and idleness.

Yet right up until the 1980s, Italy, and particularly its impoverished south, was associated more with emigration than immigration. Between unification in 1861 and the end of the twentieth century, about 26 million Italians left home for the new world, driven abroad by the neglect and plunder of rich and absent landowning families. As early as 1827 de Tocqueville, travelling around Sicily, described its interior as almost entirely devoid of human habitation. By World War I, some villages had lost most of their male population, and one out of eight Italian emigrants was a Sicilian. Though part of the new united and unified Italy, Sicily remained its most neglected area, and it was not until after World War II that it was granted regional autonomy and its own parliament.

At first, influxes of migrants into Italy were dealt with as one-off emergencies, with leniency. In 1990, the Minister of Justice, Claudio Martelli, annulled Italy's existing reservation to the 1951 Refugee Convention – which allowed refugee status only to European asylum-seekers – and set up a single procedure for deciding refugee status under a commission based in Rome, to take no more than forty-five days, during which the applicants would be housed and fed. But then came a large number of landings – Albanians in 1990 and 1991, Yugoslavs in 1992, more Albanians in 1997, Kurds in 1998, each dealt with under measures of temporary protection. Though Italy is a signatory to Europe's various immigration treaties, it was only with the Napolitano Bill of 1998 – which Italians regard as their first attempt at formulating a proper asylum policy – that rules were drawn up to govern procedures and the deportation of those deemed not to be bona fide asylum-seekers. In many ways even the Napolitano law was regarded as generous, since the right to asylum was broadened to include people discriminated against at home by virtue of their sex and their membership of particular persecuted ethnic groups.

With Berlusconi's election in 2001, much of the leniency has vanished. Those migrants seeking to work in Italy can no longer arrive and then seek employment: they must apply for work permits first at the Italian consulate in their own countries and, once their contract is over, return home. Under the Bossi-Fini law of 2003, those who arrive illegally on Italy's shores may now be held for sixty days in a CPT for processing, after which those who in preliminary hearings are judged as coming from 'safe' countries – hence the reluctance of asylum-seekers to say too much about where they come from – or as criminal, or too blatantly in search of work, are given deportation orders. (It was Umberto Bossi of the Lega Nord who declared not long ago that cannons should be set up on Italy's coasts to deter would-be asylum-seekers.) Only around 10 per cent of all who enter illegally – compared, say, to Sweden's 50 per cent or over 40 per cent in the UK – are ultimately given refugee status under the Convention. While they wait to be processed, they are released, like Roland and Mercy, to cope as best they can until summoned before the commission in Rome to put their case for asylum. However, since this process can now take a year or more, many have left their designated addresses long before the summons, to disappear into Italy's vast black economy, or to drift northwards illegally into other European countries. Only 20 per cent of those who apply for asylum turn up in Rome for their interview.

In 2001, Italy had over 1½ million legal migrants, as many as a million illegal ones and deported 75,000 people. (Only Greece expels more.) Over a third of Italy's prison population is now foreign. In 2002, it was reported that only 16 per cent of its 50–70,000 prostitutes were Italian, the rest coming mainly from Albania, followed by Yugoslavia, Nigeria and South America. The word '*extracomunitari*' has come to have distinctly racist connotations, and violent attacks on refugees, Jews, and gypsies, and especially on African immigrants, previously almost unknown in Italy, have become widespread. Officially, there are no '*Magrebini*' – people from Algeria, Tunisia or Morocco – because the North Africans have earned the reputation of being involved in drugs and crime and so tend to fail the first screening process. After September 11 2001, there was a sharp increase in the number of negative decisions handed down to asylum-seekers.

The permanent temporary centres have attracted considerable hostility among Italy's liberals, who fear that the secrecy and high walls, their rolls of barbed wire and hangar-like structures, conceal deprivation and ill-treatment. Sixty days, they argue, is a frighteningly long period to spend locked up, in total idleness, not knowing what will become of you. Migrants emerging from the CPTs complain of inedible food, extreme discomfort and a pervasive sense of despair and anxiety. Not long ago, Médecins Sans Frontières carried out research into Italy's sixteen CPTs. They found that in some of them the refugees were kept in small enclosures, freezing in winter, boiling in summer; that the guards were sometimes brutal; that there was an excessive use of anti-depressants and tranquillisers; and that self-mutilation was endemic. A politician of the left, Calogero Micciche, amid considerable publicity, insisted on being allowed into Agrigento's CPT, which is housed in a former factory in one of the town's newer concrete suburbs. Conditions inside, he told waiting reporters when he emerged, flustered from having his video camera confiscated, were appalling, with excrement all over the walls and women detainees offering their services as prostitutes.

After the fuss died down, those who are allowed to visit the centres officially – the priests, doctors and welfare officers – expressed astonishment at his words, insisting that the CPTs, though indeed without charm, since most are housed in former barracks and factories, are civilised places, the officers behaving honourably and generously towards the asylum-seekers. 'The paradox,' says Daniela D'Amico, who recently helped set up a new voluntary organisation dealing with issues of migration in Agrigento, 'is that all these new laws which are designed to stop arrivals in fact make no difference. Migration, asylum, these are a social phenomenon of our time. We have lost the memory of our history. Immigrants are the myth of our particular culture.' The truth is that many Sicilians have very mixed feelings about the asylum-seekers, although they are proud of the hospitality they accord their unexpected and unwanted visitors, remembering how it was the Italians who, of all the people of Europe, most softened the persecution of the Jews (of 60,000 Jewish-Italians, a third survived the war). They are also pleased with their apparent efficiency at dealing with such large numbers, and they are understandably reluctant to see in these detention centres anything but humane holding operations for a fair and just refugee policy. Sicilians regard themselves as rather apart from the people of the mainland, and with some reason: Cavour, the Prime Minister who achieved unification in 1860, and who had personally never been further south than Florence, once said in Parliament that he thought that Sicilians spoke Arabic.

A third of the migrant inmates have in fact served prison sentences in Italy, for a variety of criminal acts, and are sent to the CPTs to await deportation, some in Sicily and some on the mainland, for as one fills up so newcomers are shunted to those that currently have space. *Clandestini*, *extracomunitari*, illegal migrants, refugees, asylum-seekers: nowhere is the muddle that surrounds migration more apparent than on the shores of Sicily, nor the line that separates those judged worthy to enter from those turned away more blurred.

The shipwreck that killed Happy and landed her sister Mercy and her unborn child on the beach at Realmonte has had ripples all along Sicily's southern shores. Something about the intensity of the freak storm, the incredible size of the hailstones, and the way that the survivors clung for so long to the lacerating volcanic rocks touched a chord with Sicilians more accustomed to tourists enjoying the tranquillity of their beaches. In the days that followed the accident, as journalists and television reporters flocked from all over Italy, people from miles around arrived with offers of clothes and food. Dr Palumbo is the village doctor for San Biagio Platani, some forty kilometres up into the mountains above Agrigento. He was having lunch at 3 o'clock on a sunny afternoon, after a long morning with his patients, when I found him at home, surrounded by wisteria and orange trees. It was after his wife read about the bereaved Liberians in Realmonte, he explained, that he went to the prefect in Agrigento and offered to help. Dr Palumbo knows all about the *clandestini*: he is both the chairman of his local branch of the Misericordia and director of social services for the CPT in Agrigento.

After Dr Palumbo's intervention, fifteen young Liberians, five of them women, moved to San Biagio, a small town set among high summer pastures, where the inhabitants were quick to come forward with offers of help. Like Father Giuseppe in Realmonte, Dr Palumbo was proud of the way his patients were so generous towards their visitors. His wife is a teacher, and she soon borrowed a room in a neighbour's house and fashioned a schoolroom, with a borrowed blackboard, chairs and books scrounged from the local school, and began giving lessons in Italian. One of the young Liberian girls found work as an occasional maid; several of the boys were invited to help out the local builders. Though none could be officially employed, it was tacitly understood that they should be paid like everyone else while they were waiting for their claims for asylum to be heard, and that they should not stay idle and penniless. When one of the young women was found to be pregnant and had her baby, the Italian woman who had become close to her offered to adopt and care for both mother and child.

But soon the warm relationship between the Sicilians and their Liberian guests seemed to turn a little sour. As Dr Palumbo sees it, everyone understood that at first the Africans would be reluctant to talk much about who they were and where they came from, but everyone assumed that their reticence to confide in their new friends would evaporate once they felt secure and appreciated. But it didn't; if anything it grew stronger. It was as if word had reached them that they should give away absolutely nothing about themselves, not even their real names. And so they began changing their names, and then their ages and any details that they had previously let slip about their journeys. Dr Palumbo began to wonder whether some were not in fact Ivonians or Guineans after he overheard two of the young men speaking French to each other, and thought that they might have been primed by the smuggler to give Liberia as their home, a country so bedevilled by constant civil war that the refugees believe that no European nation would feel able to return them to it. Several of the girls turned out to be pregnant and when one gave her age first as eighteen, then as twenty-five, and then as twenty-two, Dr Palumbo was at first amused and then mildly irritated, and begged her to find an age and stick to it, if only for the sake of convenience. In the early autumn of 2002, when the group first settled in San Biagio, several of the young men had gone willingly to the local bars in the evening to play pool and listen to music. But as the weeks passed, they went less and less, preferring to sit in the rooms lent to them by the villagers, watching television and talking to each other in the Liberian English outsiders find so hard to follow.

The inhabitants of San Biagio and Realmonte, where much the same thing was happening with Roland and Mercy, were perplexed. They could not quite see why people on whom they had lavished genuine concern and affection, whose futures they felt personally involved with, did not appear to trust them enough to confide their true stories in return. They began to feel a little resentful when the young Liberians simply smiled when asked to talk about the terrifying boat ride, or looked vague when questioned about their families and their past lives. Even a few confidences, as Dr Palumbo says, would have made a difference. They would have been something in return for all the fruit and clothes and attention; it wasn't that his patients – or Father Giuseppe's parishioners – wanted to be thanked, but they would have appreciated, enjoyed, a little recognition; and the absence of it rankled. In Realmonte, the local people now hesitated before taking round fruit or presents for the babies. Because of the increasingly taciturn replies, the blank looks which could seem at times almost like hostility, the cutting short of any conversation leading to a question, they were soon not quite sure who to believe when Roland went on saying that Mercy was his sister, while the local midwife let it be known that Mercy was having sex with someone right up until the day her baby was born.

And in San Biagio, as autumn turned into winter and freezing winds blew through the high mountains, the Africans clearly began to suspect that the life of a remote Sicilian town, safe as it was, was not perhaps so desirable after all. Security was all very well: but what of the new life that Europe had seemed to promise? What of the affluence, the comfort, the good things they had seen on their televisions back at home? At least, that is what Dr Palumbo assumes they thought, for the young people themselves said nothing. After a few weeks' half-hearted appearance at Signora Palumbo's Italian classes, one by one they stopped attending. The day came when San Biagio woke to find three of the Liberians gone, departed on the early bus for Palermo. A few days later, another five had vanished. By January there were none left. Even the girl with her new baby had disappeared. Not one said goodbye to anyone. 'It wasn't that we wanted thanks,' says Dr Palumbo again. 'We didn't help them for gratitude. But to leave saying nothing? It made us feel foolish, used.' It also made them feel sad, thinking about these wandering young Africans, slipping quietly into the night to scatter and vanish into Europe, to lives as uncertain and precarious as those that they had left behind them. No one imagines that they will ever see their Liberian guests again.

Not everyone, of course, was able to leave so quickly. Travelling with a premature baby, or heavily pregnant, even in Italy, in dead of winter and with no papers, no money and nowhere to go, is not simple. In Realmonte, the four young Liberians and their two little girls felt that they had no choice but to wait out the weeks until their summons from the commission in Rome. Because they are Liberians – or at least claim to be Liberians – from a country still not settled, because they are survivors of a shipwreck and the parents of babies, they do not anticipate problems with their refugee status. But as the months have passed, so their irritation with Realmonte has grown. They are not content. It is as if the long wait to reach Europe has once again had to be extended; and this last wait, until they can set out for a life somewhere better, more interesting, more promising, more like the Europe they had imagined, is almost unbearable. Realmonte has become just another state of limbo.

Before leaving southern Sicily I went back to Realmonte, to the ground-floor flat with its tiled floors and television set, and the furniture and the baby things provided by the Misericordia. I wanted to see Daniel and Adrean, the young married couple who had been away in Palermo on my first visit, taking their premature daughter for a check-up with a paediatrician. I wanted to ask Adrean about her journey from her village in Liberia to Monrovia, and about the boat which finally sank, leaving her, like Mercy, clutching a rock, and about what it had been like to be pregnant and frightened and not knowing where the child would be born and whether it would survive the hours she spent in the sea. When I knocked on the shutters of the flat, I found the kitchen unexpectedly full of people, young men from Ghana and Sierra Leone, and other arrivals from Liberia. Some had been in Italy for almost twenty years, part of earlier migrant waves, and were now possessors of legal work and residence permits. The authorities had complained agitatedly about parties and noise made by the two Liberian couples, about brawls and shouting matches, but this was a muted gathering, though not a very friendly one. It was my first and almost only encounter with the rougher side of migration. Among the young men gathered in the room there was little pretence about their reasons for coming to Europe: they were in search of better lives, and they were resentful and angry that Italy seemed to offer them so little.

There was, it was immediately made clear, no question of talking to the women. Daniel, who was rather suspicious about my visit, told me that they were looking after the babies, and that in any case they were ill. What, he asked, was there in my visit that would help him? What would I do for him if he answered my questions? Wasn't it true that reporters paid for information? He could tell me nothing about the boat, he said: he had spent the whole time below deck, and since he possessed no watch he had no idea how long they were at sea. He had not noticed who was in charge. He had no idea if anyone had been sea-sick or what food they had been given. The only thing that he could say was that he had been aware of a lot of running up and down on deck just before the boat hit the rock. As it happened, I knew that the boat had no proper cabin, and that, with up to 150 people on board, wedged immovably together, there would have been no running anywhere. He soon drove me away with the truculence of his manner and his anger against the people of Realmonte. Was it true, he asked, that in Germany, at least, refugees were treated really well, given houses and money and cars, and not forced to work?

To the embarrassment of Realmonte's inhabitants, the parish had a cemetery too small and too crowded to accommodate all the coffins of the thirty-five drowned Liberians. After the bodies had lain in the graveyard of Porto Empedocle for several days and the smell of decomposition was so bad they had to lock the gates, the priests and mayors from nearby towns and villages were invited to provide burial plots for the dead *clandestini*. Agrigento, whose lemon groves, fish ponds and bird pavilions of ancient times were once the marvel of the Greek world, had no room to spare. The most generous offer, to take fifteen, came from Canicatti, a bustling, rapidly growing town some thirty kilometres inland, where the cemetery, once standing isolated in the lee of the mountains, is now surrounded by factories and the hideous, tall, square boxes that are Italy's answer to cheap housing. Sicily's destiny, Lampedusa once said, had been cast by a combination of the cruelty of its climate and twenty-five centuries of 'foreign invasion and indigenous folly', conquerors landing from every direction who had between them destroyed most of the paradise that the island had once been, though the warped grandeur of its chaotic towns and eroded hillsides still shine brighter than the drabness of the industrial north.

It was to Canicatti that Happy had been taken. I wanted to find her before I left.

The custodian, a slight man in a pea-green jacket and with a bad squint in one eye, was just locking the padlock on the iron gates when I finally located Canicatti's cemetery. I was very lucky to find him, he said, taking the key out again, for he would normally have closed long before, at sunset, but he had decided to have a shower before going home that night. He did indeed know where Realmonte's Liberians were buried, because he had gone to Porto Empedocle with Canicatti's mayor when the Guardia

Costiera was bringing in the bodies. For his own part, he thought the whole event had been tragically mishandled.

There is a brand new wall just inside the cemetery with some sixty new graves, not yet used or even promised but waiting for any arrivals, and it was here, he says, that the *povere creature* should have been put, all together, and not separated and scattered all over the place in different cemeteries, so that even the fifteen in Canicatti are not together but slotted away in ones and twos, wherever a wall had a place still to fill in. Even in death, he said, they had been given no dignity.

And there she was, Happy, three graves up in the middle of a wall, *Cittadina Liberiana, Naufraga a Porto Empedocle, 15 Settembre 2002*, though her surname on the piece of cardboard that identifies the grave wrongly lists it as 'Roland', her brother's first name. Not far from her, in another row high up on an identical wall, among the plastic flowers and the chiselled saints and shaded by the ancient cypresses for which Italian cemeteries are famous, lies Joy, another *Cittadina Liberiana*, the youngest of the drowned, said the custodian. Not far from the two girls are three other Liberians, all young men, only these have no identities, and below the words *Cittadino Liberiano* there is only a single letter of the alphabet, in bold black lettering, to distinguish one from the other, for there was no one among the survivors able or willing to give these bodies names. Happy and Joy, and three nameless Liberian boys, come to lie under the cypresses of a continent they dreamed would make their lives.

Chapter Three

The Fence: The Migrants of San Diego and Tijuana

Man is of all sorts of luggage the most difficult to be transported.
Adam Smith

One night in October 2003, when cold winds and low temperatures had already come to the bare mountains that lie along the border between northernmost Mexico and southern California, a thirty-eight-year-old Mexican woman arrived at a refuge for migrant women in Tijuana. She was very thin and very poor. With her were her children, two girls aged twelve and nine, and they, too, were small and underfed. They came, the woman told Sister Hema, the missionary nun who runs the refuge, from Guadalajara in the south, where they had been working on a ranch until the job ended. They planned now to go north, to cross into California, where they had been told there was work in the fields and on farms, and even modest fortunes to be made. The woman's husband was with them, but because Sister Hema does not take men into her refuge he had gone to sleep two doors away, in the Casa del Migrante, which is run by Father Luis from the same missionary order of San Carlos.

Sister Hema never saw the husband, but she looked after his wife and small daughters for fifteen days, trying to build up their strength with hot, nourishing food. Like their mother, she says, the little girls were remarkably fair-skinned, and with their blonde hair and pale eyes could have passed for white North Americans. The family said little, but Sister Hema kept thinking how frail and vulnerable they seemed, with their light shoes and cotton clothes and their air of uncertainty and apprehension. In her cupboards she found thick clothes for them to wear, and sturdy shoes for the long walk ahead. In the evenings, when the girls were asleep, Sister Hema would warn their mother about the journey across the border, the way it had been closed by a fence that runs intermittently for sixty-four miles towards Arizona, and how even the open stretches of mountain and desert are thickly covered in sensor wires and floodlights and regularly patrolled by US border agents. And she talked too about the *coyotes* – the jackals, as the human smugglers are called – who, for $1,000 a head, will guide groups of migrants through the wilder mountain areas, or across the canals and waterways that separate Mexico from California. The woman would listen but say only that they had to cross, there was no going back, the family had no money and no land and the job on the ranch was over, and she had elderly parents who had to be looked after; the *coyotes* and their stories of extortion and abandonment were nothing to her, as she did not have the dollars to pay for them. They would be crossing on their own.

One morning when Sister Hema came down to breakfast, the woman and her daughters had gone. From Father Luis came word that the husband had also disappeared. Sister Hema waited, hoping for news. Often, she says, people who have successfully crossed into the States telephone from California to let her know that they are safe. Then, a few days later, Father Luis heard that the husband had been caught in the mountains by a US Border Patrol after he had fainted and been found lying by a track. After a short spell in hospital he had been returned to Tijuana, and had made his way back to the Casa del Migrante. Of his wife and daughters there was no news. And a few days later the man disappeared again. This time he did not come back.

Sister Hema waited, but she heard nothing. The thin woman and her fair-haired little girls did not come back, and they have not sent word since. She thinks about them, wandering across the cold mountains in the dark, following a route they must have planned during the two weeks they lived with her, and wonders whether the bands of smugglers and robbers who prey on the migrants caught them, or whether they were picked up by the Border Patrol and are now in detention somewhere along the border. Or even whether, since the husband fainted from exposure and cold, they never reached the other side, but lost their way and died in their attempt to reach America. She worries about whether she did enough for them; whether the clothes she gave them were sufficiently thick and warm.

When Sister Hema first came to Tijuana, no one had yet put up the triangular signs along the freeways that stretch away from the border and into southern California, the signs with a picture of a man, a woman and two children running, rather like the signs you see in wooded areas warning of deer or cattle crossing. These signs, telling drivers to slow down lest they hit migrants as they run across the freeways to escape the border patrols, are everywhere now. But when Sister Hema arrived ten years ago, Tijuana was only just becoming one of the most frequented jumping-off spots for people crossing illegally. And that was before the migrants took to making their dashes for freedom across the five-lane freeways, where cars travel at well above the limit of sixty-five miles an hour, and where the light is dim and the headlights confusing at dusk. What Sister Hema thought then, seeing all the women and children hanging around the streets of Tijuana waiting for darkness to fall, bewildered, hungry, all that they possessed left far behind in southern Mexico with parents and friends, was that she could provide a small measure of safety in the hours before the crossing. The order of San Carlos works with migrants across much of Latin America, and Sister Hema had started her mission as a teacher in her native Brazil, before spending six years in the mother house in Rome. 'Wherever there are migrants,' she says, in her mixture of Spanish and Italian, 'there we will go.'

It was Father Luis who first called Sister Hema to Tijuana from Rome. She arrived in the spring of 1994 to find his Casa del Migrante not long opened on one of the steep hills that overlook the city, with beds for eighty men, who, as Father Luis puts it, had 'lost their way' somewhere on their journey north, run out of money or had it stolen, or simply been caught by the US Border Patrol. The Casa del Migrante was founded for men only, and so Sister Hema opened a second refuge, which she keeps spartan and spotless but not unfriendly, with a large courtyard of orange and fig trees where the humming birds come to feed, and where, on warm days, the women sit and their children play. Sister Hema is in her sixties, an energetic, kindly woman of great warmth and shrewdness. She wears large spectacles and her face is creased with the lines that come from laughter and smiling. She grows fond of the young women in her care, who treat her with respect and consideration, and she tries hard to provide them with the kind of guidance that will make them question the decision to make the perilous journey across the border. But she knows, even if not all of her visitors tell her so, that they have little choice: if they have reached as far as her refuge in Tijuana, it is because they have nothing left to hope for at home.

I had started my research along the border in the autumn of 2003, when forest fires were burning all down the coast of California, fanned by a strong Santa Ana wind. I wanted to see for myself the fence, and meet migrants whose reasons for crossing were to do with poverty and not flight from persecution – the so-called economic migrants – so I went to visit Father Luis, a purposeful and bearded man whose concern for the migrants who pass through his refuge is more than matched by a crusading determination to see the current border situation, with its deaths and ambiguities, reformed and clarified. Father Luis sees no sanity in a border so guarded against people so desperate and determined that they are driven away from the safer areas to cross further into the rocky and arid mountains. For him, the distinction between economic migrant and asylum-seeker has little meaning among people driven to the margins by need. 'Do people have to die in order to work? Something has to be wrong.' In the last three years Father Luis has watched the border grow more impenetrable, as new technology is invented and installed and ever larger numbers of border guards are taken on; and he has watched the numbers of those trying to cross grow. 'There are a lot of families,' he says, 'who have lost their men.' The men who are using his tidy dormitories and his generous canteen are people who have attempted the crossing again and again, only to be caught and sent back, and many of them have made it only on a fourth or fifth attempt, gone on to spend months or even years in California, returned to see their families and are now heading north once again. The Casa del Migrante is a station, a waiting room in which to gather strength and courage and to exchange news on the state of the border. It is also, though Father Luis does not say so, a place where the migrants can learn where a *coyote* might be contacted, with whom to seal a deal for a safer crossing north.

Father Luis' courtyard, with its tiers of balconies rising several storeys high, is where the men gather as night falls to sit on benches and exchange information and make plans. The air is full of expectation. They may stay in the refuge no more than fifteen days, and the pressure to be gone is strong. Visitors are young, most of them under thirty-five, and none are old; old people, as Father Luis explains, do not migrate. They have neither the strength nor the desire. Sitting on their benches around the courtyard, the men, dark and stocky and watchful, talk of Atlanta and San Francisco and Houston, of farms where cousins and brothers have found work, of the dollars they will send home and the sadness of leaving wives and small children; and of the dangers of the canal at Mexicali, where the current is strong and the Americans have built slopes into the water so that the migrants who swim across cannot find purchase in order to reach the Californian side and climb out. The Mexicali canal is famous for its deaths. Their stories, recounted as night falls in quiet soft voices and with a touch of bravado, are of chases in the desert and accidents to friends, of the venality of *coyotes* and the great hopes they have for better futures. Nowhere was I as struck by the huge ambiguities of refugee and migrant life, the way that asylum and migration overlap and complement each other, and how slender the distinctions can be. Like some of Sicily's boat people, the reasons for these men's flight were complicated and some at least were driven simply by a determination to find a better life.

It was the women whose stories I found sadder, and in Sister Hema's courtyard the mood was not so buoyant. San Diego's forest fires were still burning not far away, and the sun had turned into a small, intensely red marble, glowing eerily in the yellowish light as ash floated and drifted out of the sky. Fears of the uncertainty and the unknown, the risks of the crossing and the peril for their children preyed on the minds of the women who waited.

When I met Sister Hema, Luisa had been with her for just a day, and Sister Hema was pleased that she was there, for she would be able to tell me a story that she heard again and again from women who came to her refuge. Like the fair-skinned woman and her daughters, Luisa is from Guadalajara in southern Mexico, and she has stayed with the mission before. Four years ago, when she was twenty-five, she and her husband Pedro and their five-year-old daughter Dolores travelled to Tijuana in order to cross to seek work in the States. Their family at home – the two sets of grandparents, brothers, several sisters, many children – had a house in which to live, and a little land; but there was never quite enough to eat and the family kept growing. One of her husband's brothers had made the crossing into California earlier, and had prospered in Houston working in a factory. The stories he sent back of his new life and the dollars that came with it made the young couple decide that they should follow in his steps. At night, around the table, there were long discussions about the wisdom of such an undertaking, especially with a small child, but they were adamant that they would not leave her behind, however much the grandmothers pleaded. And the day came when they packed a very small bag, with one change of clothes each, and took a bus for Tijuana.

Just down the road in the Casa del Migrante, beyond the church where the missionaries and the migrants congregate, Luisa's husband soon learned of a route through the mountains where the Border Patrols seldom went. He discussed it with Luisa and they decided that she and Dolores should remain with Sister Hema while he went ahead to explore the journey and find work in California. Soon, word came that he had made the crossing in less than a day, and that though he had seen a patrol, he had managed to hide in the bushes until they passed. He was in Hollywood, where his brother had found him a job in a restaurant. As for her own crossing and that of their daughter, he urged them to wait while he raised the money to pay a *coyote* who would find them a safer and less arduous route across the mountains.

Luisa and Dolores waited. Then the day came when $1,700 arrived from Pedro, and with it instructions from a *coyote* network whose trustworthiness was known and tested. The route to be taken by Luisa was settled; but Dolores, said the unknown visitor who came to give her the details of their journey, was to be entrusted to a Mexican woman who had a daughter of much the same age. Dolores' name would be substituted for hers on the legal documents held by this woman, and the two would then cross the border at the checkpoint of San Ysidro, where San Diego meets Tijuana, and Dolores would be returned to Luisa on the other side. The whole experience, says Luisa now, was terrifying: all migrants know the stories of children handed over to *coyotes* in this way and never seen again, and she hesitated before letting Dolores go. But it was successful. Late one night, she put her five-year-old daughter into the hands of a total stranger who came to collect her from the refuge, promising to deliver her to a safe house on the Californian side. Luisa then set off with a *coyote*. On the way to the mountains they collected another woman with a little girl some years older than Dolores, and two men. The party spent a few hours in a safehouse just inside Mexico, and when the time was judged right by the *coyote*, set off on foot in the company of a young boy as guide, children now being preferred as guides across the border since if caught they are not detained by the Border Patrol. For several hours, they scrambled as fast and as silently as they could over the rough terrain, dodging behind bushes and rocks, stopping briefly from time to time to rest. Pausing, lying low, stopping and starting, they took almost two days to reach the safehouse on the Californian side. Twice they saw a patrol car in the distance; but the officers did not see them. Once, they came across another party of crossers, flitting silently by in the near dark. The travellers did not talk to each other. They had biscuits with them and some bottles of water. It was as if each travelled alone. Two days later, Luisa was reunited with Dolores.

But California did not work out well for the family. Luisa found a job in a factory but soon realised that she was pregnant; shortly after the birth of a little girl, she found herself pregnant again, and this time a son was born. Her husband's job in the restaurant was followed by a better one in a factory making toy bones for dogs, but the $285 he brought home each week was not enough to feed, clothe and house his growing family, particularly as, being illegal migrants, they lived on the very margins of American life. For a while, they sent money home. But there was never enough even for themselves. And then the day came when they began to run up debts, small at first, but they grew, and it made them sad and anxious.

The day I met Luisa and her three children with Sister Hema, Dolores by now a leggy, darting child of nine with fashionable American clothes and bulky, flashing trainers, the family was on its way home. Dolores spoke fluent, rapid English, interpreting for her mother who, in her four years in Hollywood, had never found the need to learn. Luisa longed to go home: she missed her family in Guadalajara. The crossing back from California to Mexico had been easy: a bus to the border, a short walk across at San Ysidro past the cars queuing for inspection, the border police taking no interest in their lack of papers. They were Mexicans, after all, going home. It was the next stage in their lives that would be hard. They had come back to nothing – no prospect of work, no savings. The afternoon I sat talking to Luisa under the fruit trees, with Sister Hema hovering in the background and the smaller children playing with a torn stuffed toy bear in the courtyard, her husband was out in Tijuana, trying to find work that would bring in enough money for the bus fare south. It was his fourth day of looking, and there was nothing to be found.

Not far from Sister Hema and the Casa del Migrante lies Tijuana's wide and white sandy beach. Here, even on a calm day, the Pacific breaks in slow, heavy waves that wash over the shore, and Mexicans with their children come to paddle and picnic and, on bright autumn and winter days, to stroll and smell the strong sea air. Behind, above, along the rocks, is some of Tijuana's most derelict housing, faded and crumbling cheap seaside hotels, a shanty town of plywood and unfaced brick, dwarfed by the enormous stadium of the bullring. On the beach, there is sand, brushwood and rough pebbles, and the constant sound of surf, and this breezy, blowy sight stretches as far as the eye can see. That is, except where it is broken by the fence, the great divide, part very real, part mythology, that separates Mexico from California.

San Diego and Tijuana could be a single city. They run, more or less without a break, along the coast from the far northern suburbs of San Diego's La Jolla and Del Mar, to Tijuana's last shanty towns to the far south, one an American city that is all freeways and neat suburbs of tranquil matching houses and landscaped gardens, the other a chaotic and anarchic Third World sprawl of run-down houses and unpaved roads. Between the two runs the fence, the structure erected and fortified over the last twenty years to keep out the successive waves of Mexicans who have longed to make California their home. For much of the border between the two cities, the fence is tidy, well patrolled and floodlit. On the beach, it is rusty, a chaotic structure of iron panels and concrete poles, a curtain of ridged iron that rises straight up out of the sand. There are gaps, and even holes large enough for a slim man to slip through. Far out into the sea stretches its extension, a wall of solid, circular iron railings. Two worlds, a tamed California wilderness on one side, with eucalyptus, cactus and bougainvillea, and horses grazing in fields; and a place of impoverished Mexican families on the other, separated by a single, rusty, crumbling fence. It seems too small a structure, too insignificant, to mean so much.

Every day, migrants gather on Tijuana's sandy beach. They come to look at the fence, to measure its height, to assess how far they will have to run on the other side before they reach the cover of trees, to observe the US Border Patrol in their four-wheel drives parked on the bluffs, to calculate when the light from the tall floodlights will be least revealing. There is no mistaking those waiting to cross. Almost all are young men travelling alone, parking their small bag or backpack on the sand as they wander up and down, looking, wondering. They test the toeholds in the fence, look through the holes at the emptiness of California and then sit quietly, waiting for dusk. Many have made the journey before, and many will make it again.

After talking to Sister Hema, I went down to the beach. It was windy, with a faint misty sun now, and the light, still yellow and odd from the fires, was beginning to fade. On the sand among the families, with their children and their dogs running for balls, sat silent young men waiting. One, with the help of a friend, was testing the fence for the best place to climb; finding a gap, he slipped quickly through and, using a stick, wrote '*pasato*', 'crossed', in tidy, clear letters in the wet sand, before slipping back, pleased with his work. He was going to make his break for it as soon as darkness fell, he said, when the patrol changed and when the fading light made figures more indistinct. He intended to run very fast along the sand towards the trees. It was his first crossing and he had friends waiting on the other side on the freeway leading up towards the centre of San Diego.

A little higher up the sand, crouching on their heels, talking in whispers to each other, were four young Chinese men. They had nothing with them, no baggage or belongings of any kind. They looked neat and rather smart, and one wore a cotton suit. They, too, were waiting for dusk. I wanted to talk to them, to ask them where they had come from and why they had chosen the beach at Tijuana, and what their journey from China had been like, but we had no language in common, or perhaps they did not want to talk to anyone. Perhaps they were computer programmers, like those I had been told about who are now using the Mexico–California route in growing numbers, smuggled from Fuijan at $60,000 a head.

Somewhere towards the middle of the fence, between the sea and the rocks that rise sharply towards the houses, is a large circle made of barbed wire, like a spider's web against the rusty iron. It is a memorial, according to a crude wooden plaque roughly tacked to the web, to those who have died in their attempts to cross into California in search of work. Further along, also fastened to the iron panels, are a number of large wooden letters, some five or six feet tall, all that is left of a slogan once written boldly by human-rights activists wanting to draw attention to the fence. 'ALT', they read; and then there is a gap; and then 'DIA'. No one on the beach that day knew what the letters stood for, but later people told me that they once read '*alto Operación Guardian*', 'halt Operation Gatekeeper', the name given to San Diego's most determined assault on the migrants that took place early in the 1990s.

On each letter in the years since, an artist has carefully drawn a number of skulls, very white against the fading yellow paint; and on each skull is the name of someone who has drowned swimming round the outer perimeter towards California, tossed back onto the shore by the waves or sucked below by an undertow that flows dangerously along this coastline. There are several Joses and many Pedros; there is a Moise and a Jaime; but most of the skulls contain just two words: '*no identificado*'.

The story of California's fence is the story of migration. Just as Europeans live with myths of departure, so Americans have myths of arrival: nearly one in ten of all US residents – 26 million people – are immigrants. The fence is part of the myth. It is about a poor country looking across a border and seeing money and opportunities, all the lure that enticed the first settlers, and wanting to have a share in them. It is about the way that, ever since anyone can remember, poor Mexicans have migrated north in search of the American dream, which for them has meant jobs in agriculture, factories, the building and service industries, and the way they have been welcomed and discouraged by turn, and have simply kept on coming, even during times of determined and brutal rejection, and the way that the Americans have feared being swamped and losing their own identities and livelihoods. It is the old and simple story of exclusion.

There have always been fences and walls. Clearly delineated and militarised frontiers have been known since antiquity. China began to build its Great Wall in the third century BC, to keep out nomadic invaders, and in AD 120 Hadrian erected his wall in Britain from the Solway Firth to the Tyne. Medieval European cities were fortified and surrounded by walls. But the idea behind the walls and fences slowly changed. With the nineteenth century, and the broad acceptance of national sovereignty, came a new vision of frontiers and border controls, with the understanding that states had the legitimate authority to dictate what took place on their own territory. To do so, they needed to control their borders. No longer were they the means of keeping out military foes, but ways of deterring invasions of unwanted people along lines that often lie like geological faults between the world's rich and the world's poor.

It has become fashionable, at the turn of the twenty-first century, to see frontiers and borders as archaic and irrelevant in the new age of globalisation and the internet. Among free-market liberals, the talk is all of a 'borderless' world; developments in communication technology, along with world market forces, are making frontiers absurd, while the peaceful interdependence of states can lead only to a further erosion of borders. In practice, of course, there is no peaceful interdependence of states and the 'debordering' of the world is all about trade and little about people. As economic borders come down in successive waves of economic liberalisation, so the physical borders themselves are actually being strengthened to keep out trespassers. Increased freedom of exit has not been matched by increased freedom of entry: people today face formidable barriers if they try to cross from one country to another. Reconciling this paradox – how to make cross-border economic exchanges easier, while enforcing border controls for would-be immigrants – is perceived as one of the most delicate and challenging political tasks of our time, a task made harder by the image peddled everywhere of the huddled masses of our times battering on the doors of the affluent world. An image, as it happens, that is false. Most people today, as in the past, are not mobile. Somewhere between 2 and 3 per cent of the world's population can be counted as international migrants – a fact seldom quoted – no more and no less than at any time in the last fifty years.

The border between Mexico and the US is just over 2,000 miles long. Ten million people today live in the twelve major cities, neighbours along the border with forty-four ports of entry between them. Around 300,000 Mexicans cross legally every day to work in the US. Cross-border trade has doubled in ten years. Tijuana and San Diego, a single urban sprawl straddling the frontier at San Ysidro, currently have a population of around

4 million, and it is rising sharply all the time. Some 60 million people and 20 million cars cross from Tijuana into San Diego every year, making it one of the busiest frontiers in the modern world. Migration across this long border, both legal and illegal, goes back a very long way. All through the nineteenth century, people moved more or less freely and unchecked backwards and forwards, and the first American attempt to restrict entry was aimed not at Mexicans but at the Chinese, who were landing by boat at the ports of Ensenada, Guaymas and Mazatlán, and paying $40 to traffickers to take them into California. The first officers appointed to catch illegal crossers were known as Chinese inspectors. In the 1920s, when the US imposed restrictions on European migration, the Mexico–US border became a back door for Europeans and when, in 1924, the first US Border Patrol was created, the primary targets for its 450 officers were European and Asian migrants. Mexicans, meanwhile, continued to cross as they had always done, informally, in response to the demand for cheap labour in the expanding agricultural businesses. Deported when the Depression hit the US, they were welcomed back once again in World War II, to make up for labour shortages.

Between 1942 and 1964, under the Bracero Program, a guest-worker arrangement provided continuing cheap labour for the new agro-businesses. By now, the presence of Mexicans in the US was enshrined in a vast and complicated web of needs and agreements and when, in the 1960s, the Bracero Program ended, the system simply moved under-ground, with the Mexicans continuing to cross, their freedom of exit guaranteed by the Mexican constitution. Undeterred by the largely symbolic presence of a small number of border agents, they joined large Mexican communities all over America, for the most part leaving their families at home. It was the passage of the Immigration Reform and Control Act of 1986, which legalised some 2 million Mexicans already working in the US (while at the same time tightening border controls), that stimulated a desire for more Mexicans to enter the US. By 1996, over 7 million Mexicans were living in the US, most of them illegally. On the wall of the briefing room in San Diego's Border Patrol headquarters hangs an extraordinary photograph. Taken around the end of the 1980s, it shows a hillside on the Mexican side of the border, somewhere on the edge of Tijuana. The entire hill is covered in men, perhaps 500 or 600 of them, all standing facing forwards, towards the camera, as if watching a football match. Caught on film by a photographer on the Californian side of the border, they are in fact migrants waiting for night to fall and the great race towards the border to begin. Facing them, not seen, are a few border-patrol vehicles, poised to arrest as many as they can.

Agent Santa Ana is a good-looking and agreeable man in his late thirties, attuned to the nuances of border affairs. He wears cowboy boots under his green uniform. A second-generation Mexican Californian, he grew up in Texas, and plans to return there. On a busy day, he told me, there would be as many as 3,000 arrests. It was unnerving to be an agent back in the 1980s, he said, waiting lonely and apprehensive for dark to fall, bracing yourself to hold back the surge of people as they came racing down the hillside towards you; but you soon learnt that if you took a very tough line with one member of a group, the rest would fall into line and go quietly. 'Even now when it is all tougher,' he said, 'Mexicans are not hard to catch: they are easily cowed by authority and they are fearful of men with guns.' They are, as he puts it, 'docile'. In those days, he went on, the men sometimes dug holes under parts of the fence for women and children to crawl through, while they, being men, insisted on climbing over.

It was in the early 1990s that life along the border changed. In 1993, the newly inaugurated President Clinton, faced by recession in California and the rise of anti-immigration groups who claimed that by mid-2050 only half the population of the US would be white, launched a programme to 'regain control' of the country's south-west border.* The most popular San Diego area, with its few stretches of weak fencing, had long been perceived as fragile but adequate: it was now seen as dangerously porous. While California became the centre for anti-immigration rhetoric, Washington hardened its approach to illegal immigrants. Generous new funds were poured into the Immigration and Naturalisation Service, the INS, and with them came more guns, more agents, more equipment. Some helicopters arrived. An electronic identification system known as IDENT, which stores the fingerprints and photographs of those caught trying to cross, was introduced at border points, and the military, bringing with them sheets of corrugated steel, sent army reservists to build a ten-foot-high fence for fourteen miles of the most vulnerable part of the border. The idea behind the Clinton administration's new commitment to curb illegal migrants was simple: they would introduce what they called 'prevention-through-deterrence', by concentrating large resources of men and technology on relatively short stretches of the border, identified as being those most used by illegal crossers, rather than taking the other

---

*This was not the first raid on the border: Operation Wetback, launched in June 1954 to stop illegal immigration of undocumented Mexicans, sent 750 patrol agents to the south-west.

possible course, which would have been to appoint large numbers of inspectors to mop up migrants once they were in.

It was also under Clinton's presidency that the first coordinated assault to frustrate Mexican immigrants was launched along the Rio Grande in Texas, where a police chief called Silvestre Reyes deployed closely spaced border-control vehicles along a number of popular crossing points. Operation Hold the Line – renamed from Operation Blockade after the Mexican government protested – was declared so successful that it was soon followed by Operation Gatekeeper in San Diego. Then came an extension of Operation Hold the Line, ten more miles of enforcement west into New Mexico. In 1999 came Operation Safeguard, to improve control along 300 miles of the Arizona–Mexico border. Everywhere underground sensors, infra-red scopes, huge portable floodlights and many new agents arrived to enforce the programme. It has become, say its critics, like a futuristic film full of gadgets; only the proposal to electrify the fence has actually been banned, after human-rights groups protested.

At first, Clinton's aggressive border policies looked highly successful. The crackdown was reported widely and with approval. Silvestre Reyes announced that arrests along his stretch of the border had dropped by a dramatic 76 per cent, which suggested to him – though not to many others – that those 76 per cent of migrants were now staying at home. Reyes left to pursue a successful career in Washington. It was true that the numbers were dropping wherever the border was now effectively enforced by men and equipment, but it rapidly became obvious that things were not what they seemed. The numbers of those crossing had not in fact dropped: they had simply shifted elsewhere. Squeezed away from the regular, safer routes, migrants were now resorting in growing numbers to smugglers, the *coyotes*, whose activities became more efficient and more professional, and who began to charge ever higher fees. Smugglers, until now operating informally, began to group themselves into highly effective syndicates, with agents all around Mexico, setting up sophisticated processes for forging and selling documents, arranging safehouses and flights and journeys by train, plane and lorry, and with carefully worked out ways of collecting fees for successful crossings. What was once a relatively simple and straightforward illegal practice has now become a complex underground web of illegality, connected to, though not the same as, the drug trade, whose members use the same routes.

And, of course, the migrants were now driven to use the more dangerous routes through the desert, with its surges in temperature, or the All American Canal, a treacherous twenty-one-foot-deep canal, in some places as wide as a football field, with undercurrents too powerful for all but the strongest swimmer, or the New River, said to be the most polluted stretch of water in the world, carrying typhoid, cholera and hepatitis. It is down this river that many of the crossers now float, holding their breath under submerged bridges and along a thirty-foot culvert. As Wayne Cornelius, Director of the Center for Comparative Migration Studies at the University of California in San Diego, sees it, there is something deeply immoral in a policy that deliberately puts people in harm's way. Like Father Luis in Tijuana, he is angry about the casualties. When he talks at seminars and conferences about the border, he tells his audiences about the 1,700 migrants who have died trying to cross between 1994 and 2001, and the many others who have lost their lives unreported in the mountains and the desert. He shows his students slides of the Berlin wall, and tells them that only 239 people lost their lives during the forty-three years of the wall's existence – a tenth of the number who have died on the Mexico–California border. Cornelius makes another point: increased enforcement has altered the composition of those who cross; fewer women, children or older people now attempt the journey. But it may also be causing those who do cross to stay longer in the US, since they do not wish to engage very often in the expense and danger of repeated crossings, and it may be encouraging a greater commerce in false documents.

While half Mexico lives in poverty and Americans depend on cheap Mexican labour, economic agreements between the two countries continue to favour the migration of goods and not people. The crucial 1994 North American Free Trade Agreement, on US insistence, omitted all mention of labour migration. Meanwhile the border remains patchily and symbolically enforced, with great shows of strength in some places and an absence of all control in others, so the migrants will keep on coming, drawn by the promise of dollars that lie just within their reach, confused but not deterred by the ambivalence with which Americans continue to view their arrival. Not deterred either, it seems, by the vigilantes spawned by this particular mixture of official encouragement and deterrence: in Arizona and Texas, ranchers carrying machine guns and two-way radios now regularly patrol the border. On their website – 'Private Property First, Foremost and Always' – which advertises weapons and combat gear and recruits volunteers for Operation Foxbat, Jaguar and Thunderbird, they quote Cicero on the moral rightness of self-protection. Ranchrescue is, they say, for people who 'believe that when government fails or refuses to act, individual citizens are obligated to act on their own' and for whom 'socialism in all its forms' as well as 'environmentalist measures' are for 'liars and fools of the worst kind'. It was the vigilantes who first used a new weapon being investigated by the Border Patrol, a manless drone which flies along the border and beams back photographs of people attempting to cross. The vigilantes are acting in total violation of federal and state laws, but they are tolerated.

The migrants are not deterred by the penalties they face if caught. Despite the Illegal Immigration Reform and Immigration Responsibility Act of 1996, which increased penalties for illegal entry and smuggling, in practice very little happens to the migrant who is arrested. So overloaded is the system all along the border that only recidivists, people caught again and again and their fingerprints recorded, are actually prosecuted. All others are simply returned across the border, in a 'humane and orderly' fashion, as demanded by the human-rights organisations active in the region, and as subscribed to by the Border Patrol. Agent Angel is proud of his district and his work. Along the border as a whole, an estimated half a million crossers are 'apprehended' each year, but no US border state has either the money or the resources to process even a fraction of them. A migrant today has just one chance in eight of being prosecuted.

It would be wrong to say that the fence dominates the border, or even that it is particularly noticeable. On the contrary, it is almost invisible. In the minds of most San Diegans, says Wayne Cornelius, the fence is an abstraction, a place where from time to time politicians make speeches, seeking votes by taking a stand against the dangers of illegal immigration, and where at others members of various churches gather to honour those who die in their attempts to reach America. Ordinary San Diegans, it seems, do not know about the fence; and they do not care.

It is, of course, possible that what is happening – a semi-closed border – is precisely what is in most people's interests. It is not hard, after all, to totally close a border if the will is there. The US needs Mexican labour. Mexicans need US jobs, which enable them to send $7 billion home each year to their families. An open and free border – as advocated by some Wall Street liberal economists – would result in an unregulated surge of new arrivals, which the US could not handle and which would rapidly lead to an even larger anti-immigrant backlash. In any case, the fears raised by September 11 2001 have introduced the spectre of terrorists using the migrant route, and there is something comforting about the idea of a fence, a barricade against the nightmare of a world out of control. The US has, therefore, to be seen to be preventing illegal immigration with showy displays of border controls, while at the same time allowing enough people through to feed the market for cheap labour.

Seen like this, the fence and the activities that surround it become like an elaborate childhood game, in which, as darkness falls each night, the two opposing sides line up, the migrants waiting to cross, the border patrols waiting to catch enough of them to appear efficient and in control. The light grows dim, the whistle goes, the migrants begin their race towards the new world. Only, of course, it is a game with a very dark side, one in which only the fittest survive, for among the casualties are many of the women and children for whom the new rules are, quite simply, too tough.

What drew me to San Diego's fence initially was a chance remark made one day by Jeff Crisp at UNHCR in Geneva. The fence, Crisp said, was fascinating because it was such a naked, unapologetic example of the lengths the West is willing to go to in order to keep unwanted people out. And he was right: there is something extraordinarily crude, even ridiculous, about these long stretches of wire and concrete that look so small and insignificant against the large landscape and arid, stony mountains of the border areas. The fence does not look as if it could really keep anything out. But it was fascinating also, Crisp went on, because the people who come across every day are not all Mexicans. Among them are Turkish Kurds and Iraqis, Sri Lankans and Nigerians, and even Chinese, like the four young men I tried to talk to on the beach at Tijuana. And indeed, when I got to San Diego, I learnt that, not long before, researchers gathering material on the nationalities of those trying to cross the border had discovered people from seventy-three different countries in a single period of not many months.

The numbers of these other nationalities, compared to those of the Mexicans who cross, are very small: perhaps no more than 4 or 5 per cent of the total. But they are enough to make an important point about modern migration: like the migratory flights of the swallows that circle the world in vast sweeps, covering thousands of miles every spring and autumn, refugees and migrants today will make extraordinary journeys in search of work and safety, journeys that on the map seem unnecessary and absurd. But unlike the swallows, which follow the same routes year after year, the journeys made by refugees can last several years, as they wander, apparently without reason, from continent to continent. In offices around the world where people study migration, there are maps charting the most used paths to freedom, with distance covered and time taken. The longest recorded journeys begin in China and end in Suriname, some 15,200 miles on the road, taking between six months and a year and costing between

$25,000 and $50,000; but Thailand to New York, at 13,500 miles, lies not far behind.

I wanted to hear about these travels, to understand the routes and the dangers, to ask questions about how the refugees decide which route to take, and what it was like travelling without possessions and with only a dim idea of the future to shape the days, guided not by their own instincts but by those of unknown traffickers whose honour they could not trust. I asked human-rights lawyers in San Diego who work with asylum-seekers if they would introduce me to some of their clients. The world of these long-distance crossers, as they are known, is completely different. Unlike the Mexicans, most have come to California not so much in search of work but to escape persecution at home: these were not the economic migrants I originally came to find, but the asylum-seekers I knew well from Europe and Africa, people so desperate that any journey, however long and arduous, however dangerous and financially ruinous, is better than likely captivity and torture at home. There are said to be about 11,000 of them in San Diego at any one time, at various stages of the asylum process.

It was from a church group in El Cajon in the west of San Diego that I heard about the Chaldeans. San Diego, like Detroit, Phoenix and Chicago, is home to a large community of these Iraqi Catholics, descendants of Sennacherib and Sargon the Akkadian, who ruled Mesopotamia with Babylon as their capital, and who still use the Aramaic language and follow the teachings of Rome. The Chaldeans did not fare well under Saddam Hussein. They were merchants, well educated and, since their religion did not forbid it, ran liquor stores. All were persecuted and thousands were arrested, imprisoned and tortured. In El Cajon, grouped into two congregations, are hundreds of Chaldeans who have fled Iraq since the early 1980s and come to settle legally as accepted asylum-seekers along its freeways and in its suburbs. They say that the landscape of southern California, with its dry air and sandy soil, reminds them of their native Iraq, and that they are happy here, though many have left relations behind. In their still oddly Middle-eastern sitting rooms, with sofas and chairs all around the walls and large floral carpets in the middle of the room, they have placed enormous television sets on which they watch the news from Iraq. When I went to the Chaldean churches, I found Iraqis who had taken remarkable routes to reach the safety of California, who had walked and driven and taken buses and ships and planes, who had spent all their savings, and left behind people they loved, people whom they mourn because they are too old, or too poor, or too frail to follow them to safety. But no journey I heard about was more dramatic than

Salaam's, and his story alone shows what people will do in order to escape persecution.

Salaam is twenty-nine and a doctor, a tall, spare, genial man with glasses and the gestures of someone who has always been at ease with himself. His dark brown hair is cropped short, and his manners are generous and open. Already, in some indefinable way, after only a few months in America, he looks American; his English has a Californian drawl. Salaam was working as a doctor in Baghdad in the spring of 1999 when his turn came to serve as prison doctor for a month in Abu Ghraib, the vast jail in the suburbs of Baghdad now known throughout the world as the place where US reservists housed and maltreated their Iraqi prisoners. As Salaam was talking, I remembered hearing about Abu Ghraib in the 1980s, when Saddam Hussein was torturing his opponents in its dungeons. Something of the horror of Abu Ghraib, horror in the voices of its victims, confined in flooded underground cells, horror brought to the West by dissidents who had escaped Saddam Hussein's executioners, has always stayed in my mind.

When he reported for work, Salaam knew little about conditions inside Abu Ghraib. It wasn't something you talked about in Baghdad in the 1990s. What he saw revolted him. He observed, but said nothing. Then one day seventy-two prisoners rebelled against the atrocities being committed every day around them. The prison governor ordered that as punishment they should be locked together in a single inner room, some four metres by five, as Salaam remembers it. The prisoners stood or sat in total darkness. On the second day, two died; on the third, thirteen. On the fourth, Salaam, as a doctor, was ordered to visit the survivors. 'I couldn't get into the room because there was no air. The people inside had become like animals. The floor was sodden with urine and excrement and sweat.' Salaam did what he could: he dragged out twenty unconscious or semi-conscious people and gave them oxygen.

Next day, the governor summoned him. Salaam could no longer hold back his hatred and outrage. The conversation did not go well. Salaam was informed that he, too, would now be punished, and that his next medical job would be to extract the eyeballs of newly executed prisoners so that the corneas could be removed for transplants. 'I was ordered to attend the executions so that the extraction could take place immediately. I refused. The governor called in a guard and had me put into a cell.'

Salaam stayed there for three and a half months. Because his parents had some influence and his sister was able to put up bail, he was released. 'After that I had to leave Iraq as quickly as I could. I was marked, as a

Chaldean and as a dissident.' As it happened, Salaam's sister Rania was now marked as well. There was no choice but for both to flee. Rania left directly for Jordan on forged papers, accompanied by their father, since as a woman she could not travel alone. With money provided by their relatively well-off parents, a ticket and visa were bought for Salaam to travel to Turkey.

It was now that the long journey into exile, that would bring brother and sister and eventually their parents and remaining sisters to California, began. Salaam and Rania knew where they wanted to go, as San Diego's Chaldean community is well known to Iraqis; furthermore, an older brother, Iman, was already settled in El Cajon. The question was how, with no genuine passports or visas, to get there.

From Turkey, Salaam travelled by bus and car to Turkestan. There, he bought another visa, a forged passport and a plane ticket for Amman. It took him several weeks but he was eventually reunited with Rania in Jordan, and the two now made enquiries and found a smuggler willing to smuggle them to Mexico, via Guatemala, for $10,000 each. This involved living for a while in a safehouse, catching a plane for Guatemala City, and making their way, in the company of a guide and four other Iraqis, up Guatemala's western coast towards the border with Mexico. The last part was through jungle. At daybreak they reached the frontier, which lay along a river. The water was high and fast flowing. Their guide directed them to the shallowest point and Salaam and Rania, hand in hand, holding tightly to one another, set out, the water swirling around their shoulders. Several times they lost their footing and thought that they would be swept away. But they reached the other side, and were taken to a safehouse to rest. They had now been travelling for thirteen days and had nothing but the clothes they stood up in.

In Mexico City, the smugglers abandoned them, but they had tickets for a plane to Tijuana. When the party disembarked, only Salaam and Rania managed to get through the immigration controls: the other four were taken into custody.

Salaam and Rania now took a room in a hotel. Their brother Iman arrived, having crossed the border at San Ysidro on his legitimate asylum-seeker papers, bringing with him a further $2,000 for each of them to pay another smuggler to get them into California. And so, very early one morning, Salaam and Rania were driven to the crossing at San Ysidro, told to walk, without looking right or left or pausing for anything, through the checkpoint, past the lines of cars waiting for border inspection, past the immigration controls. It had all been arranged with bribes. They didn't believe it, but it worked. They found themselves in California, in a parking lot near the border, where a smuggler was waiting with a taxi to drive them to their brother. Next day, they asked for asylum. In the months that followed, their parents and two sisters also reached San Diego. Rania has since married and works as a pharmacist; Salaam is studying American medicine for the qualifications he needs to practise as a doctor in the US.

What Salaam remembers most about the journey is the sense of responsibility he felt for Rania. The worst moment was crossing the river, with the current pulling at their legs and the Mexican and Guatemalan soldiers standing on the bridge, within sight, with their guns, but fortunately looking the other way. That was bad, just as it was bad leaving Jordan on a forged passport, knowing that if it was discovered he would be deported back to Iraq. The journey was hard for him, but far harder for his sister, who had no knowledge or experience of danger and hardship. As for him, what he witnessed and went through in Abu Ghraib hardened him, and in comparison his travels do not strike Salaam as very interesting. It is the past that preoccupies him.

It was from the pro-bono lawyers who handle the cases of asylum-seekers that I heard about the extent to which 'aliens' have been swept off the streets since September 11 2001. Immigrants and visitors to the US now face a barrage of legal and bureaucratic threats.* Shortly after the attacks on the Twin Towers, on the orders of the Attorney General John Ashcroft, the US resettlement programme, which has in recent years seen some 70,000 asylum-seekers granted new lives in America, was frozen. As I had seen in Cairo with the Liberians, people whose immigration had already been approved were put back into the system for new checks. Families, split between different parts of the world pending reunification in the States, moved into limbo. The infrastructure of organisations caring for them, such as the International Rescue Committee, began to crumble, as with no new arrivals there was no new funding. Then arrests of 'suspect aliens' started, beginning with Muslims and Arabs. At first, the number of detainees was conscientiously published each week. But when, before many weeks had passed, these figures reached a thousand, the bulletins stopped. All that was known was that foreigners working or studying in the

---

*There are today four main categories of immigrant in the US: relatives of US residents (69 per cent); those who come for specific work (13 per cent); refugees and asylum-seekers (8 per cent); and those who take part in the lottery, which is open to countries who sent fewer than 50,000 people in the previous five years (6 per cent).

US, many of whom had been here for many years and had families and children, suddenly found themselves picked up and charged with technical violations of immigration law, such as failing to notify the authorities of a change in the university course they were studying. On the false pretext that this was the simplest way of holding in custody and interrogating possible terrorists, some of these people have been held for months before being deported. Others have been caught under an ex-post-facto law, making immigrants who came to the US in a lawful manner subject to deportation for acts that were not grounds for deportation – such as traffic offences – when they committed them.

Another Ashcroft proposal, enacted in the wake of 11 September, requires visitors from twenty-five predominantly Muslim countries to register and submit to fingerprinting immediately on arrival, and then report back to the authorities after forty days in the US. Some forget; others misunderstand or do not take the ruling seriously. In a little less than two years, at least 5,000 people are believed to have been arrested and taken into custody – of whom just four have eventually been charged in connection with terrorism, and just one actually convicted of 'support of unsuspected terrorism'. In this context, what is taking place at Guantanamo Bay in Cuba can be seen as an extreme version of the current US hostility towards those who are 'non-citizens' – holding 650 men and boys – some as young as thirteen – in indefinite detention, incommunicado, without access to counsel, and with no hearing at which to determine whether or not they are in fact 'enemy combatants' in the first place.

The attacks launched by President Bush and John Ashcroft on America's vast immigrant population have not gone unchallenged by liberals among both the Republicans and the Democrats, who regard them as alarming warnings of an ever greater erosion of civil liberties. The USA Patriot Act has already given government agents the power to subpoena any individual's records with a university, library or telephone company. As Anthony Lewis noted in the *New York Review of Books* in the autumn of 2003, paraphrasing Pastor Niemöller, what is happening today to refugees and immigrants, the 'aliens', could very well happen tomorrow to American citizens, and the fact that such things are tolerated only makes future action against citizens that much more thinkable. And while people wait, for other terrorist attacks and yet more repressive measures taken in their wake, so the emphasis is shifting all the time, away from openness and tolerance and accountability, towards secrecy and obfuscation. Prejudices on the part of certain judges hearing immigration appeals grow more marked; postponements and adjournments become the order of the day, as do layers of investigation by one government agency after another; the appeals system becomes more meaningless; nothing is as clear as it once was and human-rights lawyers learn of changes in policy not in directives but by reading between the lines of speeches. Nuances have taken on new power.

The detention of asylum-seekers has a long history in the US. Introduced along with the first immigration controls in the late nineteenth century, it was abandoned in the 1950s, only to be revived in the 1980s in response to the influx first of Haitians and then of Cubans, arriving in small boats after many days at sea and detained in camps and federal prisons in an attempt to deter too many others from following. To this day, the rule of limited parole for pregnant women, juveniles and other vulnerable people, and blanket detention for the rest, remains in place for all those reaching the US without valid entry documents. Once they pass a screening interview, and provided they satisfy certain criteria, they are in theory eligible to be paroled, but many continue to be detained just the same. Though not criminals, they can be – and often are – detained indefinitely, for six or seven months before they come before a judge, then for the two or more years before the appeal, then many more months while the law winds along its convoluted course, only then to be denied bail and not told when they will be released. The conditions in which they are kept are often both inhuman and degrading. They can be stripped, searched, shackled, manacled, chained and denied access to lawyers and to their families. Though in theory the conditions of detention of asylum-seekers are regulated by UNHCR, of whose executive committee, EXCOM, the US is a member, these are in fact routinely breached; and, since September 11, increasingly so.

And the numbers of detained asylum-seekers keep on growing. They are to be found in state and local jails, in federal prisons, in private contract facilities and in 'servicing processing centres', formerly run by the Immigration and Naturalisation Service, but since Congress passed the Homeland Security Act in November 2002, administered by Homeland Security. Most are places singularly unsuited to long stays. Frequently denied access to interpreters or the help of non-governmental organisations, shunted from prison to prison without explanation or warning, many of these people are reported to be falling ill, the trauma of what they have fled exacerbated by the fresh trauma of uncertainty and hostility. Lawyers visiting their clients report a sense of growing helplessness and confusion and say that the women detainees in particular suffer acutely from fear, loneliness and an inability to understand what is happening to them. Physicians for Human Rights and the Bellevue/NYU Program for Survivors of Torture not long ago carried out a series of interviews with detainees who had been held between one month and four and a half years. They found that 86 per cent of them were suffering from measurable levels of depression and half were diagnosed as having post-traumatic stress disorder. Even when bail and parole are recommended, many asylum-seekers cannot meet their requirements: and so they remain in detention. 'I am tired of seeing so many depressed people,' an immigration judge told the director of one of the detention centres not long ago. 'You should do something about it.'

A number of these detainees are unaccompanied children, travelling the world alone. Like adults, they are obliged to prove that they meet the definition of a refugee under the 1951 Convention. Under a number of different international rulings, children should be imprisoned only under exceptional circumstances, and then for the shortest time necessary. Yet the number of unaccompanied children detained in the US between 1997 and 2001 doubled. And though the US has sought to draw up humane rules for these wandering children, none are in fact binding. Not long ago the care, custody and placement of unaccompanied minors was transferred to the Office of Refugee Resettlement, a separate agency within the Department of Health and Human Services which has a long history of dealing with refugee children. Guidelines were laid down for newly arrived children travelling on their own, drawing heavily on the liberal spirit of the UN Convention on the Rights of the Child. In practice, however, a third of these children wind up in secure jail-like facilities, originally designed for young offenders, where they can spend months or even years. Amnesty International, in a report on children in immigration detention published in 2003, *Why am I here?*, found widespread violations across the country, from children spending long periods in solitary confinement, to physical and verbal abuse, strip searches and the use of chains.

When William Williams was appointed Superintendent of Immigration in New York in 1902, Theodore Roosevelt was in the White House, and Ellis Island, a former navy warehouse for explosives, was processing around three-quarters of a million migrants from Europe each year. Williams was a lawyer, an unremarkable looking man with the whiskers of his day, thinning brown hair, and a mouth that showed purpose and determination. In the newspaper photographs taken at his appointment, there is little to suggest humour or self-doubt. By nature somewhat smug and deeply patriotic, Williams liked people with thrifty natures and the 'capacity for self-government'. His eye was that of a nation-builder, watchful for the future.

It was not, however, an easy job. Before Ellis Island had been set up by federal statute under President Harrison in 1890 as a reception centre for those arriving on the shores of North America by steamship, immigrants had been landing at Castle Garden in the Bowery, before being taken off to board in houses along the Battery. It was here, all through the 1880s, that Germans, Irish, Scandinavians and British had arrived in waves, to depart more or less unchecked to cities and communities across the country. To accommodate these ever growing numbers, President Harrison ordered a new depot to be built of Georgian pine and slate on the three-acre island in New York Harbour, just off the New Jersey coast, under the shadow of the Statue of Liberty, extra land provided by earth from the construction of the New York City subway. Opened in January 1892, the depot caught fire and was burnt to the ground in 1897. Williams's appointment was designed not simply to launch the new buildings erected to replace it, but to bring order and discipline to a process that was threatening to collapse under the numbers of new arrivals, and to check the graft and corruption that had spread through the system. He was believed to be just the man for the job, an iron patriot with a prophetic vision of protecting the country he loved. Williams was to be the gatekeeper to the land of opportunity. Today, wandering through Ellis Island's immense and echoing halls, where tourists come to look at photographs of the Irish and Italians and Russians who once came this way, in their strange clothes, carrying their suitcases and bundles, it is impossible not to sense something of the enormity of the futures that faced them, or the anguish of the poverty and repression they had left behind. Ellis Island is the most ghostly place I have ever been in.

Williams lost no time in making himself controversial. From the day of his appointment, he was perfectly plain about his intentions. He announced that he would be very courteous towards all new arrivals, but very tough indeed on those he feared might dilute or infect the spirit of America. There were to be 'no idiots, imbeciles, feeble-minded persons and those who have been insane within five years' among those accepted for settlement; no 'persons who at any time have had two or more attacks of insanity'; no 'criminals, polygamists and anarchists'; no 'prostitutes or procurers'; and no unaccompanied children under sixteen. And, most definitely, no one with a 'diseased condition of the spinal cord', which I only later discovered meant syphilis. No individual case aroused more of Superintendent Williams's fury than that of a nine-year-old boy with 'an organic disease of the nervous system and a double club foot'. When eighteen-year-old Bulgarian Nicola Mitroff could not tell the board how many months there were in a year, he was outraged.

During Williams's first year in office, 1902 to 1903, 850,000 immigrants arrived on Ellis Island, bringing with them on average a little less than $30 each. One hundred and ninety thousand of them were illiterate; 102,000 were under fourteen. Williams wanted America to know these facts, and he went out to tell them. Americans needed to be 'aroused', he said, in order to take an 'intelligent interest in what is going on', just as they needed to know that there were 44,500 'aliens' in prisons and poor houses, 'nearly half of them insane and one-third paupers'. These people, declared the Superintendent, had become insane after landing 'partly as a result of their unsuccessful efforts to get along in their new surroundings'. Many were Italians, and of all prospective immigrants, he liked the Italians least, saying that they were 'illiterate, impoverished and liable to lower the average political intelligence at election time'; but the chronic poverty of the Jews was 'appalling in its intensity'.

Among the yellowing and crumbling reports and letters of Williams's papers, stored in boxes in the special collections of the New York City Library, are lists. Williams loved lists. He made lists of rules, of directives, of staff, of duties and of rights. Even as I felt disturbed by so much certainty and intransigence, I wanted to like Williams: I liked the way he enjoined his officers to 'bear themselves with dignity and treat with courtesy all with whom they may have business to transact'. I approved of his orders to officers not to slouch when with the immigrants, nor smoke, nor use slovenly speech, and the way he exhorted them to 'acquire the habit of expressing themselves with directness and precision'. Neither rough language, said Williams, nor 'rough handling', would be tolerated. I felt it must have made it all less perplexing, for people already frightened and confused, who spoke no English and were pining for those they had left behind.

And I liked too the energy with which he set about transforming this immense empty space, which must have looked terrifying to the new arrivals clambering up onto the quay under the shadow of the Statue of Liberty, with the vast hangar-like building towering before them, after many weeks at sea crammed together in dark, ill-ventilated cabins, pitching and rolling, wondering what the new world would bring. Williams ordered new dormitories built to replace the hammocks strung from iron poles in tiers of eighteen, introduced a 'refrigerating plant' and a system for 'garbage cremating', and had the old engine room freshly tiled. Accused of skimping on meals, Williams was quick to publish his menus: bean soup, roast beef, potatoes, carrots, bread, and kosher meat or fish 'for Hebrews'.

But it was hard to like a man who spoke so unfeelingly about children with club feet and widows with sick children, who regarded the taking in of Italians, 'who brought forth children without reference to their ability to provide for them', as a 'dangerous experiment', and who worried about the 'wicked agencies' in Europe intent on flooding America with their unwanted people. And over principles, Williams was not a man to compromise. Again and again in his papers, he returns to the themes that made him seek the job: a belief in the need to weed out 'deficient aliens' and send them home, a conviction that America's hunger for labour must be fed realistically and not sentimentally, a determination to bring in the 'right' kind of person, 'fitted mentally and morally for good citizenship' and to keep out the very 'huddled masses' and 'wretched refuse' so eloquently proclaimed on the nearby Statue of Liberty. The irony does not seem to have struck Williams. And if occasionally a wistful note appears in his letters, it is never there for long. 'The work of inspection is difficult and arduous,' begins one of his letters. 'We are dealing with human beings, not things.' But soon he is back on his old tack: 'The existing law,' he grumbles, 'does not reach a large class of immigrant, who are generally undesirable because unintelligent, of low vitality, almost poverty stricken, able to perform only the cheapest kind of manual labour, but their competition tending to reduce the standard of living of the American wage worker.' The immigrants were coming because they wanted to come, and not because America wanted them.*

Pressure from Washington curbed some of Williams's more outspoken remarks, but it did not prevent him from establishing a highly efficient and streamlined procedure for vetting immigrants on Ellis Island, nor from rooting out and deporting up to 5 per cent of all those who came before his boards. He longed for more staff, but was obliged to make do with some 400 officers, 'gatemen', watchmen, cooks, cleaners, doctors and night inspectors. His eight immigration boards, composed of doctors and screeners of one kind and another, worked seven days a week processing

---

* It is worth remembering that Benjamin Franklin called the Germans arriving in the mid-eighteenth century 'generally the most stupid of their nation', and as ignorant as the Indians, and that Thomas Jefferson questioned the wisdom of actively promoting immigration at all.

the 'aliens' as they came off the ships, and when things were busy, they worked at the rate of an individual every two minutes. Ellis Island doctors were soon boasting that they could spot disease and mental deficiency at a glance. If there were complaints that Williams was running the place like the stockyards of Chicago, where cows were hurried towards slaughter through a series of self-locking gates, there was also considerable admiration for the speed with which he reduced detention on Ellis Island to three hours or less for about 80 per cent of new arrivals, who, once checked, passed and registered were free to move on to their destinations and waiting families and friends. But what Williams never did was to take his eye off what he saw as his main job, which was to do what was best for America, and turn away the 'scum and riff-raff of Europe'. Left to himself, he would say that he would have turned back not 5 per cent but 25, who, had they been induced to stay at home, would not have been missed in America. Even industrious immigrants, he warned bitterly, could be 'dirty, ignorant and unable to appreciate our political institutions'.

Among the immigrant communities of America, and particularly among the large German-speaking population, Williams was not a popular man. In newspaper articles and letters, filed neatly away today in the New York City Public Library, he was accused of despotism and callousness. His fine, newly tiled halls were called 'vermin infested pens', his inspectors 'ossified and grouchy bureaucrats of the first water'. A weekly paper called *Fair Play* referred to him as an 'atavistic freak' belonging to an age when 'man's inhumanity to man was a racial condition'. When he upheld a decision made by his inspectors to deport a 'comely and well-behaved' Irish seamstress called Mary Terrell, the twenty-three-year-old mother of an illegitimate child she had been forced to leave behind in Ireland after her village priest denounced her from the pulpit, even the *New York Times* attacked Williams for a 'gross and brutal misuse' of immigration law. Williams fought back. He replied to the letters and the editorials, he wrote to the newspapers, he gave speeches and he investigated all complaints. 'We all want good immigration,' he declared plaintively, 'and none of us wants bad immigration. What is good and what is bad is not always easy to tell.' Williams spoke of Ellis Island as 'the garden spot of the harbour'; his critics called it the 'isle of tears'.

Williams served two terms on Ellis Island, three years under President Roosevelt and four more under presidents Taft and Wilson. He resigned finally in June 1913, and returned to pursue his successful law practice. The newspapers, noting his departure with a couple of muted paragraphs, observed only that he had possessed a 'very broad human sympathy'.

During Williams's years in office, some 5 million immigrants had passed through Ellis Island, and all but a fraction, despite his best efforts, had fanned out across America to build new lives, most of them settling in Connecticut, New York, Massachusetts, New Jersey and Pennsylvania. It was Williams's great regret that he could never persuade more to strike out for the less inhabited regions of America, where they might have carved new outposts on the land, rather than crowding around the cities, a tendency which was, he declared, 'one of the unhealthy phenomena of modern social life'. (What happened to those he deported back to the European poverty they had fled is, of course, not recorded.) By now, most of the immigrants were coming from south and south-east Europe, and many of them were indeed the Italians he so despised.

Reading William Williams's papers in the New York Public Library, I kept being nagged by a thought that I could never quite articulate. But then it suddenly came to me: it was what was familiar that was so striking, not what was new. Writing about the ignorance and dishonesty of the immigrants, their fecklessness and greed, Williams was saying nothing different from what is being said today in London and Washington and Rome. The language, certainly, was cruder, less euphemistic; but the meaning, in 1903 as in 2003, was identical. It was not, as it would never be, that immigration as such was bad: it was the immigrants themselves who might be bad. And what was left out was also the same: the idea of what immigrants bring with them, the richness of new cultures and traditions, and what they have escaped, in terms of poverty and repression. An entire century, and all that has taken place within it, has effectively done nothing to alter the perception of a migrant as someone unencumbered with a past.

Part Three

Arriving

Chapter Four

Fair Go: Australia and the Policy of Mandatory Detention

We have to remind ourselves that geographically we are Oriental, we are not
European. We are an island just off the south-east coast of Asia, and are part
of the Oriental world. There our fate is set . . . .The decision we must make as
Australians is this: are we going to look after our coloured future or our cultural
future? . . . I could imagine a much finer race existing in Australia in a hundred
years if their colour was the colour that so many Australians seek to attain
on the beaches.

The Rt Reverend E. H. Burgmann, Anglican Bishop of Goulbourn, January 1946

In the summer of 1966, when I had just left university in London, my
father took me and my younger brother Richard to Australia. It was, in
some sense, to take us home. Born in Melbourne just before World War I,
the eldest son of a writer and journalist, my father had left Australia for
Europe in 1937 to report on the last days of the Spanish Civil War. What
he wanted to do was join the other young writers and painters drawn so
powerfully abroad by a longing for a culture and history that they felt
Australia lacked. Europe, thought my father, would be fun; it would be
where he would learn about life and music and writing. His first real story,
filed for the London *Daily Express*, whose staff he had just joined, was
about the refugees streaming across the Spanish border into France,
loyalist soldiers and their families escaping Franco's reprisals.

All his life, he would retain a feeling of ambivalence about the country
in which he was born. He loved its smells, the colour of the light and the
constant heat, and wherever he went he remarked on eucalyptus trees;
later, when he came to build his own house in Italy, he surrounded the
terrace with them. We grew up on what he called chop picnics, fires made
on the beaches of Greece and Italy over which he grilled the lamb chops
of his boyhood journeys into the bush; but he felt trapped whenever he
went back to Melbourne, by a sense of loss of people and ideas. Australia
remained both home and not home, and he would return again and again,

at first a little resentfully, later, after he became ill, with growing pleasure and recognition. Something of his ambivalence about Australia, his longings and his rejection, coloured the constant moves of our childhood.

We sailed for Perth from Naples early in July, on board the *Leonardo da Vinci*, pride of the Italian shipping lines, making its last journey to Australia. Air travel had put the long-distance passenger ships out of business. On board were 1,700 migrants, people who had accepted Australia's generous invitation of citizenship and a new life. The scenes of farewell on the docks at Naples were noisy and tearful and the *Leonardo da Vinci* sailed out of harbour festooned in paper streamers spinning in the wind, to the sounds of a brass band playing jauntily on the quay. Far out at sea, sad people continued to wave from the upper decks. The journey was very quick by the standard of most crossings: fourteen days, with a single stop in Aden. The only episode to mar the boisterous feeling on the lower decks was when the captain announced, over the loud-speaker system, that it had just been decided in Canberra that the draft for Vietnam would henceforth apply to new settlers. A mutiny threatened, but it was quietened, if I remember rightly, by an assurance that military service could also be deferred.

The migrants were, of course, all white. Most of them were Italians, in the late 1960s still among the most numerous of Australia's post-war settlers, the destination for migrants from the south and Sicily having long shifted from the United States to the suburbs of Melbourne and Sydney. 'Italians,' read a government poster of 1951, 'make good Australians.' There were some British, a few central and eastern Europeans, a handful of Spaniards; but no Asians, no one from the Middle East, and certainly no Africans. There was no sign of the small number of 'distinguished non-Europeans' the government had said they were keen to welcome.

In Perth, our first port of call, the passers-by were conspicuous by their whiteness. In the middle of the nineteenth century, significant numbers of Chinese coolies had been allowed in to work the Victorian goldfields, followed by Afghan camel-drivers and Japanese pearl-divers. But since 1901 a 'White Australia' policy, an unashamedly racist process of selection among immigrants, had been in place to keep out 'all peoples whose presence was, in the opinion of Australians, injurious to the general welfare' – people who were not, in other words, white. In the language of the day, the 7,500 Jews who found safety in Australia soon after the shameful Evian conference of 1938 became 'reffos' (refugees), as did the other 'aliens', the Balts, Czechs, Slavs and Poles whom Australia agreed to take in the post-war years of displacement and labour shortages. But still no yellows or blacks. As T. W. White, the Australian delegate to the Evian conference had said, Australia had no racial problem and 'we are not desirous of importing one'.

And the reffos did not always have much of a life, the young men living in strict, segregated camps, many having just come from the displaced people's camps of occupied Europe. They tended to be regarded little more favourably than the Aboriginals, whose harsh treatment continued to be widely disregarded even by contemporary historians. And it was now that the idea of the 'good' refugee was born: the one who, fleeing communist persecution, waited patiently in a camp far away to be selected as 'genuine' and invited to Australia.

When Gough Whitlam, Australia's first post-war Labor prime minister, finally brought an end to the White Australia policy in 1973 – six years after my visit – declaring that the country needed to 'turn a decent face to the world', it was with two important provisos. One was that Canberra's politicians, be they from the right or left, would not play the race card in their electioneering; the other that the new non-white Australians would be selected with the greatest care. As it happened, the government were given little choice in the matter. The late 1970s were the years of the Vietnamese boat people, and Australia's immigration officials chose their settlers directly from the refugee holding camps of Malaysia, Indonesia and China with a keen eye for their suitability. In the ten years that followed the fall of Saigon, Australia took 95,000 boat people, all but 5,000 of them arriving in the approved orderly manner, having been selected and processed. Australia was no longer white, but a neat and cautious system was in place. 'We are all,' declared successive ministers with pride, 'immigrants, each and every one of us.' The prior existence of the Aboriginals was seldom mentioned.

If the United States nurtured its own idea of itself as a country opening its arms to Europe's huddled masses, and Britain chose to regard itself as an early champion of political and religious dissent, Australia framed a different myth. It was that of a continent to be explored and colonised by a nation of hard-working white people with the help of a small contingent of carefully selected white foreigners, all living in the hope that the yellow hordes of Asia, growing at a terrifying pace not far from their shores, would not cast their eyes covetously in their direction. And when events did conspire to threaten this myth, Australia, the land where all but the Aboriginals are indeed immigrants, chose to introduce one of the most exclusionary immigration policies of any democracy, against a small number of people, some of them children.

*

When Sister Claudette of the Sisters of Mercy first visited Port Augusta in the 1970s, it was in answer to a call for help from Aboriginal people living in a reserve not far from what was then one of the largest ports in South Australia, transporting iron ore, lead and silver from the Flinders Ranges. Like the native Americans in the US, many were by now gathered on reserves. Reaching the camp, Sister Claudette found that the call had come from Aboriginal women who had been taken from their parents as children, all but illiterate, and sent to work as domestic servants. Some of them were members of the 'stolen generation', the generally half-Aboriginal, half-white children removed from their mothers between 1910 and 1970 and sent to remote institutions with the purpose of destroying their Aboriginal roots. Now, growing old, they wanted to learn to read and write so as to be able to help their grandchildren with their homework. It was, says Sister Claudette, who is an energetic and friendly woman in her sixties, a shocking discovery, to find these reserves full of people who had to ask permission to leave. 'I knew about poverty,' she says. 'I had been working in the townships of South Africa. But here the Aboriginals had been stripped of everything. They had no dignity left.' She stayed with them for ten years, not unhappy, though in the summer the temperature rose to 46°C. She cannot forget that good Catholics in her congregation in Port Augusta did not choose to visit the reserve.

In 2001, after an absence of fifteen years, Sister Claudette came back to Port Augusta. A detention centre for asylum-seekers was being built not far from the town, between the desert and the red streaky mountains, made out of 'dongas', prefabricated huts designed for miners, which were being shipped into nearby Port Pirie from Western Australia and set down in rectangular blocks among the eucalyptus trees. The new camp was to take detainees from a troubled and much-hated centre called Woomera, some hours' drive into the desert, which was to close down after a violent history of riots, suicide attempts and arson.

Why the authorities decided to call the new camp Baxter, Sister Claudette is not entirely sure. The name might, she says, have come from that of Sir John Philip Baxter, chairman of Australia's Atomic Energy Commission, for this was the area where the British and Australians jointly tested rockets and missiles in the 1940s and 1950s. The explanation she prefers is that the camp is named after a man who once owned the land on which it stands, a settler remembered widely for the harshness with which he treated the Aboriginals who inhabited it.

In March 2004, almost forty years after my only previous visit, I went back to Australia, landing in Adelaide and going straight to Port Augusta, wanting to see what Australia's detention policy was actually like. Sister Claudette told me that in February there had been 199 detainees, one of them a Kashmiri who had spent over seven years in detention; and that most of them were young men, from Afghanistan and Iraq, though there were also a small number of families with their children. She wasn't quite certain, the morning she took me with her to Baxter to be tagged, searched, moved from one locked compartment into another, stamped with fluorescent identification marks and then ushered through seven sets of security doors, how many detainees Baxter held that day, for the numbers change from day to day and the authorities can be evasive about exact figures. Once I was inside the camp, she said, I would see no view of the outside world other than the sky above, the camp having been designed to let no one see either in or out. That, she said, as we emptied our pockets and stowed our possessions, was what she always remembered about Baxter, the enclosed dongas and the blue sky, along with the endless sound of whining and clanging metal, as the many gates and doors opened and closed, loud and harsh in the desert silence.

It was Salem who told me most about what it is to be a detainee in Baxter. Salem is a half-Iraqi, half-Iranian geologist, a small, thin, worried man in his early fifties who looks considerably older, with thinning lifeless brown hair and very bad teeth. His wife, Emam, is thirty-eight and she too looks older, under her neat brown scarf and brown cotton gown. They come from southern Iran and are Sabian Mandaeans, vegetarians and pacifists, followers of St John the Baptist, a Christian sect neither recognised nor tolerated in Iran, and made worse in their case by Salem's mixed parentage. Salem was at Tehran University when the Shah was overthrown and the universities closed, and it was only in 1980, telling lies about his religion, that he was able to complete his degree in geology. Forbidden to apply for full citizenship in Iran during the long war with Iraq, and unable to find geological work as a foreigner, he met and married Emam and worked with his father as a goldsmith. The couple had three boys, Masoud, Majid and Youhana, and Salem paid $800 every year in bribes to keep the family's papers in order. But then the day came, early in 2000, when Salem was informed that he would no longer be entitled to a work permit or to a visa to stay in Iran. He was ordered to leave the country and move to Iraq, though that country under Saddam Hussein was known not to welcome Mandaeans, and in any case would not accept either Emam or the boys. They were now a family without a country.

Salem knew people who had already been forced into exile. In the goldsmith's shop he had heard stories of smugglers and of foreign countries prepared to give refuge to those who were persecuted. Most of all, he wanted a Christian, not a Muslim country. A friend who had fled sent him the telephone number of a smuggler in Indonesia who was known to have transported other Mandaeans to new lives in Canada and the United States. Salem waited for a while, fearful of the journey and unwilling to leave relations behind. Then, one morning at around ten o'clock, he received a call from his sons' school to say that Masoud had been gravely hurt in one eye after a fight with a group of Muslim boys, and when it took him until four that afternoon to find a doctor willing to treat a sick Mandaean half-Iraqi child, he knew he could delay no longer. He had been saving a little gold, which he sold, together with his business, his car and his furniture; he had no house to sell, being forbidden, as half-Iranian, to own property. Following the instructions he received from Indonesia, he bought tickets for a plane from Tehran to Malaysia, for which no visas were needed. From there, after a month spent waiting anxiously in a hotel, the family were told to fly on to Bali. In Bali, where Salem handed over $7,000 in cash to the smuggler arranging their journey, they waited a further month before being taken by boat to Indonesia, and then on again by car to a deserted beach. Their destination, they were now told, was Australia, a country good to refugees. They had three suitcases and two bags with them, their only possessions. They stared out across the sea and thought it looked very dangerous. 'We feared,' says Salem, 'that we would die.'

There were 126 people on board the frail wooden boat that came to collect them that night after dark fell. It was soon too rough to eat the rice, eggplants and tomatoes that Emam had prepared, and in any case most of the passengers, who had never seen the sea and could not swim, were being sick. 'Sometimes,' says Salem, 'we were sure that we would capsize. We prayed. Some of the young men on the boat fought over the drinking water, because there wasn't enough. We had brought with us some water of our own, and a little honey and biscuits, and this is what we fed to the boys.' Among the 126 passengers were twenty-seven other young children.

The asylum-seekers, most of them Iraqi, Iranian or Afghan, had been told that the boat would take them to Ashmore Reef, a fair way from Australia's northern coast. Before they reached it, an Australian navy patrol spotted them and, judging the boat to be close to sinking, towed it into shore. Salem and his family were taken to a hostel, given rice and fish, then put onto a boat for Darwin, where they stayed for a week, waiting. At two o'clock one morning, they were woken and taken to a plane. They found themselves in Adelaide, where a coach waited to drive them to the recently opened camp at Woomera. And there, for many months, they remained, confused, uncertain about their fate, questioned from time to time by immigration officials, spending each day trying to keep the boys cheerful and healthy while around them there was constant violence between detainees and guards. They witnessed fires, self-mutilation, suicide attempts.

In October 2002, the family was moved to Baxter, shortly after it opened. They had by now learnt that they had failed, after their initial interviews and without a lawyer, in their first application for asylum. In December detainees in one of the dongas lit a fire, causing Australian $2 million in damage and sparking off a rash of fires in Woomera and the camps at Port Hedland, Villawood and on Christmas Island, provoking the authorities to clamp down further on the freedom of the refugees. The boys were now aged six, twelve and fourteen. They had been behind razor wire for almost a year. In keeping with a slight softening in attitude towards the children in detention – and perhaps in response to the growing public opposition to the policy – Salem and Emam were asked whether they would prefer that the boys and their mother live in a guarded compound within Port Augusta, where they could eat home-cooked food and attend the local school, though under guard. With misgivings, hating the separation that this would entail, they accepted and were moved to a house in the town; and Salem was told that he might make two visits to his family each week, also under guard. His sons are now eating again, Salem says, which they would not while in Baxter, and they do not cry, as they did in Woomera. But he worries about them growing up without a father. Alone in Baxter, he spends the days asleep; sometimes he reads the newspaper and sometimes he smokes a cigarette. 'I am a geologist,' he says. 'What is there for me to do?'

Salem, Emam and the three boys have now been turned down definitively by the Australian immigration authorities. The 'discrimination' suffered by the Mandaeans in Iran is not deemed to amount to persecution. They have been told that, as Salem is half-Iraqi and Iraq has now been liberated from Saddam Hussein, they are safe to go there. The Refugee Review Tribunal, which hears appeals, has also turned them down. All that is now left is a last appeal to the High Court, and then to the Minister of Immigration and Multicultural and Indigenous Affairs under what is known as Section 417. If refused, the family has just two choices: to remain indefinitely in an Australian detention centre, or to return either to Iran, which would accept Emam and the boys, but not Salem, or to Iraq, where only Salem has the right to live. Neither Iran nor Iraq, even after Saddam Hussein, looks favourably on the Mandaeans. 'They have held us in prison now for a very long time,' says Salem, holding on to my arm tightly so that I will understand what he is saying to me. Emam, who has been allowed to come out to Baxter that day, speaks little English, but nods and smiles. 'What have we done?' Salem continues. 'Ordinary criminals do not live as we do, abandoned, not knowing whether we will ever be free. As Mandaeans, we need every year to be baptised. In three years, this has not once been allowed to happen. Sometimes I think that I will kill myself, but I cannot speak to my wife about this. I am an honest man. I should not be in prison.'

When I leave, back through the series of locked compartments and security checks, through the double rows of fencing and wire, and out into the yellow desert landscape, I can see Salem waving gently to me until I pass through the metal gate which cuts off all view of the outside world. Driving back into Port Augusta with Sister Claudette, we pass a minibus driven by a guard from Baxter, with another guard on board. In the back seat sits Emam, being taken home to the guarded hostel and her sons.

Salem and his family are not without friends. Sister Augusta is only one of a group of local people – schoolteachers, pastors, librarians, farmers – who now take an interest in Baxter's unhappy inmates. In October 2003, Sister Claudette told me, there were 4,000 visits to Baxter. Some of the visitors were people like herself who went out to the camp several times, and others were strangers who drove many miles across the desert to register their protest at Australia's refugee policy and to offer their support to the interned people. They do not often have a language in common with the asylum-seekers, but they bake cakes and biscuits and bring nuts and olives, and they sit together companionably under the eucalypts or, when temperatures make the desert unbearable, they retreat into a Portakabin with air-conditioning and crowd round small grey plastic tables with plastic mugs and plates. There is nothing sharp in Baxter, no glass or metal or pottery: violence has caused too much damage in the past. When Sister Claudette asked Salem not long ago what he would do first if he was released, he thought for a long time and then said that he would like to eat a meal on a porcelain plate with metal knives and forks.

Two days after my visit to Baxter, I read in the newspaper that the camp had been closed briefly to visitors. A young detainee, showing signs of disturbance and suicidal behaviour, and threatened with solitary confinement, had climbed onto the roof of the compound. The other detainees, in sympathy, had taken over the compound and barricaded themselves in. Fifty guards, in full riot gear, had forced the gate.

It was under Paul Keating's Labor government, in 1992, that Australia passed laws to lock up boat people in remote holding camps and keep them there for the entire time it took to process their applications for asylum, but the full and harsh sweep of Australia's refugee policy crystallised only much later, in the wake of a series of specific events. Had these events happened at different moments, or at a different time in the political calendar, or even not so fast one upon the other, it is possible that Australia's ways of dealing with refugees might well have remained similar to those in place throughout the West, a little tougher perhaps, but just as piecemeal, contradictory and unpredictable. As it was, the events were so dramatic, and so political, that within weeks Canberra had created a tight, clear, new and radical asylum policy. And it is this model that is now being looked at covetously by Western governments, including the United Kingdom, for whom the issue of refugees and asylum has become equally politically alarming.

It came about like this. Australia needs and welcomes immigrants. It needed them after World War II, to work in the mines and on the land. In the 1950s, there was a series of posters showing a kangaroo perched on a map of Australia, hauling towards it a boat with a beaming family on board. 'Bring out a Briton,' read the caption, 'room for millions more.' And Australia still needs migrants today to feed its prosperous economy and to boost an aging Australian population of around 20 million people. Over 6 million have come to Australia as new settlers since World War II. Since the 1970s, multiculturalism has been a pivotal plank of Australia's self-image; today, one quarter of the population was born abroad. Australia has what it calls a 'non-discriminatory' immigration policy, which means, in theory at least, that anyone from any country can apply to enter, regardless of religion or race, providing they meet Australia's rules about good character and health. In the last ten years or so, government and opposition have tended to agree over matters of immigration, and in 2002 a new migration programme was put in place, to last four years, allowing 100–110,000 migrants per year, of whom 12,000 would be humanitarian or refugee entrants, with a further 99,000 people on temporary visas for work or business. When it comes to official resettlement, Australia is generous: of the twenty-one countries that resettle through UNHCR, it takes the most people per capita – 620,000 over the last half century – but it should also be noted that Australia is only thirty-eighth in terms of refugees received. It also has one of the world's most efficient entry-processing systems, with a computer database of those they wish to exclude.

The difficulties come with asylum-seekers. There is nothing orderly about flight from persecution. Some arrive legally on a tourist visa, and subsequently apply for asylum; others are over-stayers, 'unlawful non-citizens', who fail to depart after the expiry of their visas. There are some 60,000 of these in Australia at any one time, and 21,000 are caught each year. The real problems start with those the Liberal government call 'illegals' (wrongly, as it happens, because Australia has ratified the 1951 Convention which specifically recognises that refugees are not obliged to have documents), the asylum-seekers who reach Australia's shores without a visa, most often by smugglers' boats from Indonesia, and then ask for asylum. The use of the word 'illegals' suggests criminals, people who have done wrong, terrorists, certainly people not entitled to anything. They are seen as 'queue jumpers', stealing the places of the good refugees who have been patiently waiting their turn, and having passed through a number of 'safe and secure' countries, rejected them in favour of greater affluence in Australia.

In 1992, when Keating introduced mandatory detention for these 'illegals', only about 220 were actually arriving by boat each year. They were soon processed. All through the 1990s boats clandestinely brought mainly Chinese and Sino-Vietnamese. Those found to be true refugees under the Convention – the minority – were allowed to stay; the rest were sent home. However, in 1999, in response to political instability through-out much of the Middle East, the number of people arriving by boat and asking for asylum rose to 3,274. Most of them were Iraqis fleeing Saddam Hussein or Afghans fleeing the Taliban, and almost all came with smugglers from Indonesia, already a well-established route in the migratory flow of refugee paths. And these, unlike the Chinese and Vietnamese, were 'genuine' refugees under the 1951 Convention, and as such had valid claims for asylum. It was this fact – that they could not, in theory, be turned away or deported – which posed the first problems, as well as the fact that while Canberra felt a certain sympathy for anti-communist refugees from Hanoi, it did not feel quite the same about people escaping from the Middle East.

What was Australia to do with all these people, and were there many more to come? In 1999 the Liberal Party introduced a Temporary Protection Visa, under which asylum-seekers who had been recognised under the 1951 Convention received three-year visas, which they could turn into permanent visas only if they could then persuade the immigration authorities that they were still in need of protection. Then, and only then, would they be able to apply to have their families join them, a measure that changed the nature of the boat arrivals, for whereas before men came alone and asked for their families to join them, now families, if they wished to stay together, had to travel together. Boats, once full of men, were now full of women in the gowns and veils of the Muslim world, with small children and babies. They were not deterred by a video put out by the Department of Immigration depicting Australia as inhabited by poisonous snakes, fearsome crocodiles and man-eating sharks.

And people kept coming. In 2000, there were 2,937 new applicants. In the first six months of 2001, 1,640 people arrived. These numbers were, of course, trivial compared to those who apply for asylum in Germany, the UK, Italy or France, but the Australian detention camps were packed, frantic and beset by violence, much of it involving self-mutilation and suicide attempts provoked by the uncertainty and delays. The immigration authorities let it be known that they did not want anyone to mistake them for 'holiday camps'. And the procedure for deciding who was and who was not a genuine refugee, given the changing nature of modern conflict and the outbreaks of violence across large parts of Asia and the Middle East, was moving slower and slower. Those in detention were now spending months and even years with no idea what would happen to them. And some, of course, were children.

Meanwhile, a wild political card had entered the game in the shape of a flamboyant, red-haired 'old Anglo-Australian' called Pauline Hanson, whose parents had migrated from Britain before World War I. Hanson ran a fish and chip shop in Queensland. In 1997, as an independent, she won a seat in Parliament on an unambiguously racist, anti-Aboriginal platform. Since everyone knew her feelings about the Aboriginals – she was once quoted as saying that they were cannibals who sometimes ate members of their own families – she decided to give her maiden speech on the subject of immigration. 'I believe,' she declared, 'that we are in danger of being swamped by Asians.' Though Pauline Hanson had no discernible politicial skills – her grammar was patchy, her voice grating and she had trouble reading her speeches – a large number of Australians loved her. She confirmed what they most feared about the boatloads of desperate people, clamouring to get to their shores. Hanson formed a party, One Nation, and won a fair number of votes. In response five former prime ministers – Whitlam, Fraser, Hawke, Keating and Gorton – issued a joint statement condemning her racist policies.

As it happened, John Howard, about to run for a second term as Liberal prime minister in the forthcoming 2001 elections, was not among them. And though Pauline Hanson soon lost her seat and was eventually sentenced to jail for three years for electoral fraud (though acquitted on appeal), and though the country soon got back to its usual concerns about health, crime and unemployment, she had left behind a feeling that new boundaries had been set for what was and what was not acceptable when it came to a public discussion of race. The Liberals, whose chances of winning the election were at this point dim, took note.

And then, on 24 August 2001, a twenty-metre-long grey wooden fishing boat called the *Palapa*, on its way from Indonesia to Christmas Island, was spotted drifting helplessly at sea, its engine dead. Lying below Java in the Indian Ocean, Christmas Island belonged to Australia. On board were 438 people, most of them Afghans. Children were seen, and many women. When the news reached Canberra, alarm bells sounded. There was no room on Christmas Island to take anyone else, a boat on the sixteenth having brought 345 asylum-seekers, and another on the twenty-second, 359. Australia's other detention centres, at Port Hedland, Woomera, Villawood and elsewhere, were also full. The current Minister for Immigration was Phillip Ruddock, a man described by the Australian writer David Marr as having the 'soul of a great bureaucrat' and an interesting political past, having on one occasion crossed the floor of Parliament to vote against his leader. Ruddock, as people would soon be saying, was a man of contradictions, a member of Amnesty International, yet very hard on refugees. His importance in the Liberal party had been growing with the growth of the refugee issue. Here was the very challenge he needed.

While the boat continued to drift, Australia tried to lean on the Indonesians, on whom Ruddock had already tried to bring pressure to act more firmly against the smugglers who left from the archipelago's many islands; Indonesia, a vast, poor, corrupt country with few resources, refused to be drawn in. At midnight that night, a storm blew up. Waves dashed over the *Palapa* and a hole opened in the hull. The people on board cried and clung to each other. At dawn, a man was spotted holding up a scarf on which he had written, in engine oil, SOS and HELP. Conditions on the boat continued to deteriorate. After waiting eighteen hours, the Australians realised that they could delay no longer or the boat would sink. A call went out to all shipping in the area, soon answered by a 44,000-tonne Norwegian tanker called the *Tampa*, three city blocks in length. The *Tampa*, which was on its way to China and Japan, had a crew of twenty-seven and carried a cargo of steel pipes, dried milk, food and timber. Its skipper was a highly experienced captain called Arne Rinnan, and its owner, Wilh. Wilhelmensen ASA, had done business for many years with Australia.

Captain Rinnan, obeying the laws of humanity and the sea, took the 438 people off the *Palapa*, which was now sinking. Among them were two pregnant woman and a one-year-old baby. What Rinnan proposed to do was to drop them on Christmas Island, which was precisely what the Afghans wanted him to do, some on board having already tried once before to reach Australia. What the Australians wanted was for him to take them back to Indonesia – or anywhere else, provided it wasn't Australia. Though the rules of the sea are so clear on the paramount need to save lives, there is no rule to say that a nation may not close its borders to unwanted strangers. Responsibility, argued Ruddock, lay with Indonesia, because the rescue act had taken place in the Indonesian zone of water; or possibly with Norway, whose flag the *Tampa* flew; or perhaps even with Singapore, because that had been the *Tampa*'s next port of call. But it did not, he insisted, lie with Australia, even though it was the coastal state nearest the rescue.

Following early orders, the *Tampa* put back for Indonesia, then turned back to Christmas Island, Rinnan buffetted by the pleas and threats of the asylum-seekers, the orders and counter-orders of the Australian government, and the diplomatic manoeuvrings of the Norwegian government, the human-rights lobby and UNHCR. For the next eight days, through bouts of food poisoning and diarrhoea, with near revolts and times of raging and despair, the asylum-seekers from the *Palapa* remained on the *Tampa*'s decks. They were hot, miserable, terrified and confused, treated with kindness by Rinnan and his men, and corralled and marshalled by a unit of Australian SAS men sent in to maintain order. Across the liberal world there was horror that traumatised people, many now severely dehydrated and a few barely conscious, could be treated in this fashion. Behind the scenes, frenetic exchanges continued night and day between the *Tampa*, the Norwegian shipping company, the Australian government and the navy.

Until this moment, despite Pauline Hanson, immigration had not been dominating the coming elections. Overnight, it became the only topic that mattered. The *Tampa* had unleashed an apocalyptic vision of a future overrun by the yellow hordes Australians had always feared. One of Howard's first moves was to try to push through, in the heat of the moment, new legislation that would allow Australia to return to the high seas anyone who entered Australian territory without permission. And though Jim Beazley and the Labor opposition effectively defeated the bill, Labor's slightly hesitant protests and lack of leadership combined to dash its prospects of an easy election victory. Labor, it was said, looked like 'a party trying to walk both sides of the street'. Howard and Ruddock between them gave the impression not just of being in control; they were the leaders of a party able to secure Australia's threatened borders, and as a result they were able to draw towards them voters otherwise heading for Hanson's One Nation. 'We will decide who comes to this country and the circumstances in which they come here,' Howard announced, defining what was to be the essence of his refugee policy. His words touched some chord among Australians who feared that at any time Indonesia might collapse, sending thousands of economic migrants their way. The largest Muslim nation in the world was, after all, no more than a boat ride away.

It was about now that the infamous 'Pacific Solution' was born, a strategy with a gentle name and terrible consequences. It was not new – the British blockade of Palestine in the 1930s had refused to let Jewish refugees land and pushed them to Cyprus – but in the context of modern refugee politics it was dramatic. All future boatloads of illegal people would not be allowed, Howard decided, to reach Australia. They would, if possible, be intercepted at sea and returned to Indonesia. If not, they would be transferred to 'off-shore processing centres' and to a number of designated countries willing to hold them in detention while their futures were sorted out. At no time would they have access to Australia's legal processes, and there would be no right of appeal. Like the game of tag played along San Diego's fence, getting past the guards would become part of Australia's migration process.

Nauru, in the Pacific Ocean, is a small, bankrupt republic, once famous for the richness of its guano deposits, sold off long ago for phosphates. In August 2001 it was said to owe $16.5 million on its desalination plant alone. In exchange for Australian $26.5 million, Nauru now agreed to take 150 of the *Tampa*'s asylum-seekers and hold them in detention, and then take others from other boats; Papua New Guinea agreed to do the same, and lent Manus Island for the experiment. In both places, the claims of the detainees would be assessed by UNHCR and the Australian government. At the same time, a number of islands regularly reached by the smugglers and used hitherto as spots on which to drop their passengers, such as Christmas Island and Ashmore Reef, were 'excised' from Australia for purposes of migration. Australia had effectively, by a stroke of its pen, shrunk its borders. What was so cunning about this move was that it put the *Tampa*'s asylum-seekers, and those who chose to follow their example, beyond the reach of the Australian courts, where they might have had access to lawyers, appeals and review hearings. The Australian Migration Act is now one of the most powerful instruments in the country, able to sideline even the judiciary.

When, after ten days, the fracas had died down, the deals had been struck, and the requisite administrative orders put in place, the asylum-seekers were transferred to a naval vessel, the HMAS *Manoora*. A very lucky 150 went to New Zealand, which took them as part of their normal humanitarian response to such situations, and were quickly processed. All but one were found to have valid claims under the Refugee Convention and were offered asylum. The queue jumpers were, after all, genuine. Others were taken to Nauru, to a camp hastily built by Australian military personnel on a sports field and the remains of a phosphate mine, make-shift huts built of corrugated iron, plastic sheeting and green cloth.

Howard and Ruddock now set about tightening up the whole process of asylum. The measures they took were bold, bolder in fact in their entirety than had been attempted elsewhere. In what was called Operation Relex, a taskforce of naval vessels and aircraft was assigned to patrol Australia's coast, with orders to turn back boats of asylum-seekers approaching from Indonesia, and with new powers to search boats, detain passengers and remove them, if necessary by force. Strict censorship was imposed on Nauru, which now proved virtually unreachable by journalists, human-rights advocates or lawyers, while orders went out that no press photographers could take or publish 'personalising or humanising' images, anywhere, of asylum-seekers. Department of Immigration and Multi-cultural and Indigenous Affairs officials entered into close relations with the border police of neighbouring countries to try to stem the flow of boats. And, in the wider community, the Temporary Protection Visas were changed in such a way that they could only be renewed as further temporary visas, with no chance, ever, of having families join the applicant. Labor, which could have opposed and defeated the amend-ments, endorsed them. The fact that it was illegal under Nauru's constitution to lock people up indefinitely without charge or trial was soon solved by declaring the asylum-seekers to be visitors, on special visas which confined them to the camp. That Australia had effectively bribed one of its poorest neighbours to break its own laws drew little comment.

The *Tampa* was not, however, the end of the story. For a while, at least, before Australia's message of deterrence spread, boats kept on arriving, and the navy went on turning them away without taking time to discover whether or not they contained genuine refugees. Between September and November 2001, thirteen Indonesian boats filled with asylum-seekers tried and failed to reach Australia. Four were intercepted and sent back. One sank. Of the remaining eight, either unseaworthy or actually sinking, all were intercepted and their human cargo transported to Nauru or Manus Island. Those who tried to influence or restrain Howard – the United Nations, a number of lawyers, politicians and commentators – achieved almost nothing. There was a moment's pause when the Australian government ill-advisedly released photographs purporting to show parents throwing their children overboard from an Indonesian boat, in order, so it was claimed, to blackmail Australia into accepting them. The asylum-seekers, it was suggested, were not human beings with the same values as ordinary Australians, since they were capable of treating their children this way. Howard even appeared on television saying that the kind of people who threw their children overboard were not the sort of people Australia wanted. But the pictures were later shown to be fake, the children having indeed been thrown in the water, but only because their boat was sinking. And there was a further heart-rending pause when a boat, code-named 'SIEVX', sank drowning 353 asylum-seekers; the 46 survivors later described how their boat had broken up in high seas, how they had floundered in the water swallowing fuel flowing from the boat, how they had watched those who could not swim struggle desperately before slipping underneath the waves. A young mother called Sundous lost her three daughters, Emaan, Zahra and Fatima. Another, Ronkayya Satta, saw first her five-year-old daughter Kawthar stepped on in the frenzy to leave the sinking boat and drowned, then her second daughter, Alya, who was two, slip out of her arms. A woman who had just given birth was seen drifting away, one survivor later recalled, her baby attached by the umbilical cord.* Wherever they looked, they saw 'dead children like birds floating on the water'.

It was hard to imagine that things could get worse, but they did: September 11 had put the spectre of terrorism at the front of all political agendas, and Peter Reith, Australia's Defence Minister, was able to point out that the unauthorised arrival of boats could well become a 'pipeline for terrorists'. When election day came, Howard swept to victory. Tough border protection, Operation Relex, September 11 2001, the destruction of the One Nation party, together with a new Pacific Solution, had between them proved a vote-winning formula, though the country itself

---

* David Marr and Marian Wilkinson, *Dark Victory*.

had been polarised in a way that it never had before. Neither the Australian judiciary, nor the refugee advocates, nor the human-rights campaigners, nor the many ordinary Australians who had raised their voices against Canberra's overbearing directives, had been able to do much.* What Ruddock repeated, and what Amanda Vanstone, his successor, continues to repeat, is that Australia's resettlement package is generous, and that countries taking fewer refugees as part of national policy are ill-placed to be so critical. The Liberal government said, and continues to say, with some reason, that steps must be taken to formulate coherent asylum policies that actually work, and that first among them is the need to put an end to the vast and lucrative trade in smuggled people, and that this can only happen if smugglers are shown not to be able to deliver what they promise.

Australia's new policies had not, of course, come cheap. Between August 2001 and the middle of 2003, Australia spent an estimated Australian $500 million on its Pacific Solution. But it had, in a very literal way, worked. Punishment and deterrence had paid off. Only three boats arrived in the next three years. The question people were left asking was at what moral cost it had all been achieved. What had it all done to Australia itself? And how does one justify locking up people who have broken no laws?

There was one other event that made little stir at the time, but grew later to challenge the whole spirit of mandatory detention in a way that nothing had before. It was the story of an Iranian boy called Shayan. I met Shayan, who is now nine, in a park in Paramatta, a suburb just outside Sydney. He is tall for his age, very thin, with mouse-brown hair cut short. He would look much like any other nine-year-old, fit and brown from the Australian sun, except for the extreme wariness of his expression, which makes him look rather like a startled young animal, and the way he sits or stands extremely close to his parents, stirring when they stir, watching their faces. Saeed and Zahra, Shayan's father and stepmother, drove me to the edge of a small lake in the middle of Paramatta's green and tropical park, and there in the sunshine, looking out across the water, while Shayan was persuaded to sit in the car very close by and listen to music, they told me his story.

Saeed is a computer technician, a Kurd who belongs to a religious sect,

---

*The disdain of some of the international community for Australia's stand was expressed by the award of the Nansen Medal to the captain of the *Tampa*, for outstanding service on behalf of refugees.

Al Hagh, regarded in Shi'ite Iran as heresy. He married young and unhappily, and his wife soon left him, yielding him custody of their only child, Shayan. Saeed remarried a Shi'ite Arab, Zahra, who converted to the Al Hagh faith. In 1999, Saeed became involved in student protests at his university, and though he was not among the many to be arrested, he was already marked down by the police for his religion, and for the fact that he had converted a Muslim, a serious offence under Sharia law. The family fled, arriving in Australia on an Indonesian fishing boat in March 2000. Shayan was almost five and, according to his father, liked watching the flying fish; he was bright, intensely curious, and regarded Zahra as his mother, having scarcely known his own. Zahra was pregnant.

In keeping with the immigration policy of the time, the family was taken into detention and sent to Woomera until its application for asylum could be processed. There were at this time about 500 refugee children in detention in Australia. They had been in the camp less than a week when a riot broke out among a group of detainees who had been allowed no contact with the outside world for over three months. A fence was torn down. Guards in riot gear used tear gas and batons to restore order. Shayan watched. Later, he asked his father to explain what had happened. 'I had no answer,' says Saeed. 'I didn't know what to say.' Soon afterwards, a detainee, driven beyond endurance by his situation, broke a bottle and held it to his heart, threatening to kill himself unless he received some kind of response from the Australian authorities. Shayan watched this too. 'Gradually,' says Zahra, 'we were becoming scared about him. He didn't seem to want to play with the other children, and he seemed easily frightened.' It was at about this time, she says, that Shayan's nightmares started and he began to wet his bed.

Woomera, by all accounts, was a desperate place; it was hot, crowded and when it rained the dust and sand turned to mud. By the spring of 2000, acts of violence had become common, both self-inflicted and against the detention camp itself. The atmosphere was tense and wretched. One day, a young Iranian climbed to the top of a tree and said that he would jump to his death. There were endless fights between guards and inmates. Fires were lit. Guards often wore riot gear. Shayan watched.

The centre was divided into various compounds. Sierra, a little to one side, was the punishment block, in which unruly people were placed in solitary confinement. When a batch of new arrivals was due, Shayan and his family were moved into Sierra to make room for them. This seemed to frighten Shayan out of all proportion: he believed that only 'bad' people were sent to Sierra. Apart from his new baby sister Shubnam, he was the only child in the punishment compound. He refused to eat, saying to his father: 'You eat my food. It will make you strong to fight off the guards when they attack us.'

After eleven months, it was clear to everyone that Shayan had become extremely disturbed. Doctors diagnosed him with post-traumatic stress disorder, and in his report to the authorities Wayne Lynch, a counsellor who had taken an interest in the family, listed 'bed-wetting, nightmares, anorexia, insomnia, fearfulness' among his symptoms. Shayan was now six. On 3 March 2001 the family was transferred to Villawood on the edge of Sydney, a detention centre generally regarded as calmer and better for children. By now they knew not only that they had been turned down as refugees by the immigration authorities on their first interview, but that their appeal to the Refugee Review Tribunal had failed as well. They were running out of options: again, only the High Court and a direct ministerial appeal remained.

Villawood proved no easier for Shayan. In fact, he quickly grew worse. He witnessed more acts of violence, more self-mutilation, more suicide attempts. He was taken for observation to Westmead Hospital, where a consultant psychologist, Dr Timothy Hannan, warned of the consequences of returning Shayan behind bars. His disorder was becoming chronic, he told them, and each return to detention would trigger his symptoms. Shayan was sent back to Villawood. On 30 April he watched a detainee cut his wrists and bleed heavily. He stopped eating and drinking, and soon he refused to speak. He was taken back to Westmead.

Under Section 417 of the Migration Act, Ruddock had the power to release the family on humanitarian grounds. An application by lawyers and doctors was presented: Ruddock turned it down. Shayan went back to Villawood. 'For the next forty-five days, he would not eat or drink or talk,' explains Zahra. She speaks excellent English and is a gentle and quiet young woman. Saeed, whose English is less fluent, leaves the talking to her; he is a slight, short man, with receding hair and a small moustache and, like his wife, soft spoken. 'Every four days, they took him back to Westmead and put tubes down his throat and his nose. Then twenty-four hours later, they sent him back.' Shayan lost more weight and there were fears that his kidneys might be damaged. When in Villawood, he preferred to spend his days in bed. One day, as the guards were returning him from the hospital to the detention centre, he managed to slip away. They chased him, and as he ran, he shouted: 'I don't want to go back. I don't want to go back.'

Shayan's case was now beginning to attract attention in the medical and legal worlds. Psychiatrists were writing reports and letters to the immigration authorities. Shayan, they warned, was 'acutely traumatized'. In August, a video camera was smuggled into Villawood and on the thirteenth – less than two weeks before the *Tampa* rescue – ABC's *Four Corners* put out a film showing Shayan lying in Saeed's arms, limp and apparently lifeless. Again, Ruddock could have acted. Instead, he let it be understood, on a news programme, that there was more to the family's story than met the eye, and that the fact that Zahra was only his step-mother was in some way indicative. On four separate occasions, he called Shayan 'it'. Challenged as to why he was not prepared to show more compassion, Ruddock said that he could not make exceptions to government policy. Were he to let Shayan and his family in, would other families claiming mental illness in their children not demand the same? The Melbourne *Herald Sun* and the Sydney *Daily Telegraph* both carried stories hostile to Saeed, accusing him of having kidnapped Shayan and of deliberately starving his son.

The family, nearly all legal avenues having failed, were told that they would almost certainly have to return to Iran. Meanwhile, Shayan could be fostered in the community. Saeed and Zahra hesitated. Doctors insisted that a child in so desperate a state needed above all to be with his parents, but they worried that keeping him any longer in detention might prove too dangerous: Shayan had by now witnessed three serious riots, four suicide attempts, many acts of self-mutilation, arson, fights and the repeated humiliation of his parents. One day, while discussing what would be best for him, Saeed was led into another room in the hospital. Zahra remained with Shayan and Shubnam. She described the scene: 'Shayan was clinging on to me. A guard came up and said that they were going to take him. He began to pull him away from me. Shayan screamed: "Mum, help me." What could I do? They pulled him away and locked us in a room and took him away.'

For the next few months, Shayan lived with a Muslim family in the community. His parents and Shubnam were taken to visit him two to three times a week, for an hour, always with guards who stayed with them even when Zahra went to change the baby's nappies. Their uniforms seemed to terrify Shayan. He was eating and drinking again, but his foster parents noted how he clung to them all the time, how he could not sleep unless one of them sat with him, and how he was still wetting his bed. At night, he often screamed. After four months, Ruddock granted Zahra, Shayan and Shubnam bridging visas, which meant that they could live in the community; but since bridging visas do not include financial support, they were forced to live on the charity of friends. Saeed stayed in Villawood for the next eight months.

In August 2002, the Federal Court having referred the case back to the Refugee Review Tribunal, Saeed and Zahra were found to be refugees after all, on the grounds that they would face persecution on account of Zahra's conversion if they returned to Iran. Looking back over the long nightmare, Saeed asks: 'If we are refugees now, why were we not refugees then?' He and Zahra took their case to the Human Rights and Equal Opportunity Commission, which found that their rights had indeed been seriously violated.

But Shayan's story is not over. He still sleeps little, has severe nightmares and wets his bed. When he draws, he draws pictures of people behind bars. He has few friends of his own age, saying that they do not know what it is like to have lived inside a prison, but he plays affectionately with Shubnam, who is now three. He will not watch children's television but prefers to see the news, though when he sees people in uniform, he cries. For a while, Saeed and Zahra hoped that he would get better in the flat that they have been given on a Paramatta housing estate. But since he seemed to remain so depressed and so fearful, and his screaming fits continued, they agreed to put him on medication. Every week he sees a psychiatrist, who has told them that Shayan may take a very long time to get over what he experienced and witnessed; and that, possibly, he never will. As for his parents, their story is not over either. They have been granted Temporary Protection Visas like all 'unauthorised arrivals' who are recognised to be genuine refugees. At some point in 2005, they will have to apply to have their visa renewed for a further three years, and it is not impossible that they will be turned down. If they judge it too dangerous to go back to Iran, too likely that one or other would be imprisoned or killed, then Shayan could once again find himself behind the razor wire.

As it turned out, Shayan's story pitted the Australian medical profession against the government in a way it never had before. Doctors had realised that whatever treatment they might offer their patients, it was meaningless unless they were removed from the environment causing the trauma. At no time in the past, not even over the 'lost generation', the children stolen from the Aboriginals, had the mental suffering of children been so starkly juxtaposed against political indifference. A Professional Alliance for the Health of Asylum Seekers and their Children was set up, bringing together 50,000 doctors and health workers from across the country – the largest alliance ever formed on a single social issue in Australia's history. Drawing on earlier studies from the concentration camps of the Boer War and the Nazi years, and on comparable detention-centre reports in the US and Europe, they began to submit evidence, draft appeals and draw up statements. Shayan was not the only child to stop eating and become mute. In other parts of Australia, it now emerged that other children in detention had become anxious, anorexic and agitated; they were wetting their beds and walking in their sleep. One small girl was described as wetting herself every time she saw a guard. Mothers reported aggressive and violent behaviour in otherwise placid children. One, anxious about the failure of her newborn baby to thrive as it should, was reported as saying: 'I am afraid that she takes in my unhappiness from my milk.' A young boy, deciding that he wished to die, was found digging his own grave. Another, asked why he had burnt his hand with a lighted cigarette, replied: 'Because I can't feel anything.'

I could only talk to Shayan's parents and not to Shayan himself, too wary and too young to speak to strangers. It was from Morteza, another young Iranian already in Woomera when Shayan first arrived, that I heard at first-hand what it is like to be a detained child in the Australian camps. Morteza spent three years and eleven months as a detainee, from early 2000 to his release – as a recognised refugee – on 20 November 2003. He was sixteen when he first saw Woomera. He was flying in low over the desert, after a terrifying and stormy journey by boat with smugglers, and he thought: where are we going? there is nothing there. He was right. Woomera was not yet fully built, and the first detainees lived in huts as the razor wire went up around them. There were soon 150 children in the camp, the youngest a newborn baby.

Morteza had been there about five months when the 1,500 detainees, who had had no communication with the outside world for a long time, asked for some mobile phones to be brought in so that they could contact their families. What started as a peaceful demonstration turned rapidly into agitated confrontations with the guards; tear gas was used; the detainees fought back; the ringleaders were taken to the punishment block. It was Morteza's first experience of violence, and he joined the ranks of the protestors. His younger sister Mena was by now so depressed that she became incontinent and barely spoke; his younger brother Hussein was growing thinner all the time. The months passed and the family seemed to have been forgotten. The riots multiplied. There was a breakout and Morteza was among those who got as far as the town of Woomera itself, after which concessions were made over phones and the speed of the processing interviews. There were even some releases, but not that of Morteza and his family. At some point during this period, Morteza tried to hang himself; later, he joined others on hunger strike; later again, he slashed his wrists with a razor blade. In the right-wing press, those who tried to kill themselves were labelled crazed, selfish and manipulative.

In January 2001, the family, the two younger children very troubled, was moved to Port Hedland. By now Mena was writing in her diary: 'If suicide were not a sin in my religion, I would have done it already.' One day, Morteza and Hussein watched as a Turkish detainee took out a razor blade and began to cut from his neck downwards, across his chest, his hand and arms and stomach. It was his third suicide attempt. Hussein, says Morteza, had a peculiar smile on his face. That night the little boy began to cry and couldn't stop. He started to wet himself and to stutter. 'Please God,' wrote Mena in her diary, 'if you want to finish my life, finish it quickly.' In Woomera there had been two girls her own age; in Port Hedland, she had no friends. Morteza spent his time with older boys. One night, trying to prevent his father being taken away by the guards to another compound, he was knocked to the ground and beaten with batons. There were more riots; some of the huts were burnt down.

On 21 May 2001 the family, having had their application for asylum turned down at every stage, was sent to Villawood. In a friend's room one day, the young men discussed what new tactic they could try; someone suggested sewing up their lips. The three boys did it to each other, carefully pulling the thread through; it was surprisingly unpainful, Morteza remembers, though it hurt a lot when the blood had dried. His mother fainted when she saw him. He agreed to take the stitches out when the family was promised bridging visas in the community. They did not come through, and instead Morteza spent the next nine months under observation, a guard checking on him every two minutes for the first three months. Even so, when it became clear that the promises about the visa had been false, he tried to kill himself by swallowing an entire bottle of shampoo while in the shower.

In May 2002, his parents decided that they could take no more. They had spent Australian $32,000 trying to make a new life in Australia, and had failed. Morteza's mother seemed to be aging very quickly, and neither his younger brother nor sister was thriving. They agreed to return to Iran. For Morteza it was rather more complicated. As with Shayan, a smuggled video tape had been put out on television showing him being beaten by guards, and his case had received much publicity. His father did not think it safe for him to go home. What was more, he had converted to Christianity. And so his parents flew home to Tehran and Morteza stayed another eleven months in detention, ticking off the days one by one on a calendar on his door, before he, like Shayan, was perceived to be a genuine refugee after all, in a way that he had not been three years and eleven months before. He is now living in Sydney on a three-year Temporary Protection Visa, a friendly, almost gregarious young man of twenty, his long black hair pulled back in a ponytail. If he is extremely lucky, his visa will be renewed. But there is no way, as things stand, of seeing his parents, for if he leaves Australia he will not be able to return. 'I look at guys my age and think: I have lost my family. I lost four years of my life. No education, no training. It is like a movie: the action freezes, then starts again. I think: what a terrible waste.'

Zachary Steel is a psychologist, working for the School of Psychiatry at the University of New South Wales. Soon after mandatory detention for asylum-seekers was introduced in 1992, he began to explore the possibility of investigating the mental health of the new detainees. Wherever he turned, he was blocked by the authorities. It was not until almost ten years later, in the wake of the *Tampa* and its repercussions, that he was able to start drawing together separate strands of research, joining forces with Derek Silove, a Jewish psychiatrist from South Africa, whose interest had been kindled as a medical student doing autopsies on political prisoners who bore the marks of torture, and with Dr Aamer Sultan, a medical practitioner who had fled persecution in Iraq and was a detainee himself in Villawood. Over eighteen months, Dr Sultan, who had become a confidant and counsellor to his fellow inmates, had watched their mental health deteriorate. It was with Dr Sultan's help that the camera was smuggled into Villawood to picture the listless Shayan lying in his father's arms.

What these doctors, and other psychologists, counsellors and therapists throughout Australia, put together was an alarming but altogether convincing picture. The asylum-seekers, they observed, were arriving in Australia with backgrounds of torture, violence, grief and extreme fear, and thus at great risk of psychological trauma. They believed that the Australians would treat them kindly and with sympathy. Instead, they entered a world of horror and indifference, detained seemingly indefinitely behind rows of razor wire; with multiple daily musters and head counts, sometimes in the middle of the night; subjected to a constant barrage of orders over the loud-speaker system that they could not understand; handled harshly and moved suddenly, without warning, from one camp to another, in handcuffs. Referred to by the guards by number rather than by name, they were subjected to room searches and solitary confinement. They witnessed violence, self-mutilation and the spectacle of guards wearing riot gear, and there were periods when they were locked up for a long time in their rooms, denied access to the phone, to post or to visitors. As it became clear to them that their futures depended on the credibility of their claims, and on how well they handled their interviews, so they became highly anxious about what to say, particularly as, like asylum-seekers all over the world faced by immigration interviews, they felt confused and uncertain about their memories. Many, believing that they would be judged on how they were behaving in detention, were unsure of their every move.

Faced with this new world, so different from the one they had expected to find, the asylum-seekers, as Dr Steel and his colleagues noted, behaved in a number of characteristic ways. Their initial feelings of shock and dismay were replaced, when they received news that the immigration authorities had turned down their first applications, or simply when months had passed with no news of a result, by guilt about the people they had left behind, by depression and sometimes by aggressive and confrontational behaviour. Since many arrived in Australia already suffering from post-traumatic stress disorder, the symptoms most commonly associated with this illness began to emerge: extreme anxiety, sleeplessness, fear of others. Some never left their rooms; others slept by day and paced by night. Rejection by the Refugee Review Tribunal usually comes between six and eighteen months after arrival. At this point, acute depression was common, with feelings of doom and self-obsession, paranoia, hallucinations, some-times even repetitive rocking and aimless wandering. The rate of suicide was ten times that of the normal population.

And, as the months passed, papers and reports began to appear. One, reported in a key-note speech delivered by Dr Steel and his colleagues before the Congress of the Royal Australian and New Zealand College of Psychiatrists in May 2003, concerned 10 families, consisting of 14 adults and 22 children between the ages of 3 and 19, with an average stay in detention of 2 years and 4 months. Using a wide battery of internationally accepted tests and criteria, the doctors found that a third of the adults had resorted to some form of self-harm; that every adult could be diagnosed as suffering from a depressive disorder; that all the children showed signs of at least one psychiatric disorder and 86 per cent of them had multiple disorders. More than half the children spoke of killing themselves; five had slashed their wrists or banged their head violently against a wall.

Another study, carried out by Dr Sultan in Villawood, looked at thirty-three detainees, twenty-eight of them men, the other five women. All had been inside at least nine months. Nineteen, Dr Sultan discovered, had arrived in Australia having been tortured, and nine had seen relations murdered or disappeared. In Villawood, all but one reported sleep disturbances, nightmares, loss of libido. Nineteen were on anti-depressants. Thirteen suffered from paranoid delusions; thirteen had begun to stutter; twenty-three admitted to suicidal thoughts. All spoke of feeling helpless, despairing and of being unable to concentrate or to remember simple things. It was clear to Dr Sultan that there was a strong degree of correlation between length of time spent in detention, waiting to hear, not knowing what would happen, and the level of distress and disturbance. It should be noted that it is not unusual, under Australia's current policy, to wait two years for news; some people have been in detention for over five years.

When I met Zachary Steel, his verdict on the system was clear: 'I simply no longer believe that it is possible for anyone to be kept in this kind of environment of coercive control, threat, uncertainty and fear without developing severe psychiatric consequences. Detention of this kind is a situation that cannot be rendered meaningful by anything. Even political prisoners, kept in similar circumstances, know why they are there. The asylum-seekers know that they are innocent people, and no aspect of the current structure has any care or compassion. On the contrary they feel that they are hated, and that the authorities will do everything in their power to return them back to where they fled from.'

It has long ceased to be a matter of surprise to Dr Steel when he hears that teenagers in one centre have sewn up their lips, or young men in another have gone on hunger strike. Morteza's repeated attempts to hurt and kill himself are familiar symptoms. The culture of self-harm has become so prevalent that it is impossible to prevent people from mutilating themselves. When the first studies appeared, he assumed that action would follow. Instead, the Department of Immigration announced that it was not aware of any 'independent', scientific or rigorous research to 'support claims that mental illness is endemic among detainees held in immigration detention'. Psychiatrists and doctors redoubled their efforts to produce more research, in the process putting Australia at the forefront of current medical knowledge of the effects of detention on asylum-seekers. The Department of Immigration labelled the work flawed and full of preconceptions, and Ruddock declared that it was far from certain, in his view, that you could in fact 'regard depression as a mental illness'.

And so it has continued, says Dr Steel, more research and more rebuttals, at times accompanied by personal attacks on the researchers. It makes him feel that he was once very naive. It is true, as he acknowledges, that efforts have been made to get children out of the centres and into the community, and that under Amanda Vanstone the numbers remaining behind the razor wire have dropped substantially.* His protests, and those of his colleagues, achieved at least this. But, as he sees it, the adult detainees who remain inside are getting sicker and sicker. It is a tenet of psychiatry that past traumas dealt with in safety can be mitigated and eased. In detention centres, they are only exacerbated. The environment, far from curing the pathology, is both creating and perpetuating it. 'The trauma,' Dr Steel has written, 'is not past, but present, and extends indefinitely into the future.' His words have a forlorn air: 'Our ethics require us to prevent what harm we can and to document what we cannot prevent.'

Shayan's and Morteza's stories had stirred the medical profession to anger. And though the government remained obdurate, choosing not to publicise its few concessions, something else had in fact happened. Of all the responses to the refugee predicament in the world, this is one of the most remarkable, and certainly the most heartening. Ordinary Australians, people who had tacitly accepted the fact that asylum-seekers – the 'illegals' and 'queue jumpers' – could be locked up indefinitely in detention camps in the desert, could not quite stomach the idea of children losing the will to live. It shook their image of Australia as an essentially humane place, challenged the cherished notion of 'fair go' – decency – deeply rooted in the national psyche. The publicity surrounding Shayan and Morteza, brief and contested though it was, made clear something that had not been perceived before: that Australia's camps were not the model centres described by Howard and Ruddock, but grim and terrifying places in which people were going mad.

The backlash started slowly. It has not grown to any overwhelming size, but it is evidence, to use Michael Ignatieff's phrase, of the 'expanding moral imagination' of our times. It started among writers, lawyers, actors and academics and in small pockets of the churches, with nuns, lay sisters and Jesuit priests inspired by the reports put out by Dr Zachary Steel and his colleagues, and by the growing body of critical evidence emerging from research carried out by the UN, by UNHCR, by Human Rights Watch and

---

*In the spring of 2004, fifteen children remained in detention, but there were many more living in the community under guard.

Amnesty International, and by the Australian Human Rights and Equal Opportunities Commission. And then it spread, through the cities, into towns and villages, into the outback, a surge of moral indignation carried by telephone and email. It drew in veterans of the old Aboriginal rights campaigns, and prominent barristers including Julian Burnside, a Melbourne QC, who began to question the legality of each and every process, and younger advocates, such as Deslie Billich who helps run a pro-bono law firm in Adelaide for the refugees. It prompted the birth of a now prominent human-rights group, Chilout, campaigning on behalf of the imprisoned children. It took in novelists and poets, including Thomas Keneally, Linda Jaivin, Arnold Zable, Eva Sallis and Peter Carey, who produced fiction and plays, and journalists and commentators, such as David Marr and Robert Manne, who turned to essays and books; it became fringe and street theatre; it provoked articles and poems and films. The Howard government called them the 'elites', or the 'Chardonnay liberals'.

In Port Augusta, a Catholic woman called Penny Kelly was in church on 18 October 2002 when the children in the congregation prayed for the asylum-seekers being transferred from Woomera to Baxter. She was disheartened to note the hostile reaction of the townspeople, who either wanted them sent back as quickly as possible, or pretended that nothing was happening. That Thursday, she went out to the new camp, taking with her a cake and some biscuits that she had baked. She has never really been able to believe that ordinary Germans, living around the Nazi concentration camps in World War II, maintained that they knew nothing about them, but now she began to understand. Her neighbours concentrated on other things. Friends, however, eventually listened to her stories and took to accompanying her on her weekly visits to Baxter, and when she told her husband, who works for the Port Augusta prison, that the detainees had too few men visitors, he started going too, driving out to the camp in the desert with nuts and biscuits, but really going in order to talk.

Among these very different people – country Australians and lawyers, doctors, teachers, goldsmiths, students and housewives from Iran and Iraq, Turkey and Afghanistan – real friendships began to grow. In the visitors' room, there is much laughter and affection. They celebrate each others' birthdays and remember, with amusement, the day someone brought in an enormous fish, so big that it would not fit on the X-ray machine through which everything must be checked, so that eventually it came in as a visitor instead. Like Sister Claudette, Penny Kelly feels her life to have been changed by her weekly involvement with an issue that for her raises huge moral questions. But she is also saddened. 'I grew up proud of being Australian. Though I was aware of how badly we had behaved towards the Aboriginals, I still felt we were basically a good country. I am no longer proud. I feel there is a hole inside me, like an ulcer. I think of the horrible things we are doing to these people. Australia will look back on this as a black day.'

Around the time Penny Kelly was beginning to hear about Woomera and Baxter, in the mountains not far from Sydney three women friends were watching television footage of the *Tampa*. Two of them, Susan Varga and Ann Coombs, were writers. 'We felt depressed. This was something different, something that seemed to have gone too far,' says Susan Varga. They called a public meeting in their town of Bowral and worked the streets with petitions and posters. Five hundred people turned up. Television covered the meeting. Next day, emails started arriving, many from Australians who had never protested against anything before. What was happening to the asylum-seekers, they wrote, was not 'fair'. It was counter to everything that Australia was about.

For a while, Susan and Ann kept on with their writing. More emails poured in. They put their work to one side and gave up their lives to founding what they have called Rural Australians for Refugees, drawing up a ten-point plan calling on the Australian government to overturn its current policies, disband the Pacific Solution and return to a more moral past. 'It grew,' says Susan, 'like Topsy.' By the spring of 2004, there were seventy-one groups across the country, doing whatever seemed most useful locally: writing letters, collecting money, drawing up petitions. A pharmacist called Elaine Smith has turned all her free time over to keeping in touch with the detainees on Nauru, updating her website with every legal move. It was Elaine Smith who broadcast information about a hunger strike on Nauru in December 2003, when four detainees, goaded beyond endurance by their endless, indefinite sentence, sewed up their lips. In the years of its existence, no outsider has been allowed on Nauru. What is known about it comes from relations in Australia who talk from time to time to the detainees – some of them wives and children who followed their husbands to Indonesia only to find themselves ensnared by the Pacific Solution – or from the occasional illicit reporter, like Kate Durham, an artist in Melbourne and married to Julian Burnside, who went in without permission. Others, nearer the 'front line' of the detention centres, visit prisoners. Others again invite those released into the community to stay. All over Australia, farmers have offered jobs to those on Temporary Protection Visas. The mayor of Young in New South

Wales has championed a group of Afghans to work in the town's slaughterhouses.

And, as with all other ventures concerning the asylum-seekers, the Rural Australians for Refugees has built upon its own success. This is the second most noticeable aspect of Australia's moral crusade: it was not the television images of Iranian children being maltreated that alone caught the country's imagination; it was the fact that ordinary Australians began to meet the asylum-seekers face to face. Over 9,000 are now out in the community. They all have stories to tell. As the Australians, who knew about them only from their demonised images, have discovered, they are neither scroungers nor exploitative, but anxious, troubled men, women and children who have fled torture, persecution and possible death, endured horrific journeys, lost everything they once possessed, only to spend months and even years in an Australian camp. And as they have made friends in Australia's towns and cities, and told their stories, so the absurdity and cruelty of their treatment has come to inspire and impress Australians, particularly as their temporary visas are so punishing and as so many prove hard-working and capable. What possible threat are such people to Australia's security? Why keep punishing them? Some of those on TPVs are now approaching the moment when they will have to apply for a second visa for another three years. Few of their new friends and supporters are likely to take kindly to their possible re-detention or deportation.

Australia has no Bill of Rights. But even if, at the time of the drafting of the Universal Declaration of Human Rights in 1948, it recoiled at the idea of letting people enter another country without invitation, it did sign up to the 1951 Convention. What bothers Father Brennan, a Jesuit priest, lawyer and author of a recent book on refugees, *Tampering with Asylum*, is not merely that Australia is in breach of several conventions that it has signed and ratified (one way or another, the treatment of the asylum-seekers violates several articles of the Universal Declaration of Human Rights, the Convention for the Rights of the Child, the Statute of Rome, and the International Covenant on Political and Civil Rights) but that it is becoming so hard to justify a policy that is so discriminatory and inhumane. Were every Western democracy to follow Australia's model and introduce indefinite mandatory detention – indefinitely locking up asylum-seekers who have committed no crimes as recognised under international law – the very meaning of the Refugee Convention would be forgotten.

What is more, Australia, unlike Europe, is not trying to deal with the arrival of tens of thousands of economic migrants, who need to be sorted out from the true asylum-seekers. On the contrary, those who took to the boats in Indonesia did so out of genuine need. Up to 90 per cent of unauthorised arrivals, like Morteza and Shayan, have, after years in detention, been found to be true refugees after all. Nor has a single terrorist ever been known to enter the country on a leaky boat. As Robert Manne puts it, the country is being mobilised by a spectre. With no new arrivals, it has become a policy about no one. It is an immense sledge-hammer to crack a very small nut.

Since the height of the frenetic days of the *Tampa*, the mood among the immigration authorities has remained defiant, with much talk of teaching smugglers that Australia is not a soft touch. Fewer children remain in detention. Of Nauru's peak detention figure of 1,546, all but 284 have left. Most of those remaining are Afghans, and Australia has signed an Australian $22.5 million deal to extend detention on Nauru at least until June 2005. Across the whole of Australia, 1,097 boat people are still in detention, either awaiting final decisions, or because their countries refuse to take them back, or because they have been turned down but know that if they went home they would face persecution and so have decided to wait and hope something may change. If they stay in detention, they don't get forcibly deported.

Just one man, a twenty-five-year-old Palestinian called Aladdin Sisalem, remains on Manus Island, costing Australia a reported $23,000 a day. How, asks Father Brennan, can Australia hold on to a policy that demonises a small number of innocent people and treats them with such brutality, if not in the spirit of punishment and deterrence that it so vehemently denies? A system that risks the sanity of children, he argues, makes a nonsense of the family values that Australia so prizes. What alarms him, as it alarms Dr Zachary Steel and others, is that Australia, having proved that it can get away with anything when it comes to asylum-seekers, may well become a model for countries now trying and failing to come to terms with these problems, and that far from publicising what it does well – the resettlement of refugees – as an inspiration to others, it is instead exporting all that is most shameful. Australia has seen four waves of boat arrivals over the years; there are, argues Father Brennan, bound to be others, as new Talibans or Saddam Husseins drive more refugees into exile by their atrocities: now is the time to put in place policies that, while securing Australia's borders, are also humane and decent.

For what the Pacific Solution has done to Australia itself, he says, is to divide the country in a way it has rarely been divided before, not even during the battles for indigenous recognition and rights. It has made the Liberal party more conservative, the Labor party more fractured, and battered those Australians who have long supported human rights and multiculturalism. 'Howard sang a song until the people believed him,' says Robert Manne, who has produced several excellent essays on the subject. 'It was a horrible song, and it allowed hateful things to happen in a democracy in a way that no one would ever have believed Australia would allow.' Far from expanding the world's moral imagination, as Father Brennan sees it, Australia, under Howard and the Liberals, has shrunk it.

Before leaving Australia, I went to visit Villawood, Sydney's detention centre about which Thomas Keneally wrote so bitterly in *The Tyrant's Novel*. Many of Villawood's detainees are overstayers liable to be deported, and it is here that they wait while their futures are determined. But it was also the camp where Shayan spent the last wretched months of his incarceration, and where Morteza sewed up his lips and later drank a bottle of shampoo.

The camp is in a suburb, a green, quiet area of calm streets and pleasant gardens; like most of the detention centres, it is somehow hidden away, cleverly concealed behind trees and virtually unmarked. By the beginning of visiting hours, people were making their way in ones and twos up a dirt road through the first set of gates, to join a queue inside the first wall of razor wire to be searched, screened and stamped with an ink that shows up under ultraviolet light. Inside the compound is a grassy area, perhaps an acre in size, with plastic chairs and tables and a climbing frame for children.

It was Behnam's birthday, the third he has spent in detention. He was eighteen. His family is Mandaean and their story is similar to that of most boat people. They found a smuggler in Indonesia, endured a harsh sea trip, were subjected to a slow process of interview and rejection, only then to be moved from camp to camp. Behnam's life is made tolerable by the fact that both he and his younger brother and sister attend school outside the camp, where all three are doing well. His mother is a purposeful, strong, outgoing woman. It is clear that she has played an enormous part in keeping the family together. On his eighteenth birthday, Behnam looked well.

But it was the scene around Behnam and his family that was memorable. They have made many friends during their time in Villawood, men and women who regularly make the trip from the city to talk to the detainees and to show support. To one side of the grassy compound, under a large eucalyptus tree, several plastic tables had been pulled together and a tea party was in progress, celebrating Behnam's birthday. There was an elderly woman in an enormous red floppy hat. There were several middle-aged men, some wearing baseball caps. There were two or three lawyers, some nuns, a journalist or two, a few writers. There were two girl students, new visitors to Villawood. The atmosphere was festive. There was a fine cake with candles, and plates of Iranian food brought in by other Mandaeans already settled in Sydney. Rather late, a woman arrived out of breath, carrying in her arms a great many brightly coloured balloons that rose high among the branches in the breeze. Among them all, charming and collected, wandered Behnam, receiving his birthday greetings.

If you half shut your eyes, fixed them carefully on the cheerful tea party, avoided seeing the tall banks of razor wire rising steeply on all sides, the guards patrolling, the barrack-like blocks separated by more wire fences, then you might just have believed yourself to be in an ordinary place.

Chapter Five

Newcastle and the Politics of Dispersal

It may often be easier to live in exile with a fantasy of
paradise than to suffer the inevitable ambiguities and
compromise of cultivating actual, earthly places.
Eva Hoffman, *The New Nomads*

It was on New Year's Day 2002, a still, cold morning so grey that at nine
o'clock it was barely light, that Suleiman Dialo, a thirty-year-old asylum-
seeker from Guinea, decided that the moment had come to end his life.
Though the coroner, Terence Carney, would later record an open verdict
for his death, saying that he had no way of knowing what was in Dialo's
mind when he jumped from Newcastle's Redheugh bridge to fall 100 feet
onto the towpath below, narrowly missing the waters of the river Tyne,
Dialo's friend Bertrand has no doubts.

Like Monica Bishop, area manager for the North of England Refugee
Service in Newcastle, like Katherine Henderson, Dialo's lawyer, like the
city's fast-growing population of African asylum-seekers, Bertrand knows
precisely why Dialo chose to die. He had reached the end of a legal line
he had been crawling along for the past eighteen months; and he had
finally come to believe that he had nowhere left to go. Sometime in the
middle of November he had been informed that his appeal to the tribunal
for asylum in the United Kingdom had been refused; and with it went his
accommodation, his English lessons at Gateshead College, his health care
and his money, the £38 given to him each week by the government
(calculated nicely at 70 per cent of what is deemed the minimum
necessary for a decent life, and therefore not a sum to be envied). He knew
that any morning now, probably around dawn in order to catch people in
bed, there would be a knock on his door and police would escort him to a
detention centre and from there to a plane bound for Conakry. Several
times during the year of their friendship, Dialo had told Bertrand that,
were he to be finally rejected by the Home Office and the courts, he
would choose to die. He could imagine no existence for himself back in
Guinea, however hard he tried; and sometime in those next few weeks the

Tyne must have come to seem to him a better place than the torture and death he told Bertrand awaited him at home.

This is not a plaintive tale about a cruel bureaucracy condemning a vulnerable young man to death; rather, it is a story about the loneliness and fear which are common to asylum-seekers everywhere, made worse perhaps in Dialo's case by the fact that his native language was Fula, which is spoken across parts of West Africa, and that there were no other known Fula speakers in the whole of north-east England; that his French was very poor and that he spoke scarcely a sentence of English; and that, in all his childhood in Guinea, he had never learnt to read or write. Signposts, letters, instructions, telephone calls, the television and radio, ordinary, daily conversation – none of this meant much to him in England; and his sense of aloneness was both overwhelming and shocking to him. He had not expected it. 'He didn't ever really understand what was happening to him,' says Katherine Henderson, the efficient and involved lawyer who had not long before taken up his case and at the time of his death was still hoping to redeem some of the earlier errors and misunderstandings and so win him, if not permanent leave to remain in Britain, at least some measure of breathing space. 'The world about him had shrunk to almost nothing.'

Even Bertrand, perhaps his closest friend among the Africans in the north-east, was never able to get very close to him. 'He didn't speak much,' Bertrand says now. 'It was as if he couldn't bear to talk about himself if he couldn't explain properly, if he couldn't put into words what had happened to him and why he so feared to go home. He seemed frightened in case he said a wrong word, and there was no one to know or check.'

I first heard about Dialo in the early summer of 2003 from Gaby Kitoko, a medical student who fled eastern Congo in 2000, leaving behind him a wife and two children, after he was accused of spying for the United Nations. Gaby was one of the first asylum-seekers to be sent to the north-east to await news of whether he would be accepted as a refugee, back in the days when Newcastle had no asylum-seekers living on its housing estates, and before the Home Office in London started scattering young men and women from some ninety countries around Britain. Gaby walks with a limp, from what the Congolese soldiers did to him before letting him go. Three years later, he is still waiting to hear whether he may be granted leave to remain in Britain, and with it permission to apply for his family to join him; but in the meantime, frightened on behalf of himself and other asylum-seekers of the sense of isolation and incomprehension that afflicts all who wait, he has started a small local centre for Africans in Byker, one of Newcastle's housing developments.

Patrolled back in the nineteenth century when it was still a country district by one of Newcastle's two mounted policemen, Byker, once home to Newcastle's thriving community of dockworkers, is now all battered red-brick housing and desolate streets, with shabby terracing and occasional shops protected by thick sheets of metal and iron bars. On top of the few taller buildings police have put CCTV cameras to catch signs of disorder and crime, with razor wire to safeguard them from theft and breakage. There is an air of poverty and abandonment. To open his community centre, with the help of local funders, Gaby took over three derelict shops and knocked them into a single cheerful room, in which each day he listens to the ills and worries of the Congolese, Zimbabweans, Angolans and Rwandans who come to consult him. Gaby barely knew Dialo, he said to me, while behind us on a vast television screen, donated by a local well-wisher, a portly and energetic gospel preacher in pinstripe suit and waistcoat exhorted his studio congregation to heed God. Gaby greeted Dialo when he saw him; but as a fellow African, not a friend. It was only after his death that Gaby was asked, as a leader of the Newcastle African community, to say something to journalists, and the words he produced were toned down by a local refugee officer, anxious that his valediction should not sound too accusatory. Dialo died, said Gaby, because of despair; it was threat of deportation that pushed him from the bridge. These were not words that people want to hear.

Dialo didn't have many close friends. Since he couldn't talk to them as he wished to, he seemed to prefer to stay silent. Photographs show a thin, wiry, good-looking young man, with dreadlocks and a quizzical smile; in one, he is leaning against a door, his elbow outstretched, one foot, wearing a fashionable trainer, crossed rather jauntily over the other, his head dipped to one side, the dreadlocks falling along his cheek, a half smile on his face. Monica Bishop, the good-hearted and motherly woman at the Newcastle Refugee Service, told me that hugging clients was not something that she normally did, but that with Dialo she had broken her own rules. 'He used to come into the office frequently, and we had no time to look after him. He didn't say very much. He just sat and smiled. And I would say: "Suleiman, you'll be all right. You really will be all right." And then I would give him a cuddle.' He was, Monica repeated several times, a greatly liked young man, a 'lovely lad'.

When Dialo ceased to be all right no one really knows. He reached Britain in July 2000, at twenty-seven somewhat older than many of the other African asylum-seekers, from a small Guinean village far from the capital, Conakry. He told Bertrand, whom he met that November at Gateshead College, that he had been forced to flee because his parents, brothers and sisters had been murdered. He said that he had left behind him a shop and a good life as a trader. Monica told me that Dialo had scars all over his back from being beaten by the people who killed his parents. I asked Bertrand if he knew whether Dialo had been tortured. He looked puzzled: 'Of course.' And I remembered making the same mistake before: forgetting that torture is now endemic across many parts of Africa, and that many asylum-seekers come to Britain bearing scars from cigarettes, bayonets, rifle butts, boiling water or whips. 'There was also something wrong with his feet, because when I started a football team for Africans, he would come but only watch.' *Falaka*, the beating on the soles of the feet practised by torturers all over the modern world, can leave injuries that are slow to heal.

Bertrand and Dialo met only in the evenings, because Bertrand was a regular student at Newcastle university, studying for a degree in business studies, with a French passport to ensure him smooth passage in and out of England, while Dialo was an uncertain asylum-seeker who seemed to find learning to speak English extremely difficult. But in the evenings, when the boys met and played music and talked about Africa, Dialo would sit and listen. Bertrand didn't ask him questions about his past. In any case, in those days Bertrand wasn't much concerned with refugee matters. It wasn't until Dialo's death that he really began to wonder about the fairness of it all. All he thought about then was how hard it must be for Dialo, with no friend who spoke Fula, and no more than perhaps a dozen people in the whole area who could understand his particular broken West African French, with its words of dialect and distinctive intonation, difficult to unravel even by those who speak French well. He felt worried when Dialo told him that his first legal representative had insisted on interviewing him only with a French and not a Fula inter-preter, and that Dialo knew that he had not been able to get across either to him or to the Home Office the many terrible things that had befallen him at home.

All through the summer and autumn of 2001, in her office in the middle of Newcastle not far from the statue of the eighteenth-century Whig reformer Earl Grey, under which the refugees of Newcastle like to meet, Monica Bishop worried about Dialo. She repeatedly wrote to the Home Office asking to have his hearing adjourned while she desperately combed the north-east not just for a decent solicitor to take his case but for a Fula interpreter who could understand and translate what he had to say. Even now, she cannot bear to consign his file to the archives, but keeps it buried in a drawer of her desk. She found it and gave it to me to read. 'He is extremely distressed,' says one of her letters to a reputable firm of solicitors, written in May, 'and I hope that you will be able to represent him.' This particular firm was unable to, already having more cases on their books than they could deal with. Other solicitors declined as well. I went through the file. There were other letters: to sort out problems over accommodation, to ask for travel warrants to attend hearings, to request further postponements. There is a brief note describing the fact that Dialo had been imprisoned several times in Guinea, where some of his teeth had been extracted as part of torture; and that his feet were damaged. By the time Dialo was accepted by Katherine Henderson, who has specialised as a solicitor in asylum cases for several years now, Dialo's appeal had been heard and turned down.

The last time that Bertrand saw Dialo alive was at the beginning of December, not long after he had received a letter from the Home Office telling him that they did not consider him a 'Convention Refugee'. He seemed confused, and complained that he couldn't understand how it was that some of the asylum-seekers he had met had made up stories, fabricated events and dates and even torture, and yet been granted asylum, while he had told everyone the truth and been turned down. It was at this last meeting that he told Bertrand that he would never go back to Guinea. It had taken too much to get to Britain, too much emotion and courage and too much money, and he had nothing and no one to go back to. He felt, he said, an *échec*, a failure. He had left Guinea in order to save his own life: why go back now to die? And it had all become too difficult: the language, the fact that he was not allowed to work, the way he couldn't understand anything. He wanted a private life of his own, not to be treated like a child, and he could no longer bear to depend on others for everything. And he was afraid; inside himself, he was afraid about what he would find waiting for him.

Bertrand was shocked by Dialo's death; he had not anticipated it. But when it happened, it made sense to him. Dialo was not enjoying life. He wasn't the kind of person who would ever have been able to slip into Britain's black economy and live along its margins; and he had nowhere else to go. He was, as Bertrand sees it, a strong individual with a strong sense of survival, or he would never have managed to overcome the torture, his parents' murders and his own escape to Europe. But his strength had all been used up in the waiting, the uncertainty, the humiliations and the sense of rejection. What haunts Bertrand now is that he did not see it sooner.

On New Year's Eve 2001, Dialo went to visit a group of Africans in Gateshead. Some time after midnight, he disappeared. No one knows how he spent the rest of the night. It was the driver of a car crossing the deserted Redheugh Bridge from the Gateshead side at nine o'clock the following morning who saw him jump. There was no one about. The city centre was empty; the shops and offices closed for the holiday. It was very quiet.

Dialo's funeral took place on 11 January 2002 at 1.30 p.m., in the Central Mosque on Elswick Road. It was icy, says Monica, with a terrible biting cold. Gaby was there too, and Bertrand, recently returned from a holiday in France, and a teacher from Gateshead College who had grown fond of her silent pupil. Katherine Henderson came too, reproaching herself for not having tried harder to make sure that Dialo had understood that all was not yet lost, that despite his failed appeal she might still be able to win him a reprieve from deportation by having his case reopened, based on accurate translation and a medical report testifying to his torture. In Monica's file are the arrangements for the ceremony: the cloth, towels and soap for the preparation and wrapping of Dialo's body to be provided by the Gateshead Muslim Society, the grave to be filled by members of the African community, the women mourners to 'attend at a little distance from the grave'; later, the coffin to be laid in Gateshead's Saltwell Cemetery, at the farmost end where other Muslims lie, their feet pointing towards Mecca. An imam came from London to officiate. The sum of £1,236.20 was raised locally to cover the costs.

Why, I asked Bertrand at one of our meetings under Grey's statue, did Dialo choose to jump over a bridge? 'He wanted to make certain he would die. He was not silly.' For Bertrand, Dialo's death has sent his own life in a new direction. He has become more aware of his own blackness in a white country, more conscious that to be black in north-east England is most often to be an asylum-seeker, and that to be an asylum-seeker is hardly to be a person at all. He wishes that he had known then what he knows now, that there are a number of Fula speakers in London, and that some way might have been found to bring them together with Dialo. In the weeks following Dialo's death, he began thinking about the isolation and apprehension that had borne so heavily on his friend, and he started an organisation with his friends to bring together Newcastle's African refugees to help them with some of their immediate difficulties. He has called it Baobab, after the West African tree under which villagers traditionally sit to discuss their problems; Baobab has its own football team and Bertrand talks of opening a club where the Africans can dance.

Suicides are not unusual among asylum-seekers in Britain. Not all are committed by men and women who have reached the end of the legal line and are facing imminent deportation, for the life of an asylum-seeker is precarious, confusing, beset by contradictions and reversals, subject to sudden uprooting and dispersal, all of it for the most part conducted in a foreign language. For some, the waiting and the uncertainty are already too much. For others, the loneliness is more than can be borne. When, early in July 2003, a young Iranian used a knife to try to hack himself to death in Bigg Market, just in front of Monica Bishop's offices, he left a note: 'You have to kill yourself in this country,' he had written, in large scrawled letters, 'to prove that you would be killed in your own country.'

Katherine Henderson, in the summer of 2003, had two clients she feared would not survive the wait: one was a woman from South Africa, gang-raped by soldiers in front of her family, who she was then obliged to watch being murdered; the other an Iranian, who learnt that he had been refused asylum even without an interview, and who had already attempted suicide once when the Home Office mistakenly stopped answering his letters and cut off his benefits. She believes that some 50 to 60 per cent of her clients, frantic and highly confused, traumatised by fear and grief for those they have left behind, are in need of some form of mental help. Monica Bishop has a handful of others she is keeping a close eye on. People working with asylum-seekers have become attuned to the nuances of this particular despair.

In 2002, according to official figures, 110,700 people asked for political asylum in the United Kingdom on the grounds of persecution and justifiable fear of return under the 1951 Refugee Convention to which Britain is party. This was the largest number that had ever applied (in 1993, for example, there had been only 22,370). It was also the highest number of applications in the developed world, with the US coming a long way second with 81,000, Germany third with 71,100, and then France with 50,800, although the numbers have since been dropping. Only 2 per cent of the world's asylum-seekers, however, are currently in the UK, and as a country, Britain is not generous with its contributions to UNHCR, to which it gives half what the Netherlands gives. (Nor is it generous over resettlement, recently announcing that it would be offering places to 500 people, but then allowing the plan to stall.) Just why Britain is such a magnet for asylum-seekers is something not easily explained, but it is generally attributed to a mixture of things: a cumbersome appeals procedure (which gives asylum-seekers the hope that they may enjoy longer periods in the UK, while their case is being considered, than in other countries); an awareness on the part of smugglers that the system is weak; the draw of already established communities; the fact that Britain retains its reputation of being a place of welcome to persecuted people and that English is a language many people speak; and the realisation that when it comes to deportations, the Home Office is relatively lax.

Since 1997, the rules and regulations governing the asylum process have been changed three times, on each occasion becoming tougher and more restrictive and adding to the impression, as the Refugee Council observed not long ago, that the system is not working. Asylum-seekers today (as has always been true under the Convention) may enter the country illegally – there is usually no other way – and claim asylum either at the port of entry or directly to the Home Office, but they must do so 'as soon as is reasonably practical'. Failure to do so means forfeiting all financial support, on the assumption that only a bogus asylum-seeker would not apply on landing. (This ruling, known as Section 55, is now being challenged in the courts as being in breach of the Human Rights Act article on 'inhuman and degrading treatment'.) Having completed a statement of evidence – a history of what has happened to cause flight – then been interviewed and submitting any further evidence, the asylum-seeker may be given refugee status, and eventually allowed to apply for citizenship. (Initial decisions are widely agreed to be made in an ill-informed way, and to rely on confusing and out-of-date country information.) Alternatively, he may be offered humanitarian protection for varying amounts of time, which means that though he has failed to qualify as a refugee under the 1951 Convention, there are still valid concerns about danger and security to prevent him from being sent home. If refused on both counts, the asylum-seeker can launch the first of four possible appeals to various authorities and tribunals. (A proposed 'ouster' clause, which would have removed the right to judicial review or appeal to a higher court, was recently challenged – and rejected – by the courts.) After appeals of various kinds, some half of all those who ask for asylum are refused permission to remain, and are then meant to leave the country. Not all do so. Many slip into the black economy, or simply wait and hope to escape deportation.

As I had learned from other refugees, it is not easy for people who have fled violence and persecution, or even poverty and despair, to cope with truth. When their story is their only real passport, when they have thrown away their documents and tried to reinvent themselves, it is hard not to embellish the hardships of the past. Refugee life is rife with rumour. Among those who wait to be interviewed for refugee status, word circulates about how some nationalities are more likely to get asylum than others, about how some stories are more powerful than others, and some more likely to touch the hearts of the interviewers. The buying and selling of 'good' stories, stories to win asylum, has become common practice in refugee circles, among people terrified that their own real story is not powerful enough. How easy, then, how natural, to shape the past in such a way that it provides more hope for a better future. Traffickers and smugglers transporting clients to the West are known to recommend identities, to advise nationalities known to be on the list of countries to which people asking asylum cannot be returned without breaching the Refugee Convention clause about *non-refoulement*.

In recent years, as the numbers of people arriving in the West and claiming asylum have grown steeply, and pressure has mounted on immigration officers to turn away as many applicants as they reasonably can, so the idea of what is truth and what is a lie has acquired a very particular potency. Credibility has become a benchmark on which everything depends. Asylum-seekers suspected of not telling the truth are automatically rejected, however genuine their claim may be. In fact, 'lack of credibility' has become, in most of the West, the main reason for refusal. For their lawyers, convincing their clients that they must tell only the truth has become of major importance, just as spotting a lie, however unimportant, has become a challenge for immigration officers, who admit that a falsehood, however small (such as method of travel or date of departure), enables them to throw out a case. The tragedy comes when the real story, the true story, is stronger than the made-up one and would guarantee refugee status, while the false one does not, particularly for those who receive poor legal advice or whose experience of torture makes telling their stories painful. Not easy for the asylum-seekers, certainly; but not easy for the interviewers either, to be forced to be so vigilant in their examination of the stories of desperate people, while knowing that there are among them those whose pasts contain no persecution, and others again whose stories are indistinguishable in terms of pain and anguish from true refugees but who fail to fall under the narrow definition of the Convention.

There may be as many as 25,000 asylum-seekers in Britain who, like Dialo, have reached the end of their legal road. They have been turned down on their first interviews, lost their appeals, some have failed in their attempts to win a reprieve under the Human Rights Act or before a tribunal; and some have been able to take their cases before the High Court. In every case, the immigration officers, judges and adjudicators involved have decided either that their stories lack credibility, that they have in fact nothing to fear from return to their own country,* or that their reason for coming to Britain is nothing other than a desire for a better life – that they are economic migrants and not refugees at all. Many will have suffered from lazy and exploitative solicitors – Katherine Henderson says that over half the clients who have been sent to the north-east and come to her for help bring their entire life stories, including accounts of torture and prolonged family persecution, reduced by their first solicitor to three-quarters of a sheet of A4 paper. Others, like Dialo, will have been offered poor or inappropriate interpretation, and been victims of clerical errors and misfilings. All, at the end of a process that will have lasted somewhere between four months and four years, will have been notified that their case has been rejected and that they are to leave the UK. Rejection means the end to all financial help. Deportation – ticket to home country paid for – may follow immediately, perhaps after a period in detention in case they abscond. The number of detention places stood at around 2,000 in 2003 and 2004, but the government announced not long ago that they were raising it to 4,000.

Those with special needs can apply for continued support as hardship cases, but must sign a form to say that they are willing to be voluntarily repatriated at any time. In the summer of 2003, only Iraqis were not obliged to sign this form, Iraq alone being deemed, for the time being at least, to be a country to which return was not a possibility. For all those others who leave, collected at dawn, taken to a deportation centre and put on a flight (though not, it is said, in the mid-summer months, when the planes are full and tourists going on holiday might be troubled by the spectacle of such anguish), there are dozens more who vanish into Britain's black economy, sleeping on the floor of friends' houses, working illegally for appallingly low wages in factories, farms and garages. Their particular limbo – refused asylum, always fearing deportation, the limbo that Dialo could not bear to contemplate – is not describable in figures. 'They do not sleep,' explained an acquaintance of Suleiman Dialo's when asked by reporters about those of his friends who had been rejected for asylum. 'They do not sleep because they know their futures.'

---

*In June 2003, the Home Office's list of 'safe countries' (nations from which asylum-seekers have come and to which they can 'safely' be sent back) stood at twenty-four.

In April 2000, 'interim dispersal measures' created under the 1999 Immigration Act were put into place to alleviate the pressure on London for accommodating asylum-seekers. In theory, the Home Office, through the National Asylum Support Agency (NASS), disperses people in 'clusters', sending Iraqis with Iraqis, Angolans with Angolans, to cities around the UK where there is housing available, either in council estates or with private contractors. In practice, people are dispersed as they arrive, with no time to match them up with others from their countries, which was why Dialo found himself with no other Fula speaker in Newcastle. When, in March 2003, NASS sent a first batch of asylum-seekers to Stockton-on-Tees, they sent 675 Somalis, Algerians, Kuwaitis, Pakistanis, Ethiopians, Eritreans, Macedonians, Guineans, Zimbabweans, Turks and Sierra Leoneans; all but a handful were young men, born in the 1970s and early 1980s. One result of this inchoate system is that these men are now to be found everywhere, in ones and twos, these people who no longer exist, whose legal process has run out and who do not know what to do next, and without some radical and far-sighted solution their numbers are set to grow all the time.

Both Katherine Henderson and Monica Bishop talk of the future with apprehension, as a time of inevitably rising suicides. 'It's a bomb waiting to explode,' Mohamed told me when I went to see him in his office in Sunderland. Mohamed is general manager for one of the local refugee offices, a Sudanese chemist who applied for and was given refugee status and asylum in Britain fifteen years ago, but has never been able to find a job to match his qualifications. Until 2000, Sunderland had a small Bangladeshi community, but few outsiders, and certainly none from Asia and Africa, had ever settled in the town. In the spring of 2000, Sunderland was ear-marked as a good dispersal town. Asylum-seekers from sixty countries arrived in ones and twos, all but a handful men, in keeping with the profile of asylum-seekers everywhere. When I went there in 2003, rejections were increasing; in ones and twos, like Dialo, they were losing their homes and money. 'The implications for putting so many lonely, desperate and confused people on the streets are terrifying,' Mohamed said to me. 'It will totally destroy the good work of all the refugee organisations in breaking the negative image of asylum. And what does it do to them? These people were active in their own countries. Even if they had been tortured and persecuted they were people who had work and professions and positions in society. Here they are condemned to doing nothing. They were somebody at home. They are leftovers here.'

In the summer of 2003, of the 50,000 asylum-seekers scattered by

NASS in sixty-four cities, towns and villages across the UK, there were believed to about 5,000 in the north-east at different stages of the legal process, awaiting answers from the immigration authorities. None, under legislation passed in 2002, are allowed to work, however great and necessary their particular skills – as doctors, for example, or chemists, or biologists – and however protracted their period of waiting. Lack of work was, according to Bertrand, the single hardest and most painful thing for Suleiman Dialo to bear, as he had left behind him a good and profitable job as a trader; and it is the single worst aspect of the waiting according to most of those applying for asylum. Extrapolating from national statistics, however imprecise, at least 2,500 of these people in and around Newcastle will ultimately be refused asylum. For a long time Byker absorbed first some of the hundreds of Romanians who arrived suddenly from Timişoara on Christmas Eve 2001, then Zimbabweans fleeing Mugabe's political madness, then Iraqi and Turkish Kurds escaping systematic persecution by their governments, then Afghans in flight from the Taliban; now it witnesses many departures as well.

In the UK in 2004 there may be several thousand Iraqis, most but not all of them Kurds, who have reached the end of their legal line and moved into the limbo that Dialo so feared. Because of the war in Iraq, their particular position, rejected yet not liable to immediate deportation, is more anomalous than most; though they may stay, they may not work. Cut off from the support that kept them going, they now live along the margins of the black economy, working as ill-paid labourers or in factories, or existing on the charity of those still supported by NASS. Instructed to leave, their continuing presence tolerated if not encouraged, they do not exist other than as names of people who should not be in the UK. They are, in the jargon of the trade, 'disbenefited'. Theirs is a particular limbo, no longer an asylum-seeker yet neither a refugee nor on a deportation list.

Ali arrived in Dover in a lorry full of boxes on 5 October 2000. He does not know what was in the boxes, having been ordered by the smuggler not to look. He is a Kurd from Sulaymaniyah, a short, wiry young man in his late twenties with fashionably cut hair and a pleasant grin. He speaks no English, having had neither the desire nor the aptitude to learn while not knowing his future, and therefore never having profited from the variety of English programmes laid on by local councils and voluntary organisations up and down the country. A prospering shoe-shop owner with a large family of brothers and sisters, Ali was driven from Iraq after he refused to work for a local *akha*, a powerful mafioso gang in his neigh-bourhood. Arrested on their orders by the police, detained in solitary

confinement in a cellar, beaten up and badly scared, Ali emerged from
captivity and fled to Istanbul; from there he found a trafficker to bring him
to Britain. His first application for asylum was turned down; the immigration authorities pointed out that his troubles were not with the state but
with local hoodlums, which made him ineligible for refugee status. He
appealed. On 5 June 2002, Ali learnt that his appeal, too, had been
rejected.

Within a few days, the money that he had been receiving each week was
stopped. He left the room that had been paid for by NASS while he was
an asylum-seeker, and moved in with friends. And there, fourteen months
later, he remains. When I met him, under Grey's column, he had a friend
with him to act as interpreter. He hoped I could get his money reinstated,
as he was having trouble finding even casual low-paid work now that he
had no papers of any kind. I asked him whether he thought of going home.
He looked surprised. 'Never,' he said, through his friend. 'It will never be
safe for me.' Like other Kurds in Newcastle, he is haunted by the story of
another Iraqi Kurd who, hearing that he had been refused asylum, hanged
himself in the park, on a spring day early in 2002, holding a daffodil in his
hand. Hassan Omar Saloh was an older man, of forty-seven, he explained,
and he left a wife and eight children in Iraq.

I asked Ali about his life in Newcastle. What sort of work could he find?
He looked anxious, evasive. Did he have friends? Yes, he replied, he had
many friends, nearly all of them Iraqi, men like himself, waiting; they met
when they could, they sat and talked, they watched television. Did he
have a girlfriend? 'How can I? There are no Iraqi women in Newcastle, at
least no single ones.' At night, when the Iraqis meet, they talk about work
and loss and depression, and about Halabja, the city in Iraq where Saddam
Hussein ordered 5,000 Kurds to be gassed; they remind each other of the
fathers tortured to death in special centres, and the children whose corpses
were still warm when their parents, in answer to a call from the police
station, arrived to collect them. They discuss the Americans and the war,
and whether Iraq will ever be a viable country again. They have spent
their money, and their future is not so much empty as impenetrable. They
stare at a vast blank wall. The legitimacy of their claim for asylum, in this
world of nuances and degrees of persecution, has become almost
irrelevant, and is certainly irrelevant to them. In escaping Iraq, in the long
and frightening journey to freedom, in the imagination it took to conceive
a new life and carry out the moves it required to obtain it, they crossed
some invisible barrier in their own minds. They are refugees living in an
alien land, but that land is immutably now theirs. They have no other. It

is as if Iraq has become a chimera, a place of make-believe, and the war itself, whatever its implications for the rest of the world, something that has no revelance to their lives. Going back to what was once home is not an option any longer. They have travelled too far.

The first reaction of most asylum-seekers sent to the Byker area of Newcastle is one of astonishment. They have come from all over Africa, from the Balkans, South-east Asia and South America, expecting a sense of order, predictability, tranquillity, a tangible feeling that there is some-one in charge and that that person is benevolent. This is what they have grown up imagining, a Britain in which things happen in an orderly and safe way; and because what little news that trickles home from people who have preceded them into exile is always cheerful – those who have sacrificed so much, endured so much, tend not to report poverty and failure – nothing has shaken their faith in all things British. It is a curiously old-fashioned view, frozen at another time and surprisingly little shaken by the realities of modern migration.What they find, in Byker, in derelict housing estates up and down the country, is very different from anything they expected. It is frightening, shabby and unpredictable.

When Gaby arrived in the north-east in May 2000, he was among the first Africans ever seen in Byker, apart from the few who, over the years, had jumped ship in Newcastle or been smuggled into local ports in containers. In the streets, people asked him why he was there, and how long he was planning to stay. He felt ashamed. He wanted to explain that he had lost his honour as a human being, and that being a refugee had never been among his plans. He wanted to point out that he was thirty-two, alone, separated from his wife and children, and that he was aching to work, to give something to the country that seemed willing to look after him. 'I wanted to ask them,' he says now: ' "When am I going to start my life?" ' No one, back in 2000 when the interim dispersal measures were brought in, had thought to prepare the local community for the sudden arrival of Zimbabweans, Sri Lankans, North Koreans or Iraqis, with their longing for different food, their languages and dialects no one could understand, and the far-right British National Party was quick to make gains among residents perplexed about what this influx might spell. Unemployment throughout the north-east, already high through loss of jobs in mining and the docks, created further strains. There were clashes, broken windows, stones were thrown. In Byker, Gaby was called a monkey and told to go back to the trees. Some asylum-seeker children were given urine to drink by boys in the street.

Though much has certainly improved in the three years since Gaby began his long wait in Newcastle, not least in the form of a consortium of organisations which tries extremely hard to broker good relations and better understanding for asylum-seekers, everyday life for those who wait remains extremely tough. And it is growing worse. There have been discussions about sending asylum-seekers to camps in Europe as part of a 'no nonsense' regime to prevent 'bogus' refugees flooding into Britain, while, in the wake of 11 September 2001, the Shadow Home Secretary, Oliver Letwin, has been demanding that Britain derogate from the European Convention on Human Rights, to underline the right of Britain to deport failed asylum-seekers if they represent a 'threat to national security'.

Not long ago, a report from the European Monitoring Centre on Racism and Xenophobia found Britain to have some of the most hostile attitudes towards asylum-seekers in Europe. Racial harassment is increasing, and with it the number of actual physical assaults, much promoted by the scaremongering that has become the language of the day. The website of MigrationWatch, a one-man research group run by a former British ambassador to Saudi Arabia, Sir Andrew Green, has warned that 'we can expect at least 200,000 and perhaps 250,000 non-European Union immigrants a year,' figures that I believe have little grounding but that have been much quoted. William Hague, campaigning for the Conservatives not long ago, spoke of sorting out 'criminals and asylum-seekers'.

None of this has been helped by an explosion of ill-temper in the tabloid newspapers, viewed throughout the rest of Europe as responsible for a climate of xenophobia towards refugees nowhere justified either by numbers or events, and not matched by the media in other countries. Because the articles that they carry, in which asylum-seekers are portrayed as parasites, scroungers, criminals and terrorists, are in English, they are followed with interest by the rest of the world (and copied: in Switzerland not long ago the Swiss People's Party won 26.6 per cent of the popular vote in a general election, partly, so it was said, on the strength of its poster campaign showing a black face with the slogan: 'The Swiss are becoming Negroes').

At the turn of the millennium the *Sun*, the *Daily Mail* and the *Express* sharpened their campaign against immigrants. A survey in 2003 revealed that every time one of the tabloids puts asylum on its front page, with warnings of Britain in the throes of losing control of its borders, circulation rises by some 10,000 readers. Headlines have included 'SWAN BAKE – ASYLUM-SEEKERS STEAL QUEEN'S BIRDS FOR BARBECUES', 'OFFICIAL: ASYLUM TEARING UK APART' (both from the *Sun*) and 'WIDOW, 88, TOLD

BY GP: MAKE WAY FOR ASYLUM-SEEKERS' (the *Mail on Sunday*). As the feeling grew that reporting in the British media gave undue prominence to scaremongering claims from fringe groups, portraying asylum-seekers as threatening young men with contacts with the criminal underworld, so in the spring of 2003 the anti-censorship organisation Article 19 carried out a research project on media reporting of refugee matters. They found that there were fifty-one words of a disparaging nature that were regularly being used to describe asylum-seekers. They also concluded that statistics were 'frequently unsourced, exaggerated or inadequately explained', that the tabloid press was failing to distinguish between economic migrants and asylum-seekers, and that the hostility of media coverage was provoking a sense of alienation and shame among refugees, who were rapidly becoming the '*untermensch*', the unwanted underclass, non-people, victims at best. UNHCR and the National Union of Journalists joined forces to produce a memorandum on good reporting, and in October 2003 the Press Complaints Commission issued guidelines to counter inaccurate and inflammatory stories.

Even so, hostile and bigoted reporting continues, with continued casual disregard for any distinction between asylum-seeker, refugee, failed asylum-seeker or economic migrant, and total neglect of a very simple but important fact: that in 1999–2000 alone, according to Home Office research, migrants, including asylum-seekers and refugees, made a net fiscal contribution to Britain of approximately £2.5 billion. In the *Daily Mail*, for example, Ross Benson ran a series of stories about the Roma, warning of an invasion of gypsies once the European Union is enlarged. The Roma suffer from being one of the most disliked and despised of all European ethnic minorities. In January 2004, the *Sunday Times* took up the theme, suggesting that up to 100,000 Roma were on their way. The next day, the *Sun* added that after three months in the UK, these Roma would be 'entitled to health, education, pension and welfare benefits'. The *Daily Express* then inflated the figure to 1.6 million: 'GYPSIES PREPARE TO INVADE BRITAIN'. Though two days later they amended this figure to 40,000, they predicted an 'economic disaster' just the same. Even the *Economist* spoke of the 'coming hordes'. On 22 January 2004 the *Mail* front page covered a report by the Organisation for Economic Co-operation and Development, saying that Britain, which was taking 'one in five of the Western world's asylum-seekers', had 'failed to turn the asylum tide'. The article, it later turned out, was based on figures from 2002, and ignored the fact that the UK is currently eighth in terms of the numbers of asylum-seekers it takes per capita, well behind Austria, Norway, Sweden,

Switzerland and Ireland. By contrast, there are very few articles describing what asylum-seekers are fleeing from, the violence, terror and loss that they have left behind.

It was at least in part because the mood of the country encouraged such intolerance that Jack Straw, when Foreign Secretary, raised the possibility that Britain might not reaffirm its commitment to the 1951 Convention, thereby becoming the first government in the world to threaten to pull out. Other countries, unsure whether the threat was real or tactical, watched what became known as the 'nuclear option' with interest. Though, eventually, Britain did uphold its commitment, Straw, when made Home Secretary, followed up his hesitations by proposing that, instead of processing asylum-seekers and their applications on British soil, they be sent to 'off-shore' centres (with the possible exception of some special groups, such as children), either on the fringes of the extended European Union, or in the regions from which they had come, where the whole procedure could be done in a consistent and orderly way. Coming so soon after Australia's decision to reject asylum-seekers arriving by sea, and to send them away to be processed outside Australian territory, Straw's proposals provoked strong and angry reactions in the refugee world, and were eventually rejected by other EU countries, though not before Denmark, Ireland and Austria had expressed interest. And, soon, the UK government came up with another idea: to pay Tanzania £4 million in aid in return for taking all the UK's failed Somali asylum-seekers and putting them into a 'zone of protection', thereby shifting still more responsibility to the poor countries who are already housing most of the world's refugees. Though striking bargains over refugees is far from unknown, Tanzania declined. The enormous inherent problems that would be posed by Straw's 'off-shore' centres and 'zones of protection' – would people in flight from persecution be able to proceed in an orderly manner to a designated centre? Who would run the show? How would international standards be guaranteed? – were all too obvious. What frightened the human-rights world was that they had been made at all.

In Byker, in his community centre, Gaby warns new arrivals not to expect too much, to take great care not to antagonise their British neighbours, to make no fuss, to provoke no one. 'It's very hard,' he says, 'for us Africans to accept abuse and say nothing. We knew it wouldn't be like home here, but we didn't expect to be made to feel so useless.' Gaby's office is a small, airless room at the back of the community centre, a windowless area that was once a storeroom. It is here, among the crammed desks and computers, that he listens, day after day, like a doctor discussing a diagnosis, to the fears and bafflement of those scheduled for deportation. Whether, like Dialo, they came from violence and persecution, or whether they are refugees from lives so impoverished and without hope as to make the dividing line between economic necessity and physical safety lose all meaning, their approach to forthcoming departure is one of fear. They come in search of the impossible, a postponement of the evil day.

On a Monday morning in August 2003, Gaby had two visitors. Claudette was from Rwanda, a round, nervous woman with three young boys. She is a Hutu from a prominent family, and before the birth of her sons she worked for the Ministry of Commerce in Kigali. Towards the end of the war in 1994, after the massacres of the Tutsis by the Hutus were largely over and when the Tutsi soldiers were closing in on the capital, Hutus suspected of supporting the genocide were rounded up. Claudette's sister-in-law and a niece, both Hutus, were killed in a local skirmish. Soon afterwards, her parents were killed, and with them one of her brothers and a sister. After threats were made against her Hutu husband, who was accused of having led the Interahamwe killers to their victims in the genocide, what was left of the family fled to the Congo, where they spent two years in the relative safety of a refugee camp. But then rebel fighters overran the camp, and Claudette, her husband and the children found themselves forcibly repatriated to Kigali, where she and the boys were led one way, and her husband another, into prison.

In the months that followed, Claudette was repeatedly visited by soldiers from Military Intelligence, eager to get evidence against her husband. She was raped, beaten in the small of her back with rifle butts, kicked in the stomach and forced to kneel on gravel while soldiers whipped her, tortures designed to extract from her a confession that she was indeed an 'enemy of the state' and that her husband had been a leader in the genocide. In October 2002, Claudette was detained for a fortnight and told that unless she testified against her husband, she would be held in prison indefinitely. She agreed, and was released pending her husband's trial; but she knew that the offer was meaningless, as she had no evidence to give, and other women who had been offered the same deal had sent their husbands to their deaths and remained prisoners themselves.

From earlier travels in the area, she knew the surrounding countryside well. Disguising herself as a peasant woman and taking her three small children, she walked several days through the bush towards Uganda, where a friend of her husband's helped them to escape, first to Kenya and then to Britain. Claudette and her sons reached London on a cold winter's morning. They knew no one, but were treated kindly and with respect. The three boys were now at school and doing well. Claudette recalled with appreciation how her neighbours in Byker took pity on the family and brought them, in the first days of confusion, food to eat.

On 4 July 2003, Claudette learnt that her appeal had been turned down. Refusing her case, the Home Office official allowed that her account of persecution up to her return from the Congo in 2001 was probably true; but went on to say that her assertion that the family had been targeted because they were Hutu intellectuals was not credible. Taken together with her account of her escape – which he found improbable – and the reasons she gave for her husband's detention – that he had written a hostile thesis on Rwandan prison conditions – the Home Office interviewer concluded: 'I cannot find her honest as to the core of her case.' Hard as her life would surely be in Rwanda, he believed that the country was indeed returning to normality, and that she and her children were unlikely to be mistreated again. Furthermore, given her past employment, Claudette was obviously a clever and resourceful woman, and she would manage. 'How can we go back?' asked Claudette. 'What chance would the children have with a father in prison in connection with the genocide?' While waiting and dreading the knock on the door which would spell deportation, Claudette even dreamt of finding ways of leaving her children in England, where they could at least survive.

Gaby could do little for Claudette. He was trying to find her a new solicitor willing to take her case to the High Court, but knew that this was unlikely. Nor could he do much for Nsamba, who talked in careful, measured sentences, with the precise syllables of those reared in the French legal system, and whose right leg was so badly injured during torture that the muscle has withered away and he now walks with a limp. Nsamba was a professor of economics at Kinshasa University in the Congo, a man too interested in opposition politics to remain safe for long. His account of his five-day trek to freedom in Zambia had been disbelieved by the Home Office on the grounds that no one with his injuries could have walked so far, and that, as an educated man, he would have described his journey more articulately had it been genuine. Nsamba, who has spent his months in Britain building an effective political opposition to the government at home in the Congo, learnt at the end of June that his case had been rejected. As he saw it, choosing his words with care, Britain was once a country where respect for human rights was absolute. He came, admiring what he thought he would find. Now, having lived among the refugees for many months, he is not so sure.

*

Britain's asylum world is a busy, anxious place, full of currents and hopes, misunderstandings and deferments. Nothing is as it seems, and nothing stays the same. Rules change in response to surges of hostility in public feeling, then change again as they prove unworkable, or simply too harsh to implement. In the midst of the confusion and uncertainty, those whose daily work brings them into contact with refugees – the doctors, lawyers, refugee organisations, churches, human-rights campaigners – are buffeted by a discourse that becomes more unpleasant day by day, as politicians make mileage out of scandals, as faraway countries drive political opponents into exile, as droughts and famines break out, as travellers and television programmes continue to peddle the image of a safe and welcoming West.

Before leaving Newcastle, I heard about Angel Heights, a former nurses' hostel opposite the main hospital, an imposing manor-like building, once the pride of 1930s' town development and now a home for dispersed asylum-seekers in the north-east. Angel Heights is all that is wrong and all that is right in British policy; it is both decent and dreadful; both humane and cruel. For a while, Angel Heights was home to 140 single Afghan men, but not long ago, in response to new waves of arrivals and departures, the building was turned over to single African women sent up from London and the south to wait for the results of their applications for asylum. There are relatively few such hostels for single women, reflecting the fact that few young women have the courage and money to make the journeys in search of safety, that they often have children to care for, and their movements are more restricted. As a place to visit, it is impressive: brightly painted corridors and large meeting rooms hung with prints of fruit and plants; single, comfortable rooms, with a television and a kettle and a small fridge; a large inner courtyard with plants and benches. But Angel Heights is also a waiting room, a building in which nothing happens. Few of its inhabitants speak English, and few can speak to each other. Because it provides full board and lodging, the women receive just £10 each week. Forbidden to work, they have, literally, nothing to do; nothing, that is, except to worry: about those they were forced to leave behind, of whom they seldom have news; about the torture and rape most have endured; about their cases and their lawyers; about themselves. They sit alone in large rooms full of cobalt-blue chairs in rows; they stand in the corridors; they queue by the single payphone. Angel Heights is quiet; when the women speak, they speak in whispers. Outside the window is a forlorn garden with an abandoned greenhouse and an unkempt netball court, reminders of the days when nurses strolled on the grass and organised matches against each other.

Looking for someone to talk to about life inside Angel Heights, I found Madina, one of the two non-African women then living in the hostel, the other being an older Belorussian woman in her fifties, confined to her room with severe diabetes. Madina is a geologist with a master's degree from Azerbaijan, a dark, thin woman in her early thirties, her hair lank and very black, her clothes black. She has a thin, awkward smile and speaks some English. Her story told me everything I wanted to know about Angel Heights.

Madina last saw her eleven-year-old son, Kolya, on 12 January 2003. He was then in hospital in St Petersburg with severe frostbite to his face and hands, having been thrown from a police car into the snow and found by a passer-by. Kolya is half black. He was in shock and unwilling or unable to say much about what had happened to him, beyond the fact that the police had picked him up as he was walking to a school party and that he had lost the present that he had been carrying in the scuffle. Madina was told by the doctors that he would be fine, and that she could return to collect him on the fourteenth. When she returned, his bed was empty. Kolya had severe mental problems and had been moved, she was informed, to a children's ward of a psychiatric hospital. She hastened to the hospital and was refused entry. Kolya was far too ill to see her.

Though terrified and full of panic about what to do next, Madina had long expected trouble; but not this kind of trouble. For almost a year, she had been involved with a group of campaigners protesting against the war in Chechnya, and what the Russians were doing to Chechnyan refugees. She had already had to flee her Azerbaijany home town because of death threats against her second husband, Salimov, himself a Chechnyan, and because of her own work with Armenian refugees, and she was no stranger to violence. Her first husband, Kolya's father, who was Congolese, had been killed in a bomb attack when he returned to Brazzaville after completing his studies in Azerbaijan, and Kolya had endured many racist attacks as a small boy. Since arriving in St Petersburg, the city chosen carefully by her as the most liberal in Russia, Madina had been harassed by the police, her office ransacked and her computer and files confiscated, and she had been admitted into hospital with concussion and severe bruising after being taken into custody. 'I'm not the kind of person who can sit back and do nothing,' she said to me, sitting in the empty dining room in Angel Heights, reminding me yet again of the instinctive and apparently unhesitating courage of political activists. 'I feel suffering like it's mine.' A second attack by the police had left her with two broken ribs and a dislocated shoulder. And on 19 September, four months before Kolya's abduction, Madina was admitted back into hospital with severe depression. Soon after she was released, Salimov was arrested and charged with spying.

By this stage, not surprisingly, Madina had lost what little faith she had ever had in Russian human rights. Even liberal St Petersburg was turning out dangerous for dissidents. But the abduction of her son was more than she could bear. Having been refused permission to see him on 14 January, she went home in despair. The telephone rang as she entered the apartment. Her caller did not give his name. 'We have taken your husband and your son,' a voice said, 'and now it is your turn.' Madina went to hide in her nineteen-year-old sister's flat. Later she accompanied her to the dentist. Leaving the flat, there was a shot: her sister fell into the snow, dead. Madina saw a policeman run away. 'Next time,' said the telephone caller that night, 'we will not miss.' Madina fled. Friends helped find an agent, who provided her with a ticket for London and a transit visa for Italy, where the plane was touching down. She reasoned that she must stay alive for Kolya's sake. At Heathrow, she asked for asylum. She was put into a small hotel near the airport and, three months later, sent to Newcastle.

This familiar and sad story of violence, fear and torture is Madina's reason for being in Angel Heights, waiting to hear whether the Home Office will decide to send her to Italy, for which she still has a visa, and let the Italian government decide on the legitimacy of her claim, or whether they will grant her leave to remain in Britain. All of this explains Madina's haunted look, her fragile thinness, her anxious pacing. She has no idea how or when or where she will ever see Kolya again. Meanwhile, she waits and thinks. She sleeps little, her thoughts obsessed with her son, who she knows from friends is still in the psychiatric hospital in St Petersburg, just as she knows that there is still no news of Salimov, whom she now suspects has been 'disappeared'. She spends her weekly £10 on phone calls to Russia. From dawn until late each night she wanders around Angel Heights' long bright-yellow corridors, occasionally leaving the building to walk down the hill into central Newcastle and to the main library from where she can receive and send emails. She found a book on geology in Angel Heights' small library and uses it to work on her English. Every morning, she forces herself to translate something from a newspaper, to practise her English. Had she tried any of the novels on the shelf? 'They are,' she said mournfully, 'not serious.' Most days, she spends a few hours with one of the African women, recently granted leave to remain in the

United Kingdom. This girl is too frightened to walk in Newcastle's streets on her own since some boys threw eggs at her. Asked by the Home Office whether there was a close family member she would like to apply to have join her in Britain, she replied that no, she had no one, soldiers had killed them all. At six o'clock, Madina eats dinner in the refectory, alone; afterwards, she sits in her small, perfectly comfortable, totally silent bedroom, with its bright purple walls, and thinks. And so the days pass, each one like the last, in an outer appearance of calm, and with an inner feeling of desperation and terror. I didn't feel there was much more I wanted to know about Angel Heights: a benign prison, lived in by solitary women, waiting.

As Georgina Flexner, who works for the Consortium for Asylum Support Services, sees it, the real messages spread by government go all one way. For all their pious words about integration, about preparing local communities for the arrival of asylum-seekers, about the enormous advantages to both sides of having refugees in the community, 'regionalisation', the current fashionable word, is effectively all about policing and little about care. Asylum-seekers are not meant to feel welcome; if their reception is too good, then they might want to stay. Since she started work in the north three years ago, Flexner has decided that the dispersal programme, with all its contradictions and confusions, its ever changing regulations and its arbitrariness, is designed chiefly as a deterrent to others who would follow. And there are not simply contradictions, but absurdities, which serve mainly to give ammunition to the anti-immigration lobby. Monica Bishop told me that not long ago, four young women asylum-seekers needed to be transported from a hostel in one part of Newcastle to a YMCA in another. The journey was about two miles. But because the contract for transport by bus originates in Kent, a bus was sent from Ashford to Newcastle to take the four passengers, a distance of over 300 miles. The total cost, she estimates, was around £1,000; a local taxi would have charged £5.

Georgina Flexner is not, however, altogether discouraged. What no one reckoned on, she says, are the ordinary human feelings of sympathy. The north-east, impoverished by unemployment, its housing estates vandalised and shabby, has grown fond of the strangers drifting into their city centres since 2000. Many of its inhabitants have found themselves, against their expectations, enjoying the fact that ninety new nationalities, in ones and twos, have settled in their empty houses, bringing with them new music, new customs and even new food in the markets. When, not long ago, Beamish Museum decided to draw asylum-seekers closer into the community by offering two busloads of them a free day's visit, there was outrage from the British National Party and some of the newspapers, but an equally loud backlash from local people, who liked the idea of all these Zimbabweans, Iraqis and Sri Lankans inspecting Stevenson's Rocket and early railway stock. Refugee families expelled suddenly as the result of a negative decision by the Home Office and faced with deportation from neighbourhoods in which their children have grown up, have found vociferous champions among neighbours and community groups. Georgina Flexner talks warmly of the enthusiasm of northern plans for integrating refugees. Willing to turn their hands to all forms of employment, bringing with them skills that might transform dying estates, these are the very people, as she sees it, who may contribute most to a new prosperity. Studies done in 2003 have shown that 80 per cent of asylum-seekers in the north-east would choose to stay there should they win the right to remain in Britain, providing they can find work and housing; they find the north friendlier, less intimidating, than London. As she moves between local communities and the ever growing refugee population, she observes how neatly balanced are the ancestral fears of losing England to a tide of foreigners, against the newer fear of seeing the north-east become a mere transit area.

Early in 2004, the Home Office announced that asylum figures in the UK were down by 40 per cent, to 61,050. The government's delight was not matched by those who work with refugees, who view the growing restrictions with unease and worry about all those people who, fearing rejection, are not even now bothering to try to make the journey to safety. Asylum specialists would like to see many changes, including the setting up of an independent documentation centre to provide reliable country information. They worry that the Home Office is paying far more attention to finding ways of securing its borders and building up Fortress Europe than to making the system on the ground workable for those who manage it or bearable for those who live it, and that they do little to counter the hostility fostered by the tabloids.

Lies, inaccuracies, exaggerations, untruths: this is the climate in which the current British asylum world lives, in which policy is made not so much on evidence as in response to media and public perception, and in which those seeking asylum, buffeted by the chaotic, contradictory and discriminatory procedures now operating across the Western world, scramble for a toehold using any method they can. Not long ago, Kofi

Annan, Secretary General of the United Nations, told the European Parliament that Europe anti-immigration rhetoric was 'dehumanising people'. 'This silent human-rights crisis,' he went on, 'shames our world.'

Chapter Six

Little Better Than Cockroaches: Guinea's Long-term Camps

Contemporary history has created a new kind of human
being – the kind that are put in concentration camps by their
foes and internment camps by their friends.
Hannah Arendt

It was in 1958 that Sékou Touré, Guinea's first president, won
independence from France and embarked on twenty-six years of socialist
dictatorship. Touré's isolationist views, and de Gaulle's anger at them,
effectively ensured that all through the sixties, seventies and eighties,
Guinea remained one of the most isolated of Africa's post-colonial
countries, a distant, shuttered land with a small stretch of Atlantic coast
and many thousand square kilometres of semi-tropical forest, little
touched by the material and economic developments that came to other
parts of the continent. Even today, and despite the forest region's many
natural resources, Guinea vies with Sierra Leone and Liberia – the three
Mano River Union countries of West Africa – for bottom place among the
world's poorest and least settled countries. Her 7½ million people live on
less than a dollar a day.

The capital, Conakry, is an old-fashioned and somewhat unworldly
place, with its fringe of palm trees along the shore and a wind that blows
constantly from the ocean. It is very hot and very humid and the city is
growing fast – but outwards, simply, poorly, in shanty towns that vanish
into the distance, with few of the plate-glass and steel skyscrapers that
mark other developing capitals.

Since Touré, Guinea's successive leaders have proved little more
accepting of dissent: even today, twenty years after Touré's death,
opposition politicans prefer to lie low during election time, and it is said
few of them sleep in their own homes while polling takes place. A
courageous Guinean professor of law, Dr Thierno Maadjou Sow, has since
1995 been running the Organisation Guinéene des Droits de l'Homme,

one of the country's handful of campaigning bodies. His dealings with the government are wary. '*Tout le monde ici*,' he told me when I first arrived in Conakry, '*a quelque chose à coeur*. We are all victims of terrible things.' He was talking about his many colleagues and friends who have spent months and years in prison and who expect to spend many more there.

In the year 2000, thirty-three out of the world's forty-one countries most in debt lay in Africa. Forty per cent of the world's refugees and 70 per cent of its Aids victims were also African. At its peak, in the early and mid-1990s, when civil war inside Liberia and Sierra Leone had turned some 7 million people into refugees either displaced within their own countries or driven into nearby ones, Guinea, a long fat country wrapped around its neighbours, had willingly absorbed one of the largest per capita refugee influxes in the world. Seven hundred thousand people – a tenth of Guinea's entire population – had found shelter there, either within camps run and financed by the international community, or scattered around the country. As Guinea belongs to the West African economic community, Sierra Leoneans and Liberians are allowed to reside and work there. By the spring of 2003, according to official UNHCR figures, 185,000 refugees were being protected and cared for by them in Guinea, though the true figure, including new arrivals and all those who for one reason or another had not been registered, was certainly far higher. Of all those now crossing over from Liberia and Sierra Leone, 70 per cent, over two-thirds, I was told, were under the age of eighteen.

As Cairo's Liberian boys had left their roots along this rainy belt, having fled Charles Taylor and the rebel commanders either alone or with their families and crossed the nearest border to safety, Guinea seemed to be the place to go in search of them. It would give me, I thought, not just a clearer picture of what it was that had driven them into exile in the first place, but a sense of what they had left behind. Some, like short-sighted Mamadu, working off his smuggler's fee in Tel Aviv, had spent many years here in one of the long-term refugee camps at Guekedou, and I wanted to visit for myself these camps, so established and so problematic. And Izako, the customs officer forced to abandon his wife and small son and daughter in Monrovia, believed that his family might have made their way into Guinea, so that, by going there, I half hoped that I might find them.

In Guinea's *région forestière*, so I was told, I would see the entire gamut of African refugee life, the cycle in all its stages, from new arrivals to the settled 'camps', indistinguishable, after long years, from the villages that surround them. In UNHCR's headquarters in Conakry hangs an immense map, marking with arrows and bands of colour the flows of people moving round West Africa, making me think once again, as in San Diego, of the migratory paths of birds around the world. Along the southern borders of the area, where the forest runs for almost a thousand miles, there is a swathe of red. This is refugee territory, refugees coming and going, crossing and recrossing borders; settling and dying; making lives and being moved on; it was there that I wished to go, to see for myself what Africa offered its moving populations.

The camp of Kuankan lies 700 miles from Conakry, in a clearing cut out of the semi-tropical forest that seems to stretch for ever along this part of West Africa. It can be reached by flying to Nzérékoré, the nearest town, on a twice-weekly UN and aid-agency service on the rare occasion that one of the thirty seats is not taken, or on the infrequent and very ancient commercial plane, and then by a long, slow, bumpy drive, at first along a new tarmac road laid by foreign funders to make the delivery of aid easier, and then a dark-red earth track between the tall teak and palm trees, the feathery acacias and deep green baobabs. Where there is no tarmac, the track is full of craters, deep crevices that become rivers when the rains come.

Lulled by the green and the denseness of the forest shade, the sudden clarity and light of the camp's great open space is startling. Here, in over two square miles of mud huts with thatched roofs and tarpaulin tents, live 33,000 refugees, all but a very few of them Liberians escaping Charles Taylor's long and murderous civil war. None of the Cairo Liberians had been to Kuankan, but all knew of friends here, and it was just possible that Izako's family might be among them. My visit was in March. With the start of the eight-month rainy season in February, water had begun to soak through the thatch and the torn and patched tarpaulin above the refugees' heads, and in the bright sunshine and great heat of the morning of my first day, people were laying out their possessions to dry. The air was humid and absolutely still. It seemed an isolated, hermetic place.

In the autumn of 2002, Human Rights Watch sent a mission to these borders with Ivory Coast, Liberia and Sierra Leone, where Guinea dips down into a narrow prong they call the Parrot's Beak. Researchers visited Kuankan. The report they came back with was alarming: it spoke of incursions of Liberian rebels and government forces over the border and as far as the camp, of complicity by Guinean soldiers and police, of forced recruitment of young refugees as boy soldiers and porters, of rape and looting. A third of the food that feeds the rebels in Liberia is said to have been stolen from camps like Kuankan.

The picture painted was disquieting, but it was not unexpected. Other reports, written by similar organisations in recent years, have dwelt on the violence and confusion now endemic along one of Africa's most permeable borders. In Kuankan at any one time there are Liberians who have gone backwards and forwards into Guinea in response to the fighting, Sierra Leoneans who fled first into Liberia and then again into Guinea, as conflict pursued them, and Ivorians who have spent much of their lives circling around the camps of West Africa. The fact that many come from the same ethnic groups – for the most part Mandingo, Krahn and Gio, the groups that I had heard so much about from the Liberians in Cairo – and that they speak the same language, would make the border itself almost irrelevant, were it not that soldiers from all sides use it as a place at which to threaten, intimidate and plunder those who wish to cross. Simply surviving crossing the frontier, with soldiers behind and predatory guards ahead, is a terrifying ordeal.

Reading the reports before I arrived, I had been struck mainly by the violence of these forest camps, the sense of constant vigilance, the almost casual brutality of a state of war that never seems to end. Listening to the young Liberians talking in Cairo, their long litany of loss and fear, I had expected unease, tension, a sense of anticipation. What I actually saw, when I got there, was poverty.

Ordinary Guineans, for all the vast natural resources of their country, their diamonds and gold and bauxite, are poor in material things; Guinea has limited electricity, few roads, no train service or postal system, inadequate schools and health care. But the refugees are even poorer. They exist along the very margins of life, whether inside the camps or outside, so poor that, in a literal way, they have nothing. Most of them do not even have a bucket, and they think about one and talk about one with longing. Some of the Liberians have been in Kuankan for over ten years, an entire lifetime in the case of the many small children who make up about a third of the camp's population. Poverty is very hard to describe. It is an absence, a nothingness not easy to put into words. But the poverty of camp refugees is about more than just not having things; it is about having no way in which to get them, and no means of altering or controlling one's own life. Their poverty curbs and crushes all hope and expectation. Kuankan's refugees are destitute in possibilities.

Kuankan has twelve sections, known as zones, as if a word so official could lend definition to a place of such sprawling sameness. Each zone reflects a wave of new arrivals, refugees from a fresh outbreak of fighting within a radius of perhaps a couple of hundred miles. The most recent consists of white tarpaulin tents on wooden frames donated by Médecins Sans Frontières, each one the same, and each one divided into separate compartments for different families. The tents are set up in regular lines, at a certain distance one from the next. Zone 12 stands a little apart from the others, near to the edge of the forest. Its first site, closer to the main body of the camp, was abandoned after last year's rains, when the red earth between the tents turned to deep mud and everything the refugees possessed became damp and encrusted. In the camp, there is fresh water laid on by one of the international agencies, but there is not enough to keep the children of Zone 12 free from the mud, so that by the end of each day they are streaked with red, slippery and wet.

At the time of my visit, Fatima was a recent arrival in Zone 12. She was a thin, tall woman in her early thirties, with five children, two others having died in Liberia before she was forced to flee to Guinea in July 2003. When I am taken to see her, by a refugee employed by the camp to filter the few visitors who make the journey into the forest, she is wearing a bright-yellow sarong, her black hair pulled tightly back in the plaits many of the Liberians wear; her face is gaunt and bony, but she is brisk, without self-pity. One night, while the family slept in their house, the rebels had attacked their village in Lofa County. Pulling the children behind her, carrying the two youngest on her back, the smallest still a baby, Fatima managed to get them all to the safety of the nearby forest. In the dark and the confusion, terrified by the sound of shots, she lost sight of her husband. She and her children stayed hidden for some days in the bush. I asked her what they ate. 'Bananas,' she said. 'And some leaves and roots.' From others who came to join them in the forest, she learnt that her older brother had been killed and that her closest friend had been shot in the leg.

It took her ten days to reach the border, where she found people from UNHCR waiting to ferry the refugees in lorries to Kuankan. Médecins Sans Frontières has given her, along with her ten-square-foot portion of a tent, a wooden-frame bed, four mats, four blankets, two pots and two bars of soap. Her entire home is too small for us to stand inside together. She points to a small pile of straw, neatly raked into one corner. Here, she says, two of the children, who can't fit in the bed, sleep. Not one of them has shoes. The middle girl, who is eight, has one piece of clothing, an adult's T-shirt so full of holes that it hangs half off her body. She wears it as a dress. She has no pants. Both the baby, who is now two, and her older brother, who is four, are breastfeeding. Fatima's breasts are thin and withered, like those of a very old woman.

Like all the registered refugees in Kuankan, Fatima collects food rations each month from the World Food Programme. Stored in sacks at the end of her wooden bed are bulgur, cornmeal, a little salt, a few dried beans. There is an old tin with a few inches of groundnut oil. Though in the more generous early 1990s the food package included rice, sugar and tinned fish, now these are the family's entire rations for a month. In the open spaces between the tents, some of the refugees have planted sweet potatoes. The growing cycle is too long to wait for the actual potatoes, but the leaves, which grow quickly, can be used to make a sauce for the bulgur. Neither Fatima nor her children like bulgur, which they had never eaten before they arrived in Kuankan, the diet of this part of West Africa being rice, but the refugees say that the World Food Programme has great stocks of bulgur, and bulgur is what they distribute. Later, I watch it being boiled up in huge vats of glutinous porridge. Fatima has no other food, and no means of getting any, but she accepts without apparent envy those refugees in neighbouring tents who somehow manage to buy pepper and dried fish from a market in a nearby village, or even some of the onions and tomatoes, most no larger than marbles, that are for sale near the entrance to the camp. No one has money for sugar or milk or tea, and she has not fed her children meat, fish or eggs since she left home nine months earlier. The five children, accustomed to the oranges and vegetables that grew in their garden in Liberia, to the chickens the family kept and to their eggs, are not doing well on their new diet. They miss the sugar and the fresh fruit.

Fatima has learnt that her surviving brothers and sisters have managed to escape and are now in another camp in Guinea, about a hundred kilometres away near the border with Ivory Coast, and that her parents are with them. She talks of the fact that they are alive with surprise and pleasure: she had not expected so much. Of her husband, who used to hunt small deer and wild pig in the forests around their village, she has had no news since the rebel attack in July.

Fatima's closest neighbour in the camp is Peter, an anxious and agitated former civil servant who also comes from Lofa County, which was home to almost half the young men who came as refugees to Cairo. The enforced inactivity of the camp has begun to weigh heavily on him. Escaping his burning village in the faint light of dawn in July 2002, carrying his youngest daughter in his arms while his wife took the baby, he was unable to help his elderly parents. The last time he saw them was when he looked back over his shoulder as he ran into the forest, and they were standing by their hut, watching helplessly. Peter is now haunted by what may have become of them. In Kuankan, you seldom see anyone above the age of fifty; many of the older refugees who did set out on foot gave up or died along the way. At first, Peter believed that he would find some means of contacting his parents and arranging to have them brought out to safety with friends. He questioned new arrivals, sought out the aid officials in charge of the camp, pestered the refugee organisations. But as the months passed with no news, and people coming from Lofa reported no sign of the couple, he began to accept that they were probably now dead. He sits, day after day, in front of his small hot tarpaulin tent, thinking about the past in an agony of boredom and despair, and looking out at the thick green forest into which the refugees are not encouraged to roam, for, under the terms set by Guinea's president, they may not use the land to plant crops, nor hunt the wild pig, porcupine and deer said to be plentiful in the surrounding countryside.

'I wish, at least, we were learning,' says the young interpreter lent to me by the Liberians who run some of the camp's basic chores. 'It is the fact that we sit here declining that is so hard.' This young woman, wife of an engineer with a mining company, fled for the second time from Liberia into Guinea in 2002, having spent the early 1990s in a refugee camp along the border. Her dress is Western and smart, and on her feet she wears flimsy sandals in which she picks her way through the rough muddy paths with difficulty, as if to convince herself that she does not belong here. Once a cabaret singer in Monrovia's nightclubs, she has found occasional work as an interpreter in the camp with one of the aid agencies. Her husband helps the camp's carpenters. Her manner, though friendly, is distant and a little sceptical; a muddy refugee camp in the middle of a forest clearing is not where she planned to spend the middle years of her life, and not the place she now means to stay. With the passing of so much time, and with so little to do, expectations take on an urgent and uncomfortable dimension.

Fatima, with her five children and small tent, is perhaps luckier than some, for unlike many of Kuankun's inhabitants she has not spent her adult years as a refugee, going backwards and forwards across West Africa's borders in search of safety. She and her family survived the first nine years of Liberia's civil war without being driven from home. Unlike most of her neighbours in Zone 12, this is her first experience of a camp. She takes this reduction in her life calmly, preferring to focus on a few very specific thoughts: she worries that her children may not be growing as they should on the bulgur that they find so hard to eat and deprived of everything that has a taste they know or like; and she fears that she will not be able to send the older children to the school run by an international agency in the camp, because they have no clothes and no shoes in which to go. She wonders how she can acquire the things she most needs: a bucket, a lamp and some kerosene, a mattress and one more blanket. And, just occasionally, she dreams of getting hold of a stock cube, to give the bulgur some flavour.

In the daytime, and for much of the night, the ten square feet of tarpaulin tent is stiflingly hot; the children sweat and turn in their sleep in the long hours of darkness, when the camp is lit only by the cooking fires and the occasional kerosene lamps owned by the more fortunate refugees. I can only imagine the scene. Night falls in Guinea at about seven, and it does not grow light until twelve hours later. There is no electricity in Kuankan and no generator, and, with the fighting so close and the regular incursions of rebels and soldiers from across the border, no foreigners are allowed to remain in the camp after nightfall. It is then, say the refugees, that the presence among them of rebel fighters, come to visit their families in the camp or in search of food for themselves and their companions, becomes apparent. I try to picture Fatima and her children in the dark, with the forest thick and black not far from their tent, and the quiet footsteps of people coming softly from behind the trees. I think how frightening it must be for the parents of young boys, waiting for armed men come to prey on their sons, wondering if they will ever feel safe again. I wonder too if the fighters ever come into the camp as they are said to dress for battle, in women's frocks and long wigs, their faces painted white or hidden by masks, the grotesque outfits that gave Liberia's seven-year civil war its macabre reputation, and have made commentators speculate that, together with Somalia and Rwanda, here is evidence that Africa has turned its back on progress and is sinking into barbarity and superstition. Faced with apparitions like these, of men of war said to eat the hearts of their vanquished enemies in order to draw strength from them, and for whom the invisible world of the spirits is a far more potent force than that of humankind, Fatima might well keep her children very close to her after the hours of darkness.

Though the precise origins of Liberia's savagery lie in a complicated web of politics and plunder, the events that ultimately drove Fatima and her neighbours in Kuankan into exile, and the band of young men I knew to Cairo, began with the death of President Samuel Doe, Liberia's twenty-first president, on 10 September 1989 at the hands of a psychopathic warlord called Prince Johnson, a good-looking man with a charming smile. Liberia was the first emergency in Africa after the end of the Cold War, coming soon after the dismantling of the Berlin wall and Saddam Hussein's invasion of Kuwait. To understand something of the nature of Kuankan – something of the camp's past and its continuing existence, the way it has become a place of refuge for people buffeted by a civil war that never seems to end, and how it has for many of them taken the place of everything that went before – I had to learn about Liberia. Where refugees come from and the conditions that turned them into exiles is often something that people do not want to know. In Cairo, talking to the Liberian boys, I had learned about massacres and the names of rebel leaders; I had also begun to understand the value of the past as a passport that cannot be taken away. Looking around Kuankan it was impossible not to ask: for this to be acceptable, what was it that happened at home?

Liberia, land of the free, was invented by the United States in 1847 as a country to which freed slaves, mainly from Ghana, could be returned. Samuel Doe had been a master sergeant in the Liberian army in the 1970s. He was, for a while at least, a protégé of the Americans, a small, burly man who sported an American military beret, and who came to power in a coup in 1980, after which he executed thirteen leading members of the government on the beach at Monrovia. Of Liberia's sixteen official tribes, Doe favoured the Mandingo, descendants of the ruling dynasty of medieval Mali and now inhabitants of Guinea's forest region; he took against the Gio and the Mano and slaughtered them. Despite an appalling human-rights record, and widespread knowledge that he was embezzling millions of dollars from Liberia's rich diamond and gold resources, Doe continued to be supported by the United States, for whom Liberia had been a steady provider of rubber – to counter Britain's monopoly of world rubber – since the 1920s.

For over a century power had lain with an oligarchy, sharing an American, Christian, English-speaking ancestry, and enjoying American-style institutions and American bank loans. In the late 1980s, nearby Burkina Faso became a rallying point for exiled Liberians, who, helped by Qaddafi's plans to train revolutionaries for his pan-African dreams, plotted to overthrow Doe with the help of neighbouring Sierra Leone and Ivory Coast. Among these plotters was another psychopath, Charles Taylor, who numbered among his disaffected followers many young children, whom he pressed into 'small boy units'. At one point, 20,000 out of the country's 75,000 fighters were children. Though it was Prince Johnson who closed in on Monrovia – and cut off Doe's ears before parading him in his underpants in a wheelbarrow through the streets – it was Charles Taylor who, in control of much of the country, was able to make the deals and secure the dollars with which to buy arms and followers. Between 1990 and 1994, $75 million a year was said to make its way into Taylor's war coffers through taxes levied on diamond exports, timber, rubber, gold and iron ore, as well as the marijuana that he fed to his child soldiers. Taylor might never, of course, have been so successful had it not been for the fortuitous timing of the first Gulf War, which distracted American attention away from Liberia, and let in a corrupt Nigerian-led international force called ECOMOG, who themselves plundered at will, providing arms to those warlords most open to their deals.

It was during the worst years of the civil war, between 1990 and 1997, that Charles Taylor's irregular forces, in weird and fantastic outfits and fuelled by greed, revenge, ethnic rivalry and drugs, went on frenzies of looting. They had developed a taste for Western possessions and they used drugged children to man checkpoints which became infamous for casual murder and theft. All Liberians in exile have a particular fear and horror of checkpoints, and it was at one that Mohamed saw his godmother's head hacked off and used as a football by the rebels. Headless corpses appeared in the streets of Monrovia. Not surprising, then, that Liberia's people fled. In a single year, 700,000 people left the country, for the most part taking little or nothing with them. All through the 1990s, Liberians crossed into Ivory Coast, Sierra Leone, and Guinea, where first hundreds, then thousands, then tens of thousands settled in Kuankan and other similar camps along the edge of the forest, where they were poor, but safe. And the longer the war went on, the more the splits and factions multiplied, to be manipulated and engineered by ECOMOG which dealt in looted resources and teak and other valuable hardwood with all of them, and the more the refugees fled.

It was not of course just Liberia. Though the *zone forestière* of Guinea is mainly full of Liberians, there are many other Africans there too. The 1990s were barely more peaceful in neighbouring Sierra Leone, where the largely Muslim former British colony emerged from three decades of one-party rule only to descend into a ten-year civil war triggered by an invasion of disaffected Sierra Leoneans from Liberia. Sierra Leone's own war would see executions, abductions, rape and at least 100,000 people mutilated by having limbs amputated; whole neighbourhoods of Freetown were set alight, often with their residents inside the buildings.

By 1997, when Charles Taylor brought his own kind of peace to Liberia, there were an estimated 7–8 million firearms in West Africa, transferred from one area to another as conflicts developed. UN investigators in 1999/2000 discovered a network of arms brokers and transport companies leading back to Slovakia, Moldova, Ukraine and Kyrgyzstan. The heady mixture of economic greed, ethnic tensions and ruthless warlords, and a conviction that power has its roots in the invisible world and that man's destiny can be revealed through marabouts, soothsayers, priests and 'heartsmen' (the providers of human hearts), had effectively created a generation of refugees driven to choose between starvation, life in a camp, or death at the hands of marauding soldiers dressed as women. 'I identified with those crazy people,' a former government official and later employee of a foreign food agency, Blanco Nelson, told a journalist. 'We all wear masks. Behind those masks is a mad, horrified people.'

When, on 19 July 1997, an exhausted people voted Charles Taylor, the most successful warlord of them all, into the presidency, the flow of Liberian refugees into neighbouring countries briefly stopped, and UNHCR and the international aid agencies turned their attentions to the consequences of the fighting within Sierra Leone, where rebel forces were now cutting off the arms and legs of their own citizens and driving those who survived abroad, fuelling further speculation that what was now being seen was a taste of the future – desperate, deracinated youths driven into frenzied wars by environmental degradation, vast movements of the population from countryside to city and high birth rates. Not everyone agreed, the critics of the 'New Barbarism' school arguing that, on the contrary, war was always war, whether fought with machetes or smart bombs, and that these West African wars were not different, just cheaper. For a while in Liberia it seemed as if peace might even be made to work. Taylor's victory in the presidential elections, closely observed by international experts, was accepted to be mainly fair.

But not for long. By the spring of 2002, Liberia's fragile five-year peace was coming to an end and rebel forces were once again challenging Taylor's rule; new men of war 'with no contrite hearts' and no compassion were again looting, raping and murdering, the insecurity of the country further threatened now by violent xenophobia in Ivory Coast, where leading government officials were inciting ethnic and religious hatred, and security forces were targeting victims, mainly in the Muslim north. Liberian refugees, Fatima and her five children among them, were again on the move. As they fled north into Guinea, Liberian government soldiers and rebels were moving west into Sierra Leone to abduct fighters and recruit mercenaries for the next stage in their war.

These, then, are the causes of Fatima's flight, and the flight of Peter her neighbour, and that of the Liberians in Cairo: violence, loss, grief, in comparison with which the uncertain waiting of the camp takes on a more benign aspect.

Benedict is fifteen, a lively, slender boy, watchful and old for his years. He is one of Kuankan's large population of 'single, unaccompanied children', or 'separated children', which is what the aid world calls children who have lost their families. When Benedict was thirteen, fighting broke out in Liberia's Lofa County, which borders Guinea and whose contours I had grown to know through the stories of the Liberians in Cairo. As soon as his family heard that both the rebels and the government forces were looking for boys to take as soldiers, they sent him into the bush to hide. Benedict went with others, for all the villagers, watchful of the approaching trouble, sent their own young sons with him. In the bush, the boys quickly learnt to survive. They discovered which leaves and berries were safe to eat, and which roots could be dug up and cooked. They found yams and plantains, cooking them over a small open fire, careful not to attract attention with their smoke, and adding them to the food brought out from the village from time to time by their parents. Weeks passed, and still the rebels were known to be in the area. Then one of the boys fell ill from something he had eaten; and after a few days died. Messengers from the village came to tell them that it was still not safe to go home.

Then, very early one morning, Benedict woke to see smoke rising on the horizon from the direction of his village. It was too far away to see more than wisps of white against the blue of the sky, and too far to hear any sounds, but later that day villagers appeared and told of a rebel attack. The smoke on the horizon grew thicker and newcomers now spoke of their huts being set alight, and how many of the occupants had been herded inside and burnt to death. Next morning, a neighbour of Benedict's arrived in the boys' camp. He told him that his parents, his younger brother and his elder sister were all dead, burnt to death inside their house.

It took Benedict and some of the other boys orphaned in the rebel attack four days to reach the border with Guinea. Accustomed to bush life, they had no difficulty surviving on foraged roots and fruit. Like Fatima, Benedict was welcomed by UNHCR and eventually taken to Kuankan by lorry. Offered the chance to live as a foster child with another refugee family, he asked to be allowed to live on his own, preferring the independence he had learnt in the bush. Once a month, together with the others, he collects his dried rations from WFP which he cooks for himself, together with a few onions, sweet potatoes and peppers which he has planted next to his hut. What he has left over, he sells, and buys dried fish and sugar. However much he saves, he is never able to afford a second set of clothes or a pair of shoes. When he arrived in Kuankan a year ago, the Guinean Red Cross gave him a T-shirt and a pair of shorts. Since he owns nothing else, he cannot wash them and is now embarrassed when he goes to school in such ragged and dirty clothes, though nothing will keep him from class. He wants, he says, to become a scientist. Because of the school, if for no other reason, he believes that the camp life is better than the one he was leading in the bush, though he says that he is hungry at the end of every month, just before the rations arrive. He does not like to talk about his parents or the past.

It is not easy to care for all these lost and orphaned children, those who saw their parents hacked to death or watched their homes burn down, those who got separated from their families during flight and cannot find them again, or were abducted and forced to do things as child soldiers that they are now too ashamed to confront. In the spring of 2003, there were just over 1,500 of these separated children in Kuankan. Some of them were babies, and children so small that they do not know their own names, and cannot say where they come from. They were found abandoned along the way towards the border, picked up and carried by other people escaping the fighting and given later to UNHCR. Photographs of these children are posted throughout the camps of West Africa in the hope that someone will recognise and claim them. I wonder whether Izako's son and daughter might be among them, and whether, not having seen them for so long, he would recognise them now. They make me think of the posters of the small, nameless children that hung in post offices and stations throughout liberated Europe during 1946, the year that 40 million displaced Europeans wandered in search of what had been or could again be home.

Throughout Guinea, the task of caring for the separated children falls to one of the most impressive of the international aid organisations, the International Rescue Committee, which, as implementing partner for UNHCR, runs the entire educational programme of the camps. Christian, who is in charge of the separated children, has 18 local offices and a staff of 127, who act as tracers and socialworkers; when parents are found, the children are driven or even flown to join them. These reunions can be terrifying for the children, particularly for those long separated from their families and shocked by all that they have experienced and seen. Boy soldiers in particular face the prospect of rejection, if not by their parents then by people from their villages against whom they have sometimes been forced to perform acts of great cruelty. Not long ago, Christian, whose office is in Conakry, arranged for a young boy called Sekou to be repatriated together with some of the Sierra Leoneans going home. He knew that the boy's parents were alive, and despite Sekou's evident reluctance, persuaded him that he should try to live with his family again. A few weeks later, Sekou was back, having walked through the bush for ten days to return to Conakry and the safety of the children's centre. When he was eleven, he had been kidnapped by the rebels. As a boy soldier he had been ordered to lock some people from his own village into their hut and set fire to it. The village would not accept him back into the community, and for his parents the shame of what he had done was too great for them to take him in.

The size of the task facing Christian across Guinea, and the delicate complexity of its demands, became clear to him not long ago when he heard about two refugee children living in a village just inside the border. He set off to find them in one of the white Toyota Landcruisers that have become the hallmark of international aid the world over. On making enquiries, he discovered that there were another 205 separated children in the same village. They had stopped there as they fled the war in Liberia, and were now stuck as a kind of indentured labour force for the Guinean villagers, who see nothing wrong in using these young children to work in their fields and houses in return for food and lodging. If there were 207 in a single border village, Christian reasoned, then how many more of these lost children must there be in other villages, brought to a halt by hunger along the path of their escape to safety? Few of the children had ever heard about the camps, and none knew what they were for or how to find them.

Finding ways of tracing these lost children's families, ensuring that in the meantime they are safe and not exploited, persuading the families who have taken them in and are benefiting from the work they do that the children would be better off in the camps, is a time-consuming and complicated process. In eighteen months, Christian and his staff have found 7,500 separated children along the border and in Conakry, all travelling absolutely alone. The true figure of the separated may be three or even four times as high, for it is widely accepted that somewhere between 5 and 7 per cent of children who become refugees in these flights from war become separated from their families along the way. How many never make it, but die on the way, too tired or hungry or frightened to go on, no one can say.

In Conakry, in a shabby building with a large inner courtyard shaded by mango trees, Christian runs a transit centre for the children who are on their way to be reunited with their families, or those whose problems are so acute as to make camp life too hard. He keeps it intentionally shabby; its dormitories have bare foam mattresses on the floor and ragged sheets: he does not want the children to see the place as anything but the most temporary pause between a past that they are putting behind them and a return to their families and a new life. It must not, he insists, become home. There are no toys and few books. The boys fashion cars out of old tins, ingenious contraptions of wire and cotton reels and flattened bits of metal, which clatter around the concrete at the end of strings. Some of the children who arrive at the transit centre do not speak. They listen, and will do what they are told to do, but they will not talk. It can take several months, says Christian, for them to say a single word.

In spite of the centre's transitory nature, Abu and his three brothers have been there for over a year, waiting for papers that will allow them to join an uncle in the United States. The boys are the sons of a prosperous and influential businessman and politician, a man much envied and much disliked, according to Abu, from a small town in Port Loko in Sierra Leone. When the rebels reached their town in 1997, his father was one of the first to be surrendered and killed. Their mother, eight months pregnant at the time, was shot and killed while struggling to squeeze out of a back window of their house with the younger children. The nine children, three of them by the politician's second wife, who had herself died in childbirth some months before, were caught and tied up. Abu's eldest brother was asked where their father kept his money. He did not know, so the rebels cut off first one of his hands, and then, when he still said nothing, the other. Abu's father had confided in him alone out of all the children and when it came to his turn, he led the soldiers to a hiding place in another house. While the men were clearing out the money, he managed to untie the other children and run off into the bush. He lost sight of his two sisters and two of his brothers, including the one whose hands had been amputated. When it was clear that they would not be able to go home, he set out through the bush with the four younger boys, carrying the smallest, then only two, on his back.

Once across the border, encountering no UNHCR officials, Abu stopped at the nearest village and asked for help. A farmer agreed to take in the boys and feed them in return for work. Every day, Abu, then aged twelve, worked in the house and in the market before going out into the cassava fields. One day, many months later, he heard about the camps and set off again with his little brothers, eventually reaching Guékédou, outside which there is a large camp for Liberians run by UNHCR. They had not been there very long when the camp itself was attacked by rebels coming across the border, and in a skirmish one of his brothers was killed. Abu took the surviving boys and set out again, only to be rounded up by the Guinean military, who accused them of being boy soldiers with the rebels. Eventually released, they made their way to Conakry, where they were found by Christian.

Only Abu can now remember their parents, though his twelve-year-old brother has a vague memory of their village and life before the war. The four boys sleep together on two mattresses pushed together, waiting for the moment when they may be sent to America. Two other brothers who share their room are also waiting to know their future. After many enquiries, Christian discovered that these two small boys' father was alive and living in Chicago, having escaped Liberia early in the war and gone on to make a life as a lawyer in the States. Their mother had died in the fighting, and their father had taken a new wife, a woman considerably younger than himself, and by whom he has two new children. Christian has written repeatedly but the letters that come back are vague; and to his last one there has been no answer at all.

Before I leave Conakry, I ask Christian to look out for Izako's children and give him a little money for the centre. He seems pleased. As we drive slowly back into the centre of the town in a traffic jam of overflowing communal taxis and decrepit lorries, as the extreme humidity of the day is giving way to cooler evening, he says it will go towards food for an evening of remembrance for Muna who had died two weeks before. Muna was twelve years old and Christian thought that she had died of Aids. He had found her living in the house of an elderly Guinean shopkeeper. Neighbours had told him that Muna had only been fed when she agreed to sleep with the man, and that after she had once tried to run away she had been kept locked in a cupboard for two days. At the transit centre, the other children had asked to have a party at which to remember her.

Kuankan is just one camp along a border crowded with settlements that have shifted, opened, closed, and opened again as fighting has ebbed and flowed up and down the *region forestière*. On 6 December 2000, as it was growing light, the small market town of Guékédou, a few hours' drive from the camp of Kuankan, was attacked by rebel soldiers coming across the border from Sierra Leone and Liberia and up to the Parrot's Beak. It wasn't the first attack in the area, for rebels and government soldiers from both countries had been making forays into Guinea all through the autumn. And it would not be the last, for in the months that followed, many Guineans and refugees would be killed in sudden incursions of fighters. In Guékédou, the local inhabitants fought back, anxious to defend their town, and soon the Guinean army arrived with reinforcements. When the locals seemed to be making little progress against the attackers and had been forced to allow the rebels to occupy a nearby village for several weeks, the army sent in helicopters which machine-gunned the central market square, having been informed that among the crowds were many Liberian and Sierra Leonean soldiers. The townspeople scattered and took to the bush. By evening the town was practically empty.

Guékédou happened to be one of the centres for UNHCR's eastern operations in Guinea, and several large houses and offices had been built to accommodate a substantial number of expatriate and local staff. There were also new offices and houses for the people working for the many international organisations that make up the aid constellation. It was a bustling, purposeful place. On the first day of fighting, UNHCR's office was destroyed. Then one of their staff was killed in Macenta, not far away, shot by rebels as they retreated along the road on which he lived. Another UNHCR employee was abducted, though later he was released. Seeing no signs of a quick end to the fighting, UNHCR ordered its staff to pull out of the area, and retreat, in their Landcruisers and lorries, to Kissidougou, a town further back from the border.

Until that autumn, Guinea had appeared to be a place of safety for West Africa's refugees. The armed incursions, however, brought to a head a fear that had long been simmering, that of Guinean support for the rebel factions seeking to overthrow Liberia's dictator. Faced by what looked like Liberian government reprisals for Guinea allowing the rebels to use the refugee camps as bases, Guinea's President Lansana Conté made a speech in which he called on his people to defend their country against all invaders. Widely reported in the papers and broadcast over the radio, his words were seen as a sign of a new, tough, stand against the refugees. The Liberians and Sierra Leoneans in the camps, declared President Conté, were supporting the fighters with food and arms. They should either go home or be confined to the camps, and in any case they should be controlled. Refugees were, he added, little better than cockroaches.

In the days that followed Guineans heeded his call. Vigilante groups were formed to harrass the refugees. Previously harmonious relations between Guineans and their vast foreign population were soured by attacks and accusations. There were large numbers of casualties. When the fighting died down, UNHCR and the international agencies took stock. One request made by President Conté was that the camps should be pulled back from the border areas, to make their use as rebel bases harder. Since the aid agencies no longer felt it to be safe to leave staff in such troubled places, they closed operations around Macenta and Guékédou – at the time, UNHCR's largest sub-office in the whole of Africa – and also opened up new camps several hundred kilometres further north, around Albadaria.

Early in 2003, I drove through Guékédou to see what remained of the camps that had been home to 400,000 Liberian refugees for almost six years. Mamadou, the boy who as an eleven-year-old had been dragged away by rebels from his parents and four younger brothers and sisters, had spent six years in a camp there. He had, he said, been happy. There is now almost no trace of it left. The sea of tarpaulin that once stretched across the plain as far as the eye could see has gone. It is as if it had never been there. The tents and huts have long since been pulled down, and the surrounding land has reverted to savannah and forest; only a few of the more solid international offices still stand, but they are empty and abandoned, with the look of mildew and collapse that comes quickly to these rainy areas. Guékédou itself is now poor and run down, the fine houses lived in by the expatriate staff shuttered and derelict. Not long ago, an aid worker from Kissidougou visited Guékédou to discuss the possibility of setting up a small education project in the town. The mayor greeted her with great caution. He would not wish the proposal to go ahead, he told her, unless the foreign investors were prepared to appoint a number of foreign resident staff and open a proper office. Guékédou was simply not prepared to risk a second economic collapse. It was a mark of what prosperity the refugees, however poor, bring.

Kissidougou, meanwhile, is booming. The aid organisations have built themselves offices and air-conditioned houses around central courtyards, behind tall gates. They have brought generators, installed internet and email, and improved the roads. At night, after dark, they gather in the Hotel Savannah to eat, drink beer, and talk over their day, parking their identical white Landcruisers in rows outside the door. The food is good, with distant memories of the French who once occupied this part of West Africa, and there is plenty of beer. The night I ate there, there was *steak au poivre* on the menu, and *poulet chasseur*. In Kissidougou there are doctors from Médecins Sans Frontières, logisticians and protection officers from UNHCR, sanitation experts, community workers, teachers and water engineers, men and women from several dozen different countries for whom the sense of purpose and adventure that comes with aid work offsets the punishing humidity and constant attacks of malaria and diarrhoea. At dinner, I was introduced to a woman from the Southern Illinois Trauma Center. She is in Kissidougou, she told me, to train refugees in torture care, so that they can counsel and help those among them for whom flight has included torture. 'Just do it,' reads the logo on the Nike sports cap worn by many of the foreign workers. I had known from Izako that his wife and children were not in Kuankan, but I had hoped to find some trace of them in Kissidougou. But no one knew of them, and their names were not on UNHCR's lists.

UNHCR is at its most impressive when conducting the emergency operations for which it is best known. Long-term situations, camps that endure year after year, are not its strong suit, and much of their running is sensibly left to implementing partners including IRC – who, along with programmes for separated children, organise much of the education in the camps – or Médecins Sans Frontières, who watch over the health of the refugees. All are aware of the envy among the local population under-standably created by the preferential treatment given to the refugees, and, in keeping with current thinking, efforts are made to integrate and widen services wherever possible, a challenge made easier in Guinea, where refugees and the surrounding people speak the same language and poverty is universal. Among the experts I passed along the tracks through the forest, hastening between camps and villages, were community and welfare officers, development experts and environmental consultants, come to improve conditions throughout the forest region. Refugees as 'agents of development' remains a catch-phrase from the early 1970s, when it was first noted that relief and emergency assistance to refugees, leading to dependency, was becoming an increasing burden to the neighbouring countries that took them in. But it is not an area where much progress has been made; UNHCR is not a development agency and other organisations have been reluctant to undertake expensive projects promoting self-sufficiency, particularly since refugee 'aid and develop-ment' has none of the urgency and drama of emergencies, and funds are hard to come by.

Just as it is not easy to care for separated children, whose lonely migrations have left them troubled and uncertain, so it is not easy to attract foreigners to work for very long in Guinea. The humidity and endemic diseases, the sense of imminent insecurity and lawlessness, and the widespread disinclination to stir up trouble, lest worse be unleashed, leave permanent posts unfilled or quickly abandoned. Short-term missions are greatly preferred. The idealism that drew many into the work has long since given way to despondency: hope has been eroded by the endless cutting of corners, the demands that eat into already meagre supplies, and the impossible logistics of caring for so many people with so few resources. The very nature of the daily problems – the arrival of insufficient quantities of tarpaulin, the axing of non-food items from the basket of provisions for each registered refugee, the quarrelling and rivalries of people reduced to so little – induces inertia and exhaustion. Guinea, one aid worker told me, has the reputation of being the worst country in the world in which to work.

Conakry itself has little to offer either foreigners or refugees, of whom 5–6,000 are said to live in the capital's poorer quarters, harrassed by their Guinean neighbours and prey to demands for bribes. For these refugees who do not wish to live in the camps, there is very little that UNHCR can do, beyond offering them a measure of protection against detention or *refoulement*. Danger, insecurity, is something everyone refers to, though 'fluid' and 'vulnerable' are the terms they use, as if the risks were thereby made more manageable with softer sounding words. David Kapya, who in 2003 was running the UNHCR office in Conakry, compares refugee flows to bush fires, something that may spread at any time, and that has to be contained and dealt with. Kapya's language is about the movement of populations, the raising of grants, the delicate administration of 200,000 desperate and confused people. He has little time for global policies.

Not long ago, in keeping with the world's declining budget for UNHCR and more pressing needs elsewhere, there were calls for cuts in spending in Guinea. Already pressed to the edges of necessity, UNHCR had no choice but to pare away at 'inessentials': an end to the occasional tins of sardines or bars of soap distributed in the camps, a cut-back on adult education and the gender-based violence programmes that were running throughout most of the country. But with the borders officially closed – though unofficially passable – who knows what new crisis may be bottled up beyond the confines of the camps, deep inside the forest areas that no one visits? The head of UNHCR's Nzérékoré office is a Peruvian called Cesar Ortega, who has run refugee programmes in many parts of the world. Contemplating the bridges and crossing points along the many miles of frontier, he waits and worries. 'Sometimes,' he says, 'I am lost. I think of all the people out there, who may be waiting to come in.'

In 2002, a scandal erupted in the enclosed world of Guinea's camps. Refugees, who live so close to the edge of life and are constantly alert to the possible fulfilment of wishes and needs, are particularly vulnerable to exploitation, and the news that a team of researchers doing a report on the protection of refugee children had discovered that women and young girls were being sexually exploited by refugees and aid workers alike, came as no great surprise to the foreign community. But the scale of it and the implications were shocking. It became clear to all involved that prostitution, in the sense of receiving the bare necessities of life in return for sex, had become endemic in places where small items – a few fish, a pair of shoes, a pretty scarf – can transform the meagreness of daily life to something with light and colour. Where people have nothing, even a stock cube acquires a powerful lure. In the soul-searching and recriminations that followed, seven teachers were dismissed from Kuankan's schools. When challenged, they reacted with surprise. 'This is Africa,' they said. 'This is our way.' As with the Guinean families providing the separated Liberian children with a refuge in return for work, they appeared genuinely astonished at the fuss. More worryingly, perhaps, what the inquiry brought out was the degree of sexual coercion and rape visited on refugee women all along the forest region and on their long journeys to find safety.

UNHCR, and in particular the High Commissioner, Ruud Lubbers, were not thought to have handled the situation well, initially dismissing it as something of no great importance. But later, realising the extent to which any scandal of this kind is damaging to the entire aid world, Lubbers set up a department in the Geneva headquarters to investigate all allegations of misconduct within UNHCR. In 2002, 125 separate complaints were explored, from corruption to harrassment. But what the scandal had done was to raise disquieting questions about the harm that humanitarian intervention can unthinkingly bring in its wake.

Not all Kuankan's refugees find it easy to accept the invisible line that keeps them in the camp, free and yet not free, dependent always on the whim and charity of others, enclosed in a cycle of poverty few can see a way to escape, beholden at every step to foreigners of apparently boundless power, yet often curiously pedantic and ungenerous. Something of the anger simmering among people condemned to permanent inactivity and supplication found expression not long ago in a teachers' strike. Mary is the head of education for the International Rescue Committee, a brisk and purposeful American in her fifties, from Seattle, who, having climbed in Tibet, felt the moment had come in her life to pay something back for the pleasures she had had. As an administrator and a former Peace Corps teacher, what Mary had to offer was schooling. IRC gave her a job.

Mary has 1,200 teachers and their assistants under her, having won a battle to include a woman assistant in every classroom as a way of protecting and encouraging girl pupils. Classes have seventy to eighty students in them, and it is often a struggle to keep the system flowing when the few school books go missing and have to be coaxed back with threats (and sometimes the help of sorcerers), when new pupils pop up unexpectedly in class having been sent over the border from nearby Liberian villages now that education there has collapsed and when so many students are so far behind for their ages and abilities. She is acutely conscious that she is running programmes that she herself has never witnessed, such as the evening education classes that begin in the schools after dark, long after she as a foreigner is forbidden to remain in the camps. She is also extremely aware that the children under her care would do far better in small classes in which they could overcome their fears.

Mary was in her office in Nzérékoré when she was informed that the teachers had gone on strike in Kuankan. 'Though it seemed to be about pay,' she says,

> it was really about anger. That was all I heard when I went to talk to them. 'We have no dignity,' was what they said. 'Why can't we have a plot on which to grow some food? Why will no one give us seeds?' Some of these people have been in Kuankan for ten years. They feel abandoned. They don't feel like real people any more. Our intentions are good but we do nothing for their self-esteem. It doesn't make me feel good to belong to a system that so diminishes people. So I talked to them about hope and the future and, even if I am a teacher, I began to think of ways to find them seed and hoes. These people are farmers. If you devalue and demotivate them what will happen to their children?

What struck the aid workers trying to resolve the strike was that some of the teachers had gone behind their backs and written directly to the headquarters of UNHCR in Geneva, taking the law, as it were, into their own hands. It seemed to some of them bold, even a little impertinent. To Mary, it was an excellent sign. It suggested a return to some kind of control over their own lives. But the ambivalence of the relationship between helper and helped is never far below the surface.

No one really believes in camps any longer, not in the sixty or so camps in *Guinee forestière*, not in those to be found dotted all over the world wherever refugees are on the move. Neither those who care for refugees, nor the people who live in them regard them as more than artificial constructs, designed as holding operations before something better can be worked out. The skills at which UNHCR excels, the creating and designing of these tented cities, lose their edge as months turn into years, and something of the early bustle and energy is lost in the apathy and unhappiness of unresolved situations. Once the humane and efficient answer to crises, but now forgotten by funders and resented by their hosts, these camps have become places where people wait, and where they do not want to be. Jason Scarpone, the new country director of IRC, shares Mary's longing to see more integration and development, more boosting of local economies, and less pursuit of unending crises. Like most of the new players in the international refugee world, he talks with passion about refugees as agents of development and the importance of widespread income generation.

Yet over 3 million people live in refugee camps in Africa today, in what have come to be called 'protracted refugee situations', long-lasting and intractable states of limbo in which dispossessed people are sequestered, concentrated and kept out of danger in a way that most closely suits host governments, the international community and often the refugees themselves, who feel safe in the company of others in the same position in a strange land. Camps are places dealt with by other people. However, camps are also profoundly destructive places. More fundamentally even than prisons, they are a denial of all freedoms, even the freedom to make the most basic choice. Those who service them do so humanely and with certain standards in mind; but in practice these standards are extremely low. In practice too, as an evaluation report produced by UNHCR in 2002 concluded, the 'circumstances and conditions' of these refugees are deteriorating all the time, as conflict becomes endemic, asylum ever more unpopular and the refugees themselves turn into pawns in larger political games.

In Africa, 'protracted refugee situations' are to be found where the land is poorest, the climate harshest, the conditions most inhospitable. Though peace agreements in Burundi, the Congo, Sudan and elsewhere may bring a measure of peace, violence has become a way of life for a generation of young Africans. And Kuankan, like the other camps up and down the forest, is full of children, single women and adolescents. As world attention shifts away from them, towards new, more imperative crises, so do money and rights – rights to move about, to a proper legal status, to freedom of choice, to an education. They feel truly forgotten. It was this world, of camps without seeming futures, so poor that even a bucket spelt riches, that Suleiman and Mamadou, Mohamed and Musa, had all turned their backs on when forced to flee the war in Liberia. However terrifying the journey, however unpredictable the future, staying in a camp was not an option any one of them considered bearable. I had not found Izako's family, and they were not on the UNHCR database of names, but I had seen the conditions under which, somewhere along the *region forestière*, they were probably living; and I had come to understand better the desperation of the Liberians in Cairo, their ferocious need for education, and for another life, in a better place.

The tragedy for Fatima and Peter and their neighbours goes well beyond the refugees to Guinea itself, its present and its long unfinished business with the past. Guinea as a country is neither poor nor without possibilities. It is a fertile and rich land in which four of Africa's major rivers rise. But with its economy stagnant, its borders under constant assault, its population swollen by huge numbers of refugees it has neither the resources nor the desire to care for, it is not flourishing.

In Kuankan, I asked about the extent of depression amongst the refugees, whether people so long frightened and displaced showed signs of acute sadness and apathetic despair. At the far end of the camp, in one of the single-storey brick buildings that signal its offices, is a mental-health clinic opened two years ago by a Norwegian agency. It is run by a Liberian nurse called Sophie. Not long ago, the UN carried out a survey of the health of the refugee populations along these forest regions and concluded that 12 per cent of them suffered from some degree of clinical depression. Sophie rejects the figure as grossly low. She explains that in Kuankan, depression is described by a curious phrase and imagery, brought by the Liberians from home, where any profound lowering of the spirits goes by the name of 'open mole'. In this case, the mole is the fontanelle, on the crown of the head, which remains open for many months after a baby's birth. In later life, as Sophie's depressed patients tell her, this hole can open once again and let in depression.

Sophie's treatment is simple. She asks a herbalist attached to the clinic to cut the patient's hair, clean the head, and rub in herbal potions; she herself provides paracetamol and counselling. But what she really does is listen. Behind every open mole, as she is all too aware, lies a terrible tale of rape, loss and violence. As the story unfolds, the mole is felt to close.

The day comes when the patient appears proudly in the clinic to announce that the gap has gone.

And the refugees keep coming. In the far east of Guinea there are twenty crossing-points from the Ivory Coast, and nearly as many from Liberia; but there is often little, in this hilly, densely forested countryside, to mark a frontier. At Thio, a path winds away through a clearing down towards a patch of forest, with the river beyond. It is hard to convey the richness and thickness of this tall forest, or the variety of the leaves that spread out like giant hands or whispery fronds over the bush below. This is the boundary with the Ivory Coast, and up this path, when I visit it in the early spring of 2003, are walking small groups of people, thirty to forty a day, weighed down by bundles and small children. Thirty, across a single border point, is worrying for those who work with UNHCR, for it suggests a pattern of oppression that might easily turn to panic. It is when the numbers reach the hundreds, a hastening, jostling, anxious crowd pushing its way across, over bridges and through rivers, that a state of permanent half-emergency becomes a crisis. At Thio there is a small military post with a policeman and several members of the Guinean Red Cross waiting to process the day's arrivals, the first step in this particular odyssey to safety. In the days and weeks that follow, it will involve medical checks, registration, the allocating of a tent or hut, a few clothes, a ration book, the promise of a school.

At Lola, further into Guinea along this particular journey, there is a transit centre, a former reception centre for children. Necessity has turned this immense hangar into a staging post for new arrivals. I stop to look. A young Guinean working with the Red Cross is standing by the door with a clipboard. He tells me that there are 1,002 people inside, 444 of whom are children. Reading off his clipboard, he gives me the figures: 925 Liberians, one Ghanaian, thirteen Nigerians, twenty-eight Ivorians, twenty Nigerois, eleven Malians and four Guineans, themselves former refugees in the Ivory Coast, now driven home by fighting in the country they had made their home. The hangar is busy, noisy; it makes me think of Ellis Island in New York, the great reception centre for immigrants to the New World at the turn of the century, except that it is dark, with shafts of bright light like searchlights in the surrounding dimness, the motes of dust clear in the air. On the floor, the refugees have built themselves a mosaic of small patches of territory, their mats, boxes, containers, jerry cans, baskets and bundles, the luggage of West Africa's refugees, each denoting a small, private area. Within these spaces lie small children. It is a strangely peaceful scene.

Fallah was born in a small village in northern Liberia, not far from the border with Guinea. She is a restless, assertive woman, eager to talk and full of gestures, and she is uneasy in the hangar, eager to get on and sort her life out. She says that she is not married, but that she has two sons. In 1996, when the older of the two was ten, rebels came to her village in search of boy recruits. She heard stories about women on their own being abducted and raped. Fallah took her children and fled over the border, not into nearby Guinea, but towards Ivory Coast, where she sensed that they would be safer. Being strong and energetic, the three-day walk, carrying clothes and mats on her head, and pulling along the five-year-old, was not a problem. She settled in Danane, a town well inside the border, and found work on a cassava farm. The two boys went to school. With her wages, she bought cocoa, which she was able to sell in the market at a profit. She found a friend, a younger woman, Maja, who like her had fled the fighting in Liberia. Maja also had children but no husband. After the elections in Monrovia in 1997, and Charles Taylor's doubtful victory, she thought of going home to enjoy the promised peace, but by now the two women and their children felt settled in the Ivory Coast.

Late in 2002, political unrest in previously safe Ivory Coast, sparked off by politicians fanning ethnic differences, began to spread to the countryside. Fallah and Maja watched and waited. Then the day came when Ivorian rebels began to close in on Danane, and word came that they too were looking for recruits and porters. Fallah's sons were now aged ten and fifteen. The two women packed up what they could carry, Maja put her eighteen-month-old daughter on her back, and they set out for the border with Liberia, planning to travel on to Guinea – just as I imagined that Izako's wife must have done, carrying one small child and pulling along the other. They walked for three days, stopping at night to sleep under the bushes, aware that the rebels were not far behind them, occasionally hearing shots in the distance.

On 28 January 2003, they reached the Cavally river, which separates Ivory Coast from Liberia. The bridge across, which acts as frontier between the two countries, was closed. By now they could hear persistent shooting in the forest behind them. The river was not very deep, though the current was strong. Between them, the two women managed to get their four children and baggage across. They laugh, telling me their story, two women friends who have endured much together. But then they stop laughing. They say that it had been all right for them, because they were strong and fit, but sitting alone on the banks of the river were small children, terrified by the fighting in the forest behind but unable to swim and too frightened to cross. It is then that Fallah describes watching a little girl hesitate, then slip into the water, where for a second she seemed to hold steady against the current; but almost immediately, she lost her footing and was pulled under and swept away, her yellow T-shirt bobbing brightly in the water as it was carried along until it vanished from sight in the sunshine.

Chapter Seven

The Corridors of Memory:
The Naqba and the Palestinians of Lebanon

We find stories tossed in the streets of our memory.
Elias Khoury

When Mahmut went to collect the few belongings – the mattresses, quilts and cooking pots – that his family had salvaged from their house, he brought them piled high on a camel, borrowed for the journey, over the mountains. Zainab remembers the animal well. She had not been expecting anything so exotic, and she can recall it with the sharpness of a photograph, just as she remembers with perfect clarity the earlier flight from Balad al Sheik, stumbling without shoes across the rocky hillside as dawn was breaking and the first slit of sun touched the horizon, crouching down in the gullies, dragging along her younger brothers and sisters by their hands, while behind them she could hear the crack of the rifles and see the flames as the soldiers set fire to their house. It was cold and very still.

That was New Year's Eve 1947. She was twelve. The Haganah, the Jewish underground armed organisation, was beginning its assault on the mountain villages above Haifa, flushing out the Arab fighters, of which her father was one, driving them further back up into the mountains towards the isolated stone shack that her grandfather had built for the hot summer months, when he lent his village house to guests.

The attack on Balad al Sheik, one of the first acts of reprisal in the war between Arabs and Zionists, had been prompted by the killing of forty-one Jewish oil-refinery workers the night before, itself a gesture of revenge for the deaths of six Palestinians at the gates of the refinery. Zainab's father, Mahmut, unlike many of the other villagers, owned a gun; he was a man of standing and land, some of which he had sold to buy the gun and the ammunition to go with it, for the Arab resistance was very short of weapons. He was a farmer, she explains to me when I go to see her in the autumn of 2002, who grew vegetables, carrots and cabbages, as well as corn, wheat and barley, made olive oil from his trees, and a little vinegar from the many grapes that grew on their vines; her mother supervised the making of jam, and there was a small shop in which the produce was sold. There were large black and white Dutch cows that gave milk three times a day, and some sheep. Their house had many rooms because her father was a well-known man, and many people came to call on him and drink the coffee that was always kept ready for visitors.

Zainab can also remember, and can recite, step by step, the stages of their journey into exile: the weeks in Majed al Koroum, while her father crept back to their village under cover of dark to see whether it was safe to go home; the drive by hired lorry in search of greater safety when he returned to tell them that there was little left standing of the fine house, with its two storeys and many rooms, and that many people in the village had been slaughtered, whole families lined up against the village wall and shot in reprisal for Haganah deaths. An account written later recorded that orders had been given by Haganah to 'encircle the village, harm the largest possible number of men, damage property, and refrain from attacking women and children'. After they left Majed al Koroum, they heard that twelve of those who elected to stay had been executed in the village square by the Israeli defence force. She can describe the months spent in a rented house over the border in Lebanon, waiting, trying to understand the nature of the war, while Mahmut went backwards and forwards across the border, visiting his family only by night, and the women prepared food and provisions for the fighters up in the hills; and the arrival, many months later, at Shatila, the refugee camp opened not long before on Beirut's western slopes.

Fifty-four years later, she remembers these things very clearly, particularly the family house, their lands and the way the fruit trees grew, the many celebrations of village life, and the occasional trips into Haifa by bus No. 1 from the village square to see her aunts, or to buy clothes and shoes and the fruit that could not be found in the hills. She rehearses these memories every day, savouring them as an image of lost and stolen happiness. Balad al Sheik had, she says, two coffee shops, and a school dating back to Ottoman times. And when Marwan, her eldest son, who has himself never been to the Occupied Palestinian Territories, takes his mother out on Fridays in his car up into the hills around Shatila, she points up at the bald ochre mountains that surround Beirut, their lower slopes spotted by trees and scrub, and says: 'That is what our mountain was like. That house, over there, on that hillside, was what our house was like.

Those fields, below, those could be our fields.' Memory is, and has been for half a century, the defining element of her life.

Zainab is sixty-seven, a mild, silent woman with a soft, round face and sad eyes. On her face can be seen what Edward Said once called the 'marks of disaster uncomprehended', the reflection of 'a past interrupted, a society obliterated, an existence radically impoverished'. In her expression there is a look of profound resignation and a complete absence of all expectation, as if her life has been a series of improvisations and suspended hopes. For the past fifty-four years Zainab has been a refugee, a displaced person living in the Palestinian refugee camp of Shatila which, in 1982, became a byword for Israeli violence and aggression. Among its inhabitants there are not very many today who remember the Naqba, the 'disaster', the name Palestinians all over the world give to the uprooting from their homeland in 1948, when the British pulled out of their former mandate territory and the new state of Israel was carved out of land the Palestinians believed to be theirs. There are so few survivors from the flight into exile, either in Shatila or in Lebanon's eleven other official Palestinian refugee camps, or in the diaspora that has taken Palestinians to camps in Jordan, Syria, Kuwait and from one end of the world to the other, because refugee life is hard on the elderly, and diabetes, high blood pressure, respiratory and heart diseases have all taken their toll of those who fled as children in 1948. Zainab, like all the older refugees, looks much more than her sixty-seven years. She is severely diabetic and has had a heart attack. She walks slowly, with a slight stoop. The few surviving 'notables', the men and women who were already adult and leaders in their communities when they fled, are regarded as people apart, both for what they have been through and for what they remember, custodians not simply of the Palestinian collective history, but as particular affirmation that the Palestinians exist, and have always existed, for all the attempts to make them disappear from the mind and conscience of much of the world.

Over half of those now living in Shatila are children, the grandchildren of the Naqba; neither they nor their parents, born when the camp was a rocky field of tents tethered precariously in the hard ground, have ever been to what was once Palestine, but they hold on to the dream of going home with an intensity which, like Zainab's, defies questioning. Ask a passing child in the camps where he comes from and he will reply with the name of a village, the village from which his grandparents came over half a century ago. Ask him to draw a flag, and he will draw the flag of Palestine. The 'right of return', what the Palestinians call *awdah*, the much-debated, much-disputed Clause 194* which no one except the Palestinians any longer believes could possibly happen, is more than an act of faith to them; it is an immutable fact, a necessity. 'I want to go home,' says Zainab. 'I want to go home and grow old there and be buried in our cemetery.' The fact that the village of Balad al Sheik has long since been bulldozed, that the square in which the men once sat and talked is now a concrete playground played on by Israeli children, that the marble slabs have long since been stolen from the tomb of Shaykh Izz al-Din al-Qassam, the great fighter against British rule, that a Jewish settlement stands on what were once her father's olive groves, that apples grow in place of corn and that her identity card, as a Palestinian without a state, forbids her from going anywhere, is neither interesting nor important to her. The name Balad al Sheik does not even exist anymore: it is now Tel Chanan, part of the larger town of Nesher. But what concerns Zainab is very simple: it is her right to go home and the right of her children and grandchildren to inherit the land of her father and her husband. It is that dream, that certainty that return will happen, that has sustained her for over half a century, that has held her together during the years of poverty and deprivation, through the shelling and the civil war, the fear and the uncertainty. It has made possible an entire life lived in a corridor of the mind. Like all dreams, it has become an alibi, a shadow; and like all such shadows, it does not bear disturbing.

Jabra Ibrahim Jabra, writing about his boyhood in Bethlehem, described his childhood as a 'blend of memory and dream, of existential intensity and poetic trance, a blend in which the rational and the irrational interpenetrate and intertwine'. Jabra, who spent his life in exile in Iraq, said that these memories formed a well full of water gathered 'from the rains of the heaven and the flow of experiences – to go back to when we are seized by thirst and when drought afflicts our land'. But childhood memories, as he noted, are susceptible to alteration, and when a person draws on that particular well, he can never be sure whether the water will rise cold or turbid and muddy; while the memories of the lost Palestine are frozen in time, immutable and forever happy.

Return to Palestine is not, of course, all that Zainab wants. She wants, so much that it makes her cry to talk about it, to see her third son Tariq again. Tariq was forced to flee Beirut after the Israeli invasion of 1982 when he was a young fighter for the PLO, and he now works in Oxford. In the last ten years, she has seen Tariq just once, when he was living in

*Under UN General Assembly Resolution 194, all Palestinian refugees wishing to return home were permitted to do so 'at the earliest practicable date'. But fifty-six years later, except in special cases, the refugees have not been allowed back.

Cyprus and was smuggled into Shatila for a three-day visit when she was
ill, although he had to leave early when it became known that the
Lebanese army was still looking for him. 'Tell him,' she said, when I
explained that I would soon be meeting Tariq in Oxford, 'tell him that I
am well and healthy. Tell him that you found me . . .' Then she paused,
looking for the right word, her expression of anxiety and defeat barely
visible in the dim room. 'Tell him that you found me fresh.'

Shatila, in the pale twilight of an early winter evening, is a wretched place.
Long before you reach the camp itself, walking past the bombed Gaza
hospital, once the pride of the Palestinian doctors and now home to some
900 'displaced' refugees, and through the street market that divides the
former camp of Sabra from Shatila, you begin to notice the smell. It is a
sweet, heavy, sickly smell, and it catches in your throat. It comes from the
meat, newly butchered and piled on barrows; from the chickens penned in
wicker cages and piled one on top of another; from the vegetables fallen
to the ground and rotting; and from the sewage, which seeps up steadily
from the gutters so that the earth road is wet and sticky with refuse. It is a
smell of people – too many people, living too closely together, in too great
poverty.

In 2003 there were a little over 12,300 people in the camp of Shatila,
occupying an area of 200 metres by 200 metres, where Palestinians mix
with Syrians, poor Lebanese from the south, Kurds, and Africans seeking
asylum. It has one of the densest populations outside Gaza in the world.
Walking deeper into the camp – although because there is no perimeter
fence, no army checkpoint, the residents of Lebanon's other camps
dismiss Shatila with scorn as not a true camp – among people shuffling
their way past stalls and donkeys and carts and barely moving cars, the
road narrows first into alleys, and then into passages and corridors, some no
wider than a man's shoulders. Below, where water pipes coil along the
uneven ground, and rubbish and rubble choke the gutters, lies a patina of
dirt and water. Recent plans by the UN Relief and Works Agency,
UNRWA, and the European Union to install sewage, drainage and water
systems have stalled; there is never enough water, and what there is arrives
by mains pipes laid along sewage drains, with latrines that flow into open
drains and along the pathways. Above, where successive generations of
the original families have built rooms, one above the other, in precarious
breeze-block boxes that seem to teeter as they rise, the buildings almost
touch. Forbidden to build outwards by the Lebanese, reluctant to confer
any sense of permanence on the refugees whose arrival they were forced

to accept, the Palestinians have built first into the spaces between buildings, and then upwards, accommodating children and grandchildren on the same site where the first arrivals pitched their tents in the 1940s and 1950s. Much of the inner camp is almost completely dark, the daylight reduced to a pale glimmer by the overarching buildings and the canopy of wires that dangles not far above one's head. Windows open on to walls. The air smells damp. Inside, the flickering and uncertain voltage – eight hours of electricity a day – and the 20-watt bulb are hardly enough to be able to distinguish expressions on people's faces. Talking to Zainab, wanting to learn what being a refugee means to the Palestinians of her generation, I cannot see what she is thinking. I peer at my notes, unable to make out what I am writing.

Zainab has three ground-floor rooms which she occupies with her two unmarried daughters and her husband, who, like her, fled the Naqba as a child from Balad al Sheik, and to whom she had been betrothed long before the families came to Shatila. There is almost nothing in the main room to suggest a past: no early photographs, no pictures, no ornaments. There was no time, she says, to bring them. To one side, at the end of a damp, almost entirely dark passage, lives one son, Eyad, with his family; on the floor above, Marwan, her eldest son, now fifty, with his wife Naifa and three sons. A third son, Ghassam, was knocked down by a car when he was ten; in a coma for many weeks, his speech has never fully come back. A daughter, Aziza, who is married to a pathologist, is close by. Zainab has fifteen grandchildren, two of them Tariq's daughters in Oxford. Her father was one of the first refugees to settle in Shatila, the site for his tent given to him by UNRWA when it was set up to run the camps in 1950, near to the mosque, which was a good spot in the early days. Now it lies in the dark inner heart of the camp.

Zainab remembers Shatila as she first saw it in the winter of 1949, a hostile, unwelcoming place where the winter winds blew the sand and grit into the food and the tents, loosening the tent poles and making the canvas flap with a swishing sound. Then, the hundred or so tents, of many shapes and sizes, were scattered between cactus and prickly pears, and in the daytime, when the men went off to look for casual labour on Beirut's building sites, the women would take the children to the woods on the edge of the camp and sit under the shade of the pine trees to escape the glare of the sun. At night, there was no room for the boys under the canvas and they slept outside on the sand; when they woke they found themselves covered in dew. There was very little water; what there was came by lorry, brought by UNRWA and rationed, distributed by the Palestinian men too old or frail to go looking for work. Some of the water vats had been used to transport oil: the water came out dirty, undrinkable. With the water came food rations: flour, sugar, rice, a little oil. The newcomers were destitute, wholly dependent on charity. The life was harder on the city Palestinians, educated and professional people from Haifa, Jaffa and Acre, who were not readily absorbed into the idle and impoverished existence of a camp that was closely controlled by a foreign power, and denied citizenship, working permits or travel documents.

Zainab did not go to the first school, opened in a tent not far from the newly built mosque and the separate latrines for men and women, though her younger brothers did. She stayed with her mother to look after the younger children. She never learnt to write, but Marwan says that when he was a boy, it was his mother who knew when he had failed to finish some part of his homework and sent him back to study until it was done. Two of Zainab's sons today have master's degrees; one of her four daughters is a teacher.

The first years in the camp, for all the hardship, were the best years. Then the Lebanese people in the villages around were welcoming, sympathetic to the Palestinians who, they had been told and believed, were temporary visitors, soon to go home. They saw them suffering and gave them fruit and vegetables. As the tents grew old and worn, they were reinforced, first by low walls to keep the rains out, then by tin walls and roofs, the tin taken from the drums used to supply oil and flattened with a hammer. However carefully they prised open the drums, there were always holes which let in the rain at night, and the tin was covered with the logos and names of charities and suppliers, so that the camp took on the look of advertisement billboards. It was a long time before there was anything on the ground except for bare earth and sand, which seemed always too hot, so that the children were given wooden clogs to wear. Water pipes, of a kind, were laid. Electricity appeared after two enter-prising refugees negotiated with a man who owned property near the camp to tap into his source. It was rationed, like everything else, but it was enough to power a radio and provide dim lighting after dark. Then, as the years passed and it became clear that there would always be more people in the camps – more children, more arrivals fleeing fresh fighting in the villages of Israel – and as economic conditions in the Middle East worsened, so the neighbourly Lebanese became suspicious, resentful. When those of the Naqba talked at night about all that they had left behind, there was greater longing for what had been lost. They were not just poor now; they had been betrayed – by the British, by the Israelis, by the Arabs. No one, it seemed, was willing to see in the Palestinians a people dispossessed of their land and in need of political and economic support; truly they had become objects of charity, without voice and without rights. It gave the past a sharper edge.

There is no one single culprit for the Naqba, no one cause to explain how or why, in little less than a year, 700–800,000 Palestinians – almost two-thirds of the population – fled the houses and lands where they and their forebears had been born and grew up, and went into exile, taking with them little more than the clothes they were wearing. It was not the British on their own, though the Balfour Declaration of 1917, which promised a homeland for the Jews in tandem with respect for the rights of the Palestinians, is spoken of today with the immediacy of an event that took place within the last few days, and with the full force of blame. Nor was it solely the fact that the Arab countries were irresolute when it came to supporting the Palestinians, and the Palestinian leaders divided and poorly organised, while the fighters with their few thousand rifles, of varying ages and efficiency, were equipped neither physically nor psychologically to fight side by side with others. Nor was it just the particular brutality of the Haganah and Zionist groups, though they were indeed better led, better equipped and more than willing to make the most of all weakness they encountered. By the early autumn of 1947, the Yishuv, the Zionist party, held over 10,000 rifles, 702 machine guns, and many submachine guns and mortars; and, unlike the Arabs, they had factories in which to produce more weapons. The Naqba began and grew out of war.

On 29 November 1947, the UN General Assembly voted to support the partition of Palestine into two states, one Jewish and one Arab. There were attacks by Jews on Arabs, whose leaders completely rejected partition – which would have given the Jews much of the coastal plain and Galilee – and attacks by Arabs against Jews. The skirmishes grew sharper. The exodus of the Palestinians began in late December 1947, starting with middle-class families from west Jerusalem, Haifa and Jaffa, towns already earmarked as lying within the borders of the new Israeli state. Their flight proved infectious. As household after household packed what they could into cars, taxis and hired lorries and onto the backs of mules and horses, so neighbours lost their nerve and began packing too, mindful of the spreading brigandage, the stories of attack and revenge, the outbreaks of fighting and the ominous shadow of future Israeli rule. Palestinian businesses closed, then in their wake clinics, offices, schools. Already by

January 1948, before the British left, the clashes between Arab irregular forces and the well-trained Haganah were growing more murderous; there were snipers, bomb attacks, kidnappings. A sense of imminent catastrophe clouded people's thoughts.

When, in the late spring, the Hagannah launched a number of carefully targeted attacks, it was against a people already fragmented and disoriented by departures and defeats. With every Haganah victory, the resolve of those who had determined to stay and fight weakened. Tiberias, Haifa, Jaffa and Safad fell, one after the other. Their populations joined the exodus. By the beginning of May all but 3–4,000 of Haifa's 70,000 Arabs had left. The inhabitants of the villages and the countryside, who had always looked to the city dwellers for leadership, followed them, though they, like the city people, assumed that they would soon be back. No one bothered to take much with them. Right up to April 1948, it had not been part of the official Zionist strategy to precipitate Palestinian evacuations, though the assumption had always been that the fewer Arabs remaining within Israel the better the prospects for the new state. The Haganah evacuations, which started as isolated decisions to clear areas of particular strategic concern, soon turned into conscious efforts to encourage people to leave.

Events were now moving very fast, with Israelis taking over Palestinian lands, and Palestinians continuing to leave, their departure hastened by killings. As villages were deserted, so they were destroyed to make way for new Israeli settlements. Walid Khalili, author of a study on the destroyed villages, *All that Remains*, calculated that 416 villages were occupied and destroyed. There were massacres, like the one at Deir Yassin, a village near Jerusalem, where at least 107 people were killed by the Stern Gang in April 1948. The Arabs had abandoned their cities, Ben Gurion said, speaking to the People's Council, 'with great ease, after the first defeat, even though no danger of destruction or massacre confronted them . . . Indeed, it was revealed with overwhelming clarity which people is bound with strong bonds to this land.' The rest of the world found it convenient to believe him.

By the summer of 1948, it became apparent that almost a million people had crossed the borders into Lebanon, Jordan and Syria. Count Bernadotte, the UN Mediator for Palestine, appalled by the enforced exodus, began pressing Israel to accept repatriation as part of a comprehensive settlement for the area. In December, the 'right of return' for all Palestinians was endorsed by the UN General Assembly. But by now the Zionists had perceived that an almost completely Jewish state was in fact a possibility, and that to let the Palestinians back would be to accept a fifth column in their midst. Where, in any case, would the repatriated Palestinians go? Their villages had already been bulldozed and their lands occupied by Jewish refugees, newly arrived from Europe. In the spring of 1949, while Zainab and her family lingered in the house near the Lebanese border, trying to gauge the possibility of return, the US tried to force Israel to take back 250,000 people – a third of all those who had left. Tel Aviv's offer to take 65–70,000 was judged too derisory to discuss, and the US proved unwilling to bring pressure.

In any case, it was all too late. Palestine's exiles had become refugees, to be used in the decades to come by Israelis and Arabs alike as pawns for propagandists and politicians. And not simply refugees: like Zainab's family, most had left nearly everything behind them – photographs, deeds of ownership, family records, mementoes, clothes, books, furniture, the fabric of each and every history. Only a very few have ever been able to claim back a single item. They had become a people without a past, and their minds, as the Lebanese novelist Elias Khoury, born the year the British left, wrote, 'a black cave full of obliterated memories'.

It is Tariq, Zainab's fourth son, working today as a manager in a printing firm in Oxford, who talks most easily about the violence that came to Shatila in the late 1970s. Tariq is forty-eight. Like his three brothers and four sisters he grew up in the camp, listening to his grandfather talk of Balad al Sheik; and not just his grandfather, but all the other families who came to Shatila from the villages above Haifa, united under a renowned fighter called Fakhri el Hassan, for in exile the Palestinians have chosen to keep to the configurations of their villages, neighbours often living close together within the camps. The different quarters even take the names of villages. One day, when Tariq was already a grown man, he saw a photograph on a calendar of a view overlooking Haifa: 'And I knew,' he said, when I met him in Oxford in a small trim house with a garden on the Cowley Road, 'that it was Balad al Sheik, just by seeing the photograph. All my childhood my parents had talked about it. I came to be able to almost feel it.' He has never been to the Occupied Palestinian Territories.

Tariq was born in the tent into which Zainab moved when she married. By then she was sixteen, and Tariq was her third child. He remembers his first years of tent life as perfectly normal, though even as a small child he was conscious that it was considered a temporary arrangement, something that was going to end at any moment when the family returned to Balad al Sheik. He was a naughty but loving child, a tyrant to his mother, whose favourite he knew himself to be. When she walked to collect water in a pitcher and carried it back balanced on her head, he demanded that she carry him as well.

His father, who had spent the first years in the camp as a casual labourer on Beirut's building sites, had then gone to work in the Red Crescent hospital, in the sterilising unit. The family collected the tin drums from their UNRWA rations, beating them into flat sheets to use as walls and anchoring them to wooden posts; he remembers the tent gradually being transformed into a shack, with a corrugated-iron roof and a mud and straw floor. There was always trouble with the door, the tin proving too flexible to keep upright, and his father, says Tariq, became very skilled at mending and repairing. By 1973, when Zainab was twenty-five, there were eight living children, but Tariq believes that there had also been some stillbirths. Shatila had only one midwife, and many newborn babies died. Those who survived started life in clothes made out of UN flour sacks and Tariq remembers how the women artfully used the logo of two hands meeting over the flags of the UN and the US to adorn the children's underclothes. In the summer, Shatila was full of small children running around with the flags and logos on their pants and vests.

They were the first family in Shatila to have a fridge, and a gramophone inside a wooden box on which they listened to recordings of famous Arab singers. His father, says Tariq, insisted on the boys wearing clean shoes to school, and later to work. 'He was proud of us. He made us proud. He spent all his time looking after us, working.' Their house, then as now, was 'rubbish', as Tariq puts it, 'and we all knew it. But my father made the best out of every square centimetre.' His own father, Tariq's grandfather, treated the family's tent site exactly as he treated his land in Balad al Sheik: if he discovered anything out of place, he was furious. 'He was a very small man,' says Tariq, 'very short. He sat guard on a chair and watched.'

Tariq grew up angry. He hated hearing about what had happened in Balad al Sheik, and hated the position he saw his family reduced to. 'It was the most important thing in my life,' he says, 'being a rebel.' He hated the way that the sitting room was also the bedroom and the room in which they ate, and he was ashamed at the way they ate on the floor. He wanted to become someone, someone who could fight back. His chance came in 1968, when the Palestine Liberation Organization took root in the Lebanon. It started with a football club. His grandfather, still a respected figure within the exiled Palestinian community, had a friend who had rented rooms bordering on the back of the camp which included a small backyard. Tariq persuaded him to let him use this. He got hold of some bricks and some sheets of corrugated iron and built a shack; along the front he painted the words 'Cubs of Palestine' and invited his friends to join, Lebanese boys as well as Palestinians. He managed to find uniforms and booked his team to play in tournaments. He was fourteen.

Fatah, Arafat's political group within the Palestinian resistance movement, was already active in Shatila, though the organisation itself remained secret and underground. They were looking for energetic young boys with initiative. Tariq, who sometimes walked around the open walls at the top of the half-built breeze-block houses with no fear of heights, four and five storeys up, was just the kind of boy they wanted. His father was already a member. One day, he asked Tariq to come and sit with him in the main room. They sat on the floor together on mattresses. His father showed him a gun he kept hidden in a wardrobe. This, he said to Tariq, 'is for Palestine'. The occasion stuck in the boy's mind, and though the gun was later destroyed when the camp was shelled and part of a wall fell on the wardrobe, Tariq always remembered the solemnity with which his father had spoken. Before he was sixteen he had had several brushes with the Lebanese police when they came flaunting their authority over the refugees around the perimeters of the camp.

In 1973 the eighteen-year-old Tariq graduated from school with high marks and was among the handful of boys chosen to sit the entrance exam for the American University in Beirut. To his great pleasure, he passed and began to attend the classes in the handsome colonial building in West Beirut, walking between the medieval dark alleys of Shatila and the airy lightness of the Lebanese capital each day. But the work was hard and unfamiliar, and by then Tariq was far more drawn to the political discourse of Fatah and the PLO. It was a good moment for the new generation of Palestinians, better educated than their parents and beginning to challenge the authority of the traditional elders. There was money in the camps, and work, and the freedom to meet and talk in the evenings at classes and in clubs.

Soon, Tariq was skipping classes in favour of full-time politics, drawn, like his friends, towards the increasingly influential resistance movements, each with their slightly different ideologies. Fatah, which held that the struggle was nationalist, and something apart from the overthrow of conservative Arab countries, remained a secret organisation, with cells, wings and branches. He found attractive their brand of nationalism, and their aims to free Palestinians from the arbitrariness of Lebanese control and to give an impetus to nation building. For a while, he was made a

probationary member, but by 1974 he had been selected to work in the
schools that surrounded Shatila because he was popular with the young
Palestinians. By that summer, he had recruited and was training over 200
students, and by the time the civil war broke out in 1975 he was leading
his own unit of 100 teenaged boys and girls. Fatah opened a war-
operations room and Tariq led a section of the militia, young fighters with
guns but no military experience.

There had been tensions between Palestinians and Lebanese for
years, ever since the Egyptian President Nasser had persuaded the
Lebanese to allow the Palestinians to govern their own camps. From the
mid-1960s, when it became clear that conventional warfare was never
going to be effective against Israel – the Arab forces were neither as well
equipped nor as well trained nor as united – the importance of Palestinian
guerrillas began to grow more apparent. And when the Palestinians lost
Jordan as their power base and moved their forces into Lebanon, these
tensions turned into confrontations, egged on by Christians and
Falangists who found it convenient to blame the Palestinians for
Lebanon's ills. The Israelis decided to expand their security zone, and in
March 1978 invaded south Lebanon. A thousand civilians died, and
eleven villages around Tyre were destroyed. The Palestinian fighters
adopted guerrilla tactics, withdrawing before the attacking forces, and the
Lebanese grew increasingly angry at the Palestinians for causing Israeli
aggression.

While the civil war between the alliance of the Christian Falangists and
the Israelis (Israel had been training and arming the Christian-Arab
Falangists since 1976) and the Muslims and the Palestinians was
becoming more bitter, Tariq was rising through Fatah's ranks, co-
ordinating missions against the Falangists. Wounded one day by a sniper,
he came round from a series of operations to find himself relegated by his
injuries to sitting in an office job. Fretting at the inactivity, he agreed to go
to Moscow to learn Russian.

The plan had been for him to stay seven years and take a degree; he
liked the life in the Soviet Union, and he was intrigued by Palestinians
from other parts of the diaspora whom he met in the university halls, but
he felt too distanced from the things he really cared about and before the
first year was over he was making his way back through Egypt and into
Beirut. When he got there he found that seventeen of his own recruits
were dead, killed in the fighting. He blamed himself for having recruited
them and began to drink heavily, uncertain about his own future. The
Syrians were now bombing Beirut; Tariq and the rest of his family, who

had connections in Ein al-Helweh refugee camp in Sidon, moved to greater safety along the coast.

Then, on 6 June 1982, the Israelis again invaded, in response to a series of Palestinian guerrilla attacks launched from the Lebanon. Bombing and shelling, they made their way along the coast and reached Beirut, their tanks bowling along the Corniche. The highest casualties were in Beirut itself, where up to 14,000 people died; but 2,500 died in Sidon and the Palestinian refugee camp of Ein el-Helweh, and many hundreds more in the villages of southern Lebanon. It was a while before people realised that the Israelis were using cluster bombs, having bought them from the Americans on the express understanding that they would never be used against civilians.

Tariq was in Shatila in late August when the PLO agreed to evacuate the camp under a UN-sponsored ceasefire agreement, taking its fighters into exile in return for guaranteed safety for the civilians and families left behind. He was not among the 12,000 or so who left, but instead hid himself and some weapons, fearing some dark event of retribution, but not knowing how and where it would come from. He was in the camp the night of 14 September when Bashir Gemayel, newly appointed Falangist Prime Minister of Lebanon, was assassinated and the Palestinians were blamed for his murder, and he was at home in the family house the night the Israelis began advancing on Sabra and Shatila. He tried to organise some kind of resistance, seeking out those few Palestinians who still had weapons, bringing together one with a rocket launcher, another with a Kalashnikov. Most of the night of 16 September, the Israelis and the Lebanese forces shelled the camp; inside, the rubble from the falling houses, their breeze-block walls and powdery foundations pitifully inadequate as protection, blocked the path for those trying to reach the wounded. Tariq decided that his job was to rescue the injured. His friend Jamal, shot in the head, died as he was carrying him in his arms. Talking of the killings now, Tariq weeps.

His family had scattered in the shelling. Some of his relations were taking shelter in Sabra, where the massacre would continue the next day. Others were hiding in a basement under the offices of Fatah, or behind the main water tank supplying the camp. For the next three days, the killings and arrests and disappearances continued, but Tariq and his father and uncles succeeded in getting the family together and to safety. Israeli soldiers with loudspeakers were rounding up all Palestinian men and Tariq fled to Lebanese friends at the other end of Beirut, only to be turned away. He felt bitter, but not surprised. Returning, he was arrested with his father and two brothers. A Lebanese friend, working with the soldiers, intervened to have them released. Many Palestinian men were led away to the sports stadium whose tall stands can still be seen looming over the camp; few were ever seen again.

No one has ever established precisely how many people died in the attacks, though it was later said that the Israeli offensive, and particularly the shelling of Beirut, killed 18,000 people and wounded 30,000. When reporters were at last able to approach Shatila they noted, first of all, the smell; and then the flies. As they advanced, they found bodies every-where: small children, women, elderly people, lying in the alleys, inside the houses, by the roadside, on the rubbish dumps, knifed or machine-gunned to death. When they reached a hundred corpses, they stopped counting. There were pools of blood on the ground, still wet.

Tariq escaped and was hidden by American friends in the city. Three weeks later, he took up an invitation from a college of printing in the UK. 'My mother told me to go. She was terrified that I would be killed if I stayed.' He slipped out of Lebanon and found himself in London, in the grey solitariness of a foreign autumn day. He had become not just a refugee, but doubly an exile, without possibility of return. Behind him, he left attacks and resistance against the Israelis fuelled by Amal, an increasingly vocal Shi'ite Muslim militia. He was in Oxford, not in Shatila where he felt he should be, when in 1985 the Israelis withdrew, the Syrians returned, and Amal launched an attack on Shatila, which was still largely in ruins. The 'war of the camps', pitting Amal against Palestinians, would last until the end of 1987. Sabra, and Gaza's hospital which stood along its edge, were destroyed, and patients and staff from the hospital were led away by Amal militia, many never to reappear. Those who had survived the massacre in Shatila now lived through a series of sieges which took them to the very edge of endurance. Intensive shelling drove them as far underground as they could burrow, in garages and basements. Medical services for the wounded and dying became minimal, as the one trained doctor remaining used coins and Band-Aids to stop air escaping from perforated lungs and made splints out of wooden doors. Under assault, Shatila's inhabitants grew close. Communal kitchens produced food contributed by those who still had supplies. Zainab and the other women left their dark houses with a freedom they had never had before, and carried food to the fighters. The rationed water and the cigarettes were shared until they ran out altogether. At one point, 6,000 shells a day were falling on the one square kilometre of the camp.

Unable to carry the dead to the cemetery on the edge of the camp, the people buried them in the mosque, in the concrete floor. Today it is a shrine to 350 men who lost their lives in the fighting. A flat platform of grey marble covers the place where they were laid, swaddled roughly in sheets, one alongside or on top of the other. It is one of Shatila's stopping points for visitors, with its grille looking into the makeshift tomb decorated by Palestinian flags, the names of the dead engraved down one marble wall. After the invasion and the wars, a floor was built above, where today the men gather to pray.

And in between the three sieges, which saw 2,500 Palestinians dead and over three-quarters of their houses destroyed, it was, says Marwan, Tariq's elder brother, like 1948 all over again, with the women queuing for milk powder and building materials – only now the camp was poorer and dirtier, and the women queued in filthy water that reached above their ankles, and the camp looked like a ravaged war zone. Rosemary Sayigh, a British writer and academic working on a study of Palestinian women at the time, listened as they compared massacres, the old and the new. There was a story in the camp about how someone had found the bodies of three small children blocking the drains. Children slept fitfully, wet their beds, woke screaming from nightmares. It was not only like 1948, the women said, it was worse. They were now hated by the Lebanese, who blamed them for the savagery of the invaders. And when peace finally came, Shatila was little more than rubble surrounded by a wasteland, and the road to Jerusalem, so it was said, no longer led through Beirut but through Washington.

And so, in many respects, it remains: a wasteland of garbage and ruined buildings, the jagged fragments of former houses left standing, empty, or camped in by the poorest of the refugees; a scene of devastation both utterly violent and utterly ordinary. To this day it is illegal for the PLO to have a presence in Shatila, or for the Palestinians to have their own militias. The memories of those days are violent, and when the inhabitants of Shatila talk about the massacre and the sieges, they talk about the snipers who waited in the surrounding houses to pick them off as they ventured out for food, or the day that someone found a head impaled on a pole.

In twenty years, Tariq has seen his sisters only once, the time that he was smuggled back into Beirut. 'Tell him how long my hair is,' Souha, the younger of his two unmarried sisters, said to me as I was leaving, shaking her thick black hair loose so that it fell right down her back. 'Explain to him how much it has grown.' When they last met, she said, it had been cut very short. 'That is how long we have not met: almost two feet of hair.'

Zainab has visited Tariq in Oxford once, sixteen years ago, when his first daughter Hanan was born; she has never seen his second, Rasmiyya, who is now thirteen. His father has also travelled to England once; he stayed for six weeks then said to Tariq that though he found it peaceful and the countryside green, and though he liked the fruit and vegetables, he could not bear to stay any longer. One uncle went to Libya for eight years in order to earn the money to build his house in Shatila: it had been destroyed three times by shelling. Another uncle worked in Abu Dhabi. A nephew is in Norway, where he has asked for asylum. Tariq used to keep a record of where the members of his family live, the uncles and cousins and nephews and nieces: when, three years ago, he reached thirty-six living scattered between Abu Dhabi, Britain, Sweden, Jordan, Denmark and Germany, he stopped counting.

For Tariq, too, displacement is mostly about loss, though it is also about memory. When he speaks to his mother on the telephone, he asks her what she is wearing and what she is cooking for dinner that night. 'When I think of her,' he says, 'I think of a little girl who never left her home in Balad al Sheik. Everything that happened to her afterwards is a nightmare, with happy moments. For my mother, her children became the personal possessions she had lost. It is cruelest for her. What she wants more than anything in the world is to have her four sons together in one room. She will never have this.'

Hanan is embarrassed by the insistence with which her father talks about the past. She does not like to see tears come into his eyes when he speaks of his own father, and the way that he cleaned his sons' shoes and was so proud of them. 'My daughters,' he says, 'have become English. They understand Arabic but speak very little. My wife and I speak Arabic together, but now we speak to the girls in English. They are growing up and the most important thing is that we communicate properly. I try to avoid confusion. The worst for us all is a clash of culture – one world with their friends and another with us. But I have to live knowing that if I told my mother these things, if I told her that I can accept that they may marry English boys, she would be devastated.' Hanan herself, a neat, pretty girl who seems sensible and reflective, is clear: 'I do not feel like a refugee,' she says. 'I feel Palestinian. But England is my home.'

Tariq, like Zainab, dreams of return to the Occupied Territories, where he has never been but which he feels he knows better than the orderly English terraced houses and green fields that surround him. But for him it is only a notion. The quality of his life, the possibilities for his daughters, have come to interest him more; less angry now, more accepting, he wants a settlement, the right to something if return is denied. If only, perhaps, the recognition of the world that the Palestinians exist as a distinct entity and that though they may have left the lands on which they lived, they cannot simply be absorbed without trace into surrounding Arab countries. 'I always talk about myself as a refugee,' he says. 'I will never be anything but a refugee. Even if some day I manage to go back to finish my life in Balad al Sheik, I will call myself a refugee who returned. I was born a refugee, I grew up a refugee, it is how I think.' Tariq has indefinite leave to remain in Britain, and has applied for British citizenship. Under his current status he needs a visa to travel to an Arab country, and may not go to either Israel and the Occupied Territories or to Lebanon. Laughing, a little embarrassed, he says that he has an obsession with boxes and cases, and that he keeps every container that comes into the house. 'Always I feel I might need it to pack things in. In my heart, I know that I will be moved on. I own this house, but I forget.' 'Record!' wrote Mahmoud Darwish in 'Bitaqit Hawia', the poem which has become famous throughout the Arab world: 'I am an Arab/ Without a name – without title/ Patient in a country/ with people enraged'. Where collective existence assumes the shape of a philosophical paradox, where a civilisation is regarded as essentially disposable and its people transported, dislocated and dispossessed, then *awdah*, the right of return, becomes about identity too.

For some years after the Naqba, the Palestinians were silent. The 'black cave of obliterated memories' was so shocking that no one cared to write about what had happened. It was not until 1953 that the first literary work by a Palestinian appeared in Arabic, a collection of poems by George Naguib Khalil called *Roses and Thorns*. Novels as a literary genre are not part of Palestinian cultural tradition, and it was only when the Egyptian writer Naguib Mahfuz began writing his novels in the 1950s and 1960s that a fictional voice emerged among the Palestinians, and even then it was not until the 1970s that Palestinian women began to write and publish. The voice that has developed since is distinctive, but more, Edward Said has argued, for its form than its content. The themes are those of dispossession and exile, of houses and lands wrecked, abandoned, destroyed, rebuilt and destroyed again, of collaborators – 'tails', slanderers, dangerous scorpions – and of Israeli domination through the figures of soldiers, security men, officials, employers. In Ghasan Kanafani's *Men in the Sun*, three Palestinian refugees choose to suffocate inside a tanker transporting them illegally over the border into Kuwait rather than make the fuss that would alert the driver to their existence. It is in the form these writings take, the way there is little narrative in the recognised sense of one scene following sequentially upon another, but rather a series of broken, fragmentary compositions, that the vulnerability of Palestinian life comes across, with sentences expressing instability and fluctuation, and self-conscious set pieces and testimonials in which the present is always subject to echoes from the past.

To talk to Palestinian refugees today is to understand what dispersal and loss really mean. A larger proportion of Palestinians than any other people in the modern world live away from the place they identify as home, and they can neither return to the places of their youth, nor voyage freely to where they wish to go, nor do they feel safe in countries that were once open to them.* They also live, to a great extent, away from each other. A people singularly attached to and dependent on family, for whom until recently fewer than seven or eight children was seen as a misfortune, they live separated not just by distance, but by papers. Palestinians have identity cards, not passports. They are moved around on the whim of other governments. To succeed, to be educated, to find jobs and send money home, they are obliged to travel, but not necessarily to places they wish to go. The 'stability of geography and the continuity of land', wrote Said, does not exist for them. Many are obliged to live with the certainty that they will never see a child, a parent, a cousin again. Listening to a Palestinian describe his family is a long and complicated undertaking.

Not long ago, Mourid Barghouti wrote: 'At one-thirty in the morning Mounir [his brother] informed me from Qatar of the death of my father in Amman. I was in Budapest. At two-fifteen in the afternoon, seven years later, my brother 'Alaa informed me from Qatar of the death of Mounir in Paris. I was in Cairo.' This is how Palestinians live.

There are twelve official Palestinian refugee camps in the Lebanon, of varying sizes and degrees of segregation from the Lebanese, and over 380,000 Palestinians, around half of whom are registered with UNRWA and live in the camps. No one knows the exact figure, for more Palestinians live in seventeen 'informal' camps, in conditions of great hardship. According to recent research, camp 'dwellings' average two rooms for every six people, and less than two-thirds of these dwellings are connected to any form of sewage system. Among the larger families, those with seven children or more, 96 per cent are said to live below the poverty line.

*According to official UNRWA figures, there were approximately 4 million Palestinians in exile in the Near East in 2003, and a further 428,000 outside their area of operations.

The camps in the south, near the border with Israel, are those which the Lebanese patrol most assiduously. The largest, the one people talk of as the most Palestinian, in which their original life is least diluted, is Ein el-Helweh, the camp on the edge of Sidon to which Tariq and his family fled in 1979. The name means 'sweet spring'. Here, in a dip between the sea and the mountains, surrounded by hill tops manned by Lebanese gun posts, encircled by wire and walls, entered only via checkpoints with casually contemptuous young Lebanese soldiers, live 45,000 Palestinians; or so say UNRWA, for the Palestinians themselves, for whom there is no census, put the figure at closer to 60,000. Unlike Shatila, with its 'cocktail' of displaced people, Ein el-Helweh is regarded as a pure camp, for it has no outsiders. That is, none except for a handful of wanted people, hiding out in the alleys and turned over to the Lebanese when the military search for them becomes too insistent. The camp, though poor and cramped, has none of the claustrophobic intensity of Shatila, though the former villages of Palestine are reproduced in the same way, and families live in the same kind of compounds, new rooms sprouting above and alongside the old ones on the sites of the first tents. It has a more robust, lively air. Ein el-Helweh, say its inhabitants, is truly Palestinian, a town that might just as easily be on the West Bank; unlike Shatila, it is also highly political, with eleven political parties and a Fatah headquarters, which is itself a source of employment.

To the north of the camp, on a slight elevation and some way back from the camp's main street where the market takes place each morning, lies the proxy village of Sousouf. It covers some hundred square yards of ground and contains about forty families, all descendants of men and women who fled the real Sousouf, near the Lebanese border, in the spring and summer of 1948. In Roman times, Sousouf was Safsofa, a village with many goats and beehives. In the September of 1948, Ghazi was a boy of seventeen. His family were the last to leave the village. They would have left sooner, but on the ninth his father, pressing oil from their olive crop, which had been gathered early in response to the conflict approaching from the valley below, was kicked by their horse, fell, struck his head and was killed, leaving a widow and seven children. On Saturday 18 September, not long after night fell, planes began to bomb the village. The bombing lasted all night, says Ghazi, and soon there was also shelling. At dawn, Israeli soldiers entered the village. Some of the men were lined up in batches in front of a wall and shot; others were dropped into the village well. A fourteen-year-old girl was raped. One old man was shot in his bed. In all, says Ghazi, forty-five died; he would have fought, but he had no weapon, the only gun owned by the family being with his uncle, who was away fighting in the hills. Ghazi on this point is absolutely clear: the British are to be blamed for the Naqba, for arming the Jews and repressing the Palestinians and for spreading propaganda that Palestine was a free and empty land; and for the rest he blames the Arabs for promising but then failing to support the Palestinians with arms and men. The Naqba was indeed a catastrophe: not for any one person alone, but for a whole people. The Palestinians, he says, calmly but firmly, have lived in uncertainty for fifty-four years. This uncertainty has marked his life; and ruined it. It has ruined all their lives. For him to talk to me, to tell me what the last fifty-four years have been for him, was 'like pulling off a plaster, opening a wound. I want to do it, but then I cannot stop talking.'

Like Zainab, like many of the 2,000 or so people still alive today who remember the flight from Palestine, Ghazi recalls life before the Naqba as a time of happiness and ease. His father had three wives and seven children; his mother was the middle one, and he the middle child. They were farmers, growing wheat, corn, tobacco, watermelons, chickpeas, and figs; they had an olive grove and vines. They kept the chickpeas, beans and small crops of seasonal vegetables for their own consumption, and sold the figs, olive oil and grapes. When his mother judged the moment had come when they had no choice but to flee, they crept out from where they had been hiding and ran towards the mountains during a lull in the shooting. They took nothing with them. The border with the Lebanon lay just over an hour's walk away; they crossed over to a village called Yarcun, then on to Bint Jubeil. From there, after a month wondering whether they might be able to go home, they moved on to a camp outside Tyre, Bourj el Shemali, from which UN officials were already distributing the Palestinians to camps further away in Lebanon as well as to Jordan and Syria. In May 1949 all those who had survived the killings in Sousouf were moved to the new camp of Ein el-Helweh. They were given tents close together. In 1950 Ghazi married a girl from another Sousouf family.

It was, says Ghazi, at seventy-one a strong, upright man with thick wiry grey hair cropped short, better than chaos, though it was not perfect. The two families built a fireplace near their tents and made piles of firewood they collected from the hills around the camp. UNRWA handed out flour, sugar and rice and, for the first year or so, occasional tins of fish. Water was delivered in barrels to the different village quarters: theirs was known as the 'fountain of Sousouf' and it ran out every evening around seven. Relations with UNRWA were good: most of its employees were refugee

Palestinians like themselves. The camp was surrounded by wheat fields and orchards of citrus fruit, later cut down by the Israelis when they invaded Lebanon in 1982. Ghazi got occasional jobs as a building labourer in Sidon. 'I used to roam and wander the fields looking for work,' he says. 'But it was very hard.' He was the eldest son, and he and his younger brother were responsible for his mother and sisters. Electricity reached Ein el-Helweh only in 1970. Until then, the younger children studying for their exams carried their books out of the camp in the evenings and sat along the highway, under the street lights, in order to be able to read.

It was about three years, he says, before he began to realise that they were not about to go home, and it was then that he started to talk about the need for independence, the importance of not relying on the people around them. He began to make plans; he planted a tree, and found work with local farmers. But he went on thinking about Sousouf, and at night he would dream that he was still there; in the daytime, when he was working in the farmer's fields, he would look up at the mountains around, very like his own mountains, and pretend that he was working his own fields. 'I lived in the past,' he says, 'remembering, all the time. At night, we sat and talked about what it had been like.' Ghazi was then nineteen. He has not stopped remembering since. 'Every moment,' he says,

> something reminds me. This is how I live. I remember how we used to take our olives to the press and how I used to stand around with the others and we used to laugh and joke. I remember the weddings and parties in the village and how in the summer we used to dance. I remember the way the men sat together and talked and how as I grew up I used to sit with them, listening. I remember the way the richest man in Sousouf always had coffee ready for visitors and how the women used to visit each other in their houses while the men sat in the rich man's house and talked. Yes, we live here with our neighbours from Sousouf and yes, we meet and talk. But you cannot transport the life. There, our houses were surrounded by our lands. Here, it is like a prison. The land we look out at is owned by others. There the weddings and celebrations and burials were all part of our lives, and we all shared in them. Here, unemployment and stress has driven all that away. We have become too busy thinking how to pay the rent and feed our families. We still do those things, but not with our hearts; we do them out of duty. We bring up our

children to keep to our ways. But we are frightened that they
will become thinned with exile.

It is only in the last ten years that historians and researchers have started
committing to film and archive the store of oral memory which almost
alone conserves the history of the Palestinian people. It is, they say, the
only way to preserve the meaning of what it is to be a Palestinian, and
prevent them scattering into twenty different peoples. 'Basically,' the
Palestinian historian May Seikaly wrote not long ago, 'people turn to
memory when they are afraid they have lost it.'

By the Israeli invasion of 1982, Ghazi and his family had been living in
Ein el-Helweh for over thirty years. Early in August, the camp was
surrounded on all sides, and Israeli and Falangists shelled the camp from
the hills around, before posting snipers to pick off Palestinians who were
driven out into the streets below in search of food or water. When the
Palestinians decided to fight back, they lost 100 men trying to take the hill
directly above the camp, where a lighthouse, with an ungainly stone
madonna perched high above its beacon, looms above the valley. After
houses around the perimeter had been knocked down, bulldozers were
sent in to flatten what remained.

Over loudspeakers, orders were given for all men between the ages of
fifteen and seventy to leave the camp, carrying white flags to indicate that
they intended to do so peacefully. The men fetched white sheets and bed
covers from their beds and came out, and were led down towards the
beach in a long line. It was, says Ghazi, repeating what Marwan had said
to me in Shatila, like 1948 all over again. With the others, he was taken to
Ansar, a prison camp run by the Lebanese military. In 1982, I had just
started writing about human rights for *The Times*, and I remember reports
about the camp at Ansar in southern Lebanon, about the way 9,000
Palestinian men of various ages had been rounded up, and stories of
disappearances and deaths under torture. Palestinians throughout the
country were now subjected to threats, kidnappings and attacks, and with
most of the fighters and weapons gone they had little protection from the
assaults coming at them from all sides. The Palestinians, it was said,
preferred to be arrested by the Lebanese army, from whose camps they
usually returned alive, than by the Lebanese security forces, where torture
and summary executions were common. '*Khang*', strangulation, is the
word used by people in the camps today to describe what happened to
them after 1982.

The PLO, who had been generous employers, were gone, the

Lebanese economy was in ruins, and the war had seen their homes and livelihoods destroyed. The crèches, nursery schools, clinics and work-shops had all closed down. Even so, the Palestinians were not quite crushed. The younger women in particular had been galvanised and strengthened by their role in the resistance, and a spirit of retrenchment settled over the camps. Families, long used to hardship, pulled in their belts and returned to the strong roots of their family traditions. The Palestinian flag and photographs of the martyrs, those who had died in the five years of conflict, were potent symbols of resistance. Bit by bit, new projects flowered in the ruins. The internet and email have brought the outside world into the camps, particularly to the young, who have been helped by international organisations to make contact with other teen-agers in the occupied territories, meeting online. They call it the 'electronic intifada', and the players 'global nomads'.

Ghazi is one of the very few Palestinians to have visited the village in which he spent his childhood. In 1982, at the time of the invasion, one of his daughters became very ill. The road between Sidon and Beirut was blocked, and the nearest hospital with the treatment she needed was in Haifa, across the border in Israel. He asked and received permission to take her there. On the last day of his ten-day visa, he took a bus to Sousouf, now renamed Bar Yochay. Two of the original houses, standing on the main road, were intact, but the rest of the village had been bulldozed. Piles of stones, buried by rough grass, were all that remained of the houses he remembered so vividly. His father's fields, once covered in wheat, tobacco and corn, were now planted with apple and peach trees. The olives had gone. The land around was thickly forested. It all looked absolutely different. He found the visit extremely painful. He does not want to go back; at least, not as a visitor, not before the return he believes is rightfully due to him.

But when he returned to Ein el-Helweh, he felt more like a stranger than ever. 'I had regained my sense of belonging, and now it had gone again. We are not Lebanese. We are strangers here. I cannot change.'

There is depression in the camps, though no suicide: in Ein el-Helweh, Ghazi can recall just one case, thirty years ago. And there is little or no crime, for no one has anything to steal. But there is much anxiety, and when problems arise people are quick to quarrel and come to blows. The mood is fragile and wary and conversations are full of ambiguity. Children fight and argue in ways they never used to in the 1970s and 1980s, say the teachers who work in the camps, and the noise is far greater than it ever used to be. The failure rate at school is high, and since space is so tight children seldom get a second chance. Many of the classes have fifty pupils or more. One woman in three is said to be illiterate. Fatima, who runs one of the rare successful projects in Shatila, a vocational training centre for women where they encourage each other to learn how to read, write and type, says that thirty years ago, when she was a thirteen-year-old child in the camp, there were open spaces where the children could play. Now, in the damp sunless winter days they sneeze and wheeze and their noses run. Televisions flicker in the murky light of the camp, where it is as hard to see along the pinched alleyways as inside the houses, and parents try to monitor the programmes for the violence and consumerism that they fear will only feed their children's keen sense of discontent. To these children, Fatima says, everything seems expendable, impermanent, unstable, especially where there has been so much destruction. 'Why,' asks Fatima's small daughter, seeing the Barbie dolls and tricycles on television, 'can't I have a doll with its house and its wardrobe? Why can't I go on holiday to the seaside?' Fatima's regret is that she does not know what to say to her daughter; she does not really know the answer herself.

Just as she does not know what to say to her own mother, who came as a girl to Shatila in 1949 and sang ballads about Palestine all through her childhood, and who now tells her that her one wish is that someday, someone will take her home. Fatima's mother has very high blood pressure; in the camp, she lives in one small room. Last summer, a former neighbour from their village in Palestine now living in Sweden was able to return to see what had become of their lands. He visited Shatila on his way back to Sweden and showed her parents a video of what remained of their childhood homes. Fatima's mother, who had not talked much about the past for some time, began remembering and describing her home all over again. At night, she again began to dream of when she was a girl. 'Where is home?' asks Fatima. 'We have no home. I feel conscious only of being a refugee.' Fatima has two brothers and five sisters. Her elder brother is in Utah, where he buys and sells cars; the younger is in Germany, where he fled after the war of the camps and now has asylum. One of her sisters is in Denmark and another in Canada, having moved there after working in the Gulf. The three married sisters are all in Shatila, and the last, who is single, lives in Ein el-Helweh.

Refugee populations have long attracted the attentions of statisticians. UNHCR, for many years barred from work with Palestinian refugees through its mandate and the existence of UNRWA, is now carrying out a project to identify the unmet needs of the Palestinian diaspora. Lebanon is one of the countries it plans to look at. It is said, for instance, that well over half the Palestinian men in the Lebanon are unemployed, and that what little work is to be found is only of a labouring kind; that the Lebanese camps have a particularly high number of 'hardship' cases – widows, single mothers, the handicapped – that only a handful of Palestinian children manage to go on to higher education; that the number of hospital beds available to Palestinians has dropped by half in recent years. The exiled Palestinians are the subject of countless statistics, percentages, graphs, made more poignant in their case by the fact that so much of their documentary history, their family papers and photographs, their maps and civil records, were lost with the Naqba, and the 45 million documents said to survive lie scattered, like the Palestinians themselves, through the occupied territories, in Jordan, Syria and the Lebanon, in the American Friends Service Committee in Philadelphia and the International Committee of the Red Cross archives in Geneva. History, the oral history now the subject of much attention in the camps, is coming to be seen as a potent form of resistance against the suppression and distortion of Palestinian culture and history by Israel. 'In the end,' says Edward Said, 'the past owns us.'

The events of the last decade have not been kind to the Palestinians in the Lebanon. Across the Arab world it is now accepted that they are the most unfortunate of all Palestinian refugees, for in Lebanon the once-friendly government has in recent years closed many doors against them. After the Gulf War, the rich Arab states where so many had found work and from where they sent money home began to expel the Palestinians whose labour they no longer needed. Professional people and labourers alike found their contracts abruptly terminated, the salaries that had supported large extended families in Shatila, Ein el-Helweh and Burj al Barajinah stopped. In 1980 I wrote a story for *The Times* about a Palestinian put on a plane from Kuwait because his visa had been withdrawn. He was not then allowed back into the Lebanon. Instead, he was shuttled around the world, as country after country closed their doors to him. He spent his nights sleeping on the benches of airports before being put on another plane to another country and another airport. Then, the story attracted attention; now, the odyssey of refugee life is not remarkable.

UNRWA's funds in the Lebanon, once ample for sustaining the 70,000 or so Palestinians of the Naqba, have been diminishing steadily, and make little inroads on the needs of the 380,000 and more that their numbers have now reached with the children and grandchildren of those who fled.

Like the Liberians and Sierra Leoneans in Guinea's long-term camps, their rations have been cut again and again; it is a very long time since tins of tuna and sardines made their way into camps along with the rice, oil and sugar. Today about 3,500 people live in buildings destroyed during the fighting in the 1970s, heaps of rubble patched up by cardboard or strips of corrugated iron, which they are forbidden by law to rebuild. Without sanitation, electricity or heat, without papers or identity cards, unregistered by UNRWA because not living inside the camps, they are the most dispossessed of all refugees. Like the rejects in Cairo, the 'Closed File' asylum-seekers, they are non-people, human beings without official existence.

Within Lebanon today, Palestinians may not work as doctors, dentists, lawyers, architects, taxi drivers, bankers or teachers – in all, seventy-three occupations are forbidden them. Recently the Lebanese government passed a new law prohibiting them from owning property or, if they already owned it, from passing it down to their children. There are stories of petty, idle persecution: Lebanese guards who man the checkpoints around the camps force young Palestinians to remove their sunglasses as they pass in and out, and order car drivers to remove all the wheels of their vehicles. Travelling into Ein el-Helweh with Mahmoud, Ghazi's nephew, recently returned from collecting his master's degree at Malta university, we were stopped by a stout young Lebanese recruit in battle fatigues, his Kalashnikov slung over one shoulder. He demanded to see what was in the boot. It was full of books. After a thorough rummage, as thoughtless as it was arrogant, he waved us on. Mahmoud told me that not long before his friend had been ordered to dismantle and remove all his car seats, and had to send for his wife inside the camp to bring him a screwdriver. When, some hours later, the car seats had been removed, the soldiers told him that they had no further interest in the vehicle.

Mahmoud was twelve when the Falangists and Israelis shelled Ein el-Helweh. His uncle's house was hit and two rooms collapsed. A grandchild asleep in one of them was saved because a heavy wooden wardrobe fell across his cot, making a protective cover. Too young to be rounded up with the men and taken to the beach, Mahmoud watched from the edge of the camp, and listened to the loudspeakers ordering them out. Today he has one brother in the Sudan, another in Saudi Arabia.

Those who manage to study abroad on scholarships are forced home when their visas run out, to a life with only the barest possibility of professional work with UNRWA or a foreign non-governmental organisation, while those offered the chance to visit the Palestinian Authority hesitate, fearful that the Israelis may stamp their passports and the Lebanese later refuse to let them home. They prefer to take buses to the border, where they stand behind the wire looking across to the hills of Galilee, contemplating with bitter sentimentality what was once theirs. Some, driven by poverty and enforced idleness to seek the services of human smugglers, get themselves trafficked to Europe to battle their way past asylum restrictions and onto work quotas. In the seventies their destination was Germany, crossing from the East into the West in search of jobs not even the Turks would take. Today, they aim for Scandinavia, Holland and Britain.

Until recently, Palestinians were able to attend university inside Lebanon because fees were low, and in the 1960s and 1970s Palestinians were said to be the best educated people in the Middle East, for like all dispossessed people forced to live by their abilities alone, they felt passionately about education; now fees have risen sharply and Palestinians have been reminded that they are 'non-Lebanese' and told that they must pay foreign fees, some three times those paid by the Lebanese students. With UNRWA's funds falling, a decision has been taken to pay for no major health care beyond the age of sixty – thereby cutting off older people with cancer, heart conditions or strokes. One bad illness can now cripple an entire family. Into this hermetic world, encircled by prohibitions and restrictions, it is not surprising to find that the Islamic fundamentalists have made inroads, and that the young Palestinians are once again joining political groups, where they receive a little money and a sympathetic hearing. In Lebanon, Hamas is said to be second only to Fatah in size, though no one speaks openly of its activities. In the camps, the language of politics is about power, not ideology; survival, not democracy.

'The Palestinians are resigned to suffering,' explained Bassam Jamil Hubaishi, a Palestinian in his fifties working for a human-rights organisation. 'But for how long will they be willing to watch their well-educated children working as manual labourers? We need to find a solution to this soon. No one is living as a human being should. No one meets even the minimum requirements.' It was Bassam who pointed out to me that while those born in the camps and now in their forties and fifties are more interested in a decent life than unquestioning return to Palestine, the young by contrast are growing up more militant. 'If they are given no chance to improve their lives, who can blame them for talking of a homeland? They feel precarious, unwanted. They don't belong anywhere. When they look around them at the hovels and alleys in which they grew up, they think: at least that isn't home, home is somewhere better, home is where I can live in dignity and where I will be wanted.'

Not long ago the Palestinian political scientist Khalil Shikaki, questioning 4,000 Palestinians about where they would choose to live, found that the overwhelming majority wanted to live, not back in what is now the state of Israel, but in a Palestinian state, a finding that has been used and interpreted in different ways in the Arab world. Another researcher asked the Palestinians what they felt about the right of return. A little over three-quarters did not hesitate: it was their entitlement, they said, and not something any one of them would be prepared to negotiate about. Their words were both sad and chilling. It is many years since the right of their return to the lands they left over half a century ago has been anything but a bargaining tool, useful in talks conducted by people who themselves live far from the camps, something to barter in return for political leverage. It gives the Palestinian refugees, over 5 million people spread out today through Jordan, Syria, the Lebanon and the whole Arab world from the Gulf States to Iraq, a true feeling of abandonment, an almost biblical sense of betrayal and forsakenness. The notion of redemption by return is an absurdity, a game played by politicians. There can be no homecoming for those of the Naqba.

Ghazi, who had farmed his father's fields of olives and vines in Galilee as a boy and imagined that one day they would be his, tried to work as a farmer in the fields around Ein el-Helweh, and for a while was even able to rent some small fields of his own. But they were not his fields. Before I left the camp, having spent nearly a whole day listening to him describe his life, with more anger than self-pity, he took me up to the top of his house. In old kerosene and petrol cans on the roof he grows onions, marjoram and mint. He picked some herbs and gave them to me, saying that he would willingly have given me an onion, except that since I was travelling I would probably have no use for one.

'All those who have been destined to exile share the same features,' wrote Mourid Barghouti, not long ago. 'For an exile, the habitual place and status of a person is lost. The fortunate ones are looked upon with suspicion, and envy becomes the profession of those who have no profession except watching others . . . The calm of the place of exile and its wished-for safety is never completely realised. The homeland does not leave the body until the last moment, the moment of death.'

Chapter Eight

The Illness of Exile

Exile was not so much a geographical dislocation as a state of mind,
something that consumed and branded and left one maimed for life.
Mandla Langa, *The Naked Song*

Lamine is his mother's only child. When he was seven and living in a
suburb of Algiers with two younger half-brothers, his father was assassinated. It was a killing carried out in error, and the military men who ruled
the new Algeria did what they thought was best for the eldest son of a
martyr: they put him in a uniform and sent him off to military cadet school
900 kilometres away, across the desert and near to the border with
Morocco. And there Lamine stayed, year after year, bewildered,
frightened and lonely. The descendant of an Armenian Orthodox
Christian, he was the only boy in the school who was not Muslim, and
though he agreed to read the Koran, he would not convert, and this added
powerfully to his sense of apartness. The freedom fighters who came to
train the little future officers were hard men from the Atlas mountains,
more used to guerrilla warfare against the French than to the ways of small
boys. When Lamine went home to see his mother in Algiers for two ten-
day holidays each year, much of that time spent on the journey there and
back, he found her always in tears, lamenting the loss of his childhood. He
did not cry himself, having quickly learnt that to survive among soldiers
emotions must be suppressed. 'I had lost my loving,' he says. 'You can't
hold on to love when no one treats you gently.' But when his twelve-year
penance was coming to an end and he had been made an officer, he began
to dream of another kind of life, one that was not circumscribed by
bullying, orders and desolation. Behind the outer shell of impassivity, he
nurtured a longing for a gentler life.

Today, Lamine is no longer so innocent; he is a watchful, taut figure,
precise and knowing. But in those years there must have been something
innocent about the slim, boyish officer who stares boldly out of graduation
photographs, because when he was just eighteen, about to embark on the
next rung in a military career of which every twist and turn had long been

ordained, he questioned his superiors about his future. Was it absolutely necessary, he asked, for him to remain in the army? Might he not now return to civilian life?

It was 1983. Algeria had not yet embarked on its long descent into civil conflict, but the military rulers who held the country in their grip were not in a mood for vacillating young officers with who knew what dark plots and secrets in their minds; particularly as Lamine was not alone in his protests, but one of a group of similarly troubled young cadets, boys who had been together since the age of seven and shared a profound revulsion for the military life. Lamine was accused of wanting to overthrow the government, of being a ringleader with contacts abroad. He was sent to spend the next three years in secret military detention, sharing a cell with twelve other prisoners, men like him deemed to present a threat to the stability of Algerian military rule. From time to time, in order to extract the names of fellow conspirators, guards put electrodes on his genitals, kicked him with their heavy military boots, and sprayed him with freezing jets of water. They told him that he was a rebel and that he deserved such punishment. They said that he was an animal, and should not exist on this earth. One day, they kicked him so hard that they broke his leg and knee; most days, he was carried unconscious from the torture room, blood pouring from his nose, mouth and ears, and zipped back into the overalls they had stripped from him before they began their work. He survived, Lamine says now, for one very simple reason: he was accustomed to ill-treatment. He knew all about punishment. One morning, as his torturers prepared their electrodes, Lamine laughed out loud. He had, he says, realised a profound truth: either they would kill him, or they would stop torturing him. Either way, he had ceased to care; he was free. After this, they tortured him all the more: the pain became so great that he deliberately moved to another room in his mind and tried to imagine himself another person. Since they had teams of torturers working around the clock, they came for him at random moments of the day and night. 'They wanted us to die,' he says.

But the time came when the military was forced to recognise that there was in fact no plot afoot, that they were dealing simply with a group of disaffected boys. All but a handful were released. Lamine was among the seven supposed ringleaders to be sent for court martial for plotting against the security of the state, since all these years of punishment could not be allowed to appear a mistake. He received a six-year prison sentence, with hard labour. He was greatly relieved: he had heard from a cadet friend that the supposed ringleaders would be shot as an example to others, and believes now that they were spared because of a campaign mounted on their behalf by Amnesty International, who had long regarded them as conscientious objectors and convinced the Algerians that their deaths would bring worldwide criticism. In his prison life, he had seen many others lined up and shot against the wall of the courtyard where they exercised. Sent to a civilian prison – but obliged to keep wearing his military uniform – he offered to teach and write letters for illiterate detainees in exchange for extra rations of coffee and cigarettes. He learnt a lot about death, he says now, for many of those he helped were due to die, and often in the mornings, when he went on his rounds, he found their cells empty.

After six years, Lamine and his surviving friends were set free. One had died while in detention; another had gone mad, and a third would shortly die from the effects of the treatment he had received. A fourth had agreed to work for the regime. Lamine had lost almost ten years of his life, though he tends to look back on his twelve years in cadet school as lost years too; but now, at last, he was allowed to become a civilian. He applied to the ministry of health to train as a paramedic, and though they kept a close eye on him lest he show any signs of political activity, they taught him about epidemiology and tropical diseases and sent him off to work for the World Health Organisation in Africa. He was constantly in pain, all down his spine and around his neck, as well as from his broken knee. In the years that followed, while he kept his eye on the military rulers in Algeria, hoping and waiting for the day when his country might become a safe and free place for him to live, Lamine roamed on behalf of WHO: the Congo, Zaire, Guinea, Ivory Coast, Mali and the southern deserts of Algeria. For a while, he was based in Djanet, an outpost deep in the Algerian Sahara, where early nomadic hunters had painted antelopes on the walls of their caves, and where he went in search of the missionary fathers of Père Charles de Foucault, to whom he was drawn because of their spiritual certainties, even though he sensed that they did not have quite enough to offer him. Until 1994, when the political tensions and pressures of the civil war caused those in power to begin to fear even shadows from the past, Lamine came and went between Algeria and the rest of Africa, restless, always alone, but free. But his record stalked him. 'They wanted,' he explains now, 'to do away with the silent opposition. They saw me as hostile.' When he felt the threat growing ever closer, when he saw others arrested and imprisoned for milder pasts, he slipped over the border into Morocco one day and crossed to Spain. With his existing file, his story and Amnesty International's testimonial, he was granted asylum.

Lamine had become a refugee. And it was now that his real problems began.

Somehow, people have forgotten a very simple truth: no one wants to be a refugee. Exile is a terrifying, lonely, confusing experience. 'Imagine,' said a psychiatrist I went to talk to one day, 'being a baby in a loving, happy family. Your mother loves you, feeds you, smiles at you, hugs you. You wake up one morning to find that she no longer appears to know who you are. She doesn't smile. She doesn't even look at you. You cry, you laugh, you make noises. She remains withdrawn and silent. All that was familiar and safe has gone. That is my image of what it feels like to be a refugee. A world without known contours, its geography hostile and alien.' No surprise, then, that exile can become a form of mourning, as memory invades the present, as traumatic events – torture, flight, death and the loss of those you love – flare up, like sudden fires, into despair.

For Lamine, the descent into grief was slow. In Spain, he started teaching French and Arabic, and Russian, which he had studied at military school. When he ran out of money, he washed plates in a restaurant. In his spare time, he interpreted for other refugees, helping them to prepare their applications for asylum; he reminded himself how fortunate he was to have papers no one could challenge. He felt neither happiness nor misery, though looking back on those years today, he knows that, day by day, he was growing sicker. When he worried, it was about the constant pain in his knee, spine and shoulders, which no doctor seemed able to cure. He did not feel part of his new life, but he had friends and work, and when he woke in the middle of the night with tears on his face, from dreams about cadet school and prison, he pushed them firmly to one side. He dismisses the word 'integration', saying that it is actually the bane of every refugee's life and that it means nothing in the vocabulary of displacement, but has been invented by those who like to pretend that the past is a country easily left behind. He was helped by his nature, he says, which is to struggle and look for solutions, though he wonders now how far his refusal to confront his sense of alienation paved the way for what was to come.

Lamine might have lived out the rest of his life as a refugee in Spain, speaking his many languages, helping other refugees, placating his demons with willpower, writing occasional articles for a Catholic magazine about the poor and the dispossessed of the modern world. But late one night, going back to his room, he was stopped by a group of men. They were Algerians and they had come to find him. They had knives. He was stabbed, but survived.

When he recovered, friends urged him to move on, to leave Spain but to avoid France, with its large Algerian community. The UK agreed to take him, and a transfer of his refugee status was swiftly arranged; he was not even interviewed by the Home Office. Late in December 1996, Lamine arrived in London. 'It was cold, so bitterly cold that I thought I would die,' he said to me, soon after we met. 'Believe me, I didn't see how I would ever be warm again.' Though fluent in five languages, he spoke no English. He found a small room in a cheap hotel in King's Cross and lay down on his bed, his bones still aching from the prison torture, and the wounds from the recent stabbing raw and painful. Days passed. When he could, he slept. The rest of the time he lay still, staring at the wall, thinking. He was assailed by flashbacks – of being bullied as a small boy, of having his leg broken, of the electrodes – and now he could not keep the thoughts away. His life had been fractured, the word he uses again and again, and this time, he feared, he would not have the courage to start over. He was forty-two. 'I had reached a black hole. I was lost. I had friends, a life, work in Spain. In England I had nothing. There I had been wanted, useful. Here, I did not exist. I could see no point in going on.'

The literature of exile is full of pain. 'We, the exiled survivors,' Virgil has Aeneas lament, as he flees the burning city of Troy carrying his father Anchises on his back, 'were forced by divine command to search the world for a home in some uninhabited land.' In these journeys into loss and the unknown, the past, as Nabokov wrote in a long essay about memory, overshadows the present and dims the future 'into something thicker than its usual pea soup'. Like the false prophets of Dante's 'Inferno', Nabokov saw the exile's head 'forever turned backward, and his tears or saliva . . . running down his shoulder blades'. And like Edward Said, he remarked on the ambiguities of the state itself: exile, he wrote, 'is strangely compelling to think about but terrible to experience.'

Whether Greek or Roman, European or Arab, whether today or in the past, all those who write of exile describe a world in which the past is safer territory than the present, even when the former was full of horror, for at least it has already been experienced. One of the most frequent themes of exiles is that of recapturing and reliving their lost past, earlier images providing a solid counter to the fluidity and rootlessness of the present. The native shore, observed Milan Kundera, the Czech émigré writer, is after all the only known shore, but the exile, to survive, has no choice but to step off onto a precarious, rickety bridge from the land where all is familiar and where he speaks a language known to him from childhood –

his real world – and grope his way across to a new country – a world hitherto only of the imagination – in which nothing is understood or familiar. In the process, by some sleight of hand, he must reverse these two worlds, the real and the imaginary, so that all that was once familiar becomes imaginary, and the imaginary, real. Both to remember too much and to forget too quickly is perilous; a 'fetish of exile', as Said described it, distances the refugee from 'all connections and commitments'. Willing himself to forget his cultural background, he finds that he has nothing to put in its place. The bridge is fragile and terrifying. Yet this profound dislocation of the spirit has to be borne, because it cannot be avoided. When Eva Hoffman coined her haunting phrase, 'lost in translation', she was describing what it means to live not only linguistically but spiritually in a new language. 'The words I hear now,' she wrote, 'don't stand for things in the same unquestioned way they did in my native tongue.' For all of us the word 'exile' resonates as an ultimate image of loneliness and need, touching an atavistic fear of losing all we most cherish, and all that we feel has shaped our identities and continues to define our tenuous image of ourselves. For Mandla Langa, one of the African writers to have put the experience of exile that has dislocated his continent for the last half century into the written word, exiles are branded and maimed creatures, condemned like animals who have left limbs in a snare to wander through life 'crippled, their minds locked on that fateful moment of rupture'.

It was not until after World War II that systematic attempts were made to link the experience of exile with that of the traumatic events that so often led to it. As the stories of those who had survived the Holocaust became known, so a literature of trauma began to take shape, and with it a realisation among doctors that terrifying and destructive events have the power to cripple and maim, even if apparently survived at the time, and to come back later as illness. None of this was new, of course: Freud had written extensively on childhood trauma, and Bowlby about the lasting effects of loss and bereavement, but something about the intensity and similarity of the symptoms reported by many different patients began to attract attention beyond psychoanalytic circles. Exile, it became clear, particularly when accompanied by brutal experiences, overwhelming loss and torture, was a potent and disabling event, leading often to sickness. When Primo Levi and Bruno Bettelheim, who had survived Auschwitz and Dachau, killed themselves at the end of long and productive lives, people were quick to say that the past had finally caught up with them. As survivors of the concentration camps began to reach retirement, when the huge efforts to keep the past at bay through work and activity began to lessen, so it was then that their minds were invaded by all that they had lost and endured. And it became clear, too, that the after-effects of the camps were being handed down to a second generation, the heirs of the Holocaust, who seemed to share an anguished collective memory in their dreams and fantasies, waking up at night with terrifying images of gas chambers, firing squads and extermination camps. They live, as a psychiatrist put it to me, in the reality of their parents' past, identifying with parental behaviour and patterns of thought caused by experiences they feel they share but did not in fact themselves experience.

Like the children of Holocaust survivors, the children of refugees grow up in a world circumscribed by fear, unrealistic expectations and over-protectiveness, with parents whose profound sense of powerlessness in the face of annihilation and loss expresses itself often as self-blame and guilt. Because they are in limbo, and because all their concentration and energy has to go into surviving and helping their children survive, they feel they have no permission to mourn and grieve. Seen this way, exile and the memory of trauma and loss is an experience of bereavement many times over: loss of country, status, activity, social networks, reference points and family, all compounded by a sense of lost time, the lost hopes and ambitions of youth and young adulthood. Yet delay in mourning, psychiatrists have long agreed, is known to increase the difficulties of adjustment. 'That which cannot be spoken cannot be treated,' wrote Bruno Bettelheim not long before his suicide in 1990. 'If they are not treated, these wounds will continue to ulcerate from generation to generation.'

As an understanding of this became more common towards the end of the 1970s, so there came a move to encapsulate this experience of breakdown, to give the condition a name and a label. As more and more clinicians saw patients who had suffered traumatic events, either recently or in the past, whether of sudden unexpected horror or of self-inflicted harm, they began to document a number of precise emotions. Their patients – not all, of course, refugees – told them of feeling depressed, fearful, sleepless, irritable, unable to concentrate; they said that they felt estranged from other people and that they kept forgetting the most obvious and important things. They reported flashbacks of great intensity, and terrifying dreams that woke them night after night. They returned, again and again, to their feelings of guilt about the people they had left behind, and those they had failed to save. A new term, post-traumatic stress disorder, was invented to cover all these symptoms, which seemed to occur, disappear and then recur, sometimes with no apparent reason, sometimes triggered by a smell, a few notes of music, an unexpected encounter. Most people reported a feeling of profound worthlessness. Some spoke of suicide. Others came to their doctors complaining of headaches and constant pains in their arms, legs and necks. Others again described seeing shadows or hearing screams. They spoke of 'frozen memories', obsessive and intrusive thoughts that came back, unchanged, again and again. Many had panic attacks. A few became hostile, paranoid, and turned to alcohol or drugs. Some wanted to talk, and then could not stop talking. Some said little, preferring to retreat into silence, where the past was buried deep. 'Some stories,' wrote Anne Michaels in her book *Fugitive Pieces*, 'are so heavy only silence helps you to carry them.' When physiological studies were made, physical changes were found to have taken place in neurotransmitters, hormones and the immune system. And these various symptoms, twice as common in women as in men, and particularly present in women who had been raped, seemed to occur in people from every ethnic and cultural background. Rape has its own particular horror, especially among people whose culture views it as extreme dishonour: to overcome the feelings of shame, to survive in a new world where there is no shame attached to rape, may mean rejecting the culture and faith of the past, and with it much that once lent comfort and support.

By the 1980s, post-traumatic stress disorder was attracting the attention of many researchers, drawn not least to the apparent existence of a disorder that seemed, uniquely, to be triggered by a single specific event. More discoveries followed. Patients, it seemed, appeared to alternate between re-experiencing, and then avoiding, their traumatic memories. They were using different defence mechanisms to keep away what felt so acutely painful, to lock into the unconscious what they could not bear to experience. But then the moment would come when the conflicting need to integrate this information into their existing cognitive world became too powerful, and it would break through these defences and into the conscious again. These two tendencies, argued the psychiatrist M. J. Horowitz in the early 1980s, the tendency to complete what was missing and the tendency to repress, led traumatised people to oscillate. It was when they proved incapable of processing the traumatic material, so that it remained permanently in active memory, that chronic post-traumatic reactions followed. Criticised for failing to explain how it is that some people seem to survive traumatic events relatively unscarred, while others react to the same situations by becoming disturbed, Horowitz's theory nevertheless found interested supporters in a world in which terrifying and destructive events seemed to be such a feature of the times.

And nowhere perhaps has the term post-traumatic stress disorder become more used than among those who work with refugees, who argue that the asylum-seekers of modern days are those who undergo some of the most extreme events that life can deliver: torture, killings, violence, loss. Lamine's story is not unusual in its horror or despair, something that explains the difficulty people experience in believing the stories of asylum-seekers, preferring to find them exaggerated or untruthful simply because they are too painful to absorb or comprehend. Exile, once the fate of individuals, is today the fate of millions – some 40 million people, perhaps, driven abroad or made refugees within their own countries.

In a field known to be short of reliable statistics, a few figures nonetheless stand out: depression has been observed in up to 90 per cent of people who have been displaced, and post-traumatic stress disorder in about half of them; many people who have been tortured have also suffered injury to the brain from beatings to the head, suffocation, near drowning and starvation. There is, it appears, something singularly traumatic about the combination of forced exile and extreme violence. At no moment is it more disabling than at the moment of arrival in a safe place, when the asylum-seeker – frozen in a state of insecurity, not knowing whether he will be allowed to stay or be deported, be allowed or denied access to work or study, and assailed by memories of loss and brutality – oscillates on his bridge, unable to go back or to proceed forwards. And it continues to be disabling during the long limbo of the asylum process, when those who wait, condemned to passivity and uncertainty, experience feelings of being disliked and despised, which in turn feed existing feelings of failure and loss of self-esteem.

Torture is now documented in 124 countries. Two-thirds of those are countries recognised as nation states by the United Nations, whose Convention against torture most have signed and ratified. Torture alone – that is, physical pain and degradation inflicted as acts of gratuitous punishment in order to achieve social control through terror and coercion, to obtain information, or as expressions of loathing – is enough to produce consequences; but the severity of these consequences will be influenced by the duration and severity of the ill-treatment, by the age of the person being tortured, by his biological vulnerabilities and pre-existing personality, by his expectations and perception of torture and by the models of the world that the individual brings to the experience. Victims of torture are individuals: but they are not alone. As with the survivors of the Holocaust, the effects of their torture will be felt on wives and husbands, parents, children, neighbours. As with the Holocaust, torture involves societies which appear on the surface to be civilised, societies in which people who could be expected to treat their fellows as human beings turn on them as individuals, brutally stripping them of all dignity, safety and humanity, while continuing to behave apparently normally in other ways. This duality and the way that seemingly mindless persecution destroys the deepest-rooted expectations about human behaviour are understood to be among the cruellest aspects of torture. Helpless and without purpose, unable to protect either oneself or others – these are the things that refugees who have been tortured talk about.

In May 1984, two doctors from the Chilean medical association travelled from Santiago to Washington to appear before the House of Representatives Committee on Foreign Affairs. They had come to testify to the activities of some of their colleagues who were collaborating with the military dictatorship in the practice of torture. As the torturers beat their captives into unconsciousness, the two doctors explained, suspending them by the arms and shoulders from poles and hooks, clamping electrodes to their testicles and stubbing their cigarettes on their bare arms, so these medical colleagues stood by to make certain that the prisoners did not die, but instead lived on to be tortured another day. Disgusted by what they had heard, the committee issued a report. They called for a worldwide campaign to make these facts known, so that torturers everywhere would be shamed into abandoning the practice, and they urged doctors to study the long-term mental and physical effects of torture itself, and to set up centres where it could be documented and treated.

As it happened, the committee's concerns, though important politically, had already been voiced. Eleven years earlier, in 1973, Amnesty International had organised a conference on torture in Paris. To it came interested doctors, lawyers and researchers from many parts of Europe and North America. Among them was a Danish doctor called Inge Kemp Genefke, who set up the first medical centre for the study of torture in Denmark; others soon followed in Canada, America and France. Bit by bit, torture's insidious legacy was unfolded: the way that, by attacking the body and leaving physical scars and deformities, the pain is prolonged far into the future. Some physical injuries were discovered to be susceptible to treatment; but others were not. Few victims, it was found, had in fact been tortured only one way: most had known many variations, thus reducing the chances of recovery. Torture also destroys the mind. Listening, recording, analysing, doctors began to discover how clever torturers had become, tailoring their methods to cause most pain and distress while leaving the fewest traces. They learnt that while the Turks preferred *falaka*, beatings on the soles of the feet, the Chileans liked to administer electric shocks. Soon, they came to certain conclusions: three-quarters of people who have been tortured suffer from severe mental consequences, and often this is accompanied by extreme physical pain. And they discovered something else: that treatment to mitigate the effects of torture is virtually always extremely difficult.

In 1945, a nineteen-year-old British girl had gone into Belsen with the Allies as a volunteer and had stayed on for two years to work with the survivors, before spending the next seven helping children who had been through Auschwitz. Now living in London, and working as a medical secretary, she had long been interested in the after-effects of horror and grief. Her name was Helen Bamber; she was rather short, with a pretty, innocent face and a light, soft voice. Working as a volunteer in her spare time for Amnesty International in the 1980s, she set up a medical group to document the stories of refugees arriving in England from countries like Argentina and Greece. Amnesty was a campaigning organisation; it could lobby and collect material, but it could not treat. And so in 1985 Helen found the backers and the money to open a medical foundation to treat survivors of torture, and when I first met her, she was working in two rooms in the National Temperance Hospital not far from Euston and King's Cross stations.

Because she believed so passionately in what she was doing, because she is a persuasive and remarkable woman, she was soon acting as a magnet for a whole range of doctors, psychiatrists and therapists, who came to her after their days in hospitals and surgeries to treat, for free, people with dislocated shoulders and disfiguring burns, with agonising pain to the soles of their feet, and with terrors and flashbacks that stalked them day and night. 'The majority of those tortured do not survive,' Helen would tell people who came to hear about the work of the foundation. The testimonies of those who did 'cast a shadow on us all'. Arthur Koestler, waiting to be executed in a prison during the Spanish Civil War, described himself as so restricted in time and space, so deprived of hope by the imminence of death, that he lacked even the substance to cast a shadow. Helen borrowed his image. The shadows of those who had been tortured, ethereal miasmas of agony and loss, the pain so real that it had destroyed even the will to live, needed addressing. And in her quiet, soft, reasonable voice, Helen would explain how it was our duty, as people who had not suffered this way, to bear witness, to reclaim time and space for those who had lost both, and in the process counter what she calls the 'climate of disbelief' that colours the attitude of the West towards those who seek asylum.

Those who came to work with her would document the experiences of those who had been tortured, and they would help them to live again. The question for her, though torture itself is full of nuances and ambiguities, was always fundamentally simple: how do you coax back to a bearable existence people whose bodies have been attacked, whose brains and memories have been weakened by blows to the head, whose privacy and pride have been invaded by rape and sexual assault, who have seen their families destroyed and lost everything that once mattered to them though they have done nothing wrong? Torture, she would say, is about isolation and chaos; about the disintegration of the psyche. Tortured people have to be helped to reclaim their lives; they have to be freed, not cured, for the concept of cure is seldom appropriate; they have to learn to cope again. And those she could not immediately see how to heal, for whom the scars of memory were so deeply embedded that they obscured all possibility of brighter realities, these she would 'accompany'. Accompanying, travelling alongside, in Helen's view, is a crucial part of the process.

When I went to see her early in 2003, Helen talked about a middle-aged Rwandan woman sent to her not long before. For several weeks, Mrs M. did not speak. She cried, she rocked backwards and forwards, but she said nothing. Helen sat and held her. Week after week, she appeared in Helen's room at the appointed time and on the correct day, and cried and rocked. Then one day she began to talk. She said that she was a Hutu, the wife of a Hutu businessman who sold spare parts for cars, and that she had three children, a girl of thirteen and two boys of ten and six. In 1994, some years before the birth of her youngest child, civil war came to her village. One day Tutsi soldiers arrived. They assumed that her family had been responsible for the deaths of Tutsis. They killed her father and her two brothers with knives and machetes. Then they attacked her, using machetes and bayonets, and slashed her from side to side, almost amputating her right foot, and leaving her stomach and groin with open gashes. They raped her, vaginally and rectally. Leaving many villagers dead or mutilated, they dragged her husband away with them. Later, she heard that they were holding him in a prison, and later still he suddenly appeared at home, having escaped. For a while, the family lived quietly, without trouble. But one day the soldiers came back and, finding her husband there, beat him very badly and took him away with them again. Mrs M. was again raped, by four men. When she fought off a fifth, she was again slashed and beaten. Her husband did not come back; a neighbour told her that he had been killed. One day, a villager came to tell her that the soldiers were looking for her, and that they were on their way to get her. Mrs M. fled. She hid in the bush and then with friends, until money was raised to send her abroad. She left her children with her mother.

As Mrs M. related her story, she told Helen that every day, lying on her bed in her lonely hostel room in London, she saw her children sitting near her. They were always there. Talking about the three children she has no news of and has not seen for many months, Mrs M. cried and rocked. One day, Helen asked her what she said to her children. Did she tell them that she was always with them in her thoughts? Did she tell them what disgusting food she was forced to eat in her hostel? Mrs M. laughed. It was the first time she had laughed or smiled in all the weeks she had been coming. And after this, things changed. The two women talked. It was the beginning, a breakthrough. Now Helen hopes that the day will come when Mrs M. can leave her children behind. 'But her reality is still that they are sitting on her bed. I cannot destroy that. I can't delve into her inner world. She wants not to live, but does not know how to die. I can only accompany her.'

Over the years, the Medical Foundation, growing steadily in response to the victims of torturers in Colombia, Sri Lanka, Kosovo, Iraq, Turkey, Zimbabwe and Liberia, has developed into a loose federation of doctors and therapists, with many different skills and therapeutic methods, presided over, until her retirement as director in 2003, by Helen's accepting and benevolent eye.* Drawn to the work by their feelings of sympathy and recognition, bringing with them disciplines that range from Freudian analysis to cognitive therapy, the clinicians have discovered the freedom to listen and treat as they see best, feeling their way into methods that owe as much to instinct and common sense as to orthodox medicine. It is, say its admirers, one of the last bastions of eclectic medicine in a field which grows more specialised and narrow all the time. While most of them accept post-traumatic stress disorder as a useful diagnostic label with which to arm their clients in their requests for asylum with the Home Office, few regard it as more than a very broad diagnosis. As a recognisable set of symptoms shared by many people who

---

*Between 1986 and 2004, the Medical Foundation saw 37,000 clients from 80 countries.

have been badly tortured, post-traumatic stress disorder provides a therapeutic base from which to start work. But recognising the symptons is just a beginning. The damage done by torture, its particular perversion of human relationships and intimate violations, leaves echoes not easily comprehended or dispelled. Listening always for the nuances of the possible, assessing the degree to which confrontation and direction are wise or premature, becomes part of an everyday process in which to the skills of doctor, psychiatrist and therapist need to be added those of social worker, housing officer and lawyer, for the needs of refugees are without bounds. For clinicians trained in precise disciplines, the very flexibility and imaginativeness of their sessions with clients is extremely attractive.

Though not, of course, to everyone. Some years ago, the senior clinician at the Foundation was a psychiatrist called Derek Summerfield. The longer he worked with clients, the more Dr Summerfield came to feel that his skills as doctor were in fact less important in dealing with asylum-seekers and refugees than his ability to find them homes and work. Torture, he accepted, is a devastating event, and can and does leave traumatic effects. But most people who came to the Foundation seemed to him to process and handle the experience themselves with extraordinary resilience. What they needed was not medical help, which perpetuated their sense of being victims, but practical assistance in putting their lives onto a tolerable footing. To call them 'ill' was to detract from their many social problems. As his impatience with what he saw as the 'medicalization' of the problem grew, so Dr Summerfield decided to leave and forge his own path. Though the Medical Foundation felt bruised by months of debate and discussion, the feeling did not last long. In the warren of offices and consulting rooms that spread across three buildings in north London, lawyers continued to take down initial testimonies and work on submissions to government, physiotherapists to ease the pain of fractured bones, psychiatrists to evaluate the effectiveness of different interventions, and therapists to guide clients through the minefields in their minds.

Talking about the work of the Foundation, Helen tells a story. A young man from a Central American country was sent to her one day, several months after his arrival in England. They started sessions together. He had been profoundly tortured, and been forced to watch others tortured. No one in England, he explained, had been able to imagine the degree of his anguish. Instead, he had found a forest, and there, in the beech woods, he would run about and shout and cry. The forest, he said, became his doctor. After some months working with Helen, he told her that the Medical Foundation was now his forest.

And in other clinics and counselling rooms, and in some parts of the National Health Service, other doctors, many of whom have done their stints at the Medical Foundation, are attempting to come to grips with the hideous legacies of torture and the long unhappiness of exile. Yet the fact that the Foundation is forced to rely on a team of interpreters, built up over the years, whose knowledge of torture and its many variations is enormous, has long troubled some of the specialists who feel the need for more direct contact. A new centre to tackle precisely this question of the gaps in language and interpretation was started in London in 2001, by two women who themselves have personal experience of oppression and exile. The first, Josephine Klein, is the only daughter of a Polish Jew who fled to Holland at the age of seventeen to escape persecution at home, and who herself became a refugee at the age of thirteen when the Germans invaded Holland. She, her parents and a disturbed older brother fled to England. They had hoped to make their way on to America, but when several convoys lost ships on the crossing, they accepted refuge in a village in the Midlands. England treated Josephine well. All she knew about the country came from *The Scarlet Pimpernel*, and she was not disappointed. The local authority found her a place in a good school and paid for her uniform; and she began to study. Soon, she moved to the top of her class. Later there followed a successful academic career in psychoanalytic psychotherapy. It was a world in which chaos had been contained and regulated, and she was grateful. Josephine is now in her seventies, a smiling, understanding woman.

In 1993, after she had given a paper at a memorial conference for Bowlby, the psychologist famous for his work on attachment, a young woman came up to her. She was Armenian and her name was Aida Alayarian. She was a refugee from Iran studying for a master's degree and she needed a supervisor for her dissertation on torture. It was, Josephine says now – as the two women tell me their story, interrupting each other frequently and affectionately – her day for good deeds. She promised Aida that when she had a vacancy she would accept her as a student, and she kept her word. It took her just three sessions to realise that Aida had no need of a supervisor. Trained in Iran in clinical psychology and child therapy, Aida needed a collaborator. After that, as Aida wrote her dissertation about torture, the two women talked about their own lives, about Josephine's extended family, almost all of whom disappeared into the extermination camps, and about Aida's escape from Tehran's

notorious Evin prison; and they told each other how they would like to
start a treatment centre for refugees, for those traumatised by terrible
events, and how they would recruit and train therapists who could work
with clients in their own languages, without need of interpreters.
Interpreters, however sensitive and good, it seemed to them, inevitably
blunted a process almost too fragile for words, and they were appalled
when, in the work they were already doing, they noticed that people
preferred to bring and use as interpreters their own children, who had
learnt English quicker than they had been able to, rather than tell their
stories through strangers.

Aida knew all about torture. As an Armenian from a vocal and politically
active family in Tehran, she had seen her father imprisoned and lose his
sight, and her brother and several cousins executed. Iran, in the late 1970s
and 1980s, was a brutal and terrifying place, with revolutionary courts and
committees presiding over a regime of torture and summary executions,
many of them carried out in Evin prison. Writing about human rights for
The Times at the time, I remember talking one day to an Iranian physicist
who had escaped to London. We met in secret; he was too frightened of
the long arm of the Iranian secret services to tell me his name. Talking
about the months he had spent in Evin, he described being taken one day
by a guard along a corridor towards the torture rooms. On the way they
passed an open door. I have always been haunted by what he said next. 'I
looked into the room. It seemed to be a hall, stretching for many metres in
all directions, with a high ceiling. All I could see were legs and feet,
hanging from hooks in the ceiling, rows and rows of them. Men's legs, with
trousers; women's bare legs; children's legs and tiny bare feet. Bodies,
hanging, dead, dozens of them. I realised that this was where the torture
ended.'

When her daughter was four, and she was heavily pregnant with her
second child, Aida was arrested and taken to Evin. She was tortured. Her
guards wanted the names of Armenian activists. When the time came for
her baby to be born, nothing happened. She laughs now, sitting in north
London, as she recounts her story.

> A month passed, and then a second. Still no baby. This is
> medically extremely rare in human beings but it happens in
> bears. When there is danger, they simply hang on to their
> unborn cubs. When I reached the end of the eleventh month,
> one of Evin's doctors took pity on me. He was a young man,
> and he was terrified of the system himself. They were still

torturing me, and I begged him to help me die. Instead, when at last it was clear that my son was going to be born, he diagnosed me with puerperal fever and transferred me to a hospital outside the prison. A guard accompanied me, but he was not allowed inside the women's ward. The young doctor told me to pretend that I was Turkish, from a village far from Tehran, and that I was a simple peasant girl. When the doctors discharged me, I telephoned my sister from the hospital telephone and she came to collect me and the baby from the back. The guard never knew that I had gone.

After this, heavily veiled and living in hiding with her two children, her mother having forfeited her house on account of her disappearance, Aida returned to her underground work with refugees and dissidents, until the day came when it was simply too dangerous for her to stay in Tehran. With the help of friends, she and her children escaped to Turkey – she had parted by now from her husband – but as an Armenian in Istanbul she was again suspected of having dissident connections, and again arrested and tortured. A United Nations commissioner heard about her and secured her release. The family now moved on to Holland, and then, in 1991, to England, where they were given refugee status and where Aida started work with HIV patients and asylum-seekers.

By 2001, Aida and Josephine had gathered enough funders and volunteers to open the centre they had dreamt of. They found therapists able to work in seventeen different languages. Both are practical, realistic women and they share a similar vision of the effects of torture. Terrible experiences, they agree, can and do lead to trauma; but trauma is cloudy, not solid like measles, and how it will be experienced owes much to how an individual perceives himself, and how resilient his past has made him. Good parenting, they say, that leaves children feeling loved with a strength that lies beyond words, will make a vital difference to the way a person is able to process torture. For Aida, the help she seeks to provide is all about trust, the breaking of isolation, and allowing people to feel safe. 'We provide,' she says, 'a space in which people can be while they learn to trust again.' As she sees it, not all people who have been tortured need or are able or want to relive the experience; rather, they need to be helped to build up structures that contain and imprison it. Then they need to learn to live. 'Until recently,' she argues, 'the accepted view was that in order to get better, people have to talk about what has happened to them. But for some people, the best thing is to build a wall around that particular moment in their past, and then move on.' Aida, like Helen, 'accompanies' her clients. And they know, she says, when the time has come for them to end their therapy. They get bored and they simply stop coming.

The image of victim and survivor is always present in this field. Doctors working over long periods of time with people who have been tortured marvel at the spirit and dignity of their clients, and at their enormous powers of self-regeneration. Much, they note, depends also on the expectations of torture victims. 'When people come from societies where repression is severe and where torture is routine,' says Dr Michael Peel at the Medical Foundation, 'where they have witnessed others disappear and heard stories of torture, these people tolerate it better. It is not a catastrophe, striking from nowhere. It is part of their map. They assimilate it because it does not shatter their feelings of what is predictable.' Cultural differences have become important to him, as has the need to gauge, person by person, what works best. For many, it is a question of reducing the traumatic past into 'bite-sized chunks', which can, one by one, be assimilated.

And people find their own strategies to survive. Helen told me about a man in a Middle-eastern country who had been arrested and severely tortured. One day, he was made to watch a friend being tortured. Afterwards, he tried to comfort him. 'Old man,' he said, 'we cannot strike them back now. But whilst we are here in prison I shall teach you to read and write and that will be our victory over them.'

The first time Michael Korsinski saw Lamine, he was lying on the floor of his office at the Medical Foundation, scrunched up like a foetus, racked with pain. He could neither sit in a chair, nor walk normally around the room. That day, the two men, Lamine an Algerian former military cadet and refugee in his mid-forties, Michael an American therapist some ten years younger, embarked on what would become a very long and very arduous programme of work. The therapist, a tall, thin, gangling man who uses his hands a lot, would lounge in his chair, his client crouched over and cramped, or shuffling around the room looking at his feet, unable to meet his eye – because in prison, as Lamine would tell me, there is no horizon, and to look into people's eyes is to invite trouble. Michael is an ideal example of the Foundation's eclecticism: a dancer who learnt about physical pain through a bad accident; a practitioner of the Alexander Technique who came to Jungian analysis through his need to bridge what he saw as an uncomfortable gap between his own mind and body; a somatic psychotherapist who came to the work not through the theories of earlier doctors and analysts working with functional disorders like Reich and Charcot, but through his own interest in the body. At the Medical Foundation, among people stunned into chronic pain and despair by torture, Michael discovered the setting he needed in which to do his work. In the early 1990s, recruited by Helen, he began to listen to people's bodies.

In many ways, Lamine was also Michael's ideal client. He was a clever, articulate, reflective man who had reached a moment of such profound desperation that the vast edifices of his defences were weakened just enough to allow them to be breached. Safe at last from threat and danger, he could permit himself to collapse. He was caught, as Michael saw it, in that quasi-world familiar to all who work with tortured refugees, in a state of pain that is neither all physical nor all mental but some complicated amalgam of both, trying to dissociate himself from his body in order to survive as a psychic entity; and the two, the mental and the physical, needed to be brought together again. And so, while Lamine rocked and groaned, Michael got down onto the floor next to him and did exactly what his instincts told him to do: he took hold of Lamine's head and supported it. 'I could feel this huge tension,' Michael says. 'I had to do something to release this unbearable physical pain.' For Lamine, the moment was both shocking and intensely moving. He felt humiliated; but he also felt comforted. Never, he says now, had he lain on the floor in this abject fashion, not even during the worst of the torture. However, lying on his bed in his bleak hotel room in King's Cross, he had decided against suicide and knew that he needed help: medical help for his old injuries, and above all mental help, though he could not imagine that he would ever meet anyone he could trust. Particularly not in this alien country, where he could not speak to anyone and where he felt permanently cold. Through Michael's hands, in a room full of brightly coloured rubber balls and odd objects that are some of the tools of his trade, with an interpreter looking on, Lamine wondered whether he had found his man.

Nothing happened quickly. It had been luck that had taken Lamine to the Medical Foundation, in the form of a perceptive nurse at his local doctor's office in King's Cross, who remarked on his wounds and suggested that he try the place up the road that she believed looked after people who had been tortured. It now took great courage to go there. Helen's flash of humour helped release Mrs M.'s story: now it was a single act by Michael that would open Lamine's first door. 'He promised me something. And he kept his word.' Lamine did not expect people to do this. He had been betrayed since early childhood. That sudden feeling of trust became his key.

Though the doors opened only very gradually – and not all are yet open – Lamine returned week after week to see Michael, longing for the day when he would not need an interpreter; and slowly, the pain began to ease. 'There were,' he says, 'two aspects to talking. One was talking or not talking. The other was really talking.' It was his whole, painful life of lovelessness and violence that Lamine was forcing himself to face, of which torture was just a part. Michael knows all about doors. He knows that they cannot be opened brutally, just as he knows that torture may do many different things to people, but that one thing it always does is alter them. Lamine was looking for the person that he had been, Michael for ways to help him metabolise his experiences, to face up to and question his own carefully constructed defence mechanisms and find the strength to let them go, and then move on. As he saw it, his job was to decide when Lamine was ready to confront the past, when he was sufficiently strong to start rebuilding. He was listening for the signal. 'You need,' he says, 'a very broad palette to work in this field.'

When I went to see him, Michael, like Helen, told me a story. 'There was an Asian man who was blind. One day, he found himself by an elephant but did not know what it was. "This," he said to himself, stroking the trunk, "must be a snake." Then he felt the elephant's body. "And this is a breathing mountain." After this, he ran his hand along a leg. "And this is a tree."' No one, says Michael, 'knows the whole picture. All we have are the pieces of a complex puzzle which says that people don't react well when they are badly treated.'

On Friday afternoons over several years I have listened to refugees at the Medical Foundation talk about what torture has done to them, and about their sense of exile. I have heard about rape, about burns and electric shocks and what it is like watching children and parents die; often, describing what has happened to them, people cry; sometimes, they barely speak. I have come to learn that rape, of both men and women, and betrayal, both real and perceived, cause a particular kind of pain and grief neither easily conveyed nor ever eradicated. In Muslim societies especially, the shame of rape is so profound that many of the women have never told their families, or mentioned the fact to the immigration authorities when asking for asylum. Easier, by far, to describe survival, the steps to safety, than to confess.

There is Mary, a neat, contained Ugandan girl who speaks good English from her days in missionary school in Kampala. Mary is twenty-two. Her mother died of Aids when she was a child. During her first holidays from university, she volunteered to take some food and clothes to northern Uganda, to distribute in a camp for displaced people. One night, asleep alone in a tent, she was attacked by fighters from the Lord's Army. They raped her, took her away with them to their camp, and held her prisoner. Every night, often by several different fighters, she was raped. She was also beaten. Three months later, the camp was attacked by government forces. Mary was freed, but then taken back to a military barracks. Here she was kept for two months. She was again raped. One night, she managed to escape and make her way back to Kampala. She found that her widowed father had died. An uncle bought her a ticket and put her on a plane to London. She arrived in England six months pregnant, too late to have an abortion, and when she came to the Medical Foundation she showed me her swollen stomach, disfigured by the blotchy scar of a huge burn: the Lord's Army fighters had poured boiling water and porridge over her. Mary cried when she first came to see me on a Friday afternoon at the Medical Foundation; she cried because she was alone, with no friends, and because she could not get in touch with her sisters and brother in Uganda, and because she had just been refused asylum in Britain and didn't know what would become of her, and she cried because she did not know whether to keep her baby after the birth.

There is Luis, who arrived in London in 1976 from Chile, a young political supporter of Allende and a rare survivor of Pinochet's death squads and torture centres. Luis's friends and pregnant wife had been murdered in secret detention. For many years, he had pressed on with his life, held the memories at bay, laughed when strangers told him he needed psychiatric help. He couldn't sleep and ached and coughed, but he studied sociology at Middlesex Polytechnic and earned his living washing up, cleaning, repairing fridges and washing machines and selling shoes in Camden Market. At night, he became a cleaner in Somerset House, where he fantasised that refugees were only permitted to clean during the night so that the staff would not be forced to meet their eyes. When, on and around people's desks, he saw combs and boxes of Kleenex, cigarette packets, hats or pairs of shoes, he would try to imagine their lives and their families, picture them in the pub or at home after work cooking dinner with their children. When he was sent by the agency to clean people's homes he would feel their beds and their half-empty cups of tea to see if they were still warm. And in the little time that he wasn't cleaning, or mending people's cookers and fridges, or writing his essays for Middlesex,

Luis busied himself helping other Chilean refugees. Like Lamine, he has thought a great deal about exile. At this period, he says, he was running very fast to keep thought at bay; but inside, he was falling apart, 'atomised, shattering'.

Luis met Helen Bamber on a bus. They travelled the same route in the mornings and they began to talk. In her immediate, forthright way, she told him that he looked terrible; he told her that his left side ached unbearably where the muscles had been torn by the torturers, and that his nights were filled with dreams of the people he had left behind, his wife and comrades, tortured and now dead, whose faces he saw in the darkness, smiling, alive, sad, asking him questions about why he had lived while they had died. In Chile, he had often beseeched his torturers to kill him; now, in between the work and the fullness of his crowded life, he thought often of suicide. Panic attacks engulfed him, like black holes in which he lost all sense of what was real and what was not. For several years he stayed at home, giving up the studying and cleaning people's houses only when sheer financial necessity drove him, bringing up a daughter he had fathered by another Chilean refugee, and her daughter by an earlier relationship, enjoying the safety and happiness of being at home with the small children, pushing away thoughts about himself. That is, until the day when, like Lamine, he could push them away no longer.

With Helen's help, he found a therapist to work with; and, very slowly, he opened the past and began to reshape the present. His girlfriend had begged him to talk, saying that she was afraid, in the night, of what was happening in that part of the mind that he kept shut; now he could not stop talking, week after week, to a therapist in Brighton, though it was many months before he stopped imagining the moment that he would jump from the cliffs of Dover, and stopped remembering always the heavy shadow of the dead, those who had been alone when tortured and 'alone, their bodies mutilated, abused and broken, defeated when they died'.

In a passage of a memoir that Luis wrote when he decided that he should record his experiences for others, he mirrored Helen's words: 'I know their last words and their last sounds, because I was there too, because I accompanied them to the threshold.' He thought that he would never survive the day his girlfriend took his daughter back to Chile, fighting to win custody but being told that as an ex-convict he had no hope of keeping her. And, in time, he stopped denying the past and knew what it felt like to be angry. And in time too he became a therapist working with refugees himself, and was able to return to Chile to give evidence at a trial of his torturers, confronting them at last, terrified that he would fail, shaking, sleepless, but elated – though when he came back to London again he felt himself a stranger once more, with nightmares and memories he could not control, and which only more therapy helped put behind him. In his memoir, Luis wrote about the torture, the beatings and the threats to the three-year-old daughter he had had by his wife in Chile, the mock executions and the solitary confinement, and the day when, like Lamine, he found a gate somewhere within his mind that the torturers could not enter. 'Here, I said, pointing to my head, you will not enter. The rest of my body has been all yours and you have violated it, abused it, humiliated it and tortured it. But this is mine, only mine, and when I am gone, after you kill me, it will go with me, with all the secrets and my secrets and all the secrets before me.' And now, much in the same way as Lamine had laughed aloud at his torturers, Luis had told his tormentors, 'You can leave the room.'

Today, almost a quarter of a century later, as we talk in a café in Victoria Station, from where he is about to catch his train home to his new wife and two young sons, with the sound of the trains and the clatter and din of a large station drowning some of his soft words, what Luis wants to talk about is loss: 'the loss of all the people I loved. I want to be with them, the people I met in the camps, the ones who disappeared, the two who were machine-gunned in front of me in their car, those I heard screaming day after day in the torture centre of Villa Grimaldi. I don't feel guilty. I wasn't a perpetrator and I begged them to kill me and they wouldn't. But I remember, and I think always of the loss. I keep company with the dead.'

Another refugee who talks to me is Tesfay. Tesfay is Eritrean, a tall, very thin figure with greying hair cut short and glasses that give him a distinguished, professorial look. He is neat and trim. Tesfay never imagined, in all the years of his childhood and adolescence, living outside of Eritrea. On the contrary, Tesfay knew that what he liked best about his life was the sense of community that came to him from his large family, many relations and small village. He would tell friends, when they talked about the world outside Africa, that perhaps, when he was old, he might travel for a look at Europe.

In the winter of 1995, as a twenty-six-year-old teacher and occasional political activist, Tesfay realised that unless he acted quickly he would be arrested and possibly executed. He knew all about prison and torture: he had already been taken several times into custody, sometimes at the same time as his father. And he had lost two brothers and seen a sister wounded in the long war with Ethiopia. Now, on this bright, sunny, winter day, Tesfay fled. He told only his father of his plans. He said goodbye to no one

else. Late one night, on foot, taking nothing with him, he followed a
smuggler through the hills and across the desert. They walked for six days.
In Sudan, he was put onto a plane, still in the company of the smuggler.
He thought he might be gone for two years. By the time I met Tesfay, in
a café near his small council flat in Hammersmith, he had been an exile for
eight, with little prospect of being able to go home. As he told me his story,
he kept stopping to breathe deeply and steady himself. 'You see,' he said,
when he could breathe again, 'whenever I talk about it, my chest becomes
too tight to speak.'

Like Lamine, Tesfay knew no one in London. It was January and, again
like Lamine, what he remembers best is the grey and the debilitating cold
after the light and sun of the high plateaux of Eritrea. The smuggler, who
accompanied him all the way into the city, left him on a street corner in
Finsbury Park towards the north of the city, telling him that it was an area
frequented by Eritreans. Tesfay walked around the streets, stunned and
shocked by the feeling of unfamiliarity, terrified by the chaos in his mind.
But, in the way that many of the stories that refugees tell about themselves
are lit by sudden episodes of luck and generosity, so something
unexpected and good happened to him. Looking into a shop window, he
saw an elderly woman inside who seemed to him unmistakably Eritrean in
appearance. He went in and spoke to her. It turned out that her family
came originally from his father's village in the mountains. She took him
home with her, to her flat in Finsbury Park where she had lived for many
years since becoming a refugee herself in the 1970s, and she let him sleep
on her sofa while he found a solicitor and applied for political asylum.

Because his flight had been so precipitate, Tesfay had not had time to
prepare himself for London, to visualise what it might all look and sound
like. He wandered the streets, fighting off his sense of panic, trying to
understand what people were saying; he felt very cold and very lost;
sometimes, overwhelmed by memory and desolation, he fell over and lay
under a car or along the pavement. Passers-by assumed he was drunk. And
though his Eritrean friend did her best to make his life tolerable, though
the Home Office eventually granted him asylum and gave him a hotel
room in which to live, his sense of loss and isolation grew stronger. His first
hotel was inhabited by prostitutes and drug dealers, and he found them
terrifying and strange. The shared kitchen was very dirty. He stayed in his
room. One day, he bought a kettle and sometimes, when he felt weak from
lack of food, he boiled pasta in it, switching the kettle on and off until it
was cooked. On several occasions he came back from walks to find his
room ransacked, his few possessions gone. He moved back to spend the

night on his friend's sofa, but spent the days in his hotel room in his pyjamas, remembering the past, going over what he had lost and the life he would have been living had he stayed at home. 'I felt everything as a shock, a pain, a loss,' Tesfay says now. 'At home I had always felt safe. I was respected, popular, I had friends, I had money in my pocket. Here, I knew no one. Days went by when I did not speak to anyone. The more time I spent alone, the more I needed to be alone. I dreaded having to tell my story again and again, to lawyers, to the doctor, to the Home Office. The only place I could find to live was the past.' He grew thinner. Constant, agonising stomach pains and feelings of nausea sent him to see doctors. Some, he says, treated him well; others were impatient and callous and he left them feeling that he was not good enough to receive their care. From time to time, a new doctor would wonder whether some of his pains might not be psychological in origin. 'I thought they were telling me that I was mad. I became defensive and insisted that they simply try to address my symptoms.' In time, he says, his hotel room came to look like a little pharmacy.

It took almost two years for Tesfay's life to improve. Slowly, he learnt English and began to make friends. The Eritrean lady went back to Asmara for a visit, and took letters to his family and brought back replies. Now he knew that they were alive and well, and they knew that he was alive. I asked Tesfay if he had ever been able to speak to them. He said that his village had no telephone. He moved, first to a better hotel, then to his room in Hammersmith, where the kitchen is clean. And the day came when he was referred to the Medical Foundation, and though he kept telling everyone that he wanted to forget, not to talk, he did begin to talk about himself, very slowly, often having to leave his sessions to vomit. 'The therapist would say to me: "How do you feel?" And I would say: "I feel terrible, I have a headache and a stomach ache and I feel sick." And then I would quickly begin to generalise. "Like everyone else, I . . ." And the therapist would say: "I don't want to know about everyone else. I want to know about you." Then he would ask me why I thought this or that, and I found this terrifying. I felt silly.'

As Tesfay began to talk, so he began to remember his dreams. He dreamt about police and soldiers coming to get him, and about the President of Eritrea arriving in his village by helicopter; and he dreamt about his family. He felt bad all the time, and whenever anything upset him, he was sick. He gave up drinking coffee or tea or eating anything but the blandest food. He could not be in a room with anyone smoking, and still cannot tolerate cigarette smoke. But, bit by bit, session by session, he began to grow more aware, to anticipate what gave him pain and made him sick. He learnt to control it. And, after some time, he began to train to become a counsellor himself, working with those whose sense of shock and alienation he felt to be part of himself. 'It changed,' he says, 'my frame of reference.'

But Tesfay, like Lamine, is alone. When I asked him whether he had a wife or a girlfriend, he pulled a bowl of sugar lumps that was sitting on the table between us towards him, picked up a single lump and threw it, almost violently, to one side. This, he said, was what his life was like: apart, not in a group, not close to anyone. 'At home, you meet someone like you. To have a relationship, you need a network or a group, and there you find someone who shares your values and understands you. I want someone who can communicate with my mother. Here, I never know the extent to which people understand me. I have friends, but I have to work hard to communicate with them. I have to think, very carefully, about concepts. It is very, very hard work.'

For Tesfay, for Lamine, for Luis who accompanies the dead, and for Mary, who is shocked by her sense of aloneness, home has become an elusive idea, haunting and dangerous. Home was what defined them, and what they were forced to abandon. The image is always that of abandonment, their own and that of others. And home, in a place of exile, rarely exists. It is a thought most find too frightening to dwell on. But Tesfay thinks about it often. 'If I were to play with words,' he says, 'I would say that I was homeless. Even if I go back to Eritrea now, I will not belong there. I will be strange to people, and they will be strange to me. Eritrea does not now have everything to satisfy me: I have acquired new habits and manners. But here, I lack what I need to feel at home. Wherever I am, for the rest of my life, I will never be entirely at home again.'

Part Four

Afterwards

Chapter Nine

Going Home: Afghanistan

As a political unity, it is nothing but a chewed bone left over
on the plate between Imperial Russia and British India.
Peter Levi, *The Light Garden of the Angel King*

In July 2002, the Taliban not long gone and the Americans still pursuing
al-Qaeda in the high southern valleys, I went to Kabul to talk to refugees
returning to their country after many years of exile. I needed to see for
myself what return meant to a people who had been gone so long that little
was remembered, who were going back to a country petrified in time, a
quarter of a century earlier, and what it was like for a country so new and
so fragile to welcome and absorb so many expectant people, bringing back
with them so many new skills and foreign ways and so much hopeful
memory. I wanted to learn what it felt like to travel backwards in great
numbers all at once, and about what people who had spent years – in many
cases all their lives – in refugee camps expected and hoped for.

Dubai in the summer of 2002 was still the gateway to Afghanistan from
the West. Ariana, the Afghan state airway, owned a single elderly jet
coaxed into service by foreign engineers, but it had as yet no booking
system. It was a question of turning up and waiting. At midnight, Dubai's
modest second airport was humid, quiet and very hot. Along one wall, with
its single row of plastic seats, gathered the passengers hopeful for Kabul's
dawn flight: a German television crew, with furry booms and metal boxes;
women aid workers, incongruous in Afghan dress and neat Western
haircuts, leaning on their trolleys reading fat paperbacks; a group of
bearded Afghan men, standing apart, talking to each other. And there was
Nasir.

Nasir stood out from the others because he didn't quite belong. He was
dark, clean shaven and wore light woollen pale-grey trousers and brown
loafers and a checked poplin button-down shirt, newly ironed; and his hair
was cut short and very neat. He was in his early sixties. Nasir had glasses,
unmistakably Western, which gave him a mild, scholarly air, a mobile
telephone in his shiny leather briefcase, and a new belt that was probably,

like his loafers, made in Italy. His manner was tentative; like his faint
foreign overtones, it had something unsure about it, almost wary.

As the night wore on, as a second and then a third television crew joined
the queue, and then some more aid workers, Nasir and I began to talk. He
told me in his uneven American accent that he was an Afghan who had
been forced to flee Kabul in 1979, when, as the son of a prominent family,
he had been suspected of political interests inimical to the incoming
regime. One by one, all of his large family had been driven abroad, for fear
that their homes and livelihoods would not escape the repressions of the
communist regime. No one expected to be gone for long. Nasir, his wife
and two sons went to America. There he did well as a businessman in
electronics, and his wife gave birth to a third son. All three were soon
fluent in English as well as in their native Pashto and Dari, and all later
graduated with master's degrees. Though Nasir's marriage did not survive
the long exile, he built himself a large house in the suburbs of Washington
and described to me with pride the fine tall trees in his garden. His
business thrived. Year by year, he watched from afar the mujahideen's
struggle for power, observed the Taliban's rise, and later celebrated their
defeat. Now, he was intrigued by the new Afghanistan and what it might
have to offer. He wondered what he had to offer his country himself, since
he had money and a good house and an American passport, and his sons
were grown men. He had come to look. Afghanistan needed trained and
professional Afghans, he said to me, as the night wore slowly on; it needed
people who spoke the languages, who remembered the past and who
wanted to shape the future. With his easy Americanised ways, Nasir
believed he might be the kind of person who was wanted. And he had
cousins he had not seen for over two decades, men who had endured the
communist and mujahideen and Taliban years in quiet, unobtrusive jobs
at the university or in the civil service, making no enemies. Nasir had
houses in Afghanistan too, one of them a large compound in the centre of
old Kabul where his grandparents had lived and his father had grown up.
He had, he told me, plans to open a factory and possibly broker a series of
deals between foreign organisations and the new administration to provide
water for the city. He was excited by what was waiting.

Kabul lies a little over two hours from Dubai by plane, over an unbroken
landscape of ochre and beige mountains. There are almost no trees,
though occasionally, far below, you can trace the course of a river cut into
the rock, edged with a long strip of green valley with wheat fields and
orchards. The airport, six months after the allied invasion, was pitted with
deep holes where shells had landed; just off the runways lay the burnt-out

aeroplanes of Afghanistan's small military airforce; beyond, by the ruins of hangars, were tanks destroyed in the last weeks of fighting. The air was clean and clear, the tawny mountains, tipped by snow which descended in thin rivulets of white along the cusp, stretched away for ever in patterns of colour that seemed to grow darker with distance; and the sky was very blue. The airport hall was cramped, noisy, frenetic; there were soldiers and UN posters about landmines and security precautions. 'Do not travel,' said one, 'to places that other people are not going to.' Arriving passengers were given forms to fill in, with questions about identity and address. Not knowing what to write, I looked for Nasir and found him leaning silently against a pillar in the chaos. He was biting his lips, his pencil poised in the air above his form, hesitating. There was only one blank left on his form. What, asked this last question, is the reason for your visit? As I watched, Nasir's pencil descended. In English, in a firm, large, rounded hand, he wrote: 'Coming home'.

The Afghans know about exile. Until recently, they were the country with the largest number of its people dispersed, as refugees in neighbouring Iran or Pakistan, or, further afield, in America, Germany, Britain and the Gulf States. During the 1980s and 1990s, when Afghanistan was almost totally cut off from the world – first by the Soviet invasion, then by the mujahideen fighters conducting their own civil war, and later by the Taliban – I read about the refugees and wondered what it was like to come from a country in which almost one in four of its inhabitants had fled. From 1979, when Nur Mohamed Taraki declared Afghanistan a democratic republic and Moscow moved to shore up the insurgency with military equipment and advisers, Afghans had left in waves, via precipitate flights on foot, by car, lorry, donkey and camel, leaving behind houses and lands and possessions and, sometimes, elderly grandparents too frail to make the arduous journey over the mountains to safety. During the confused years of warlords and mujahideen, and then the reign of the austere and punishing young Talibs, bent on imposing their own brand of implacable Islam, I heard about derelict and abandoned villages, empty except for a handful of elderly people, sometimes sharing a single room for warmth and safety. The young, for the most part single men in their twenties and thirties, but families too, the women silent and watchful, came to the West with stories of torture and executions.

By the time the Allies attacked, on 6 October 2001, those who had stayed behind had endured twenty-three years of lawlessness, rape, killings, looting, expulsions and displacement as, one after the other, groups of fighters, often aided by foreign powers, had destroyed their fabled irrigation system, mined their orchards and fields, levelled their cities, closed their schools and hospitals, plundered their possessions and driven the brightest and strongest abroad. One in four Afghan children could expect to be dead before the age of five. Kabul was virtually destroyed, and sewage ran along open gutters. The handful of tarmac roads that once linked the larger cities – Afghanistan is the size of Texas – had become all but impassable due to neglect, erosion and the effects of war. The water supply, once the pride of Afghanistan, flowing in underground canals and irrigating wheat fields, orchards and vineyards, had collapsed under mines and shelling. There was no postal system, no telephone, no national newspaper, and all the law books were said to have been burnt by the Taliban. There never had been a railway. And there were said to be up to 10 million unexploded landmines – down wells, in fields, among the ruined houses. A country once self-sufficient had been reduced by war and drought to penury.

After the Allies began their bombing, and the warlords, assisted by the Americans, began their advance on Kabul, UN agencies, long in waiting over the Pakistan border in Islamabad and Peshawar, started to prepare for what they assumed would be a new wave of refugees. For a while there was confusion: Pakistan and then Iran closed their borders and there were descriptions of terrified and destitute families clinging together in the rocky, barren no man's land, unable to move either forwards or backwards. But the predicted exodus never happened. When the borders opened, there were not many people wanting to leave Afghanistan. Most Afghans preferred to sit this conflict out.

On 13 November 2001, Kabul fell. The remnants of the Taliban took to the mountains to the east, along the North-West Frontier Province of Pakistan, and to the south, where the valleys and high passes were full of tunnels and secret caves. An interim authority was sworn in to prepare for a *loya jirga*, a grand council of elders, and for eventual democratic elections; in Bonn, the international community pledged $4.5 billion in aid to rebuild a country in the grip of a four-year drought, and where, in its capital city, 70 per cent of the buildings had been reduced to rubble.

In November, when the first humanitarian experts flew cautiously in to assess the lie of the land, they found Kabul silent, empty and eerie. The university lay in ruins, and in the library ancient religious tomes had been punctured by bullet holes. Nothing moved on the streets. Round the airport at Bagram, not a single house was standing. By February 2002, the UN agencies and the non-governmental organisations that had been looking after the Afghan refugees for over two decades in Pakistan, were frantically shifting their operations from Peshawar to Kabul in anticipation of the waves who would now come home. In keeping with a report drafted by Lakhdar Brahimi, the UN special representative, Afghanistan was to be regarded as a model for a more co-ordinated and sensitive approach to UN assistance. Consultation, involvement, a 'light foot-print', became the catch-phrases of foreign involvement. Overnight, Kabul became hectic, its residents boasting wanly of traffic jams, though apart from ancient yellow taxis, bicycles and the jeeps carrying heavily armed militia and the peacekeeping forces, ISAF, the traffic was all white Toyota Landcruisers, the logos of the aid agencies and non-governmental groups painted on their sides. Kabul had become a place of expectations.

And the refugees did start to come home. They came because President Hamid Karzai asked them to, and promised that in the new Afghanistan they would prosper and be safe. They came because the UN High Commission for Refugees told them that they would pay for their journeys, and give them food and money with which to rebuild their lives. They came because Iran and Pakistan were growing weary of their long-term guests and had started to make their lives uneasy with threats and random attacks and demands for bribes. And they came because they wanted to come home, because after years in a foreign land they wished to grow up, or die, in the place that their families remembered as their own, where they belonged, and where they were beholden to no one. They were tired of being unwelcome.

By March 2002, though al-Qaeda still controlled some of the mountain areas, though landmines littered their fields and their houses had been reduced to rubble, they were on their way back, for March is traditionally the first month of migration in this part of the world, when the snows have melted sufficiently to make the high roads passable, and when enough months of light and sun remain to plant and build before the bitterly cold winter weather descends. By June they were coming in thousands, by July in tens of thousands. They arrived at the outskirts of Kabul, where UNHCR had set up one of its reception centres, in buses and lorries that streamed up over the high plateaux in clouds of dust at first light, piled high with quilts and bales and buckets, their metalwork brilliantly decorated with peacocks and lovebirds, camels, palm trees and leopards, and lions stalking in jungles. By July, it was clear to everyone that this was likely to be the largest mass return in modern history.

When Robert Byron visited Kabul in the 1930s, he found strongly scented yellow and white roses in the British Minister's garden, along with sweet williams, peonies, canterbury bells and columbines. Set in the middle of a great green plain, the town, he noted, was small and shady, with long avenues of poplars, and the houses surrounded by well-irrigated and well-tended gardens.

Three-quarters of a century later, the city was a ruin, a shell of houses open to the wind and dust, with flies hanging in clouds over the deep gutters that act as open sewers along the roads. There were very few roses anywhere. The city was crowded with Jeeps that contained soldiers with their rifles at the ready. Boys in the streets were selling long green cucumbers that hung like fat worms from their barrows, and flat sheets of bread that looked like loofahs, pinned up by pegs, much as the Chinese hang up their ducks in the windows of restaurants. Half the women were wearing sky-blue burkas with their small mesh panels for their eyes, while the rest wind scarves around their heads.

After dark, when a curfew confined foreigners to their hotels and guest houses, the talk was of warlords, weapons, opium, and the assassination of a vice president, shot, it is said, on the orders of another warlord. The electricity supply was still erratic, there was not much water and the telephone did not work as a result of the UN having installed one system for itself and the government, and aid agencies another, incompatible one, for everyone else. It is heady work, this creation of a new country – for those who sweated out the Taliban years, for those who went into exile and spent the time dreaming of a better future, for the aid world which perceives a virgin land for its new theories, for lawyers who plan to draft a constitution full of the human rights so long denied the Afghans, for women escaping the terrible isolation imposed on them by the misogynist Talibs, and for the UN, for whom Afghanistan may provide redemption after the debacles of Rwanda and Somalia. Playing at new countries is fun.

Not many districts of Kabul were as badly shelled as the west, traditionally home to the Hazaras, among the most persecuted of Afghanistan's main ethnic people. They are descendants of Mongols and Turks who fought with Genghis Khan and lost their lands and lives in successive brushes with Tajik and Pathan warlords, who killed or enslaved over half their number in the late nineteenth century. Wanting to learn what the returning refugees were up against, I went to west Kabul, which in July 2002 still looked like photographs of Berlin in 1945. Mounds of earth and dirt mark the spot where houses once stood, and the jagged remains of more solid buildings line the main roads; the rafters for the roofs have long since gone, taken by the Taliban for firewood.

But west Kabul was already a place of purpose. The Hazaras, accustomed to conflict and defeat, had planned their exodus two decades earlier with foresight. Fleeing the civil war and the Taliban, they had journeyed for the most part together, over the mountains to the east, to the cities and refugee camps of Pakistan. There, they had regrouped and waited. Twenty or more years later, they were still there, and when news came that Kabul was again safe, they hired lorries with the money promised by UNHCR and travelled back together to reclaim their part of the city. While in Pakistan, they had become renowned weavers of carpets, and now whole factories decided to make the journey home together, the owners and middlemen as well as the weaver families (whose young children provide the bulk of the workforce), bringing with them their vats, dyes and wool. And because the weaving day for the children includes several hours of schooling, the Hazaras brought their schools with them, the teachers accompanying their pupils in the peacock- and leopard-covered buses and lorries.

Since there was no building standing for the school to occupy, they held the first lessons in a shell of a compound, teachers and children crouching in the remains of former rooms, swept clean and divided one from the other by curtains of bright cloth. Within three days of their return, looms had been erected in houses that were hastily being rebuilt around them, and children as young as six and seven were sitting in their rows, on a single low stool, plucking threads through the taut string. I found twelve-year-old Abdul Hakim, a thin, energetic boy with the quick movements of a small animal, eager to practise the English he had acquired in Peshawar. He led me from the school along dusty tracks between the ruins to where his five brothers and sisters were at work, chattering and weaving like a row of brightly coloured little birds. It was their turn to go to school later in the day. The family had been lucky: they came home to find their house, though partially ruined, at least unoccupied. Their neighbours had found theirs intact, but inhabited by a family able to produce deeds proving ownership: the house had changed hands many times in twenty-three years, starting, after the original family's departure, with a new set of deeds forged by a local warlord.

The teacher who walked with us was Jawad Wafa, a slender, gentle young man, with soft brown hair. He is twenty-two. Jawad comes from Bamiyan, in the high mountains of the Hindu Kush, and his family have spent the years of exile in Iran. Jawad himself had been forced to stay in Pakistan.

'My father,' said Jawad, in his soft, precise English, 'was a farmer, with many fields of wheat, and a religious scholar. When fighting came to our village in 1988, he decided that we should leave and go abroad, though my two married sisters were to stay behind. We left one night on foot, with a donkey and a horse to carry our things to Quetta in Pakistan. But my eldest brother had heard that things were better for refugees in Iran, and he went ahead to see. He sent word that he had found well-paid work in a factory making loaves of sugar, and that there was work there for my other five brothers as well. I was only eight then. Even though the work was enough to support all of us, I hated Iran. In the street, people used to insult us and call us names. Our accents were different. At last, I was given a place in a religious school in Kom, but one day the religious police picked me up and held me in jail for a month and shaved my hair.

Jawad was never safe. He has the distinctive flat face and slightly slanting eyes of the Hazaras, and during the long years when Afghans were living in great numbers in Iran – 2 million people at its peak – there were periods of mass expulsions back into Afghanistan, particularly of young men, picked up in the streets or late at night, held in camps near the border, then pushed across with orders not to return. The day came when this happened to fourteen-year-old Jawad, and he found himself in Herat, alone, with no money and no friends. 'The Taliban were just starting to be powerful. I saw them in the streets, with their great turbans and their scissors to cut the hair of men they thought wore it too long. They stopped me all the time to ask if I had said my prayers. After a few days I found a way to go back to Bamiyan, but it was six years since I had left and my married sisters did not know me. I got ill and didn't know what to do. I tried to get back into Iran, but I was stopped at the border and pushed back.'

Jawad now had little choice but to find a home in Pakistan. He heard of a religious school in Peshawar, founded by an Iranian cleric, and for the next five years he lived and studied in the madrassa. He saw his parents only once, when he got word that his father had had a stroke and slipped across the Iranian border by night to see him, returning the next day to the madrassa. But in Pakistan the mood was changing, and soon confrontations between the traditional religious teachers and their secular young pupils, who wanted to be taught to speak English and use computers, led to bitter fights and expulsions. Jawad was one of eighteen young men deemed to be the ringleaders and expelled. He was trying his hand as an apprentice tailor when he met Aziz, an energetic and somewhat older Hazara, who was then in the process of setting up a school for Hazara weaving children in Peshawar. Aziz offered him a deal: he would coach the younger man in English and political science if Jawad would join his school and teach the children to read and write.

Jawad was one of Aziz's teachers sent on ahead, as the Taliban were pulling out of Kabul, to prepare for the transfer of the school back to Afghanistan. He found an abandoned and derelict building, bought some whitewash, acquired tables and chairs. In May 2002, the school travelled together across the mountains in a lorry with their textbooks. They missed just three days of schooling. 'I am very anxious,' Jawad said to me. 'I am anxious but also hopeful. I need a proper university education if I am to help my country. But I have too little time to study and no one to help me. I plan to become a lawyer. If we don't have social justice, we will never become men for ourselves: our destiny will be that of people who carry wheels on their shoulders for others.'

In 1836, Lieutenant Colonel Sir Alexander Burnes, visiting Kabul with a British military expedition, set out west from the city on a journey into the mountains. From Kareez-i-Meer, where he and his party halted for the first night, he noted in his journal that he could see 'in the hazy distance, a vast vista of gardens extending for some thirty or forty miles . . . No written description can do justice to this lovely and delightful country. Throughout the whole of our journey we had been lingering amidst beautiful orchards, the banks of which were clustered over with wild flowers and plants in profuse abundance.' Among the 'wide spreading plane-trees' and the grapes, 'which imparted a purple tinge to the hills', Burnes spotted porcupines, hedgehogs and marmots, though he observed, with his sportsman's eye, that 'everything that yields a fur' was hunted by the Afghans. What Burnes had seen was the fabled Shomali plain, the former orchards and vineyards of Kabul, a rich plateau irrigated by deep wells and the snow melt which flowed along 'qanats' or channels buried far underground. Babur, the Moghul Emperor Zahiruddin Mahomed, descendant of Genghis Khan and Tamburlaine, loved the Shomali plain, and came in the sixteenth century while on his way to India to picnic underneath its mulberry trees. He had already spotted sixteen varieties of wild tulip growing in the hills around Kabul, one of which bore the scent of red roses, and here he remarked on the excellence of the quinces and plums, and observed that the valley was home to parrots, mynah birds, peacocks and monkeys, and that the local people laid snares for migrating herons and cranes in order to decorate their turbans with their feathers.

But the Shomali plain was also where, during the 1980s and 1990s, the mujahideen fought each other and the Soviets for the approaches to Kabul, and where the Taliban decreed a scorched-earth policy to level the ground for self-protection. Over a period of several years, acting alone or ordering others to do their work, the Taliban shelled the leafy Shomali villages into ruins, set fire to the vineyards to starve their economy, destroyed the avenues of planes and poplars to prevent the rebuilding of roofs, chopped down the mulberry trees that gave shade and fruit to passing travellers, dropped mines down the wells and the qanats and laid others in the fields of wheat. The Shomali plain came to be a symbol of Taliban savagery. By the summer of 2002, when I saw it, it was a derelict, deserted, silent wilderness, broken only by the red printed warnings about unexploded mines, and by the clusters of green flags waving on the ends of poles, each marking the grave of a martyr, a man who had died a violent death. It was a barren, desolate, place.

But not, as it turned out, entirely empty.

Searching for signs of Babur's earthly paradise, I saw two men, with white beards and the flat felt hats the Afghans wear, at work in a half-burnt vineyard close to the main road to Mazaar-i-Sherif. Behind them were the ruins of a once large village and the great stumps of what must have been a magnificent row of mulberry trees. The men were gently picking up unexploded shells and putting them on a pile, ready for collection by a de-mining agency working in the plain. It was hot and still and very dusty.

The men are cousins. In the early 1980s, as Haji Kamal, the older of the two men, explained, the village of Logar (taking its name from the province of his great-grandfather, who had planted these lands) had been home for forty families, most of them related to one another. With its avenues of trees, its orchards of apricot, apple, plum and pear, Logar had been a tranquil and shady place. Haji Kamal and his three brothers had owned 12,000 vines, from which they produced 600 sacks of raisins and many table grapes, sold in the bazaar in Kabul together with wheat, melons, maize, apricots, walnuts and several kinds of cherries, as well as an abundance of the sugary white mulberries which the Afghans eat dried during the winter months. Haji Kamal himself had grown eleven varieties of grape, drying most of them in the sun during the month of October, on the roof of his house or spread out on the ground. The Kandari red grapes were the sweetest, Haji Kamal told me, but the most valuable were the white ones, which he dried slowly inside the house. In the late 1970s, Chinese farming technicians had visited Logar and introduced pomegranates to the valley, and these too had made him a fine crop. Haji Kamal's family, with his children and his brothers and their families, had grown to eighty people by the time the mujahideen came, and they shared between them eight milking cows and a donkey, as well as a small tractor. When the Soviets invaded in 1979, he had just opened shops in Kandahar and Kabul, and made a deal to sell fifty tonnes of raisins each year to China.

After the Soviet shelling started he began to fear for his family's life, and sent his wife and children to Pakistan. They left by truck at dawn, taking with them the cows. It was a morning so cold that there was heavy snow in the passes and one of his pregnant daughters lost her baby. He stayed on, fighting with the mujahideen, then joined his family in a rented house in Peshawar, where he sent his young sons, but not his daughters, to school. From time to time he made the journey home across the mountains to check on his abandoned fields and crumbling house. Until the Taliban were defeated, he had not judged it safe to come back, but here he was now with his cousin Amir Jan – also one of several brothers – planning, with the help of UNHCR and various foreign aid organisations which were providing rafters and windows, to rebuild the compound in which they had once lived. In the years of exile his family had grown from eighty to two hundred people; but if the fields could be made fertile again, there would be enough food for them all.

The two elderly cousins, with their lean bearded faces and elegant pale-grey turbans, took me to see their compounds, now mounds of dust and rubble around the stumps of the mulberry trees that had once provided such dense, green shade. In one, a large white tent donated by UNCHR sheltered some of the women and children who returned with them; there was a cow, tethered to a pomegranate bush. It was a bleak, but not despairing scene. The water from his well alone, Haji Kamal said, gives him great pleasure: very cold and very pure, it reminds him that he has come home from his borrowed life in a rented room in Peshawar, where he had always felt hot and cramped. 'Though I found everything ruined, I knelt down and kissed the ground. I don't expect a harvest for two years. But at least we can walk along the road in safety, even at night. We feel safe.'

Before I left Kabul, I went to watch the families arriving early one morning at the UNHCR reception centre at Pulicharki, site of a notorious Taliban prison, under a fold of the tall ochre mountains. UNHCR has put up tents and hangars, where they hand out rations of wheat, buckets, bars of soap and plastic sheets, and where doctors from Medécins Sans Frontières monitor the health of the new arrivals and vaccinate against measles and polio. UNHCR gives small sums of money to every returning refugee, though they are conscious that they must not show too much favour to them, thereby causing resentment among those who endured the Taliban years. The money men, who are all Afghan but supervised by UNHCR, sit crosslegged in a low row behind wire cages, counting out the dollars. One tent has been made into a simulated minefield, and the families are walked past the weapons they might expect to find, unexploded, in their fields. Over the mountains to the east, in swirling bursts of dust, come the trucks and lorries, their painted sides catching the sun, swaying under their loads of mattresses and blankets, mats and sewing machines, bicycles and cooking pots, all accumulated in exile. The families who climb out talk about how hard life has been in Pakistan, and about the perils of the journey, preyed on by police and guards in search of bribes. Farmers in the 1970s and 1980s, they have since become cobblers and builders, shop-keepers and mechanics. The young boys speak little, but the girls are bold: egging each other on, they talk of the education many have received and about their plans to become doctors and teachers in the new Afghanistan. A small, robust, outspoken girl of fourteen, who can remember almost nothing of her village, having spent ten years in a refugee camp, said that her plan was to attend Kabul university. On her head, she wore a plain scarf. 'I am not in the habit of wearing a veil,' she said.

By midday, the process of arrival was over; it had been an orderly, cheerful procedure. The morning's 5,000 returnees, with their buckets and bars of soap, were on their way, by taxi or in the cars of relatives come to collect them, to discover what was left of home; or what they had come to call home, for it is estimated that over half of all those returning to Afghanistan in 2002 had in fact been born outside the country. In the other direction, the brightly decorated lorries and buses were climbing the mountain passes again, to collect more returning families.

Before I caught my plane back to Dubai, Nasir took me to see a friend in government, Nabi Farahi, deputy minister of finance, whom he had known a quarter of a century earlier when both were students at the university. Farahi sat out the Taliban years as a professor of Pashto, lying low when others provoked the Taliban. He is a charming, bespectacled, bearded man in his sixties, who offered melon to counteract the intense heat of his un-air-conditioned office, and apologised for the lack of lift, telephone, computer, carpet or fan. To wipe up the melon juice, he sent his assistant to look for unused forms from previous times, taken from the top of an ancient filing cabinet and now used as napkins. Farahi is appalled at the speed with which the refugees are coming home. 'We have nothing for them yet,' he said. 'No jobs, no houses. This country doesn't work. It is too soon.' Like all Afghans in positions of authority, he worries when he sees the few good jobs going to men who have come back from exile with skills those who stayed behind had no chance to learn, and at the way that the foreign aid organisations are so casually poaching the best people, with salaries that can run to fifty times those the bankrupt Afghan state can offer. 'I would like to see some dignity in the way people are returning,' he said, licking the melon juice from his fingers. 'It is only chaos.' It was Farahi who first mentioned the resentment many Afghans feel about the way so much money has been promised, and so little visibly delivered.

By the summer of 2002, well over a million people had listened to Karzai's calls and UNHCR's promises and had come home, more, in less than six months, than had been expected for the entire year. At this rate, there would be 2 million by the time the snows came, arriving back to a country without houses, roads, schools, hospitals, water or electricity to sustain them. 'I see our job as software,' said a man working for the UN. 'We are trying to provide the rewiring of the system, but we will not be here to run it. The Afghans have to learn to do it for themselves.' For their part, the Afghans fear that the West will not fulfil its promises. As they watch the white Toyota Landcruisers speeding along the dusty roads, they remind each other that the West has promised things before, when they wanted the Soviets out, but that once the Soviets had gone they did not seem quite as committed as before.

Out on the Shomali plain, Haji Kamal is very conscious of the fragility of the transitional government, the power of the encircling warlords, and of the coming winter, when snow and winds, no longer broken by trees, would turn his valley into a harsh and forbidding place. It would be in the next few months, he said, that Afghanistan's future would be decided.

Almost exactly a year later, I went back to Afghanistan to see how the refugees had survived their first winter. It was again summer, and I wanted to find Abdul, the ebullient small boy who had led me through the dusty alleys of west Kabul, to see whether Jawad had won his place at university, and whether Haji Kamal and Amir Jan had rebuilt their houses in the Shomali plain and were growing raisins once again. I had heard that the weavers' Hazara school was flourishing. Nasir, to whom I spoke from time to time on the telephone, told me that he had reoccupied his family home in the centre of Kabul, but that there was nothing but confusion over the awarding of the lucrative contracts for roads, telephones and electricity. He was still hesitating, flying in and out of Kabul on Ariana's ancient jet, trying to gauge the stability of the new Afghanistan. He could not quite make up his mind how far to commit himself, he kept saying over the crackling line. Money was pouring into the city, houses were being built and fetching enormous rents, but there was no certainty anywhere. No one felt safe. Only the foreign aid world, he said, negotiating the now crowded roads of the capital in their Landcruisers, seemed in control, and even they would soon be leaving.

Flying in low over the bare mountains, I found the airport still pitted with the same shell holes, the burnt-out tanks still in their places along the runways. Inside the terminal, the chaos was unchanged, but pictures of General Masood, the Northern Alliance warlord assassinated in the closing days of Taliban power, had replaced the earlier notices about landmines. On my plane were two middle-aged Afghan brothers who had fled the city twenty-four years before, and who were now bringing the body of their father home for burial to a Kabul he had never been able to visit in his long years in exile. They were uneasy, talkative. In their pockets were the deeds to the family house, long since occupied by others, over which they anticipated one of the fierce property wrangles in which many returnees have been ensnared.

We landed in Kabul soon after a flight from Frankfurt bearing more prosperous returnees, businessmen and engineers and academics who have made their lives in the West and are now, like my friend Nasir, coming back to see how the land lies. An elegant Afghan woman in her forties, fashionably dressed in a stylish combination of Afghan and Western dress, struggled to find her many trunks. '*Entshuldige*' ('sorry'), she was saying loudly, pushing her way through the Afghan porters with their turbans and flat hats, '*Entshuldige, entshuldige*'. A young Afghan with a strong American accent, crew-cutted, cocky and bemused, was telling all who would listen that this was his first visit to Kabul, and that he had come to meet a grandmother he had never seen. His real name was Mohamed; but he liked to be called Mo. Born and bred in Manhattan, Mo was incredulous and a little scornful of the chaos. 'This is not really my place, you know. I don't belong here.'

Kabul, I wrote that night in my diary, is much changed in a year. There was more razor wire on foreign and United Nations buildings; there were more women wearing burkas, sign of the little faith most Afghans now have in an independent future; the crowds were thicker and the city was dirtier and dustier, Kabul having apparently doubled to 2½ million people in a single year. And the white Toyota Landcruisers, the ubiquitous symbols of an aid city, were now lost in a permanent traffic jam of taxis, lorries, old cars, donkeys and bicycles. The pollution was so bad that to live in Kabul today, so it is said, is to smoke the equivalent of forty-five packets of cigarettes a day. There were many more beggars, mostly women in burkas with babies, and small boys were selling tattered copies of the US Marine training manual by the roadside. A hundred thousand returnees were apparently squatting in the ruins of the city, destitute and homeless. Afghanistan was still, in the language of the aid world, a SCCPI, a Situation of Chronic Conflict and Political Instability, its people short of food and vulnerable to disease, physical assault and forced displacement.

But there were roses out along the avenues leading into the city, and over a garden wall there was a pink lavatera in flower, and the fruitsellers had watermelons and mangoes, and the policeman was still where I left him, directing traffic from a purple plush sofa perched on a raised dais in the middle of the road. In the UN compounds were growing geraniums and zinnias, watered by channels cut out of the earth, and in the bazaar were new photograph shops showing the unveiled faces of young women. Masood's hawkish, brooding, unsmiling face was on every billboard.

Though the city was bustling and full of energy, in a state of constant rebuilding and activity, the returning refugees have become cautious. When the snows had melted and the migrations had begun again in March 2003, they did not flock home in anything like the same numbers as the previous year, as it had been feared they would, despite a greater climate of intolerance in Pakistan and Iran and promises of work and houses in Afghanistan. The tales of resettlement that had travelled back over the mountains had not been altogether happy ones, and the numbers arriving at Pulicharki daily in their brightly painted buses were, according to the UN, down to 600. And something had been done to curb those who travelled backwards and forwards across the border again and again, each time collecting money and rations from the World Food Programme and UNHCR. A sophisticated machine that photographs the iris of each returnee and keeps a print on a database had been introduced.

The Hazaras have been hard at work rebuilding west Kabul. Along the road leading out to the weavers' school, timber and brick merchants were doing a brisk trade. If the city buildings were still shells, their jagged walls in ruins, the side streets were by contrast full of builders and carpenters, the reconstruction of the capital said to be in the hands of wealthy returnees, or warlords and their commanders, eager to control the money and the patronage all this reconstruction entails. Aziz, the energetic young Hazara who is much involved in his people's return, had come to the airport to meet me and the friend with whom I was travelling, Frances D'Souza. He said that some 300,000 Hazaras have already returned to west Kabul. His school now had 870 pupils, studying in two shifts, and had moved to a new compound, a series of classrooms built in breeze-block, an innovation brought back with returning refugee builders from Pakistan, and judged greatly superior to the old Afghan mud and straw. More than half his pupils, Aziz said with pride, are girls, and in the evening, when the rooms are given over to classes in literacy, he could fill his centre six times over with women queuing for an education denied them by the Taliban. Aziz noted these numbers with delight. 'People have come home from Pakistan and Iran believing that education is their passport to a better life.' He is teaching humanism, human rights and what he calls a benevolent interpretation of the Koran to his top class, tightly packed rows of serious young men and women.

In the alleys behind the school, in among the building sites and timber merchants, the carpet trade is booming. Aziz believes that there are at least 600 firms, some employing as many as 500 weavers, mostly working in their own homes, the patterns drawn out by young apprentice draughts-men on squared paper and quickly memorised by the children at the looms. The work is slow: five to six hours' weaving every day except for Friday, precise, meticulous work that needs small fingers and affects the eyes and lungs – but it brings in enough money to support the entire family. The looms stand in the cool, under the pomegranate bushes and vines. It takes four months for a family to weave a carpet three metres wide and four metres long. In Aziz's school, the children talk of their futures as doctors, teachers and engineers.

Not all the foreign experts who have made Kabul their base – there are said to be over a thousand registered non-governmental organisations alone – are as sanguine as Aziz about the country's future. In February 2003, four months before my return, a Brazilian working for the International Committee of the Red Cross was stopped on a busy road outside Kandahar by a militia group. The commander, recognising the red cross painted on the front of the Landcruisers, pointed to his false leg and thanked the Brazilian for saving his life during an earlier skirmish. A Red Cross team, he told him, had been on hand and amputated his leg, without which he would surely have died. Then, taking from his pocket a mobile telephone, the commander called his warlord. He spoke, listened, came back, drew out his gun and shot the Brazilian dead.

Incidents like this have made foreigners wary and no one, now, felt safe. Within the UN compounds, behind the razor wire and the concrete pillars, there was talk of how much can be achieved for Afghanistan and how quickly, before the money runs out and with it the political will to restore such an ailing country to a semblance of democratic rule. Only, they add, it is of course not so much a question of restoration as imposition. Afghanistan never was a democracy; it was, and remains, a loose federation of tribal fiefdoms ruled over by powerful warlords, and thus it seems set to remain. Andrew Wilder is a British academic, a man who has lived in Afghanistan off and on for many years. Early in 2002, Wilder arrived in Kabul with a small monitoring unit funded by the Swiss and the Swedes, and a remit to do what is seldom done in UN circles, and that is to analyse data on the spot. Wilder is not happy with what he sees around him. Over fourteen months, he has watched the UN agencies bicker over priorities and chains of command, non-governmental organisations proliferate and go their own ways, and more attention and money go to the easier and more visible problems than to the more difficult and necessary ones. Sitting in his prefabricated hut in the grounds of a former prime minister's residence, Wilder fears for the future. The theories behind development and the delivery of aid become more complex and sophisticated all the time, he points out, but they are not matched by performance on the ground, where disillusion and disappointment fester over how few expectations have been realised. Security, argues Wilder, was always known to be the major issue in Afghanistan, the question of how to make the country safe from the warlords and free of weapons. 'Everyone, from Karzai down, knew that security should be addressed first. So what did we do? We provided assistance first, with the assumption that security would follow. It hasn't.'

On my first day back in Kabul, I found a driver and went out to the Shomali plain to see how Haji Kamal and his family had survived the winter. The dog roses were out along the hedgerows and the fields around Logar were full of men working at the vines, now watered and pruned and sprouting once more. The UN tent had gone and in both Haji Kamal's compound and that of his cousin, Amir Jan, there were signs of building. Seven long whitewashed rooms had been finished, with windows and rafters donated by a foreign aid organisation. The walls were lined with felt carpets and pillows in reds and greens. From the cool of Haji Kamal's main room, which he has painted a bright blue wash, visitors can look out over pomegranate bushes and chickens pecking in the dirt. There was a new outside bread oven, and a second cow and four sheep had appeared.

All his children and grandchildren who have reached the size and strength to walk half an hour there and back, are at the village school, and he and his cousin have planted tomatoes, radishes, potatoes, eggplants and onions. Along the avenues of mulberries, destroyed by the Taliban, new shoots are growing from the stumps of the trees.

Of Logar's forty original families, all but six have come home. Haji Kamal, the former mujahideen freedom fighter, is a man of peace now, and talks of his new orchards, of the apples and plums and almonds from which he expects a first crop in three years' time, and of the lessons he gives his grandchildren about the mines, still plentiful and unexploded across his land. But he is pleased, every day, to be home. Not long ago he turned down the offer of a job for his eldest son in Dubai, saying that he no longer wished to have his children live away from him. He fears only the weakness of the central government in Kabul, and the power of the warlords, grown strong and lazy on their looting and extortion. 'What do I miss from my years in Pakistan? Nothing. There is nothing to miss. I have no single good memory of exile.'

Since on my first visit it had been too dangerous to move far outside Kabul, this time I planned to go to the Hindu Kush to see for myself how the people returning from exile to the high mountain villages had fared during the long snowy winter. I knew that the numbers coming home had dropped with the cold season, but that the refugees were again arriving, by bus and lorry, over the passes, worried that unless they came soon, their homes and lands would be occupied by others.

When Nancy Dupree wrote her guide to Afghanistan back in 1972, before the Russians arrived and foreign visitors still came to sightsee and fish for trout in the high mountains, she travelled up into the Hindu Kush. She wanted to visit the valley of Bamiyan, where a Buddhist sect in the fourth century cut two immense buddhas out of the mountain face, and a third smaller one in a niche between them. For the journey, she described two decent roads, not paved but passable. Either one, she wrote, whether across the 12,000-foot Hijigak Pass or skirting the lower Shibar mountain, watershed between the Oxus and the Indus, would take no longer than seven hours, and it would be a delightful and memorable journey. The journey is delightful still, but twenty-six years of neglect and fighting have reduced the roads to little more than river beds pitted with huge craters and strewn with rocks; and the few cars and lorries that make the journey now prefer to travel in convoy, for fear of breakdown or attack.

Eleven hours of painful bucketing over the stones takes the traveller through some of the most dramatic scenery in the world, the bald peaks of the Hindu Kush, tinged for most of the year with snow, stretching for ever into the distance in shades of beige, ochre and purple, against a sky of deep, pure blue. There is a constant sound of water from the snow melt down the river bed. The million or so Kuchi nomads, who once regarded the highlands of the Hindu Kush as their summer pasture, have not returned to their grazing lands, for they have lost their herds to fighting and to the drought; there were no animals to be seen. In any case the Hazaras, who occupy this part of Afghanistan, do not want the Kuchis back, for the Kuchis famously sided with the Taliban in their battles, and many Kuchi leaders became Taliban commanders whose savage ways are remembered all too well in the Hindu Kush. The summer grazing, say the Hazaras who have returned home, will be excellent for the herds they now intend to build up for themselves.

Before you start the long climb towards the pass, having left Kabul along a fine tarmac road, a brief but smooth legacy of the Taliban years, you come across a lush valley with water racing down a river, irrigating orchards and plantations of poplars. In the fields grow potatoes and wheat, and, in neat rows between the crops and trees, in plots of their own, are the poppy fields, white and pink against the bright surrounding green of the grass, the rocky mountains and blue sky above. They have a festive air. From far away, the poppies look like wild flowers, growing in profusion in this green and fertile valley; from close to they look like rows of tulips, their petals large and firm. The nearest laboratories capable of transforming the poppies into heroin lie far to the south, around Kandahar. In the Hindu Kush, they are smoked as opium, though all but a very small part of the crop is sold to traders in Kabul. Before the Taliban came, Afghanistan was the world's main producer of heroin. The Taliban, for a while, curbed production. When the UN arrived in the winter of 2001, it offered grants to farmers willing to substitute their most profitable cash crop for any other. But today Afghanistan's heroin yield is again at the top of world production, the farmers having understood that by growing poppies they cannot lose: they are paid equally well to dig them up or sell them on to warlords and their middlemen. Among much else that the refugees are bringing back from their years in Iran and Pakistan is a taste for drugs – especially, so it is said, among young Hazara men.

I wanted to see Bamiyan because I had heard that Jawad Wafa, the young Hazara teacher from Aziz's school in west Kabul, was now working with the UN there; and because Bamiyan, which once lay on the silk route between Samarkand and Kabul, is a place of return for the internally displaced, refugees who did not have the money to make the expensive journey across the borders into Iran or Pakistan and so had remained in Afghanistan, exiles in their own land. These internally displaced Afghans, like IDPs the world over, are not eligible for the dollars and the bars of soap going to those coming back by bus and lorry across the mountains. UNHCR is doing what it can for them but in a country of such overwhelming want, the very ambiguities of the IDP stories do not lend themselves to easy bureaucratic assistance. In Bamiyan, I hoped the predicament of the displaced would become clearer.

Had the Taliban ruled for very much longer, the Hazaras claim, then their people would have been wiped out altogether. The Taliban considered them inferior and hostile. Finding them weakened by the Soviet and mujahideen years, they persecuted them with particular ferocity, and nowhere more so than in the province which is traditionally home to most Hazara people, finally bringing to Bamiyan and its valley the heavy artillery with which to destroy their buddhas. The valley of Bamiyan itself, with its escarpment running down the middle, is faced along one side by a long and sheer sandstone cliff, perhaps five kilometres from end to end. The sky and the light, at this altitude, is startlingly bright and clear. The air is pure and sharp. I tried to imagine the Taliban fighters laying the mines, then lining up the tanks that now lie scattered, rusting and broken, around the escarpment, positioning their heavy artillery, then giving the order to fire, the shells booming out in the silence until the two great buddhas – each standing well over a hundred feet tall in their sheltered niches, with the faded touches of their once red and blue painted robes still visible – crumbled and fractured into the valley below.

In the caves and grottoes that surround the buddhas, pitting the rock face like the holes inhabited by the swallows that flit through the valley, there once lived a community of yellow-robed monks, said to number over a thousand people at its peak in the seventh century. By the summer of 2003, the cliff caves had become shelter to those coming home to Bamiyan who had sat out the Taliban savagery in the high, secluded valleys of the Hindu Kush. Though not regarded as refugees, they were exiles none the less, returning in the spring and summer of 2003 to homes looted and burnt down by the departing Taliban, to fields long since gone wild. Like the poppies in the green valleys lower down the mountain, their bright clothes – vermilion, turquoise and many shades of yellow and purple – stand out dramatically against the dull rock face as they flit up and down the perilous tracks cut by the monks through their mountain monastery. From the caves, the view over Bamiyan is sad: the old bazaar lies far below, reduced to rubble when old scores were paid off, and the handsome buildings which once dotted the valley, surrounded by magnificent gardens, have been razed to the ground.

By the time I reached the valley early in July, 260 returning families were said to inhabit the caves, six or seven people sharing holes once occupied by a single monk. They are cool in the summer but damp and cold when the snows come to Bamiyan in late October. Inside, the frescoes of flowers, griffins, ducks and musicians that once covered their walls and ceilings have long since been blackened by cooking fires. All but a very few of the cave dwellers are Hazaras, farming families who once lived in some comfort and prosperity on their lands in the valley, growing wheat and potatoes and raising small herds of sheep and goats. Many of them are single mothers, their husbands and fathers having been killed by the Taliban as they fled. As the cave dwellers gathered around to talk, the children solemn and staring, the women breaking in to add their own memories, Amir, one of the older men, told of the final flight for most of them in the winter of 1997. The snow was already deep and the winds bitter, and they had put off leaving too long, hoping that the Taliban's attentions might be turned elsewhere.

> Then the day came when we knew that we could not wait any longer. We hid what we could, carried a few necessities with us, like quilts and cooking pots, but there were many small children to help. The old people came with us, but many did not survive the journey. We don't know quite how many died, simply giving up in the high mountains and dying quickly of the cold. We dug mass graves for them at the foot of the mountains. When we found safety in the distant valleys, where the Taliban never came, the farmers there helped us by giving us flour and shelter. We survived, but that is all.

It was from a woman in the caves that I first heard a story that would come to haunt me.

Mira is an energetic, handsome, wiry woman, tall and black-haired, in a purple dress with much embroidery. She has a son of six, a lively child with cuts and bruises from falls along the cliff face, and two older girls, silent, pretty and watchful. Mira's husband, the father of the children, was taken hostage by the Taliban in 1997, after a Hazara attack. She has had no news of him since that day. When her neighbours decided that the moment could no longer be put off to flee, she gathered up her four children, the youngest a girl of six months, and followed her friends across the fields. It was soon clear to her that she could not keep up with them, carrying on her back both a baby and a child too young to walk. 'We got to a road, and I knew I couldn't go on,' Mira said, telling her story briskly, without emotion. I began to dread what I knew must follow. 'It was snowing lightly, and dark. I wrapped the baby up in all the clothes that we could spare, and I put her down by the edge of the road, propped up against a rock. Then I picked up my son and, pulling my daughters behind me, I went on with the others to look for shelter for the night in the mountains. Later, I left the children with my neighbours and went back down into the valley to look for the baby. I found her quickly, still propped against the rock. But she was dead.'

Mira is not the only woman to have left a child by the wayside in her flight from the Taliban. Talking quickly, pointing to surviving small boys and girls, other women began to talk of babies abandoned and never found again, or discovered dead from exposure when they went back to get them. They had no choice, they said. They always picked out the youngest, the one who could not stray and whose cries would be the least loud. I became obsessed by this image of small, silent babies freezing to death alone in the dark and the snow.

As it became clear that the Taliban had left Bamiyan, in the winter of 2001, and that many of their men had disappeared for ever, executed in the closing weeks of fighting, so the survivors made the journey back over the mountains, better prepared this time, leaving no children or old people behind. They returned, however, to destitution, some of them grand-mothers who had lost five or six sons to the Taliban and were now caring for their grandchildren, others women with husbands mutilated in the fighting, others again children on their own: there are many small orphans in the dank holes in the cliff. In Bamiyan's caves, by the time of my visit, they were living in a curious vacuum, an existence that they have grown used to and that many believe will never end. They send the fitter young men to work in the new bazaar in the plain far below, visible from the caves, where they pick up a little money as porters, and the young girls to make the daily trek in search of water, found in the river almost half a kilometre distant. The younger children are dispatched to collect firewood in the mountains. Because of the sheer cliff face, each small child requires a constant minder, and it is usual to see babies and small children who are starting to walk harnessed and bound to the older girls.

All along Bamiyan's lush valley, where the first crops of wheat and potatoes were again growing, there were other families reduced by the war and exile to the edges of hunger. Many of them are widows unable to reclaim their farms after so many years of neglect, either because their lands have been appropriated by others or because, as women alone, they do not have the strength or knowledge to farm them again themselves.

For all this, Bamiyan is not a sad place. Twenty-two experts representing every form of foreign aid – from Médecins Sans Frontières to Save the Children – and many nationalities – Japanese and French, Germans and British, Swedes and Americans – are busy bringing water, electricity, schooling, family planning and women's cooperatives to the area. Bamiyan's dusty tracks are full of boys wobbling on their new bicycles, gifts of UNICEF to encourage children to make the journey to school. Along the higher ridge, where the ground flattens out to provide a runway for the aid world's planes, the American military have put one of their outposts, a unit called a Provincial Reconstruction Team, composed of a mixture of soldiers and reservists sent to offer both security and a campaign for the hearts and minds of Bamiyan's people. Surrounded by the safety of open space, towered over by the great mountains that stretch away behind, the American base appears like a stockade from the Wild West, with its watch-towers and flag poles, its row of concrete fortifications and rolled razor wire. Just to see the Americans walking around, with their radios and walkie-talkies and their army boots, makes them feel safe, say the people of Bamiyan, when they have not felt safe for years.

I found Jawad Wafa, as neat and courteous as ever, in the UN compound, where two aid workers were playing ping-pong. His life had not worked out as he had hoped. With the growth of the school in west Kabul, Jawad had lost his sleeping quarters to a new classroom, and, on a salary of $15 a month, had found it hard to survive. Dreams of entrance to Kabul university had been lost in the ever increasing demands on him as a teacher. With his family reluctant to return to Bamiyan from their now established and comfortable lives in Iran, Jawad had accepted a job with the UN in the hope of becoming one of the first undergraduates at Bamiyan university, which the Americans have promised to rebuild. His pay in Bamiyan is good – over $300 a month – but he is very wary about the future, and disillusioned with the materialistic ambitions of the Hazara leaders, whose motives in exile had once seemed to him so pure, so far removed from personal power. The politics of returnees, their greed and desire for personal gain, have saddened him. He feels rootless, separated from a family he cannot visit: as a former refugee, he has no passport and no ID card, and he fears that he would be arrested and ill-treated by the Iranian border guards if he were caught crossing over into Iran. He says that he has never seen the five nieces and nephews born since he was last at home, five years ago, though his mother has written to tell him that she has hung a photograph of him on her wall. Jawad has been a refugee since he was eight; he feels himself to be one still.

I went to two more villages before the long journey down through the mountains to Kabul, and I heard more stories about babies abandoned along the road to exile, and about men executed by the Taliban, their widows pointing out to me the green flags that stand out bright and clear against the rocky mountains, marking their violent deaths. And then I set off down the rocky track again, past the wrecks of lorries that have slid over the passes and fallen into the ravines far below, past the valley where a dragon is said to have devoured a daily tribute of maidens until a warrior turned him to stone, a mountain stream marking for eternity the tears of remorse that he weeps. The road leads down along the stony river beds where wild rhubarb grows in profusion, and through the pink and white fields of poppies and the orchards of late-flowering Lebanese apple trees, which are said to produce the sweetest fruit.

It seemed clear that Kabul, in the summer of 2003, nineteen months after the arrival of the liberating forces, was still an aid city, the strings pulled by foreign forces and foreign money, and the city protected by the 1,500 men of the peacekeeping forces – more wary after a suicide bomber killed six of their men – and ruled over by a fragile government. A great deal was happening, in terms of income generation and cash-for-work projects – wells dug and mines removed, lawyers and teachers trained and a new currency floated – but the city had, as Nasir had warned, an uncertain air, as if the players were constantly looking over their shoulders and wondering what was about to happen. Nasir had spelt out their fears: the possible departure of the 15,000 American soldiers from their head-quarters at Bagram, along the Shomali plain, the dismantling of the UN operation as donors are lured to newer emergencies and able officials are posted to more sensitive troublespots, the moving away of the now bustling foreign organisations, as money and the interest of backers go elsewhere. 'No one reads the history books, and no one listens to those who do,' said one weary and seasoned aid worker. 'It's all about quick fixes and we do those very well. But we don't stick around for the real work.' Like others, he feared that donors, agencies, the aid organisations with their high salaries and white Toyotas, were in danger of overwhelming the fragile administration, distorting the economy and losing sight of their most important task, that of building up institutions owned by and accountable to Afghans. Money is being spent almost arbitrarily, more in keeping with the whims and desires for a high profile by the funders than in response to what is needed. Though most Afghans now see themselves as Afghans first – hence the vast numbers coming 'home' – it remains a country of some twenty ethnic groups, the largest being the Pathans, the Tajiks and the Hazaras, ruled over by warlords (who like to call themselves 'commanders') who control their fiefdoms with absolute authority and fill the vacuum left where the state should be.

In the summer of 2003 there were still over 2,000 UN people in Kabul alone; but there was talk of how there would soon be no more than a few hundred, plans to 'downsize', in the language of the aid world, being already far advanced. The young men and women, experts in water and refugee returns and gender studies and protection, the missionaries of the modern world, are veterans of these particular campaigns. They know each other from Kosovo and East Timor and will doubtless meet again in Iraq, the Congo or wherever the next emergency calls them. Flitting about Kabul, they provide a bustling, efficient, cheerful service. They are fit and full of enthusiasm, and they work extremely hard, stopping only on Fridays to exercise in the UN's new gym, its treadmills and rowing machines flown in not long ago; but they are growing restless. UNHCR's budget for 2004 has already been set at a quarter less than that for 2003. No one doubts the need for a stable Afghanistan, but the politics are unlikely, they say, to allow it. Nor will there be enough money. Somewhere between $14 and $18 billion are needed in the next ten years to put Afghanistan on its feet: $4.5 billion has been promised, rather less than $2 billion delivered. 'It is not,' one official told me, 'a question of whether we are going to pull out of Afghanistan. It is a question of when. In some senses, you could say that we are pulling out already.' Lachdar Brahimi, the head of the UN operation, a man widely admired and respected, was on his way to Baghdad. He left behind him, say the sceptics, a tinderbox with echoes of Vietnam.

Not surprising, then, that the professional Afghans who spent their years of exile studying and training in the West, waiting for the day when they would cease to be refugees but could return home to rebuild the new Afghanistan, are hesitating. They feel they have been deceived, explains Nasir, led to expect things that are not there. It is the poor who are coming home, many of them forced home, either expelled by the Iranians or put onto planes by the British, whose assertion that Afghanistan is now a safe and fit place for return, designed to placate the home market, has sent alarming messages to Iran and Pakistan – although both countries have recently signed temporary agreements that they will force no more refugees home, despite the huge numbers who remain.

Still in search of the internally displaced, trying to find some line of definition in this persistently hazy field, I wanted before I left to visit the camps set up by UNHCR outside Kandahar for the Kuchis, the now herdless and unpopular nomads reported to make up the greatest part of the 300,000 or so IDPs estimated to be still adrift within Afghanistan. But the shooting of the Brazilian delegate in February had made the roads around Kandahar unsafe, and I was taken instead to meet a young Afghan social worker called Amira, a woman who had trained in her years of exile in Pakistan and come home to offer her skills to the interim administration. Amira had agreed to take me to visit three women living with their young children in the old city, widows and their families who are, in her book, the truly displaced of Afghanistan today. We drove to the old quarter, where once fine houses, with courtyards and porticoes, are now derelict and ruined. Down one alleyway, through what looks like a mine shaft propping up a crumbling roof and up the remnants of a steep flight of stairs, live Anja, Fatima and Salima, perching in the ruins in squalor and destitution. The three women have known each other for a long time. They come from the same village in the highlands of the Hindu Kush, not far from Bamiyan. Anja is in her early sixties, and the two younger women barely in their thirties, but all three look considerably older. Fatima's face is thickly lined and Salima is thin and listless. Their husbands were killed at different times in the fighting, when the Taliban came to their valley and laid waste to their homes and fields. Together with nine children under the age of fifteen they occupy two dark rooms. The smell of faeces and rubbish is overpowering.

On one wall in the room Anja and Fatima share with Fatima's two young daughters, high up in the style of Afghan pictures, hangs a single photograph of a young, scholarly-looking man, in spectacles and city clothes. Though there is very little light, the picture stands out, for there is almost nothing else in the room beyond a neat pile of mats and quilts in one corner, and two burkas hanging on a peg. 'That is my son,' said Anja. 'He was called Husein. When the Taliban attacked the mujahideen in our village, he was caught in the crossfire. There was a bullet in his neck and another in his kidneys. He had been in Iran as a refugee, but we were all here in Kabul because we couldn't afford to get to Iran, and he had gone back to the village to see what the situation was. We hadn't seen him for many months.' Fatima was Husein's wife. Too poor to make the journey into exile during the civil war, they are now too poor to go home to their valley, where as women alone with small children they do not feel able to reclaim the lands that were once theirs. In any case, their houses have been destroyed in the fighting, the rafters stolen for firewood, their fields long since claimed by others, and they are sceptical that they would receive any of the international help promised by foreign donors.

Salima's husband Mustafa was the first to die. In 1998, when the Taliban attacked their village, the family was preparing to flee to safety with other villagers when a stray bullet caught Mustafa as he was carrying a first load of belongings out of their house. 'There was no hospital to take him to,' she said. 'I simply held him in my arms and he died. We just sat there staring at him, because we couldn't believe it: one moment he was alive, and then he was dead.' Because she stayed behind to bury him, Salima and her seven children were forced to make the journey to safety alone. 'We were the last to leave. The village was deserted. It took us a week to get to Kabul, sleeping out in the mountains, and I had to carry my youngest child on my back. We left behind us a good and happy life. We were all farmers, and we grew potatoes, barley, beans, wheat, cucumbers, onions and tomatoes. We had apple and apricot trees. We managed well.'

When Salima and her children got to Kabul, she found work doing washing for the more prosperous families, and began spinning and sewing quilts, skills she had used for the family at home. She found a room in the same building as Anja and Fatima. 'Kabul was very empty then, and there was no landlord. We simply moved in and cleaned it up a bit and lived here. But when the Americans came and the landlord came back, he told us that we would have to pay $10 a month for each room and now I wonder every month how to pay the rent.' Salima's rent buys her a single room, some fifteen-foot square, which she shares with her seven children. It has a cement floor and a wooden ceiling, a window with glass looking out over the derelict courtyard, the use of an open latrine, and a small extra area she uses as a kitchen. Her eldest son, who is fourteen, sells soap and shampoo in the bazaar, but in recent months demands by police for bribes have reduced his profit to nothing. Other than the little Salima makes from her sewing, the family has no income. I asked her what they eat. 'For breakfast and lunch we have bread, and sometimes a little tea. For dinner, I cook potatoes and sometimes the cheapest rice. Sometimes I have to buy the food already cooked because it is very hard to find fuel. The children search for pieces of paper or cardboard, or old shoes, to use as fuel.' At night, a very small kerosene lamp gives them a few hours of light.

The children, say the three women, are healthy, and some of them at least are now going to school. The women themselves do not look well.

Rheumatism from the damp and cold, TB, scabies, gastritis and kidney problems from the polluted water and poor diet have hit the returning refugees hard. Anja has constant toothache in her few remaining teeth, and Fatima suffers from recurrent bouts of untreated malaria. Anja and Fatima cry when they talk about Husein, saying that he would have looked after them, and that they had pinned all their hopes on him. 'If he had lived,' they say, 'we would have gone home. We would have been all right.' While the Taliban were still in power, Fatima travelled back to the village to find Husein's grave. But they were still fighting in the neighbourhood and she had to flee back to Kabul without seeing where he was buried. She has not been back since. Her misfortune now, she says, is that she has two daughters and no sons: with no male figure to look after them, what future do they have?

Afghanistan, said Amira as we left, has become a country of displacement, people drifting from one end of the land to the other in search of safety or food. Half the population no longer lives in the place they once knew as home. The European Union plan, drawn up to monitor the returning refugees, spoke of a people coming home 'in safety and dignity'. The Belgian Médecins Sans Frontières, who have opened the only clinic for mental-health problems, have been overwhelmed by cases of anxiety and depression, men and women shocked and traumatised by events they were forced to witness, by loss and deaths, and by the utter desolation of the life they are enduring now.

I asked Amira who she considered to be worse off in the new Afghanistan, the families who had had the resources to become true refugees abroad during the years of fighting, or those who, like the three widows, could not find the money to reach the borders. She looked surprised. 'Kabul is full of displaced people like these women. There are hundreds, perhaps thousands of women just like Anja and Fatima and Salima, in cities all over the country. Unlike the refugees who are coming back with new skills and languages and education and even possessions, they have nothing to offer. They have lost everything – husbands, lands, homes. They are entitled to nothing and they have nothing. What little money they manage to earn all goes on food for the children. It is hard to see how they will survive.' It is hard, too, in Afghanistan, to see where the internally displaced end and the urban poor begin, a distinction that is increasingly blurred among those who work with them, who say that the ever growing numbers of people displaced by extreme poverty and moving to the big cities are now indistinguishable from the beggars and squatters who have long filled the capital.

*

Before leaving Afghanistan, I went to visit Babur's tomb, fabled as a place of greenery and peace. The greatest and most civilised of the Islamic warrior-kings, conqueror of Delhi and founder of the Moghul dynasty, Babur asked to be buried in Kabul, whose gardens of shady trees and the cool of its summer months he loved. Babur's last wife was an Afghan, and after her husband's death she brought his body home. In 1640 his grandson Shah Jahan built him a tomb on the hillside above the city, looking out across the river, under mulberry and plane trees. Babur wanted his tomb left open to the winds, but sometime later a memorial pavilion, with delicately carved panels of pink, green and black marble, was erected to protect the site. The writer Peter Levi, who visited Babur's tomb in 1972, had expected to find the place in ruins. Instead all was tranquillity and elegance, the gardens stretching away in formal parterres, with the fountains of bubbling water and the avenues of mulberries the philosopher-warrior had so loved.

The civil war has not been kind to Babur. His garden today lies in chaos, the fountains dry, the pavilion chipped and pitted by bullets, and the plane trees blackened stumps. Babur's tomb is said to be a place where young returnees come after dark to take drugs, but by day two municipal pools nearby are full of children swimming, coming out of the water to eat hard-boiled eggs sold from baskets, their shells dyed russet brown with the skins of onions. The occasional visitor to Kabul still makes the long, hot, dusty walk up through the former gardens, where now only marigolds grow, to where Babur and his obedient wife Bibi Mobaraka lie, Bibi in a more modest tomb not far from his feet. The inscription above his tomb alone has not been harmed. This tomb, it says, was constructed 'for the prayer of saints and the epiphany of cherubs.'

At the airport, Red Cross and UN flights were leaving for Kandahar, Herat and Mazár-e Sharíf, Ariana was bringing back refugees from Dubai, professional people keen to observe their reclaimed homeland, and there was a new sign saying that no one may traffic in precious saplings, threatening devices or 'Knife-Swords'. Here I found Mo from Brooklyn. He was still chewing gum, but now he was very cheerful. Kabul was a great place, he said, and he loved his mom's family. He planned to stay around and see what it has to offer him, when he got back from a quick visit to Dubai to meet a cousin.

Chapter Ten

Dead Dreams: The Dinkas of Oulu

An exile reads change the way he reads time,
memory, self, love, fear, beauty: in the key of loss.
André Aciman, *Shadow Cities*

'What,' asked Shinfig, who is nine, 'is this?' He was pointing to a picture
of a mountain slope covered in thick white snow somewhere in northern
Finland, down which people are skiing between the fir trees. Shinfig is a
Dinka from southern Sudan, the second son of Mary and Maum Awol,
whom I had met in Cairo in the spring of 2001 soon after I started working
with the refugees. Mary had been brought to see us by our Sudanese
interpreter, David Deng, another Dinka, a huge, genial man whose fluent
English made him a leader in the large Sudanese community of asylum-
seekers in Cairo.

Mary was well over six-foot tall, with large front teeth and hair neatly
braided in thin plaits that lay in stripes across her small head. She had a
limp, which made her gait slow and awkward. She spoke no English and
was often solemn, but when she smiled it was with great warmth. Mary
was a 'Closed File', David told us, an asylum-seeker not just refused
refugee status by UNHCR, but informed that any further appeal would be
useless. Would we, he asked, consider interviewing her and trying to put
together a new case for UNHCR? Without it, she faced not deportation –
there was no money to send Mary and Maum and their four children back
to Sudan – but a state of permanent limbo on the margins of Egyptian life,
her children without education and often with little to eat. I still have the
first lines of the testimony she brought to us. 'My name is Mary Agum
Masayo Kou,' she had written. 'I am from southern Sudan and a member
of the Dinka tribe. I was born in the Rumbek Lake States in 1963. My
father, Mayo Kou, worked as a medical assistant in Rumbek hospital. My
mother was a prison warder in Rumbek while my grandmother looked
after me and my many brothers and sisters. When I was very small, I
contracted a childhood disease, which left me lame in my left leg.'

But there was more that she hadn't thought to explain to UNHCR, or had said badly or too fast. Mary and her family had been forced to flee Rumbek when it was captured by the Sudan People's Liberation Army, and her father had died of heart failure before they reached the safety of nearby Wau. Later, when she was a young married woman working as a dental nurse, fighting had broken out between the Dinka and the Fartit, and her husband and small daughter had been shot dead. She had fled to Khartoum, taking her remaining child, a boy, with her. There she had met a childhood friend called Maum and married him and had four children, before being harrassed and pursued by the security forces, anxious to use her services as a spy on other southerners. When she refused, they arrested both her and Maum in the middle of the night and took them to security headquarters. 'I was kept for two days and given torture,' Mary explained carefully through David. 'Many times I was beaten with leather lashes all over my body. I was beaten on my feet. I was burned with lighted cigarettes. For all these punishments, I have scars. I was all the time insulted because I am a Dinka.' Down the corridor, the security forces had also been torturing Maum. When Mary and her husband were allowed to go home, she saw that he had a tooth missing, and that the front of his body was covered with welts from a whip. Six months later, having been constantly followed and watched, the family bought false passports and early one morning slipped out of Khartoum and made their way to Egypt. Mary had to leave behind her eldest son, who had been forcibly conscripted into the army.

Having heard her full story, we helped Mary to prepare a new statement for UNHCR, then persuaded them to reopen her case. And then she waited, for month after month, to hear what they would say. Each time I returned to Cairo I would go to see her and her children: Majok, the eldest boy, who was eleven, then Shinfig, the boy who had marvelled at the snow, then a girl of seven called Anwen and last a little boy of three called Nuomshett. For several months, the six of them lived in two rooms in a shanty town on the edge of the city, sharing the small space with David and another young Sudanese man. Maum could not find work, but Mary found occasional jobs as a cleaner, always badly paid since as an asylum-seeker she was not officially allowed to work and was often exploited by her Egyptian employers. When she was away from home, the children stayed indoors because Mary feared for their safety on the streets. Most months, she expected to be evicted for paying the rent late, and the children seldom had much to eat besides beans, rice and onions. When I went to see her, I took with me clothes, oranges and milk, and a tray of the pastries that Egytians love to eat. Mary never complained about her life.

Once, she was indeed evicted. By now she was also looking after her thirteen-year-old nephew Joshua, who had fled southern Sudan to escape forcible conscription as a boy-soldier. I heard from David that she was living in a new apartment in another part of Cairo, and when I went back the next time, I found her in an empty shell of a flat, due shortly for demolition. There was no electricity or running water, the floors sloped and the ceilings sagged, and it was completely bare except for a few tattered velvet hangings and two enormous damask sofas without springs, remnants from a more splendid past, abandoned by their Egyptian owners as they moved on to better things. In this dark and cavernous flat, Mary, Maum, their four children, Joshua, David and another young Sudanese man, all lived on the very little Mary earned as a cleaner, and on the money David brought back from occasional jobs as an interpreter. They slept on the floor. Mary's health was often poor and weeks passed when she could not work. From time to time, Father Anastasi at the Coptic Church gave her a little money and some secondhand clothes for the children. Still, Mary was always cheerful when I saw her. 'Oooooooooh,' she would say, a long, drawn-out sound of pleasure which was the greeting she gave to visitors, and which I had grown used to down the phone on the few occasions I had managed to reach her from Europe. Her embrace was enormous.

Late in 2002, Mary heard that UNHCR, against all probability, had decided to grant her and her family refugee status. With it came the much-prized blue refugee card, which gave them a measure of protection against the Egyptian police, and a small monthly allowance of around £12 which helped buy food. This was also the year that Finland decided to open its quota of resettlement places for refugees to people from Sudan, and early in 2003 Mary learnt from the Finnish Embassy that they were being offered new lives in Finland. They visited the embassy and listened to the orientation talks for refugees who were about to be resettled, about Finland's weather and education, work and living conditions. It was the brochure about the snowy Finnish countryside that Shinfig showed me when I went to see them. Snow is not easy to describe to a nine-year-old boy accustomed only to varying degrees of great heat. Only much later, when I went to Finland, did I hear an immigration officer describe how she tries to convey what snow and ice will feel like to refugees who have never even worn a coat. 'I ask them,' she said, 'whether they have ever seen a freezer. If they say yes, I tell them to imagine putting their hand inside and keeping it there for a few minutes. Then I tell them about the way that we deal with the cold, about the thermal underclothes and the padded jackets.'

Describing his first encounter with snow when he arrived to live with the Eskimos in Greenland, the Togolese writer Tété-Michel Kpomassie wrote: 'So thick were the flakes, you'd have said that all the white birds in the world were shedding their feathers.'

Though they had taken in a few hundred Chilean asylum-seekers fleeing Pinochet's persecution in the 1970s, it was not until 1989 that Finland adopted a formal resettlement programme. The Vietnamese boat people became their first experiment. Resettlement was not an option then widely offered in Europe, which, throughout the 1980s, had remained a place of refuge principally for 'good refugees', those fleeing communism. It was only Australia, Canada, New Zealand and the United States who had opened their doors to UNHCR's Convention refugees, people for whom there was no possibility of ever going home. In Finland, the Vietnamese – taken in, cared for, eventually granted citizenship – flourished. They seemed to adjust without too much pain to the freezing darkness of Scandinavia and soon began to open restaurants and small shops. Other South-east Asians followed, and they too appeared to thrive and to meet with their hosts' approval. There was something pleasing in their temperament, something about their quiet reticence that ordinary Finns, quiet and reticent themselves, found soothing. Kielo Brewis, who works for the ministry of immigration in Helsinki, has become interested in what she calls the inter-cultural exchanges between the Finns and the resettled refugees, the way that the Finns and the Asians share patterns of non-communication that are both subtle and remarkably similar. 'We Finns take a long time to talk,' she says. 'We never talk very much and when we do, we really take our time. We are never too explicit. The Asians too take their time. It has worked very well here.'

But Finland is not immune to the new cross-currents of refugee politics. Its borders, with Russia to the east and Sweden to the west, make it vulnerable to the arrival of asylum-seekers by train and sea, and all through the 1990s, when a direct train service linked Helsinki and St Petersburg, refugees arrived in their hundreds in search of work and asylum. The numbers have dropped in recent years now that the border with Russia is heavily guarded, thickly mined and the train has been stopped, and people trying to enter Finland without papers are swiftly returned. However, Finland still has about 3,000 asylum-seekers entering its territory every year – for the most part using the services of smugglers – to begin a process of interview, appeal, acceptance or rejection, followed by deportation, that closely mirrors what happens in other parts of the

European Union. But with at least one difference: Finland is both small – under 6 million in population – and orderly. It is not a country in which it is possible to disappear. Failed asylum-seekers – some 60 per cent of all who apply on arrival – are sent speedily home, often accompanied by police to see them returned to their original countries. 'We are good at clarity here,' said Leena-Kaisa Aberg, head of the Finnish Red Cross refugee team, when I went to see her in Helsinki. 'There is no one in Finland who is just in limbo. We like to have things orderly.'

I had come to Finland not to look at asylum, but at resettlement, the acceptance of refugees given status by UNHCR under the 1951 Convention as eventual citizens with full rights. The main countries for resettlement remain the United States, with some 70,000 places each year, followed, at some distance, by Canada, Australia and New Zealand. The Scandinavian countries have been generous in proportion to their small populations, both Norway and Sweden taking around 1,000 people every year. Finland too has always said that it intends to honour its obligations under a convention that it was one of the first countries to sign and ratify. Unlike the US and Canada, which are accused of creaming off the best of the refugees, those most educated and most likely to contribute to their new country, the Finns offer homes to the most vulnerable and the most needy. Around 15 per cent of the Finnish quota, which started at 500 people each year in 1989 and has since built up to 750 (though there has been talk of more), goes to single mothers with many children, to the elderly and to the sick. For some years, Finland steered away from Africans, particularly after a large influx of Somali asylum-seekers in the 1990s – arriving without warning via a direct flight from Mogadishu to Moscow and on by boat via Estonia – caused tension and unease. These Somalis, unlike most of the Asian refugees, struck their hosts neither as reticent nor quiet. Then, in 2001, mindful of Africa's apparently unsolvable problems, the Finnish government took the decision to offer 500 places, spaced out over several years, to those escaping Sudan's long civil war. Mary and her family were among them.

Over the past fifteen years, the Finns have made an art of resettlement. Having realised their initial mistakes – for example, sending three Kurds to three separate towns far from each other in order to avoid a ghetto of foreigners, thereby making them miserably confused and lonely – they have come round to the idea of communities. They study the needs of their new guests carefully, and prepare their own inhabitants for all eventualities. Before the arrival of a number of Burmese not long ago, talks, which were enthusiastically attended, were arranged in the municipalities where the newcomers were to go. Police, librarians, school cleaners and mayors flocked to learn about Burmese politics, culture, dress and food. Municipalities – of which twenty-five have now joined the resettlement programme – have considerable autonomy in Finland, and are invited by the government to make offers to resettle refugees, for which they will get generous national support, and interest-free loans for any new housing they will need to provide for them. For the refugees, the package is also generous: at least three years' guaranteed full support, and many years beyond that if necessary, on a par with that given to unemployed Finnish citizens, as well as help of every kind from the Red Cross, from municipal social workers and from the various ministries of education, health and labour. 'Sometimes,' said Ann-Charlotte Siren-Borrego, who has worked in resettlement affairs since the programme began, 'we say that this is just like a laboratory. We can test things out. We are a microcosm of what resettlement can provide. And because we know each other, and talk and cooperate, we iron out problems before they arise.' As Argentina, Chile, Brazil, Burkina Faso, Benin and Ireland are all considering resettlement as a policy, Finland, whose experiment is small and neat, is being looked at as something of a model for other countries to follow.

It took me a while to find Mary and her family. Between UNHCR and the Finnish Embassy in Cairo, who processed her papers, her family names underwent a number of changes. But the Red Cross tracing methods are impressive and eventually I was informed that Mary, Maum and their children had gone to Oulu, in Finland's far north, not far from Lapland, where it is totally dark for several months each year and where it is not unusual for the temperature to sink below –35°C. Born in heat, colour and light, the family was to be resettled in ice and universal winter greyness.

Oulu was once famous for its tar. It was here, among the lakes, ponds, bogs, marshes, rivers and creeks of northern Finland, that in the seventeenth century enterprising loggers built ships to sail the world. A fire, impossible to control in the middle of so much wood and tar, destroyed the fine old timber city in 1822, and what was left of the painted wooden houses was bombed by the Russians in World War II. Since then a new town has been laid out on a grid system, a town of square, flat-roofed, box-like buildings with cement and stucco facings and metal-frame windows. Oulu – windy, icy, perched on the edge of the Gulf of Bothnia facing Sweden, and on a latitude with Siberia, Greenland and Alaska – has little charm. Logging has long since given way to technology, and Nokia is Oulu's main employer, though there is still a paper mill, and as you drive in from the airport along a wide, flat, empty highway between the fir trees and the silver birches, you can see the smoke from its chimneys curl slowly into the still, clear sky of winter. In summer, tourists come to cycle along Oulu's paths and by the side of the water, and to sit drinking in the market square until late into a night that never grows dark. In winter, the town is quiet, empty, dark and very cold. The sun never rises. Ice makes the pavements lethal. No one moves on the streets, and very few cars go by.

Oulu has 123,000 inhabitants. Contemplating the scarcely imaginable contrasts, the move the resettled refugees have to make, and the extraordinary journey through climate and culture, Heike Estolen, area manager for the Red Cross, tried to imagine what it must be like adapting to surroundings in which nothing is like anything you have ever known. If Oulu had become a world apart for him, a world of silence and difference after a two-year posting among the refugees in Bosnia, what, he asked, might it be for people who had travelled many thousands of miles, from colour into grey?

Though Christians make up most of the seventy-one Sudanese sent to live in Oulu, all but a very few from the south, among the first to arrive was a Muslim called Malish. Together with eight other Sudanese families, Malish reached Oulu on 15 October 2001. It was snowing. He was on his own, having left his pregnant wife in Cairo, and by the time he went to bed the first night, he had been allocated a small, warm, pleasant flat with pale wooden floors. The town office that looks after the refugees – the Sudanese had been preceded by some Iraqis, Bosnians and Somalis – gave him a few pieces of basic furniture and his first allowance, enough to buy warm clothes. Malish had been a teacher in Sudan, with a hankering after a degree in philosophy. He had studied for some years in an English-speaking seminary, and in Cairo, because his English is so good and because he is ambitious and energetic, he had even managed to get a little work teaching. 'I had no real idea of any kind about what I was coming to,' he says. 'In junior school, I had read about Finland but it didn't actually mean anything to me. In Cairo, the Finnish Embassy told us about the weather, but how do you describe great cold? I was shocked by the dark; that is what I felt and that is what I still feel: shock. I couldn't understand why it was all so quiet, why no one spoke in the street.'

Malish came to interpret for me with the Sudanese, who, alerted by Mary, gathered to talk in the community centre. Like all the Sudanese, he is finding Finnish, which they all study every day for six hours, extremely hard. It is a language with immensely long words and no prepositions, in which pronunciation counts for everything; even the Swedish minority in Finland seldom speak it without an accent. As Malish talked, describing to me the way in which the Sudanese in Oulu are living – the little flats they have been allocated all around the town, the television channels they watch, the friendly distance shown them by their Finnish neighbours, the lack of spices and dried fish or okra on sale in the local shops – so other Sudanese arrived to join us, slithering along the treacherous pavements, immensely tall and dark and absolutely improbable in their woolly hats and down jackets and thick boots. A few brought babies with them, for there have been seven births in the Sudanese community since 2002.

Sitting in the small, hot hall, warmed by an old-fashioned, tiled wood-burning stove, the Sudanese talked. From time to time, their mobile telephones, the absolute necessity of the refugee existence, as important here as on the streets of Cairo, rang. It was not easy, the Sudanese said, one after the other, as they described how they filled their days. The Finns were generous and always pleasant. The Dinkas were short of nothing. They liked their new gadgets and their television sets, and they liked feeling safe and knowing that their children were safe. But the language was very hard, and they were not quite certain what they were doing in this dark, northern city. All would have preferred Canada or the United States had they been given a choice, and those with relatives already settled in North America are puzzled about why they have not been allowed to join them. Then they talked about their year's compulsory Finnish-language course, and how they wished they could learn English, for they still believe English is the only possible language of their future. They talked about not having understood the restrictions on their papers, that it will take them at least eight years before they can become Finnish citizens, and until then they will not be allowed to travel abroad, not even briefly to visit friends or relations. Alem, a man in his thirties with deep tribal scars carved across his forehead, said that he had believed that he would be given the proper schooling and then university education, that war had prevented him acquiring in Sudan. He spoke of education as something concrete, something that could be handed over as a gift. The Finns have indeed given the Sudanese education, but it is not the education they dream about.

Later, at a church service in a classroom lent to them by the Lutheran Church, sitting at desks in rows, their long legs folded awkwardly around the tables, the Sudanese sang revivalist hymns, the African beat loud in the utter silence of an Oulu Sunday afternoon, and they prayed, for the government of Finland, for one of their congregation soon to undergo an operation, for a newborn Dinka boy, and they prayed for peace to come to Sudan, so that one day they could go home.

And throughout the time that I spent with them in Oulu, the Sudanese talked about work. Work, their failure to find or have it, is a subject that never goes away. As they know well, as they tell each other every day, of the 250 refugees who were resettled in Oulu before them – Iraqis and Iranians, Bosnians and Somalis, Afghans and Burmese – only two have found work, and both of these are interpreters for social workers. Among the seventy-one Sudanese are teachers, electricians, nurses, farmers and university students. Talking about their lives, they say that they had simply assumed that resettlement would bring with it education, and with education would come work and a future. Now, it seemed, they would learn Finnish but not much else. They had never imagined, never conceived it possible, that there might be a life without an occupation. 'We watch television, we eat, we sleep,' said Malish. 'We visit people. And we sit. This is really useless for me. I had a dream. It was about how I would work, and learn things, and become someone. If I don't succeed in my dream, I don't know how my life will be. My dream is dead. I have nothing to look forward to. All of us talk about work and education. It is all we talk about. We eat and we sit and we talk about work.' I asked some of the other men what they did to fill their days. 'Actually,' they said, using the word in a way particular to Africans speaking English, 'actually, we do nothing.'

Oulu has no work. It has employment for skilled IT specialists, and it has a little work for men in the paper mill, but 12 per cent of the workforce are unemployed, and levels of alcoholism are, as elsewhere in Finland, high. For the Dinkas, there is no work; and it is very unlikely that there ever will be. A few may find employment eventually as cleaners or looking after old people, if their Finnish is judged good enough by the authorities. But for the engineers and the teachers, the nurses and the would-be university graduates, there is nothing.

And so the Dinkas in Oulu wait. Like the Palestinians in Shatila and the Liberians in Sicily, they wait for real life to begin, the dream of a life which, like Malish, they carried with them into exile, about work and education and knowing who they are. Having held tight to this dream during the transit years in Cairo, where it became a form of protection against an unacceptable present, they are trying to come to terms with the fact that what surrounds them in Finland will never really provide it. Like Malish, they fear their dead dreams, and like Malish, they prefer to start dreaming again, to plan for the day when they will become Finnish citizens, with Finnish passports, and will be able to move on, to the life they hope for, in another country.

Yet even if Finland is now just another stage in a journey towards another future, the Dinkas in Oulu still worry about those friends and relations who have not passed the first hurdle. By the time I left Oulu, I had a list of those still in Cairo or Sudan and in need of help. The refugees brought these names to me one at a time, written on little scraps of paper. They included the younger brother and sister of Jeremiah, who has multiple sclerosis. They had joined him in Cairo from Sudan when his illness grew severe and, not invited to accompany him to Finland, are now alone and on the streets in Egypt. There was Elizabeth Zacharia Arop, Simon Maderi Agei and Peter Dhykwan, all still in Cairo, all penniless, all with 'files closed' many years ago. And there was Amina's young son, eighteen-year-old Johannes Peter, waiting in Cairo to hear whether he would be allowed to join his mother in Oulu (at eighteen, he is no longer a dependent child). Talking to Amina, an imposing, matronly woman in her early forties whose pastor husband was killed in the fighting in Sudan, and who has five young children with her in Oulu, I thought again of the diaspora of the Palestinians. Amina's eldest son is still in Khartoum, having been, like Mary's son, forcibly conscripted into the army. She has a cousin in Cairo with five small children, whose husband and three brothers are all dead, and a niece in Australia. Her uncle is in America. When interviewed by UNHCR in Cairo, Amina said that she would be grateful to be sent anywhere she would find peace and safety for her children, so that they would not be attacked and abused. And she is grateful, she says, very grateful, for she has found both. But then she adds: 'Help is not just running away from death. In the end, that is not enough. Life has to have many different things.'

Sitting after the service in the Lutheran church, I asked Malish and Jeremiah, both of whom had talked with such passion about their education, whether there were books I could send them from England. Malish asked for Bertrand Russell's *History of Western Philosophy*, Jeremiah for Paul Burrell's book about Princess Diana.

In the night, when he cannot sleep, Maum thinks about his brothers, still in Rumbek, and wonders whether they are alive. He dreams often, dreams that turn into nightmares, and he wakes sad. As a small boy, the youngest in his family, he accompanied his eldest brother to watch over their cattle, and when he grew old enough, his brother taught him to mould little animals out of the black soil, and to colour them with ashes from the fire. The two boys, sitting while the cows grazed, made flocks of goats and herds of cattle, and figures of people carrying spears to watch over them. They preferred to make the animals they knew best, and seldom tried their hand at wildebeest or warthog or even the lions who, from time to time, would seize one of their cows and drag its carcass off into the bush. They were less frightened of the lions, who preferred cattle to attacking humans, than of the snakes, which were plentiful around Rumbek. Remembering the long vigils in the bush, Maum talks about the snake he most dreaded, over a metre in length and very black and shiny. Its body, he says, was as thick as the thermos flask that sits between us as we talk, and he describes the day his friend went down to the river to fish, and was bitten as he moved through the long grass by the water's edge. But he has heard, from a cousin who was able to contact him one day from Khartoum, that there are fewer wild animals around Rumbek these days, ever since the frequent sound of gunfire from the civil war frightened them away. It is when Maum talks about his childhood, when he describes with precision and tenderness the daily events of a life that lasted until the day that he and his family were forced to flee in 1984, that the enormity of the journey he has made takes shape.

Maum was born in a small, square house with a thatched roof in 1961. His family had neither water nor electricity, Rumbek's one generator supplying just enough for the police station and the small hospital. He is not sure of the exact date of his birth, because births in Rumbek were registered casually, and it was often many months before anyone bothered to seek out the proper authorities and have them written down. His father was a farmer, with fields of wheat and cows. The week that Maum and his twin sister were born, the second set of twins in the family, he was killed in a tribal skirmish near the town. The absence of a father was a defining element in Maum's childhood. He was taught to miss him as one might miss a person one knows and loves. Because his grandfather had five wives, and his mother was one of eight brothers and sisters, Maum's boyhood was passed in the midst of an enormous clan, in households that merged one into another, among children of all ages, related to each other by ties of blood.

Though Maum finished nine years of schooling, it is his free time that he remembers most vividly, when he wandered around the surrounding countryside, fishing in the local rivers with a spear, or with a net left in the river overnight to catch dink, a fish the colour of mud with no bones apart from its backbone, considered by his mother the most digestible and delicious of all the river fish. The boys in the family, Maum says, were not encouraged to hunt until they were fully grown, but as a young boy he accompanied his elder brothers when they went out in search of antelope, taking with them long spears with metal tips. When he thinks about his childhood, Maum thinks about the seasons blending mildly one into the other, about the cattle grazing quietly in the bush, and about the days that he was sent to market to sell a cow and buy new clothes for the family. Maum is very thin, with a wispy beard, two long, pointed front teeth, and a large gap where the tooth was knocked out by Khartoum's security forces. It was a good life, he says, sitting on the family's new sofa in a bare room in northern Finland, except for not knowing his father. Maum was living with an uncle, studying, dreaming of a day when he might follow his cousins into a university education in some foreign city, when fighting came to Rumbek and he was forced to go north.

Mary's memories of her Rumbek childhood are less clear. One of eight children, she too helped watch her family's cows, and when she was free she went with her friends to swim in the river that ran not far from their home. On weekends, when there was no school, she would walk the thirty-three miles to a village called Shomek, her father's village, where her grandparents still lived and where she helped pick olives. Mary loved her grandmother, and she was particularly fond of one of her brothers, who resembled her so closely that people took them for twins. She says little about her decision to become a dental nurse, or the studies that she did, or her first husband and firstborn child and their deaths in the raid on Wau. Nor does she like to talk about the death of her much loved brother in the fighting, nor the loss of her second child, taken by government forces to serve as a child soldier. Talking about her marriage to Maum, Mary says that she chose him because he was a good boy with a good mind, and that despite the objections of his parents, who would have preferred a wife with no previous husband, they 'entered into love' with each other.

When Mary and Maum and the four children reached Oulu from Cairo on 17 March 2003, there was still snow on the ground. Shinfig ran to touch it. Mary remembers the sense of shock, the way the cold made her catch her breath. In Cairo, she explains carefully, she had known cold indoors and out on the few winter days when the evenings were cool. But there was no difference in the temperature, wherever you went, in or out. What struck her at once in Oulu was something she had not thought about: that inside the buildings it would be hot. Going from cold into heat, heat into cold, was something she had not expected.

*

The Finns are extremely conscious of the contradictions in which the resettled refugees live. They understand about the need for work and occupation, and in the offices in Helsinki where these things are discussed, they try to find ways to make generous provisions for language classes and further education of every kind. They worry that the refugees are not sufficiently prepared, and so they give them pamphlets describing frostbite and how to deal with it, and they are concerned with the way that Sudanese men, accustomed to being in control of their families, will adjust to a society as equal-minded and feminist as Finland. They foresee, too, problems with resentment, when the Finns may grow angry at so much being given to people who now pay no taxes. Across the country, planners are trying to anticipate the racism now endemic in other parts of Europe, with publicity campaigns about the benefits brought by people from other cultures and societies. They worry too about these lives in limbo, and the way the refugees keep dreaming of what will happen next. 'It is,' they say, 'a wasted life. If you dream too much, you forget to concentrate on living.' When, not long ago, a young Iranian in another northern town hanged himself, despite having been given his own apartment and living comfortably, the authorities were shocked. 'We thought,' they said, 'that we had done so well.'

It is in the second generation of resettled refugees that the authorities see real hope, the children whose bilingualism will ensure that they start their working lives equal in opportunity to their Finnish classmates. These young people will reach working age just when Finland's population tips heavily towards pensioners, the post-war boom generation grown to retirement, and jobs, particularly in the service industries, should be plentiful. In Helsinki I met Ekhias Osman, a Sudanese woman who has worked for the Finnish refugee council and for one of the municipalities most active in resettlement. Ekhias's story is different in that she is not a refugee, but the Finns who work with her point to her experiences as a hopeful message for the future.

Ekhias has lived in Finland for fourteen years. She arrived in 1990 with her husband, who had a scholarship to study forestry at Helsinki university. It was November and almost completely dark. What she remembers is her sense of surprise at finding no leaves and no green trees. When her husband's degree was finished, he decided to stay on to teach at the university; Ekhias, who had brought two small children with her from Sudan, and arrived pregnant with a third, now had a fourth. There was no one for her to talk to, for she was the only Sudanese woman in the whole of Finland, and it took her five years to learn Finnish. She decided that she could cope perfectly well when the temperature was at –10°C, but that what she really hated were the days when it sank to –20°C. There was also then nowhere for her to buy the spices she craved. Now, she says, everything is easy. At least twenty shops selling Middle-eastern food have opened in the last five years. She has many Finnish women friends. Her only regret is that, whatever she does, she can find no way for her elderly mother to pay her a visit – the Finns will not grant her even a temporary tourist visa – so every two years she takes the children and returns home to Sudan to see her. 'I need to see my mother,' she says, 'and the children need their grandmother.' Her husband is reluctant to go back to Sudan even on a short visit, though he has learnt no more than ten words of Finnish in his years at the university, where he is able to teach in English. Not long ago, to show her new friends something of her past life, Ekhias invited two Finnish women on a visit back to Khartoum.

For her children, Ekhias has no doubts about the wisdom of their decision to stay. The eldest two are fluent in Finnish, Arabic, English, Swedish and French. Their education has been excellent, and if the eldest, who is a boy, is currently talking about becoming a footballer, the three girls have their minds already set on more stable careers: the eldest, says Ekhias, is planning to be a paediatrician, the second a heart specialist. As for the youngest, she talks of entering the army, or perhaps the police force, enjoying the idea of being the only black woman soldier in the country. The girls are, as their mother says, affectionate and family-minded. They are also Muslim, which separates them from most of the new arrivals. It is only when talking about the future that Ekhias hesitates. The girls, already nearing the end of their secondary schooling, wonder if they will ever meet a boy whom they might marry, and Ekhias has already begun to plan for the day when she will have to send them home to live with her mother to find husbands. What this spells, she knows, is the very arrangement that she most dreads: her family scattered across the world.

At every stage in the journey that led her ever further from her first home, Mary shed her possessions. Like most refugees, she has almost nothing from her past. But sitting on her table in Oulu, in the neat new flat with the sauna that she uses to air the children's outdoor clothes, I saw the photograph album that I had been shown when I first met her in Cairo. Its red flowered plastic cover, with the inset silver heart and its photograph of a younger Mary, is a little more battered, but there inside were the portraits I remembered: of adults and children, babies and elderly men and women, in turbans, printed gowns and shawls of brilliant colours, many posed in photographers' studios, alone and in groups, serious, unsmiling, smartly dressed, so many of them, belonging to another time and another place. Turning the pages, telling me their names and who they were, Mary paused. This man, she said, is dead; this woman has fled to Khartoum; this couple have disappeared; this family is now in Cairo. It was as if nothing could ever be right again.

But Mary is not unhappy. She has accepted that it is unlikely that her Finnish will ever be good enough for her to work again as a dental nurse, because that would involve first the language, then seven years' retraining. She is in her forties, yet learning each day how to cope with new devices and contraptions, how to catch a bus to her Finnish lessons or make her way round the supermarkets, has brought her pleasure and laughter. She makes one of her long exclamations of disbelief and humour as she describes trying to work out the identity of electrical gadgets she has never seen and the contents of packets of food that look utterly foreign. She likes the way that her children can bicycle along the bridle paths and the way that she is sure that they will come home safe. She is touched by the generosity and warmth of a Finnish family who have befriended them and who not long ago came to collect them in a car and drove them out to a farmhouse in the country, sending them home with a present of a Christmas tree and decorations to hang on its branches. Before that, she had only ever seen Christmas trees in pictures and wondered what they could be. And she talks with pride about the sports that the children have been learning at their schools and the delight they take in being taught to ski. Both she and Maum talk often to the children about Rumbek, about the house and land that they have never seen, and the relations they have never met. Anwen, the only girl, is more curious than her brothers; she wants to know what it was really like. But Rumbek is a long way in the past now, and Mary does not dwell on those days; Majok's future, the safety of her daughter and her two small sons, these are what concern her now.

Mary has brought doughnuts and large plates of cake for us to eat while the children watch a toboggan race on television. I found her quiet, almost subdued, though her smile is always affectionate. It is as if she has undergone a journey of a kind that can barely be comprehended, that has tested the very nature of adjustability. In the heat of the flat, with the dark and the cold of Oulu in winter kept out by heavy white net curtains, the children go barefoot.

Epilogue

A Mode of Being

'It becomes ever more urgent to develop a framework of thinking
that makes the migrant central, not ancillary, to the historical process . . .
It might begin by regarding movement, not as an awkward interval between
fixed points of departure and arrival, but as a mode of being in the world.'
Paul Carter: *Living in a New Community*

When Jeff Crisp joined UNHCR in 1987, migration was a dirty word. It was certainly not something that anyone was allowed to confuse with the legitimate claims of refugees forced to flee persecution. But at the beginning of the 1990s, he thinks, all this began to change. The end of the Cold War drove people abroad in search of work and better lives, and almost overnight, international migration became a key topic in world politics. People began to warn of uncontrollable floods of people, and the threat to national identity that all these culturally different and impoverished people might pose. As Crisp remembers it, it was at the Cairo Conference on Population and Development, in 1992, that UNHCR first presented papers about migration as a global issue that involved all people on the move, from asylum-seekers to those in search of better lives. And it was in 1995 that the words 'managed migration' found their way into the second edition of *The State of the World's Refugees*, with the assumption that it was no longer right or possible to ignore migration as the crucial debate of the age, within which asylum occupied a particular corner. The pity, as Jeff Crisp and others like him see it, is that all this was not understood and addressed long ago. For managed migration may prove a large part of the solution to the problems that lie ahead.

Like internally displaced people, like refugees, there have always been migrants. Ever since the sixteenth century, people have moved to work, to explore, to travel, to find better lives. What no one quite anticipated was the emergence of new multicultural societies, nor the new patterns that migration has taken. The history of migration since World War II is one of unforeseen developments and unplanned consequences. No one, for instance, would have predicted that the remittances migrants send home would reach around \$92 billion in 2003* – virtually double what is spent globally on overseas development. Globalisation has meant not simply flows of goods, services and capital, but a parallel flow of people and ideas.

The figures themselves are revealing. According to UN statistics, only 175 million people – around 3 per cent of the world population – are actually outside the countries of their birth at any one time, considerably more of them from the developed than from the developing world. What is more, the West needs them. The picture, say demographers, is now becoming clear. The populations of the developed world are aging, and fertility rates in some Western countries have fallen to as low as 1.2 children per woman. The West needs migrant workers. In the UK, for instance, though the so-called 'demographic deficit' between aging population and declining numbers of workers will not actually have an effect until 2020 – later than its European neighbours – there are already labour shortages; the National Health Service would collapse without overseas staff.

The idea that migration must, somehow, be 'managed' is now beyond doubt. All Western democracies have modulated their recent language to reflect this view. The worry is how to do it, given that September 11 increased the perception of a world under threat, that some of the Western public have been hijacked by the stories peddled by the far right, and that even demographers are not able to predict precise labour needs. Even as the speed of change has challenged people's sense of identity across the Western world, the necessary policy decisions to confront the new realities are judged as too unpopular; and public confidence has evaporated in the face of inefficient handling. The UN General Secretary, Kofi Annan, personally very interested, and aware that the UN needs to be seen to act on this challenging issue of twenty-first-century politics, has set up a Global Commission on International Migration, though its budget is small and its lifespan short.

Within the EU there already exists a cross-border labour market for several million workers, and EU policy has been moving towards opening more doors to both high- and low-skilled migrants. But while those with high skills are perceived as necessary, there remain doubts about the numbers of low-skilled workers the West will be able to absorb, particularly as current migrants are finding it harder to prosper economically than those who came before them. No one disputes that increased

---

*In 2003, Sudan, for example, received \$638 million in remittances and \$225 million in aid.

migration brings economic gains at a global level: the migrant moves from a place where he is less productive to a place where he is more. But migration works best when workers have different skills to the existing workforce and complement rather than replace those who are already there. Fears of attracting skilled people away from where they are needed in a brain drain is only one element in a debate which, say economists, has many still largely unexplored avenues, such as the remittances sent back to provide capital for investment and job creation. The links between diasporas and development, they say, may prove promising.

However, migration can only provide one answer to the needs of a future labour force, for migrants age too. People may also need to work longer, more productively and to save more. In the UK there are plans to tap the 2.8 million men and women aged between fifty and state-pension age who are currently not working. Across the EU, there are now new immigration programmes, guest-worker arrangements and migrant quotas drawn up both out of self-interest and in order to relieve pressure on overburdened asylum systems. There is also the suggestion, outlined not long ago by Timothy Hatton of the University of Essex, that immigration and asylum could be integrated at EU level by adopting a points system, to include humanitarian criteria.

At the beginning of 1999, 500 people from different backgrounds, disciplines and countries came together in the Hague under the auspices of the Society for International Development to discuss the future of migration and refugee policy. Starting from a shared conviction that the present situation is no longer tolerable either for asylum-seekers, migrants or for the countries on whom fall the burden of caring for them, and that the threats posed to stability and security are alarming, they produced a Declaration of the Hague in November 2002, a document with a more hopeful tone and outlook than many that have preceded it. A coherent and genuinely international migration policy, they argue, must go hand in hand with development policies and programmes to combat disease, poverty and illiteracy; the root causes of forced displacement have to be tackled – such as the flow of arms – and the corporate sector, as well as governments, must play their part in conflict resolution and post-conflict reconstruction. The Declaration comes at a good time: refugee numbers dropped by 10 per cent to 9.7 million between 2003 and 2004, according to UNHCR, the lowest figure in a decade. In the past few years, over 5 million people have gone home – to Afghanistan, Angola, Burundi, Iraq and elsewhere.

Apart from the demographers' calculations and their uncertain predictions, more intangible questions arise. Why should something as arbitrary as where one is born determine where one is allowed to live?* Entrance restrictions, borders and boundaries, often themselves accidents of history, stand as barriers to a more equal world, protecting the privileges of those who live in the richest, safest, least crowded states. Against the moral claims of liberals, who argue that current restrictions on immigrants constitute a gross violation of human rights, and point out that it is ethically inconsistent to support the free movement of goods and services while restricting the free movement of people, come the counter-claims of the anti-immigration lobbies, arguing for the need to preserve by state boundaries the unique cultural communities of people who share common practices and understandings. To demand of a state that it shows equal concern for those who live outside its boundaries is to ask it to pursue policies which may undermine the very institutions that provide social justice and cultural autonomy for those who live inside them. If to restrict entrance is to accept a world in which differences of citizenship correspond to differences in quality of life, then the arrival of large numbers of people can undermine the existing 'provision of collective or public good' and profoundly alter the nature of a state. It is hard to halt entrance flows at just the right moment, before social disharmony breaks out; once started, migration flows, with people following in each other's footsteps, are extremely hard to stop. By the same token, as migratory chains develop, so young people leave villages, thereby causing vast change in community life. And migration can only increase, say demographers, as high levels of insecurity and increasing disparity between rich and poor in so many parts of the world make families keen to send their children to safer and more stable economies.

In the mid-1970s the anthropologist Theodore Schwartz used the phrase 'migrants of identity' to describe the search among young people in America for an identity they considered both 'acceptable and authentic'. Since then, much has been thought, debated and written about the relationship between space and time in the construction of modern cultural identities. Wars, market forces and environmental change all uproot people – not only refugees and migrants, but tourists, travellers and businessmen – and that movement can more and more be seen as the determining experience of the age. In the twenty-first century, 'non-places' such as waiting rooms, refugee camps, stations, airports and hotels,

*See Matthew Gibney, 'Liberal Democratic States and Responsibilities to Refugees', *American Political Science Review*, Vol. 93, 1999.

have become temporary abodes. The idea of 'home' is no longer that of a fixed and safe place, there to leave and return to, and giving form to memory and anticipation. Rather it has become a more fluid idea, something to carry in one's head. Home, argues John Berger, is located in a set of routines, a repetition of habitual interactions, in styles of behaviour and in dress, in memories and in myths, and in stories carried around in the head. 'We dream in narrative,' Barbara Hardy famously observed not long ago, 'day-dream in narrative, remember, anticipate, hope, despair, believe, doubt, plan, revise, criticise, construct, gossip, learn, hate and love by narrative.' For Mamadu in Tel Aviv, Abdularam in Maryland and Mary in London, for whom their original homes have disappeared into memory and for whom no return to a fixed place of the past is possible, these narratives, testimonies to their own histories, become a form of safety. As cultural anthropologists describe it, the modern age is an age of exile; displacement between worlds, existence between a lost past and a changing present, presents the most fitting metaphor for modern consciousness. In his constant state of transit between so many different worlds, the modern traveller is at home in none, a 'homeless mind' constantly subject to nostalgia for a past, fixed time, when identity was rooted, safe and communal.

After the Wannsee conference of 20 January 1942, and the launch of the Final Solution, Jewish refugees began to arrive in ever greater numbers to beg for asylum at Switzerland's western borders. Nearly all were turned back. Heinrich Rothmund, the head of the Swiss police, warned of the 'menace to our spiritual identity if too many foreigners live here'. Rothmund would later describe his twenty-year battle against the *enjuivement* – the 'Jewification' – of Switzerland. Regarding the decision to keep the frontiers closed in the summer of 1942, Rothmund repeated a phrase that was much used in Switzerland during the late 1930s and early 1940s. 'The boat,' he said, 'is full.'

Even if the flows of migrants now trying to make their way to Western Europe, North America and Australia were to be realistically addressed by an increase in working permits and a better understanding of labour needs, there are always going to be more people wanting to migrate than the developed states will be willing to take. Why they persist in such numbers given the increasingly restrictive policies is not altogether clear, beyond the fact that asylum-seeker networks are growing and that smugglers are becoming ever more skilful. There will be migrants in search of better lives; there will be refugees fleeing death and persecution; and there will be a huge grey area in the middle, growing all the time, where people move because of poverty, because they have been driven to the margins of life by ethnic tensions, because a new dam has flooded their village. It is this grey area that makes UNHCR's position so hard, bound on the one hand to insist that refugees are different from other migrants and deserve different treatment, without which their entire house of cards will collapse, while on the other hand having to acknowledge that people move for many different reasons and need respect and rights. Migrants need protecting too.

Migration, as Gervase Apave at the International Organisation for Migration in Geneva sees it, is the unfinished business of globalisation. It is threatening because it challenges the last defining national characteristic: the ability of a country to say who comes in and who goes out. And it is threatening because by its very nature it is disorderly and unpredictable. While Australia has gone further than any other country in its efforts to make migration orderly, its draconian solutions are not possible on continents with many countries and many borders.

The paradoxes of the West are what make migration so uncertain. Western states are driven by the democratic will of their people, who are often hostile to refugees and migrants, but also by the rule of law which makes excessive exclusion impossible. Since research for this book began, ever tighter restrictions on asylum are being debated throughout the EU, where recent elections reflect growing, but unfounded, fears that terrorists are using the asylum route to reach the west, while in the US the many made homeless by the New Orleans hurricane have caused the very word 'refugee' to take on new and confusing meanings. There is, as has been argued in many papers, speeches and articles, no magic panacea. There are things worth trying, from the speeding up and improving of the asylum process to the spreading of more accurate and realistic information about conditions in the West and the dangers and pitfalls that await immigrants, to the setting up of regular programmes so that people can travel legitimately and not take the asylum route. But none, in the absence of addressing the root causes – the poverty, violence and instability that send people abroad in the first place – can ever achieve enough. Meanwhile, there is very little alternative but to follow the proposals of the Declaration of the Hague and to take steps to manage migration with clarity and imagination, while upholding the 1951 Convention so that true refugees are treated humanely and generously. The whole refugee apparatus – rules, conventions, organisations – exists to offer substitute protection for people whose governments cannot or will not protect them. UNHCR's task remains that of preserving asylum for those who need it and ensuring that those who are driven from their homes do not have to resort to clandestine means; it should not depart from its original mandate of protection by taking on activities that others do better.

No one denies that it would be best if the situations that create the world's flow of refugees could be prevented from happening. The diaspora Sudanese in Uganda, Ethiopia, Congo, Kenya and Central Africa, or the diaspora Somalis in Yemen, the UK, the USA and Djibouti would rather not be there. But until the improbable day comes when they are able to return home, refugees will keep on moving, and governments have no alternative but to find policies which protect their borders, but which are also humane and protect the rights of those who seek asylum. Some acts like torture are not negotiable; the prolonged detention of refugees, particularly refugee children, comes close to torture. Protecting people who flee persecution is a responsibility all nation states have to share if collective sovereignty is to have some moral worth.

And there is something more at stake. No one, in the end, wants to be a refugee. Exile is an unhappy state. Refugees seldom want to leave home, and when forced to do so they dream of the day they can return. The best 'durable solution' for any refugee is to go home, but to a home and a country that are safe; if that is impossible, the next best option is resettlement. It has to be accepted that not all asylum-seekers will ever contribute anything to the West's economy: some will be too frail, too damaged, too inflexible to achieve a productive life. But to rail at that is to misunderstand the nature of asylum, because asylum in the end is not only about responsibility and interdependence but about morality; in an age of globalisation, it is simply not possible to ignore the world's dispossessed. How a state deals with its refugees should be a measure of its social and political health.

By email, letter and the occasional phone call, I was able to keep in touch with some of the asylum seekers and refugees I had met on my travels, just as I was able to follow the progress of Mary, the Ugandan girl who had fled to England after her long abduction by both rebels and government forces. In June 2003, Mary gave birth to a baby girl, and decided not to put her up for adoption. On appeal, she was given four years' leave to remain in the UK, and, slowly, cautiously, she began to recreate her life. Then, just as she was settling down with friends and a possible college place in south London, she was 'dispersed' by the Home Office with forty-eight hours' notice to the twenty-fourth floor of a block of flats in Glasgow. In Glasgow, she knew no one; while she was out one day, her flat was broken into. Soon after, she received a letter from the Home Office. They had made a mistake: the UK was not willing to accept her as a refugee after all, on the grounds that she would be in no danger if she returned to Kampala. In the current ungenerous spirit that governs asylum decisions, Mary's fear and horror of return to a country in which she was repeatedly raped apparently no longer counts. While a new application is being prepared, she is moved, randomly, from flat to bedsitter to hostel, with her baby and her few possessions, sometimes two or even three times a month. Her old terrors have returned.

The refugees I had no news of were those I had twice visited in Afghanistan: Jawad Wafa, the studious and solemn Hazara teacher in Bamyan, and the raisin farmers in the Shomali plain, Haji Kamal and Amir Jan. Afghanistan, largely forgotten by the West and without the money or the security promised by the Allies, was again on the verge of anarchy. Poppies were now being cultivated in twenty-eight out of the thirty-two provinces and opium production is said to account for over half of Afghanistan's GDP. The Taliban and the warlords are back in control of huge areas of the country.

As for the camps of West Africa, there were new reports of young women refugees resorting to prostitution in return for food and shelter. In Liberia, Charles Taylor, the president whose soldiers had driven the young Liberians into exile, had gone, but the country remains lawless. Of Fatima and her five surviving children, I could discover nothing. In the Mediterranean, rough seas continue to take the lives of asylum seekers who put out in leaky boats from the coasts of North Africa, hoping to find work and safety in Europe. And Madina, the young Russian woman geologist I had met in 2003 in Newcastle, had been sent to Italy, as she had feared, because it had been her first port of call on leaving Russia. After a year in Sezze Scalo, a cheerless railway town in Latina built by the Fascists in the 1920s on land reclaimed by Mussolini from the malarial Pontine marshes – where Horace once complained that he was kept awake at night by the croaking of innumerable frogs – her application for asylum was turned down on the grounds that it lacked credibility. She has filed an appeal and been told that it may be more than a year before it is heard. The last time she saw her son Kolya, he was in a children's ward in a hospital in St Petersburg, recovering from frostbite to his face and hands. When I went to Sezze Scalo to see Madina early in 2005, she was wearing an enormous, handsome and very mothy mink coat – which she had brought with her on her flight from Russia and clung to throughout her many moves – to keep out the bitter winds that sweep down from the mountains across the plains.

In the spring of 2003, the young Liberians who had stayed in Cairo suddenly heard that they had been accepted for resettlement in the West. Their years of waiting, their powers of survival, their absolute determination not to give up, had paid off. Their lives could now be split in two: the past, before Cairo, when they had lost everything and everyone once familiar and safe to them and the future, when they would find an education and work and make families of their own. Cairo, a long, unhappy interlude, was the marking line.

Canada offered a humanitarian visa to Kono, the thick-set boy with the gap between his front teeth who had seen his mother raped and murdered, his father bayonetted, and the uncle and aunt who took him in killed while he was still a small boy. Though Christian, Kono had tried to pass himself off as a Muslim at Al Azhar University in return for somewhere to sleep. Hiding in different parts of the city since his escape, Kono had been growing ever more desperate; an Italian psychiatrist, visiting Cairo, had worried that his level of depression was now so acute that she was uncertain whether he would be able to pull out of it. Now, from Canada, came emails that made me think of the early Christian travellers. 'Great thanks and appreciation to bro. Daniel', he wrote, soon after his arrival in Toronto. 'He welcomed me like a motherly brother'. Over the phone he told me about his own induction into the Canadian way of life. At the Canadian Embassy in Cairo, when he went for his second interview, not knowing whether they would accept him and hunched and mumbling as was his custom, an official had said to him: 'When you are in Canada, you must stand up straight, pull your shoulders back, look people in the eye and speak out loudly.' She paused, then went on: 'Welcome to Canada'. Kono, used to making himself as inconspicuous as possible in a city in which to be black invited endless attacks, recalled the conversation with delight. 'I suddenly understood', he said, 'that I had possibilities again'.

The other Liberians, one by one, were called for interview at UNHCR and went off to new lives in different parts of America. 'Hi. This is Mohamed, from Texas, sending you greetings', wrote the moon-faced young man who had watched his godmother's head kicked about like a football, and who was now working as a garage mechanic in Austin. Abdularam, whose lack of back teeth had made his English so impenetrable, was sent to Maryland, where he was offered work as a caretaker in a laboratory by day, and classes in accountancy and computer studies by night. 'I haven't been engage in any social life', read his first email, in the English particular to the Liberians. 'As I have no friends. 2 days ago I met a Sierra Leonean guy in school and a Zambian guy. They are going to be my first friends'. Abdullah went to Iowa, to a factory making spare parts for cars; Bility, the good-looking boy in the brown woolly hat, who called all foreign women 'Ma'am', to Dallas; and Abudu, the tall, self-assured young man, who coped with the years of poverty and uncertainty by pretending they weren't happening, went to start his American life in Texas, but soon moved to Seattle, which he said he found more to his taste. Amadu had an American accent even before he got to America. Over the phone, their voices sounded light, buoyant.

At first anxious about being so far from each other, after the years of enforced and sometimes claustrophobic proximity, the Liberians kept in touch, obsessively, by mobile phone, ringing around the group two or three times every week. They still never talked to each other about the past, and nor did they talk about the present, beyond saying that they had a job and that life was easy – 'Life is not easy' was a sentence that each repeated again and again while in Cairo. What they talked about, between Dallas, Ohio and Seattle, was the future. Across the huge distances that now separated them, talking often late into the night, they discussed night school and college entrance, law degrees and openings in business and management. It was as if their horizons had become so immense that there was nothing, now, that might not be possible. 'All of us', Kono said to me with pride, 'have a plan'.

Maryland has a long tradition of resettling Liberians, many of whose ancestors made the first journeys as freed slaves to colonise the new Liberia, land of the free, founded with US help in 1822. Some 4,000 Liberians live in the Baltimore area alone, and forty-six, resettled here from their places of flight and exile all over the world, arrived in 2004. Among these was Omar and his wife Maikan.

Omar was one of the eldest of the young men in Cairo. A contained, solemn figure, he worried about the others, helping those who did not get enough to eat, keeping an eye out for trouble and despair. He had been a teacher briefly before being imprisoned by Charles Taylor's soldiers in a warehouse in Monrovia and kept for a week without food or water. He had fled to Cairo only after learning that he was to be detained again and this time probably executed. In Taylor's Liberia, there did not have to be a reason for the killings. When he first presented his case to UNHCR in Egypt, he was turned down, in the way that many asylum seekers are turned down, on grounds of insufficient evidence. It was only when his wife Maikan turned up in Cairo, having herself fled Monrovia after being raped by armed security men in front of her children, that their case was reconsidered jointly and then accepted. Unable to take the children with her as she fled from Liberia, Maikan had left them with her sister.

The couple arrived in Baltimore on a snowy afternoon in November 2003; just over a year later, on another snowy afternoon, I went to see them. Neither one of them had ever seen snow before reaching the USA. When they talked about that first moment of arrival, they stretched out their arms and showed how they watched the snow settle on their hands, touched it and felt it dissolve.

Maikan soon found work in a hotel, making over $400 a week in wages and tips; Omar was given a job in a mail sorting office. They have applied for their son and their daughter to join them; Omar has not seen his children for over six years. When they talk to them on the telephone, the children often cry, such is their longing to reach the country which in their minds has come to represent not only reunion with their parents but the consumer goods – the bicycles, mobile phones, computer games – that have become symbols of the stability they have never known. In their gleaming flat on an attractive housing estate on the outskirts of Baltimore, with its fitted white carpet and enormous fridge, there is a new television and video set and a computer, proof that life has again, after so many years of poverty, become predictable and prosperous.

Soon after they arrived, they were told about their rights: rights to education and medical care, to food stamps and an allowance until they found work, to green cards and eventually to citizenship, and above all rights to have their children join them. Entitlement is heady to people who have lived for so long with no rights at all, on the casual charity of others, and the sense of being worth something again is what all the resettled refugees talk about. Maikan, who never spoke in Cairo, now cannot stop exclaiming over the new horizons in her life. 'Being given things, just given them', she says. 'I still find it impossible to believe. With our first food stamps I went into a supermarket and bought all the food that I had never seen and never eaten'. Not that the threads that tie them to their childhoods are quite broken: Omar has long suffered from some kind of neuralgia in his jaw. It started when he was caring for the Liberians in Cairo and it continues to mystify the American medical profession who have sent him to see many specialists. Walking along in the snow, near his modern estate, Omar said, with an air of slight defiance, that he personally believed it was black magic and that one of the young Liberians, in the edgy days in Cairo, when each watched the others for signs that they might be getting a better deal, had put a spell on him.

By some act of serendipity, for such neat pairings are not planned by the computer-driven process of selection and allocation, while homely Omar and Maikan were sent to orderly, slow-moving Baltimore, Ansu, the most canny and street-wise of the group, the young man whose step was almost jaunty even when in despair, was directed to New York. To understand Ansu's joy in his new surroundings, to comprehend the enormous luck and randomness of resettlement, one has to know something more of his past.

In the 1980s, Ansu's father, Siaka, owned a large coffee and cocoa farm near the town of Bahn in Liberia's Nimba County, though he spent most of his time in Monrovia, where he was employed by the Ministry of the Interior. Ansu lived with his mother and six brothers and sisters in Bahn. They were Mandingos. The civil war reached Nimba in March 1990, when he was twelve. Charles Taylor's rebel forces, letting it be known that they intended to kill all Mandingos – the ethnic group containing the largest number of educated and successful people – began rounding up and questioning everyone they could catch. Ansu escaped and hid in the bush, but he was soon caught by the rebels and taken to a camp with other able-bodied boys and young men. Every day, the captives, tied to each other with rope, were led off to a diamond mine in a nearby swamp, and there, up to their waists in water, they dug for the diamonds with which the soldiers paid for their weapons. Boiled cassava leaves formed the basis of the prisoners' diet, and the boys often felt faint from hunger.

Because Ansu had grown up speaking not only Mandingo and English, but Gio, Jula and Bambara as well, he was useful to the soldiers as an interpreter. After four months, one day he was taken deep into the forest to forage for food. Nonchalantly inching away from the others, he managed to untie the rope and escape, though he was shot in the leg as he ran off. Though lame and in some pain, he reached Monrovia, where to his immense relief he found that his entire family had survived. Once his wound had healed he returned to school and completed his education, and though university was not available in Liberia, still in a state of prolonged civil war, he went to work in his father's office.

By now Samuel Doe – the president favoured by the USA – was dead, and Charles Taylor had officially come to power, promising that there would be no further discrimination or witch-hunts against Mandingos. Just the same, one morning in the late spring of 1998, after saying goodbye to his mother in the kitchen and driving to work, Ansu and his father were arrested by the security services and taken to the prison at Salt Beach. Their arms were bound tightly behind their backs and they were tortured by men in black hoods. Ansu's feet were held over lit coals and burnt. First, Siaka's fingers were slashed with a razor blade and then his head was plunged into a cauldron of hot melted rubber. When I went to see him in New York, seven years after this took place, Ansu described the scene:

'When my father's head was pulled out of the cauldron, he couldn't see anything. he seemed to have gone blind. I begged the men to stop torturing him. One of them said: "He has lost his eyesight? OK. Now he will lose his soul". Then he shot my father in the back of the head, and when he didn't die, but lay on the floor screaming with pain, they took a chainsaw and cut off his hands and feet'. When the guards turned their attentions to Ansu, he fainted.

When he came to, his father's body had been taken away and all that was left was a pool of blood. Eventually, helped by a guard who was a Mandingo himself, Ansu escaped. Hearing that his mother, as well as his brothers and sisters, had all been arrested and had since disappeared, he accepted a friend's offer of a lift in a lorry to Guinea. From there, in 1998, he accompanied another family friend, whom he met in a refugee camp, to Cairo, to act as his driver in Alexandria. He was certain his family was now all dead. Left alone in 2001 when the friend died suddenly of a heart attack, Ansu joined the small band of Liberians in Cairo in search of refugee status and resettlement. A clever, good-looking boy, he appeared as a solitary, wary figure, who went to great lengths to avoid all talk of the past. To keep questions and concern at bay, he laughed and told jokes in the American voice that he had picked up from tourists in Alexandria. Sometimes he vanished for weeks on end; when he returned to the group, he brought back more jokes. In New York, looking back at that time when we met, he said: 'I was thinking of committing suicide. No one could have stopped me. No one at all'. Even then, his long passage of persecution and bad luck had not ended. Learning one day that one of his brothers was in fact alive and living in the USA, he learnt a week later that he had been killed in a car crash.

In the autumn of 2003, having by now spent almost two years penniless on the streets of Cairo, Ansu was informed that he was to be resettled in New York. His first weeks were very lonely. The city seemed too big, too frenetic. But then the parents of a young legal intern he had known in Cairo and who had recently lost their own son, befriended him, and he started to feel better. Talking about himself, with charm and self-mockery and in the lilting cadences of West African English which stay long in the mind, Ansu often refers to himself by name. 'And then' he says, 'Ansu thought to himself: I'm a city boy. New York is the perfect place for me. I'm going to make it here'.

At times, it seems that asylum seekers and refugees exist in a world almost exclusively governed by luck, good as well as bad. When Ansu's luck finally turned, it set in train a series of events so improbable that they belong better in fiction. Once he resolved to make the most of New York, he determined to make money in order to put himself through the college education the Liberian civil war had denied him. He found a first job as a restroom attendant, and a second as a cleaner, after advertising his services on the web with the words: 'I can make your house clean beyond all your expectations'. People believed him and he soon had enough saved to join the highly competitive two-week course to train to be a yellow cab driver, emerging at the end of it as one of the few to get through on a first attempt.

Ansu's weekly contract with a cab company costs him $1,250, but as soon as he has earnt that money each week, with something over on which to live, he goes to act as an interpreter for new West African arrivals. Not long ago he was invited to join a performing company staging shows to introduce New York children to foreign lands and foreign cultures. The children, who found his name hard to remember, christened him 'African Child'. When Ansu reflects on the future, he toys with the idea of business or public relations, and sometimes, when he is feeling philosophical, he talks about joining the CIA, where he senses some of the unseen power that intrigues him about public life might lie.

Meanwhile, his life has again changed course. One morning, driving his yellow cab down Central Park West, he picked up an African passenger heading for the airport. From her clothes, a smart Western coat over a lapa – a tied cloth skirt worn by West African women – he thought she might be Guinean or even Liberian. She asked him, as many of his passengers do, where he came from. They fell to talking. It turned out that she was a business woman from Conakry in Guinea and that her name was Khalidatu. Idly, Ansu remarked that this was also his mother's name. As she paid her fare, his passenger gave him her card, saying that she worked with a Liberian woman, who traded in textiles across West Africa, and that Ansu might like to contact her, in case she had news of other Liberians who had survived Charles Taylor's massacres.

Several attempts to reach his passenger by phone failed, and Ansu lost the card on which her number was written. A few months later, while he was cleaning out his room, the card fell out of a book. This time, his passenger answered and gave him a number to call. He dialled. A woman answered. He tells the story: 'My heart stopped. I knew the voice. I said: "Mom, it's me, Ansu". There was silence. Then cries, laughter, screams. She couldn't believe it. I couldn't believe it'. All that day, impervious to the cab company's pleas that he pick up passengers, Ansu and his mother talked. She told him that she had managed to escape Monrovia with two of his sisters and one brother, and that she was now caring for them in a rented flat in Conakry, together with two orphaned nieces. Ansu suggested that he should immediately apply to have her join him in New York. (Resettlement allows for family reunification of a parent, a child and a spouse). 'Ansu', his mother told him, 'I've got a boyfriend, I'm 49, and I'm not going nowhere'.

Ansu and Khalidatu now talk five to six times every week. 'I started to get happy when I got hold of my mom', says Ansu. They talk as he ferries passengers up and down Manhattan and as he walks home to his appartment in the Bronx, having parked his cab in the company garages. They talk late at night and early in the morning, as if to make up for the six years they have lost. With the money that he sends her – $150 every two weeks – she has bought a plot of land in Conakry, and the foundations of a house have already been laid. But it is only when the roof is on that he will go to visit her, for by then he will have fulfilled his duties as an eldest son and provided for his widowed mother and younger brothers and sisters. The thought that he is now in a position to do so gives him pleasure every day. But just as the Liberians do not talk to each other about their pasts, so his mother does not talk to him about what happened to her in the weeks that followed his and his father's arrest. He fears it was something terrible, and fears, too, that he might not have the strength to listen. 'If I knew', he says, 'maybe I wouldn't be able to drive.' And so, with his baseball cap set at a boyish angle and his dark blue Ralph Lauren woollen jacket, bought with the first money he earned – for clothes, like mobile phones, are crucial to Ansu's image of survival, just as they are crucial to all the young Liberians – he rides the city in his yellow cab, loving the early mornings when Central Park is full of mist. 'African Child, I say to myself, you're a lucky guy. New York, where everyone says the F– word, that's the place for Ansu'.

The first time that I had bought glasses for Mamadu was late at night in a poor district of Cairo where the shops stay open until after midnight and where a few generous-minded doctors and opticians see patients for free after their salaried working days. That was in the spring of 2002. Mamadu was then twenty-one, a thin, anxious, scholarly young Liberian, sole survivor of the massacre that had seen his parents and four younger brothers and sisters murdered in front of him, and so short-sighted that the optician could not believe that he was able to see his way across Cairo's frenetic streets. I explained that Mamadu had spent six years in a refugee camp in Guinea before being helped by a family friend to come as an asylum seeker to Cairo. When he tried on his glasses, on that still, warm

night, Mamadu marvelled at a world he had until then perceived only as a
blur.

The second time that I bought glasses for Mamadu, having at last
tracked him down after more than a year of silence, during which I had
feared that he might be dead, it was on a brilliantly sunny afternoon in
January 2005. We were in a shopping mall in Tel Aviv and the Israeli
optician, like his Egyptian counterpart, could not believe that a boy so
short-sighted could negotiate the hazards of everyday life without help.
What I didn't tell him was that Mamadu had lost his first pair of glasses
during his flight from Egypt across the Sinai, jostled and harried by the
people traffickers to whom he had promised $3,000 for a one way passage
to Israel. It is through Mamadu's tale, and that of the other eleven young
Liberians who fled to Egypt in 1999 and 2000, with their sequences of
brutality and violence, fear and loss, hardship and poverty, that the other
story of modern asylum and refugee life can be told, in which luck can play
so poignant and so harsh a part.

It was the arrest and torture of Amr in a police lock-up on the outskirts
of Cairo in the autumn of 2003, and his appearance in court, evidently
fragile and confused, with bruises on his face and neck, that had first
unnerved the young Liberians. Not long afterwards, Mustafa was picked
up and spent three weeks blindfolded in a police cell in Cairo. Mustafa
was the wiry, bookish boy who had been seven years old, and out fishing,
when the rebels attacked his village in Liberia's Grand Capemount
County and killed his parents and eleven brothers and sisters. Then Iziako
was arrested after an argument with an Egyptian neighbour and deported.
Hearing these stories, the young Liberians began to lose their nerve.

It was soon after this that the departures started. Though cautioned by
the others not to panic, the sense of fear became overwhelming for some
of them. People traffickers are not hard to find in Cairo. In the last few
years, a highly lucrative network of Africans and Egyptians, using the
Bedouin nomads for the passage across the Sinai desert, has started
trafficking groups of refugees from Egypt into Israel following the routes
traditionally used to smuggle drugs and arms. (In 2002, the Israeli paper
Ha'aretz published the log of a border policeman who patrols the frontier.
'July 22,' it read, '3 bags of marijuana; July 24: 6 bags and 25 prostitutes;
July 26: 10 prostitutes; 5 Africans; July 31: 4 Egyptians, 4 foreign workers,
1 woman.') In twos and threes, twelve of the young Liberians now agreed
to pay middlemen for the traffickers $3,000 each for a passage to Tel Aviv,
to be taken out of their wages on arrival. It was Mamadu who had the
easiest journey but the worst arrival.

Transported by car and truck, then put across the border on foot in only a pair of trousers and a tee shirt and with no documents, Mamadu had immediately found himself locked up by his smugglers in a bakery on the edges of Tel Aviv. He was woken at four in the morning to start work and kept working until seven at night. He was fed mostly bread and cakes. At night, he slept on a concrete floor with a single blanket. The dust and the flour got into his lungs and made him cough. After a month, during which time he had not been allowed outside, the middleman for the smugglers, who was a Russian, moved him to a road construction unit, giving him a uniform so that he would not be questioned by police. Together with a dozen other Africans, also paying off their smugglers, he was closely guarded, locked at night into a warehouse and given food but no money. He was told that the fee would take eight months to work off and he counted the days, one by one. Allergic to some chemical in the machinery, he developed sores on his face, arms and hands, which bled and became infected. These were the months I did not hear from him.

The smugglers' fee paid off, Mamadu joined the other smuggled Liberians from Cairo and applied to UNHCR in Israel for refugee status. Elsewhere his case would probably have won recognition and resettlement in the USA or Canada. In Israel the process is different. Though in theory a new immigration and refugee law, enforced by a special commission with the help and advice of UNHCR, regulates policy, in practice, as elsewhere in the world, asylum remains a murky area. Broadly, those who enter illegally from countries hostile to Israel, who are known as 'infiltrators', are either quickly resettled in a willing third country or deported. Palestinian refugees have separate laws of their own. All the others – except for Liberia, Sierra Leone, Ivory Coast and the Congo, which are 'conflict' countries – are examined and either given refugee status or rejected. The nationals of the four current 'conflict countries', providing they can prove that they are who they say they are, are given six-month visas, renewable until the moment when their country is declared 'safe', and they are deported. Not long ago, Sierra Leone was declared 'safe' and Sierra Leoneans are now on their way home. 'The moment the weather looks better', an immigration lawyer said to me, 'the Liberians will be on their way too'.

Mamadu and the other eleven Liberians live and work along the margins of Israeli life. They wash dishes in restaurants, clean lavatories, take the most dangerous and dirtiest of the construction jobs for wages that fall below the national level. After the government, worried about the failing economy and rising unemployment, embarked on a crackdown of illegal immigrants in 2002 – said at their peak to number a quarter of a million, mainly made up of Africans, Asians and Eastern Europeans drawn by the demand for cheap labour in Israeli construction and agriculture – a new immigration police force was set up, which periodically carries out raids on poor neighbourhoods. Most of these take place in the middle of the night, and those without papers are taken into detention and deported. All the Liberians have stories of being stopped, questioned and taken into custody. One day, coming back to the room he shared with another young African from his job washing up in a hotel, Mamadu was picked up by the police and handcuffed. When he asked to be allowed to urinate, the police refused; when he eventually did so in the police car, he was punched in the stomach.

Not one of the eleven young Liberians can forget that, had they waited in Cairo, they would now be resettled in the USA or Canada. It haunts them. Mamadu, in particular, is tormented by all he senses that he has lost. In October 2004, while cleaning a house, he started to hear voices murmuring in his head. They told him that he was being watched, and they sounded angry. 'Sometimes', he told me when I saw him in January 2005, 'I can hear people reading in my head. I shout abusive things. I see people laughing at me. I do believe people tried to use supernatural powers to destroy me'. These episodes are followed by blinding headaches. 'I am hungry for recovery', he said to me.

'Any time am out in the streets I see angry faces', he wrote not long ago, in one of the many emails that followed my visit. 'But am tired of living as such. I've always been running away from threats and intimidation. I am really tired'. For the first time, he began to talk of going back to Liberia, to Monrovia, where as an eleven-year-old boy he had heard his family being murdered in the road behind him.

Acknowledgments

Lyndall Passerini, Frances D'Souza, Janet Powney, and my son Daniel
Swift came with me on different parts of my journey: I would never have
travelled anywhere, and this book would not have been written, without
them. I would like to thank them very much.

I particularly want to thank the following, who read different chapters
and gave suggestions and advice: Anne Chisholm, Jeff Crisp, Beth
Crosland, Michael Davie, William Hopkins, David Marr, Philip Rudge
and Kirteen Tait. I am also very grateful to the Society of Authors, for their
grant from the Authors' Foundation.

The book would never have been started without the young Liberians
in Cairo, and I owe them thanks for the many hours they spent talking to
me about their lives. In Cairo, I would also like to thank Magda Ali, Fateh
Azzam, Barbara Harrell-Bond, Sofi Elg, Enid Hill, Heba Kasseem, Mulki
al-Sharmani, and Nachoua El Azharí for her generous hospitality. Just as I
would like to thank Diana Allan, Virginia Duigan, Gill and Robb Lodge
and Dawn Sparks for very kindly having me to stay on my travels, as well
as the staff of the International Rescue Committee, Refugees International, Amnesty International and UNHCR, who made my journeys in
Guinea and Afghanistan possible. The archivists and librarians of the
Refugee Studies Centre in Oxford, the Medical Foundation for the Care
of Victims of Torture, the London Library and the Refugee Council
Archive at the University of East London were extremely helpful.

Many people talked to me for this book, helped me, drove me about and
showed me things. I am very grateful to them all. They are: Ghassan
'Abdallah, Leena-Kaisa Aberg, Eleanor Acer, Rafaelo Alarcon, Daniela
D'Amico, Kathi Anderson, Gervase Apache, Paris Aristotle, Sister Bridget
Arthur, Karim Atassi, Gian Luca Avanzato, Kenneth Bacon, Helen Bamber,
Peer Baneke, Christina Bennett, Jean-Francois Berger, Paul Bergue, Deslie
Billich, Tony Birch, Monica Bishop, Professor Geoffrey Blainey, Father

Frank Brennan, Kielo Brewis, Sir Nigel Broomfield, Michelle Brown, Sandy Buchan, Julian Burnside, Sherman Carroll, Stephen Castles, Jean Chandler, Deirdre Clancy, Sister Claudette of the Sisters of Mercy, Rupert Colville, Marguerite Contat, Wayne Cornelius, Sarah Covington, Mark Cutts, Nomita Dave, David Deng, Damtew Dessalegue, Kate Durham, Jean-Francois Durieux, Ann Durst, Sue Emmott, Daniel Endres, Heike Estolen, Nabi Farahi, Erika Feller, Giovanni Fiannaca, Georgina Fletcher, Julian Fountain, Ana Liria-Franch, Joung-Ah Ghedini, Matthew Gibney, John Gibson, Brenda Goddard, Nate Goetz, Monica Gonzales, Guy Goodwin-Gill, Mariette Grange, Stefanie Grant, Ahmed, Aziz and Ayda Halime, Luke Hardy, Wendy Hartman, Ahmed Hawri, the late Arthur Helton, Anne Henderson, Katherine Henderson, Professor Louis Henkin, Taryn Higashi, Liz Hodgkin, Louis Hoffmann, Andrew Hogg, Christopher Horrocks, Bassam Jamil Hubaishi, Jurgen Humber, Linda Jaivin, Lucy Jones, Tania Kaiser, Maija Kajava, David Kapya, Rose Kasusky, Penny Kelly, Josephine Klein, Michelle Klein Solomon, Michael Korsinki, Kristina Kumpula, Margaret Ladner, David Lambo, Comfort Lamptey, Nick Leader, Philippe Leclerc, Eve Lester, Gil Loescher, Anne-Sophie Lois, Ruud Lubbers, Dr Thierno Maadjou Sow, Charles MacFadden, Ewen MacLeod, Dennis McNamara, Monique Malha, Robert Mann, Lucia Marghieri, Delphine Marie, Peter Marsden, Anne-Charlotte Martineau, Roberto Martinez, Pablo Mateu, Laura Maxwell, Peter Maxwell, Nicholas and Kerry Minchin, Robert Montgomery, John Morrison, David Murphy, Nancy Murray, Kathleen Newland, Clementine Nkweta Muna, Sayre Nyce, Pia Oberoi, Comfort Ofolabi, Grainne O'Hara, Patricia Omidian, Ekhlas Osman, Dr Biagio Palumbo, Alison Parker, Mervyn Patterson, Dr Michael Peel, David Petrasek, Charles Petrie, Margaret Piper, Michael Pugh, Ian Purves, Archi Pyati, Cesar Pastor Ortega, Ron Redmond, Rachel Reilly, Marianne Reiner, Ngareta Rossell, Aziz Royesh, Katherine Sainsbury, Eva Sallis, Angel Santa Ana, Rosemary Sayigh, Jason Scarpone, Ed van Schenkenberg, Col. Mark Schnur, Nasir Shansab, John Shattuck, Zainab Sheik-Ali, Alanna Sherry, Ann-Charlotte Siren-Borrego, Russell Skelton, Malcolm Smart, Elaine Smith, John Spooner, Dr Zachary Steele, Barry Stoyle, Derek Summerfield, Tim Swett, Larry Thompson, Robbie Thomson, Steve Tull, Volker Turk, Dr Stuart Turner, David Turton, Amanda Vanstone, Susan Varga, Fulvio Vassalo, Sally Verity Smith, Andrew Wilder, Sara Wills, Arnold Zable, Monette Zard, and Abu, Ali, Hussein and Mahmud Zeidan.

As always, I am most grateful for the help and encouragement of my agent, Clare Alexander, and my publishers, Penelope Hoare, Jennifer Barth and Vanessa Mobley.

Sources

Much – perhaps most – of the research in this book comes from interviews with asylum-seekers, refugees and migrants in different parts of the world. It is their stories that form the heart of the book. Many have preferred not to be named and for them I have invented new names; others were happy to be identified and I have accordingly done so. I also talked to many people who work with refugees.

The main human-rights and refugee organisations publish regular reports, country profiles, press releases and publications and have websites with up-to-date information about the countries and places I visited. I found the following particularly useful: Amnesty International, the British Medical Journal, the British Refugee Council, the *Economist*, the European Council on Refugees and Exile, *Forced Migration Review*, the Global Internally Displaced People project of the Norwegian Refugee Council, the UK Home Office, Human Rights Watch, *Index on Censorship*, the Information Centre about Asylum and Refugees, the International Rescue Committee, the Lawyers Committee for Human Rights, Opendemocracy, Refugees International, the Refugees Studies Centre, Reliefweb, the United Nations Commission on Human Rights, the United Nations High Commissioner for Refugees, US State Department Country Reports, and the World Refugee Survey.

Chapter One: The Homeless and the Rightless
p. 27 'Louis Henkin was a young . . .' Conversation with author 3 November 2003.
p. 29 'No international organisation . . .' For an excellent overview of UNHCR's work, see Gil Loescher, *The UNHCR & World Politics: A Perilous Path*, Oxford University Press, 2001. See also the newsletters of the International Council of Voluntary Organisations.
p. 33 'And Ogata's interests . . .' The following pages are based on

interviews with UNHCR in February 2004.

p. 34 'The new millenium . . .' See UNHCR: *The State of the World's Refugees*, 1995, 1997, 2000.

p. 36 'Not the least . . .' See the publications of the Global IDP Project, Norwegian Refugee Council.

p. 38 'Among them were many . . .' Conversation with Sally Verity-Smith, 25 October 2003.

p. 39 'Some $10 billion . . .' See websites of the UK Home Office (www.homeoffice.gov.uk) and UNHCR (www.unhcr.ch).

Chapter Two: The Extracommunitari

p. 51 'Lampedusa is popular . . .' See David Gilmour, *The Last Leopard*, London, 1988.

p. 55 'Europe's earliest migrants . . .' See Raleigh Trevelyan, *The Companion Guide to Sicily*, London, 1999.

p 56 'At first, influxes . . .' See Michael Pugh, *Europe's Boat People: maritime cooperation in the Mediterranean*, Challot Paper 41, WEU Institute for Security Studies, Paris, July 2000.

p. 56 'With Berlusconi's election . . .' See publications of ECRE. Also the Commission for the politics of integration of immigrants, Department of Social Affairs, Rome. Also: Stefano Vincenzi, *Italy; A newcomer with a positive attitude*, Journal of Refugee Studies, Vol. 13 No. 1, 2000. John Morrison & Beth Crosland, *The Trafficking & Smuggling of Refugees: the endgame in European asylum policy?* UNHCR Working Paper, No. 39, April 2001.

Chapter Three: The Fence

p. 73 'It has become . . .' See Philip Martin & Jonas Widgren, *International Migration: Facing the Challenge*, Population Bulletin, Vol 57. No. 1, 2002. *United States of America: Human rights concerns in the border region with Mexico*, Amnesty International, 1998.

p. 75 'It was in the . . .' See Peter Andreas, *Border Games: Policing the US–Mexico Divide*, Cornell University Press, 2000.

p. 76 'And of course . . .' See Wayne Cornelius, *Death at the border. Efficacy and unintended consequences of US immigration control policy*, Population and Development review, Vol 27, December 2001. Also: *Anti-immigration vigilantes on the US–Mexico borderlands*, Centre for Comparative Immigration Studies, October 2003. Also: *Policing the border: US immigration control strategy*, November 2003.

p. 78 'The migrants are . . .' Author conversation with Nate Goetz, 28

October 2003. Also: *Reports in Migration World*, 1998–2001, Centre for Migration Studies of New York inc.

p. 85 'The detention of asylum . . .' See reports by Amnesty International, Human Rights Watch, Lawyers' Committee for Human Rights.

p. 86 'When William Williams . . .' William Williams papers. Manuscripts and Archives Division, New York Public Library. See also: Thomas M. Pitkin, *Keepers of the gate: A history of Ellis Island*, New York, 1975.

Chapter Four: Fair Go

p. 96 'Italians . . .' For documents on early immigration, see Melbourne's Museum of Immigration.

p. 103 'It was under . . .' See *Not for export*, Human Rights Watch briefing paper, September 2002.

p. 103 'It came about . . .' See the website of the Australian Government Immigration Department (www.immi.gov.au); also that of the Refugee Council of Australia (www.refugeecouncil.org.au).

p. 106 'And then, on . . .' David Marr & Marian Wilkinson, *Dark Victory*, Sydney, 2003. Also Robert Manne & David Corlett, *Sending them home*, Quarterly Essay, 2004. Don McMaster, *Asylum Seekers: Australia's response to refugees*, Melbourne, 2003.

p. 108 'It was about now . . .' See *Australia-Pacific: Offending human dignity – the 'Pacific Solution'*, Amnesty International, 2002.

p. 112 'Woomera, by all . . .' Tom Mann, *Desert Sorrow: Asylum seekers at Woomera*, Sydney, 2003.

p. 118 'What these doctors . . .' There are a great many papers and reports on this subject. See, in particular, J. P. Wilson & B. Drozdele (eds), *Broken Spirits: the treatment of asylum seekers and refugees with post-traumatic stress disorder*, Melbourne, 2004. Also Aamer Sultan & Kevin O'Sullivan, *Psychiatric disturbances in asylum seekers held in long term detention*, Medical Journal of Australia, Vol 175, 2001.

Chapter Five: Newcastle

p. 134 'In 2002 . . .' For up-to-date figures see the websites of the Home Office, the British Refugee Council and the Information Centre about Asylum and Refugees (www.icar.org.uk).

p. 138 'In practice, people . . .' See *A trans-national network: hearing the voices of refugees in policy and practice in the European Union*, North of England Refugee Service, 2000.

p. 142 'None of this . . .' *What's the story?* Media Representation of Refugees and Asylum seekers in the UK, Article XIX, 2003.

Chapter Six: Little Better than Cockroaches

p. 155 'In the autumn . . .' *Liberian refugees in Guinea: refoulement, militarisation of camps and other protection concerns*, Human Rights Watch, November 2002. Also *Guinea and Sierra Leone: no place of refuge*, Amnesty International, October 2001.

p. 160 'Though the precise . . .' For an excellent recent history of Liberia, see Stephen Ellis, *The mask of anarchy: The destruction of Liberia and the religious dimension of an African civil war*, London, 1999.

p. 171 'UNHCR is at . . .' See Tania Kaiser, *A beneficiary-based evaluation of the UNHCR programme in Guinea*, UNHCR Working Paper, 2001. Also Jeff Crisp, *No solutions in sight: the problem of protracted refugee situations in Africa*, UNHCR Working Paper, 2003.

p. 175 'No one really . . .' Robert F. Gorman, *Refugee aid and development*, London, 1993.

Chapter Seven: The Corridors of Memory

p. 183 'a blend of . . .' Jabra Ibrahim Jabra, *A Bethlehem Boyhood*, Arkansas, 1995.

p. 187 'There is no . . .' For good accounts of the history of the Palestinians in Lebanon, see: Rosemary Sadigh, *Too many enemies: the Palestinian experiment in Lebanon*, London, 1994, and D. Gilmour, *Dispossessed: the ordeal of the Palestinians, 1917–80*, London, 1980, and Robert Fisk, *Pity the Nation: Lebanon at war*, London, 1990. See also the archives of the International Committee of the Red Cross, Geneva, and those of the UN Relief & Works Administration.

p. 188 'As villages were . . .' Walid Khalidi, *All that remains: the Palestinian villages occupied and depopulated by Israel in 1948*, Institute of Palestinian Studies, 1992, Washington.

p. 189 'a black cave . . .' Elias Khoury, *The kingdom of strangers*, Beirut, 1996.

p. 197 'The voice that . . .' Edward Said, *Reflections on Exile*, London, 2000. Also, *The Politics of Dispossession*, London, 1994.

p. 198 'At one-thirty . . .' Mourid Barghouti, *I saw Ramallah*, London, 2003.

p. 202 'Basically, the Palestinian . . .' May Seikaly, *Al-Jana file on Palestinian oral history*, The Arab Resource Centre, Beirut, 2002.

p. 208 'All those who . . .' Mourid Barghouti. Ibid.

Chapter Eight: The Illness of Exile

p. 213 'The literature of . . .' See Paul Tabori, *The Anatomy of Exile*, London, 1972.

p. 215 'As an understanding . . .' For the literature on torture see the publications of Amnesty International and the Medical Foundation for the Care of Victims of Torture.

p. 221 'Over the years . . .' See Jane Kramer, *Refugee*, the *New Yorker*, 20 January 2003.

Chapter Nine: Going Home

p. 239 'The Afghans know . . .' See David Turton & Peter Marsden, *Taking refugees for a ride? The politics of refugee returns to Afghanistan*. Afghanistan Research and Evaluation Unit, December 2002.

p. 241 'And the refugees did . . .' Amnesty International and Human Rights Watch have excellent reports on Afghanistan. See, in particular, *Afghanistan: Out of sight, out of mind: The fate of the Afghan returnees*, Amnesty International, 2003. Reports of the British Agencies Afghanistan Group (BAAG). Michael Ignatieff, *New York Times*, August 2002. Nicholas Stockton, *Strategic Coordination in Afghanistan*, Afghanistan Research and Evaluation Unit, August 2002.

p. 241 'When Robert Byron . . .' Robert Byron, *The Road to Oxiana*, London, 1937.

p. 245 'In 1836, Colonel . . .' Sir Alexander Burnes, *Cabool, a personal narrative of a journey to and residence in that city, 1836, 7 and 8*, London, 1842.

p. 245 'here, he remarked . . .' The Banurnama, *Memoirs*, London, 1921.

Chapter Ten: Dead Dreams

p. 269 'Describing his first . . .' Tété-Michel Kpomassie, *An African in Greenland*, London, 1988.

Epilogue: A Mode of Being

p. 283 'Asylum-seekers may . . .' See Stephen Castles & Sean Loughna, *Trends in asylum migration to industrialized countries, 1990–2001*, UNU/Wider, 2003.

p. 284 'Meanwhile the idea . . .' Author conversation with Peer Baneke, 10 January 2003. See also reports of the European Council on Refugees and Exiles.

p. 285 'When Jeff Crisp . . .' Conversation with author, February 2002. See also Jeff Crisp, *A new asylum paradigm? Globalization, immigration and the uncertain future of the international refugee regime*, UNHCR Working Paper, December 2003. See also: *Refugees: human rights have no borders*, Amnesty International, 1997.

p. 287 'Not long ago . . .' Philip Rudge conversation with author, 15 March

2004. See also Philip Rudge, *The need for a more focused response: European donor policies towards IDPs*, London, January 2002.

p. 287 'Why should something . . .' Matthew Gibney conversation with author, October 2003.

p. 288 'In the mid . . .' See ed. Nigel Rapport & Andrew Dawson, *Migrants of identity: perceptions of home in a world of movement*, Oxford, 1998.

p. 289 'Even if the flows . . .' For good overview, see Stephen Castles, *The International politics of forced migration*, in ed. Leo Planitch & Colin Leys, *Fighting identities: race, religion and ethno-nationalism*, the Socialist register, London, 2002.

p. 290 "UNHCR's task . . .' Voker Turk, *Refugee Survey Quarterly*, Vol 20, 2001.

Index